Editors
Seamus Deane
Ciarán Deane

Design
Red Dog Design Consultants
www.reddog.ie

Fonts
Headlines — Gill Sans 24/28
Body Copy Essays/Reviews — Sabon 9/12

Paper Stock
McNaughton's Challenger Offset

Copyright © 2012 by the contributors and Field Day Publications

Field Day Review is published annually by
Field Day Publications in association with
the Keough-Naughton Institute for Irish
Studies at the University of Notre Dame.

ISSN 1649-6507
ISBN 978-0-946755-54-7

Field Day Review
Keough-Naughton Institute for Irish Studies
58 Merrion Square
Dublin 2
Ireland

fieldday@nd.edu

www.fielddaybooks.com

FIELD DAY REVIEW
2012

Angus Mitchell	5	**'A Strange Chapter of Irish History':** Sir Roger Casement, Germany and the 1916 Rising
Roger Casement	23	**Diary of Roger Casement, 1914–16** Part I: *My Journey to the German Headquarters at Charleville*, annotated by Angus Mitchell
Roger Casement	47	**A Last Page of my Diary,** with an Introduction by Angus Mitchell
Angus Mitchell	85	**'Phases of a Dishonourable Phantasy'**
Amy E. Martin	127	**Representing the 'Indian Revolution' of 1857:** Towards a Genealogy of Irish Internationalist Anticolonialism
Willie Smyth	149	***Atlas of the Irish Rural Landscape* (2nd Ed) and Historical Geography**
Joseph A. Buttigieg	167	**The Alternative Communism of Lucio Magri**
Ronan Sheehan	181	**'Sub Nomine Columbae / In the Name of Columba'**
Seamus Deane	207	**The End of the World**

We Are Making a New World, painting by Paul Nash (1889–1946) from WWI series. Courtesy Imperial War Museum © Lebrecht Music & Arts/Corbis

'A Strange Chapter of Irish History':

Sir Roger Casement, Germany and the 1916 Rising

Angus Mitchell

These two previously unpublished excerpts from the diary kept by Roger Casement during his eighteen months in Germany, from October 1914 to April 1916, provide some critical insight into the international context of the 1916 Rising. They show Casement to have had a candid, prophetic grasp of the tragic turmoil of his age and Ireland's historic location within that turmoil. Why then, in the writing of the history of the First World War, has Casement's voice been so unremittingly ignored and sidelined? Part of the reason lies perhaps in the narrative of these two essential moments on his path to the gallows: his journey to the Western Front in November 1914 and his negotiations with the

Roger Casement, 1915.
© Hulton-Deutsch Collection/CORBIS

German government in the weeks before his return to Ireland aboard a submarine in April 1916.

Independent Ireland has found it hard to incorporate into its foundational history the narrative of this decorated imperial official who played a pivotal role in both the intellectual and practical formation of the Irish Volunteers and then returned to Ireland to try and stop the Rising. Equally, Britain has turned its back on the renegade traitor and done its utmost to forget the inconvenient truths exposed by the clear logic of his 'treason'. Both these positions are expediently simplified in and by the toxic dualism of his reputation as British 'traitor' or Irish 'martyr'. From his years working within the inner circle of imperial power, Casement had developed an intimate knowledge of international diplomacy and an acute awareness of the intensifying use and power of propaganda and of covert actions as instruments of state control. His insight into the modern mechanisms of transnational power had been deepened by his involvement with Irish revolutionary politics in the build-up to the Rising. His unique composite of establishment and revolutionary experience provided an international dimension to Ireland's revolution and bequeathed to it an ineradicable anti-colonial dynamic.

After undertaking two investigations into crimes against humanity in the Congo and northwest Amazon during twenty years of official service, Casement resigned from his post as the British consul general in Brazil, in August 1913. His energies were then channelled into the Home Rule crisis and the paramilitarization of Irish politics that followed the signing of the Ulster Covenant. He was a key figure in the founding of the Irish Volunteers in November 1913, taking part in a series of recruiting rallies across Ireland over the next six months. In the summer of 1914, his plan to run guns into Ireland for the Irish Volunteers—hatched with the collaboration of the historian Alice Stopford Green, and the authors Erskine Childers and Darrell Figgis—was successfully accomplished with the landing of the arms shipment at Howth on board the *Asgard*. The success of the plan so elevated him within Irish-American revolutionary ranks, that when Britain declared war on Germany a week later, Casement was already in the US, headlining a series of fund-raising rallies and being fêted by the IRB veteran John Devoy and the Clan na Gael chief Joseph McGarrity. In early October, with the support of the German ambassador in the US, Johann Heinrich von Bernstorff, he left New York under a false identity. Having successfully foiled an assassination plot in Norway hatched by the British Minister (ambassador), Mansfeldt de Cardonnel Findlay, he arrived incognito in Berlin on 31 October 1914.

During his years in the British Foreign Office, Casement had built up an extensive network of international support: this included a number of German friends and officials in positions of influence. Some, like the Celtic scholar and philologist Professor Kuno Meyer, were involved in the Cultural Revival and Irish language movement; others, such as Count von Blücher and the Baron von Nordenflycht, were friends he had made during his consular postings. Within days he had established contact with some of these people, and with the German Foreign Office. Over the next few weeks, he met with some of the most senior officials in the German government. He remained in Germany for the next year-and-a-half, engaged with the German government in discussions of strategy and inciting anti-imperial subversion amongst the groups of itinerant revolutionaries who passed through Berlin during these months.

Casement had three fundamental aims during his mission to Germany. His first priority was to secure German help for the cause of Irish independence. This was partly achieved with the *Declaration of Goodwill*, circulated on 20 November 1914, in which the German government openly expressed its peaceful and non-belligerent intentions towards the Irish people. Over Christmas 1914, a more comprehensive treaty of ten articles was agreed to, which set out the conditions for the formation and deployment of an Irish Brigade. Casement's second priority was to work as a propagandist and to educate the German people about the situation in Ireland so as to obtain public support once the German government threw in its lot with the Irish people. This propaganda campaign involved Casement in a crusade against the British government and a number of its senior statesmen; the viciousness of the response had important and disfiguring effects upon the status of his own earlier official investigations into crimes against humanity. His third objective was to raise an Irish Brigade from among captured POWs and turn them into an efficient fighting unit to help in the independence struggles in Ireland and in Egypt. Some years later, when reflecting on these three dimensions of Casement's

Johann Heinrich von Bernstorff, German ambassador to Mexico and the US 1908–17.

German mission, John Devoy commented: 'Casement did his best in all these things, but did the first ineffectively, succeeded admirably in the second, and failed badly in the third.'[1]

The two diary extracts published here conveniently bracket the beginning and end of his eighteen months in Germany. The first excerpt covers the days, from 17 to 19 November 1914, when Casement made a secret visit to the German headquarters at the Western Front to meet with senior representatives in the German Foreign Office and at the German General Staff. His presence in Germany was still officially unacknowledged and he travelled under the assumed name of 'Mr. Hammond'. After successfully convincing the necessary senior officials of the sincerity of his purpose, his

1 John Devoy, *Recollections of an Irish Rebel* (New York, 1929), 432.

identity was revealed on his return to Berlin on 20 November.

The news may have taken the public by surprise, but the British security services had been on Casement's trail for many months by then; well in advance of this public admission of his treason, Casement had become a priority of different intelligence agencies in Britain. Such was the urgency of their need to capture, overthrow and subsequently control his legacy, that it drove British intelligence chiefs into a vortex of conspiracy and intrigue. The recent releases of intelligence files held by different security services show that Casement was prioritized as the first serious counter-subversion target of the war, and considerable resources were deployed to unveil his plans and capture him. The efforts to buy the loyalty of his manservant, Adler Christiensen, by the British Minister Findlay, provided Casement with plenty of ammunition for his propaganda campaign against the nefarious activities of the British Foreign Office; he spent much time and energy exposing the assassination plot.

By the spring of 1915, as the plans to raise the Irish Brigade had largely failed and as Germany began to pull back from its support for the cause of Irish independence, Casement's health began to deteriorate under the increasing pressure of the worsening situation. Much of his time was consumed in writing articles for *The Continental Times* and the *Gaelic American*, revealing secrets about the British state and contesting Britain's justification for going to war. In an effort to improve matters, the Supreme Council of the IRB in Ireland sent out Joseph Mary Plunkett to try to revitalize relations with the German General Staff. Plunkett's mission was followed by the arrival in the autumn of Robert Monteith, who took over the day-to-day running of the Brigade. But the Brigade never attained the proposed target of two hundred volunteers and the German General Staff lost faith in the project.

During these months, a combination of tropical fever and nervous exhaustion forced Casement to retire to a sanatorium near Munich, where he spent several weeks in early 1916; it was then that he heard the news that the plans for the Rising were well advanced. Despite various ailments and low levels of energy, he made one last effort to exert his influence to stop the Rising or, failing that, to return to Ireland to take part in it. The second extract—covering the period from 17 March to 8 April 1916—is the diary he kept in the last weeks of his mission to Germany. It details his high-level meetings with representatives from the German General Staff, the German Foreign Office and the Admiralty, before he embarked on board a submarine bound for Ireland.

In the sixteen months separating these two extracts, it is apparent how his attitude to Germany's political authorities had undergone a sea-change. His initial belief in the sincerity of the support of the German General Staff for Irish independence had evaporated well in advance of his departure from Germany. Negotiations with some of the most senior officials in the German Foreign Office and German General Staff had turned acrimonious and were undermined by suspicion and distrust. At times, Casement's inner reflections border on the paranoid. His sympathies lay with the German people who were in thrall, as he saw it, to the curse of Prussian militarism. In November 1914, Casement had believed Germany would win the war; this was a view he no longer entertained when he boarded the submarine in April 1916.

The Mystery of the Casement Diary

Shortly before leaving Germany for Ireland, Casement left extensive and explicit instructions with his friend Charles Curry for the safekeeping and eventual publication of his German diaries.[2]

[2] Correspondence is held in NLI MSS 17026 & 17027.

Casement believed that by publishing his version of events explaining why he went to Germany, and why he was determined to internationalize the issue of Irish independence and to raise an Irish Brigade, the manifest honesty of his motives and the sincerity of his beliefs would add to the logic of his 'treason' an appealing, affective dimension. But ultimately, his political views were rooted in a reasoned response to imperial violence. By the time he set sail for Germany from New York, his reputation was so enmeshed in the impasse of First World War propaganda and the ramifying intrigues of the confrontation between British secret services and Irish revolutionary conspiracy, that the most straightforward 'truth' was impossible to distinguish or decipher. Casement was well aware that there were special forces at play determined to undermine his reputation and, by deliberate misinformation, to shape public opinion about his aims and purposes. He realized that the publication of his own version of events was therefore vital to his eventual exoneration from the calumnies that besieged him.

Curry followed Casement's instructions, and the diaries were carefully stowed away until after the war. In 1922, Curry published a carefully edited version in a small Munich edition *Diaries of Sir Roger Casement: His Mission to Germany and the Findlay Affair*.[3] He chose to edit out quite significant parts of the complete diary, including the narrative of Casement's trip to the Western Front reproduced here. The aim of Curry's edition was to highlight the 'Findlay Affair'—the efforts by the British Minister in Oslo to bribe Casement's comrade Adler Christensen to have Casement either captured or assassinated.

The fate of his papers became an increasing concern to Casement in his last days in Berlin. He distributed different parts of his German archive to various friends. Some of these papers were eventually deposited in the New York Public Library among the William Maloney papers, others reached the National Library of Ireland [NLI]. It is clear, however, that a certain part of this correspondence was picked up by British intelligence. A typed list of documents, compiled by N. C. Harrington of the G-2 Branch of the Department of Defence after the war, lists the German papers intercepted and carefully scrutinized by the British intelligence services, before they were returned to the family.[4] Like so much of Casement's extensive archive it is often difficult to trace the precise provenance of papers and what happened to them before they were made available for independent scrutiny.

There is compelling evidence to suggest that Casement kept diaries at many of the critical junctures of his life, although a number of them have disappeared. The extended diary of his 1903 Congo journey, for instance, has not survived. His 1910 Amazon voyage was covered in immense detail in a daily journal, which was later submitted as evidence to the parliamentary select committee inquiry.[5] Casement admitted to throwing 'diaries overboard' on leaving the US in 1914, fearful that they contained incriminating information, which might fall into the hands of the British authorities. In Germany, he deliberately faked pages of his diary in a strategy of misinformation against the British Foreign Office—an incident referred to in the extract published here. He realized that the rationale of his revolutionary turn would one day be explained through his version of events—and much of that explanation was evident in the narrative of his diaries. But he could not have predicted that British secret services would fabricate a sexualized diary narrative of his investigations in the Congo and the Amazon, with the sole purpose of assassinating his character and thereby denying him the moral authority necessary for the impact of his investigations into crimes against humanity and, ultimately, for the creation of an authentic and coherent historical legacy to which his recognition of imperial criminality in Ireland was integral.

3   There was also a German translation of the diary *Sir Roger Casement: Meine Mission Deutschland während des Krieges und die Findlay-Affaire* (Altenburg/Thüringen, 1925). Extracts from the Curry edition, with some supplementary materials, were serialized in the *Nation* between 30 November 1921 and 8 February 1922.
4   NLI MSS 13085
5   Angus Mitchell (ed.), *The Amazon Journal of Roger Casement* (London and Dublin, 1997).
6   Roger McHugh, 'Casement and German Help', in F. X. Martin (ed.), *Leaders and Men of the Easter Rising: Dublin 1916* (London, 1967). McHugh also published some excerpts from *A Last Page of My Diary* in his edition *Dublin 1916* (London, 1966).
7   Reinhard R. Doerries, 'Die Mission Sir Roger Casements im Deutschen Reich 1914-16', *Historische Zeitschrift*, Bd. 222, H.3 (June 1976), 578–625; 'Hopeless Mission: Sir Roger Casement in Imperial Germany', *The Journal of Intelligence History* 6 (Summer 2006), 25–39.
8   John Devoy, 'Sir Roger Casement and the Irish Brigade in Germany', *The Gaelic American*, 28 June 1924. Timothy Quinlisk, 'The German Irish Brigade: Diary of Casement's Lieutenant', in *Land and Water* (6 November 1919). Also see Bureau of Military History Witness Statement 551 Thomas Canon Duggan.

Both extracts published here are held in the original manuscript in the National Library of Ireland. The journey to the Western Front is excerpted from a diary notebook [MS 1689], which forms part of the larger diary published by Curry in 1922. The entries are written in reverse: the narrative begins on folio 97 and ends on folio 46. The second extract [NLI 5244] was written on 134 numbered sides of script with additional comments and marginalia added on 8 April 1916. At the start of this extract, Casement contextualized his situation at this critical juncture by recounting some of the most important events from the previous months. He was aware that these last three weeks would prove crucial in determining the historical fate of the Irish Brigade and justifying his own break with the German General Staff and their intelligence chiefs. However, this narrative is selective and deals predominantly with Casement's meetings with German officials; it does not record Casement's liaisons with members of the Irish Brigade.

Much ancillary correspondence relevant to both these extracts, but principally to the second of them, is held among the Maloney Papers at the New York Public Library. This includes copies and originals of the 1916 correspondence between Casement and Robert Monteith. Casement's extensive correspondence with the German Foreign Office is held in Politisches Archiv des Auswärtigen Amtes Berlin (Archive of the German Foreign Office). Roger McHugh undertook comprehensive work on Casement in the build-up to the 1966 commemoration.[6] Much of the more important correspondence by and about Casement's months in Germany appears in Reinhard R. Doerries, *Prelude to the Easter Rising: Sir Roger Casement in Imperial Germany* (London, 2000). This is an indispensable supplement to both these diary extracts and I refer to this work extensively throughout. Although Doerries has pioneered scholarship on Casement's activities in Germany, especially from the specialized perspective of intelligence history, his studies have tended to marginalize the diary narrative and the propaganda war waged by Casement against the British Empire that is contained in a series of quite inaccessible essays written in 1915.[7] Doerries's defence of the German Foreign Office and German General Staff is founded on his belief that Casement's mission was 'hopeless'.

The history of the Irish Brigade has been treated in several essays and memoirs.[8] On the Brigade itself, there has been good recent scholarship, most notably by Andreas Roth.[9] Various memoirs were written by volunteers about the organization. The most extensive published account is by Michael Keogh, *With Casement's Irish Brigade*.[10] An intriguing memoir by Sean Kavanagh is yet to be published.[11] Two accounts of the Irish Brigade were written by Joseph Zerhusen, who served as interpreter and liaison officer to it.[12] The most reliable and most intimate witness to Casement's last weeks in Germany was Robert Monteith, who wrote a gripping version of events.[13] The important chronicle of the propaganda war fought between Britain and Germany for American support is intriguingly told by Thomas St John Gaffney, with chapters on Casement and his last weeks in Berlin.[14] The memoir of the politically biased, English-born, Evelyn, Princess Blücher is atmospheric but untrustworthy.[15] Karl Spindler, the Captain of the arms ship, the *Aud*, wrote his account of events soon after the war; it was translated into French and widely read.[16] Most recently, the journeys of the *Aud* and the U-19 have been exhaustively researched in the work of Xander Clayton.[17] Casement's time in Germany was treated in various studies. The often sentimental hagiography by Dr Franz Rothenfelder, *Casement in Deutschland*, includes important information about Casement's network of German friends and contacts in Dresden, Hamburg, Munich and Leipzig.[18] Eduard Meyer, Kuno Meyer's brother, also left

9 Andreas Roth, 'The German soldier is not Tactful': Sir Roger Casement and the Irish Brigade in Germany during the First World War', *The Irish Sword* 19, 1995, 315. Joachim Lerchenmueller, "The wretched lot"—a brief history of the Irish Brigade in Germany, 1914–1919', in *Yearbook of the Centre for Irish-German Studies* (University of Limerick, 1998–99), 95–113.

10 Michael Keogh, *With Casement's Irish Brigade* (Drogheda, 2010), originally published in the indispensable *Catholic Bulletin*, (January–December 1928). See Bureau of Military History W.S. 741.

11 A typescript of the memoir of Sean Kavanagh, *The Betrayal of Roger Casement and the Irish Brigade*, circulated among publishers in Dublin in 1998, but has yet to find its way into print.

12 NLI MS 43 570/1–2 contains a 98-page typescript of Zerhusen's recollections about the Irish Brigade from 1915 to 1918. A second, shorter reminiscence is held in NLI MS 31 728.

13 Robert Monteith, *Casement's Last Adventure* (Chicago, 1932) republished and revised edition (Dublin, 1953), with a foreword by Franz von Papen. His diary was published in the biographical study by his daughter Florence Monteith Lynch, *The Mystery Man of Banna Strand: The Life and Death of Captain Robert Monteith* (New York, 1959).

Kurt von Lersner (1883–1954), German diplomat and politician, whom Casement met in New York.

a memoir.[19] The understanding of Casement's internationalism—evident in his subversive dealings with other revolutionaries residing in Berlin in 1915, notably Virendranath Chattopadhyaya and Rosa Luxemburg—was greatly amplified with the publication of a biography of Casement by the anti-colonial, Weimar intellectual, Balder Olden. The work was banned by the Nazis and hastened Olden's exile, first to France and later to Buenos Aires and Montevideo.[20] Despite the extensive literature on the Irish Brigade and Casement's adventures in Germany, this gripping supplement to the Irish revolution has yet to be properly integrated into the wider history of Ireland and of the First World War.

14 Thomas St John Gaffney, *Breaking the Silence: England, Ireland, Wilson and the War* (New York, 1930). Another relevant study is James K. McGuire, *The King, the Kaiser and Irish Freedom* (New York, 1915), which begins with a chapter explaining Casement's mission to Germany within the wider republican movement.

15 Princess Blücher later wrote a memoir, *An English Wife in Berlin: A Private Memoir of Events, Politics and Daily Life in Germany Throughout the War and the Social Revolution of 1918* (New York, 1920).

16 Karl Spindler's memoir was published originally as *Das geheimnisvolle Schiff: Blockadedurchbruch S. M. Hilfskreuzer 'Libau' zur irischen* (Berlin, 1921). This was first translated into English as *Gun-Running for Casement in the Easter Rebellion, 1916* (Glasgow, 1921) and into French as *Le Vaisseau Fantôme* (Paris, 1929). Spindler wrote an introduction to a new updated version, published as *The Mystery of the Casement Ship [with authentic documents]* (Berlin, 1931). This was republished in a paperback edition (Kerry, 1965) with an extensive foreword by Florence O'Donoghue, where he takes issue with several aspects of Spindler's account of events.

17 Xander Clayton, *Aud* (Plymouth, 2007)

18 Dr Franz Rothenfelder, *Casement in Deutschland* (Augsburg, 1917). Also, Karin Wolf, *Sir Roger Casement und die deutsch-irischen Beziehungen* (Berlin, 1972).
19 Berlin-Brandenburgische Akademie der Wissenschaften, NL Eduard Meyer 357.
20 Balder Olden, *Paradiese des Teufels: Das Leben Sir Roger Casement* (Berlin, 1933). Balder Olden and his brother, Rudolf, wrote some of the earliest books attacking the Nazi Party, criticism which cost them dearly.
21 Jérôme aan de Wiel, *The Irish Factor 1899–1919: Ireland's Strategic and Diplomatic importance for Foreign Powers* (Dublin, 2008) is a vital study for understanding the continental context for Casement's months in Germany and the relevance of Ireland as a determining factor in European foreign policy in this period. Aan de Wiel acknowledges his debt to Wolfgang Hünssler, *Das Deutsche Kaiserreich und die Irische Frage 1900–14* (Frankfurt am Main, 1978), and Hans-Dieter Kluge, *Irland in der deutschen Geschichtswissenschaft, Politik und Propaganda vor 1914 und im Ersten Weltkrieg* (Frankfurt am Main, 1985).

Over the years, the Irish-German connection has been the subject of several important studies, which were never translated into English. Fortunately, much of this scholarship has been recently synthesized and expanded by Jérôme aan de Wiel.[21] Aan de Wiel has persuasively illuminated Ireland's strategic value in the diplomatic discussions between France, Germany, Austro-Hungary and Russia with Britain and the tangled web of espionage, subversion and propaganda linking Ireland's revolutionary network to other anti-imperial networks across Europe and Asia—often supported clandestinely by the agencies of different European powers. The situation of Casement within these wider, interlinking national and anti-colonial associations raises important questions and opportunities for further research into the overlapping and interconnecting European, Atlantic and global contexts for 1916.

The journey to the Western Front

Roger Casement's journey to the German headquarters at Charleville-Mézières, just inside the French border with Belgium, was arranged less than three weeks after his arrival in Berlin. The journey was made incognito, with Casement travelling under his adopted pseudonym of 'Mr Hammond', an American from New York. This secrecy reflected both diplomatic sensitivities and lingering suspicions about his true purpose in Germany. The brief, three-day journey was undertaken in the company of Count von Lüttichau of the German General Staff, Richard Meyer, his Foreign Office 'assessor', who would advise Casement during his eighteen months in Germany, and a driver, Herr Meckle, with considerable local knowledge of the area. Count von Lüttichau organized the trip and had orders to take Casement on a detour through the region to witness for himself the condition of the people less than three months after the German army occupation of Belgium. On the route to Charleville the car passed through the frozen, forested hills of the Eifel region, before crossing through Luxembourg into the valley of the Meuse.

Negotiations were still underway between Casement and senior officials of the German Foreign Office about how they might co-operate in Casement's plans to further the cause of Irish independence. Casement met with two officials: Kurt von Lersner, a senior German diplomat, whom he had contacted in the US during his dealings with the German embassy in advance of his departure from New York, and Wilhelm von Stumm, the head of the Political Department at the German Foreign Office. The conversation with von Lersner was largely about the Irish Brigade, but the meeting with Baron von Stumm ranged widely and covered the larger, geo-strategic implications of the war and the future balance of power in Europe. Casement was determined that the German government should recognize Ireland's right to independence in the event of any negotiated peace settlement. It was and is well known that Casement pointed out that the British Government's justification for its going to war to defend the rights of small nations was wholly contradicted by its policy towards Ireland.

The discussion with von Stumm also disclosed attitudes held at the highest level of the German command structure, most notably the view that Germany did not believe Britain would go to war in August 1914. This prompted Casement to express his view that a conspiracy and crisis within the inner circle of the Liberal government, combined with Britain's desire to defend its global economic interests, were responsible for the escalation of a European crisis into a world crisis. His arguments on the causes of war had been expanded in his volume of essays—*The Crime against Europe*—which had already appeared in English in the US and would soon be translated into German. Here, Casement argued why Ireland should stay out of the war and why Britain's justification for going to war was false.[22] The essays asserted the case for a German-Irish alliance able to work towards the peaceful and negotiated reconfiguration of European, Atlantic and global power relations. While these essays have been casually dismissed over the last century as Sinn Féin propaganda, his arguments have unavoidable parallels with later analyses on the origins of the First World War made by the Marxist historian, Arno Mayer, and, more recently, by Niall Fergusson in his controversial *The Pity of War*.[23] Ferguson's argument that Britain could have stayed out of the conflict had it not been for reckless imperial policy carried out in secret over many years is a recurring theme in Casement's writing:

> England fights as the foe of Europe and the enemy of European civilization. In order to destroy German shipping, German commerce, German industry, she has deliberately plotted the conspiracy we now see at work. The war of 1914 is England's war.[24]

It was British aggression and not German militarism that was the real *causus belli*. Enmity was founded upon economic concerns and supported by an insidious publicity campaign conducted by the popular press in Britain, deliberately aimed at demonizing Germany and German culture and at stirring up feelings of hatred. Irish independence and neutrality, to Casement's way of thinking, served both the interests of European relations and the greater cause of international humanity. The independence of Ireland was and would remain critical and central to the balance of power. For its day, this was a remarkably European position to take; much of Casement's speculation in this book has, with a century of hindsight, proved both relevant and prescient.

Casement's experience as an advocate for a revolutionary humanism within the circles of European power supports Arno Meyer's argument that domestic policy was a key factor in determining foreign policy in the months before the declaration of war. Meyer's reading of the First World War as a determined counter-revolutionary strike by conservative and reactionary interests in Europe to protect their economic and hegemonic interests is confirmed by Casement's rapid disillusion with a specifically Prussian militarism in Germany and by his ruthless treatment at the hands of the Conservative and Unionist bloc in Britain after his capture. Casement's efforts to merge different revolutionary forces within Ireland and internationally were anathema to both sides. They contributed towards his alienation from the German General Staff and explain why the British security services—in the widest sense of that term—were so anxious for his capture and silencing by assassination.

Yet in November 1914, Casement still believed that Germany held the key to Irish sovereignty. Once he had reassured senior military officials of the sincerity of his intentions, he was escorted back to Cologne through the towns and cities of Belgium that had stood in the front line during the German advance through Belgium in August 1914. His journey included brief stops in Dinant, Andenne and Liège. Along the way, he noted the physical destruction—of bridges and buildings—and the socio-economic condition of the people reduced to prostitution, vagrancy and destitution. His escort car passed to the south of Brussels, close to the royal palace at Tervuren, founded by King Leopold II as an architectural monument to his colonial policy in central Africa. At Andenne, the driver, Herr Meckle, recounted the story of the *franc-tireurs*, who had opened fire on a column of German soldiers taking ammunition to the front. In reprisal 350 men were arrested and shot against the wall. On hearing this story Casement was provoked to consider and review his own feelings about the war, about the politics of atrocities and German atrocities in particular. He did not deny that appalling incidents had happened, but he saw then in the light of what his

22 Andrew McGrath's forthcoming critique of Casement's political writings in the light of just war theory are touched on in his essay 'The Anglo-Irish War (1919–1921): Just War or Unjust Rebellion?', *Irish Theological Quarterly*, 77 (1) (2012), 67–82.

23 Casement's essays might be usefully read alongside Arno Meyer, 'The Primacy of Domestic Politics', in Holger Herwig (ed.), *The Outbreak of World War I* (Boston, 1997) and Niall Fergusson, *The Pity of War: Explaining World War I* (New York, 2000).

24 Roger Casement, 'The Crime against Ireland', in *The Crime Against Europe* (Belfast, 2003), 62.

25 The 'demographic deficit' of 10 million lives resulting from the rubber wars in the Congo was most recently made by Adam Hochschild in his best-selling history *King Leopold's Ghost* (London, 1998). The figure was also referenced in the dramatized documentary by Peter Bate, *White King, Red Rubber, Black Death* (BBC 4, 2004). The claim provoked an official response from the Belgian Embassy in London 'Congo under King Leopold II', which categorically denied the estimated figures, claiming that they are 'very inaccurate and, at worst, totally incorrect.' The matter was widely dicussed in the Belgium press. For a discussion of the debate see Geert Castryk, 'Whose History is History? Singularities and Dualities of the Public Debate on Belgian Colonialism', Csaba Lévai, *Europe and the World in European Historiography* (Pisa, 2006) and Adam Hochschild, 'In the Heart of Darkness', *New York Review of Books*, 6 October 2005, 39–42.

own official investigation of crimes against humanity had exposed. In a particularly revealing moment, as he stood before a wall in Namur, site of a notorious atrocity perpetrated by German soldiers against Belgian civilians, he reflected:

> Sometimes, I must confess, when the present 'agony of Belgium' confronts me—and it cannot well be minimised, it is in truth a national agony—I feel that there may be in this awful lesson to the Belgian people a *repayment*. All that they now suffer and far more, they, or their king, his government and his officers wreaked on the well nigh defenceless people of the Congo basin.

In this comment, Casement instinctively dismantles the colonial hierarchy of humanity: in British propaganda, gallant little Belgium was being subjected to the unprecedented inhumanity of the 'Hun', while the Congo—or any of the sites of European massacre in Africa—had no place in the accepted hierarchy of suffering 'humanity'. Some estimates claim that the casualties resulting from King Leopold II's administration in the Congo Free State were as high as the death toll of the First World War.[25] Comparison of such statistics is hazardous, but the question of violence and its concealment within the concept of 'humanity' arises directly from Casement's visit to the Western Front. His comments on German atrocities and the 'agony of Belgium' are central to understanding his career and to the hypocrisy of the atrocity claims of the First World War and the propaganda struggle for ownership of the terminology of civilization by the warring colonial powers. He had shown the merciless nature of colonial rule in sub-Saharan Africa and in South America. The First World War was being fought by the perpetrators of those 'crimes against humanity'; the phrase was then and continues to be a central trope of the propaganda of colonial and imperial powers. Casement's pioneering interrogation of colonial power and the destructive capacity of international venture capitalism had a revolutionary impact that was at the heart of his dedication to Ireland's struggle.

As a leading authority on the investigation of crimes against humanity, Casement was well placed to observe the allegations made against the German occupation of Belgium. He had journeyed through part of this region during a European holiday in May 1912, enabling him to make an informed comparison between the territory as it was then and in 1914. In 1914, he was of course aware of how images and rumours of German atrocities were being used by Britain to sway public opinion, both domestically and internationally, against Germany, to justify Britain's own entry into the war, and to help in the conscription campaign. At one point in his diary, on the road back to Cologne, Casement commented:

> Of all the lies England has distributed in recent years throughout the world, by her admirable system called 'free trade', I guess this lie of German barbarism and 'German atrocities' is the most wilful, the most perverse and the most evil intentioned.

This is one of many such attacks on the strategic use of German atrocity stories to influence world opinion, especially American opinion, in the battle for hearts and minds. In his writing and correspondence during 1914 and 1915, Casement claimed forthrightly that much 'official' evidence in Britain was manufactured and invented. In his opening essay in *The Crime Against Europe* he claimed:

> To find the causes of war we should turn not to Blue Books or White Papers, giving carefully selected statements of those responsible for concealing from the public the true issues that move nations to attack each other, but

should seek the unavowed aims of those nations themselves.[27]

Casement's determination to reveal the deceptive practices behind officially sanctioned truths was a principal theme in his political writings in the last three years of his life. It was not only the atrocities in sub-Saharan Africa and the Amazon that had shocked him; it was the difficulty of reporting them that alerted him to how such allegations could be manipulated for political ends. His innovative use of graphic descriptions and images of atrocities to expose oppressive administration in the Congo, Putumayo and Ireland had involved him in acrimonious disputes and accusations of inventing evidence, distorting truth, exaggeration and fantasizing. But Casement skilfully defended his investigative practices and procedures and placed them indelibly on the official record. In 1913, as he harnessed his own investigations of crimes against humanity to the cause of Irish independence and his own overtly political purposes, a counter-strategy was implemented to deny him moral authority and undermine the truth of his accusations. Nevertheless, in the exposure of colonial atrocities that would feature prominently in the advanced nationalist and socialist press in Ireland in 1914, Casement's hand was clearly at play.[27]

Casement's earliest comments on the politics of atrocity can be traced back to 1894, when he undertook survey work along the contested frontier between the emerging British administrative district of the Oil Rivers Protectorate (Niger Delta) and German Cameroon. His later investigations in the Congo Free State and the upper Amazon prompted European diplomacy to rethink aspects of international trade and the question of native rights. His Putumayo report had been deployed in the switching of international capital away from the extractive rubber economy to the plantation economy of Southeast Asia. Unofficially, Casement had used his investigations to draw attention to the degenerative and destructive capacity of empires and to justify his own path to rebellion. Therefore, the account of his brief journey through war-torn Belgium is an important and vivid report because it is by the man who had investigated more atrocities at first hand than any other official of that era. Despite his pro-German and anti-British sympathies, no one better understood the potential for the use and abuse of atrocity claims. Casement had been fastidious in his own reporting of crimes against humanity and rigorous in substantiating claims, corroborating testimony and investigating allegations at first hand. He was well placed therefore to critically evaluate the official investigative practices into German atrocities in Belgium.

The historiographical controversy over the allegations made by agencies of the British government against the German army in their invasion and occupation of Belgium is extensive and endures.[28] From August 1914, Britain launched a highly effective publicity campaign detailing the brutal treatment of the civilian population. The Rape of Belgium, as it was called, contained graphic accounts of gratuitous violence—rape, infanticide, the cutting off of hands and mass executions. Many of the rumours were later shown to have been black propaganda, most notably the story of the German corpse factory.[29] Several figures who campaigned most vigorously against the distortions of the truth and the unhealthy alliance between state agencies of propaganda and the press were members of the Union of Democratic Control (U.D.C.). The U.D.C. was the anti-war organization established on the outbreak of war in 1914 by Casement's main collaborator in the Congo Reform Association, E. D. Morel. It lobbied against secret diplomacy and worked as a pressure group for a more democratically accountable foreign policy. Numbered among its cohort of recognised supporters and members were

26 Roger Casement, 'The Causes of the War and the Foundations of Peace' in *The Crime Against Europe* (Belfast, 2003), 64.

27 See, for instance, James Connolly, 'Belgian Rubber and Belgian Neutrality', *The Irish Worker*, 14 November 1914, and an anonymously written article, 'Atrocities', in *The Hibernian*, 1: 16, 18 September 1915, 2–3.

28 See the studies which have reignited the issue: John Horne and Alan Kramer, *German Atrocities, 1914: A History of Denial* (New Haven, 2001) and Jeff Lipkes, *Rehearsals, The Belgium Army in Belgium, August 1914* (Leuven, 2007).

29 Joachim Neander and Randal Marlin, 'Media and Propaganda: The Northcliffe Press and the Corpse Factory Story of World War I', in *Global Media Journal (Canadian Edition)* Vol 3: 2, 2010, 67–82. For a contemporary analysis of the treatment of war crimes and the political use and abuse of the word 'humanity', see Danilo Zolo, *Invoking Humanity: War, Law and Global Order* (London, 2002); *Victor's Justice: From Nuremburg to Baghdad* (London, 2009).

Edmund Dene Morel (1873–1924) c. 1905, British journalist, author and socialist politician. (Photo by Images of Empire/Universal Images Group via Getty Images).

30 *Report of the Committee on Alleged German Outrages* (London: HMSO, 1915)

the philosopher, Bertrand Russell; the journalist, H. N. Brailsford; the activist, Norman Angell; and Britain's first Labour Prime Minister, Ramsay MacDonald.

The critical document in establishing both the legal and historical claims for German atrocities was the Bryce Report, named after the historian, jurist and diplomat, James Bryce.[30] From the spring of 1915, as Casement began to channel his energies towards writing about the war and revealing secret dimensions of British power, he spoke out vehemently against the manipulation of truth and the circulation of falsehoods and exaggeration of German atrocities. He took issue in particular with Bryce for lending his name to the commission officially appointed by Prime Minister H. H. Asquith to report on the nature and extent of German war crimes in Belgium.

'I knew Lord Bryce well—he used to be an honourable man—but this lending his name to a faked and obviously fraudulent investigation, undertaken for one object only, is beneath contempt.'[31]

When serving as British ambassador in Washington, Bryce had helped Casement broaden his Putumayo investigation into the U.S. State Department and had arranged a meeting in early 1912 between Casement and the U.S. President, William Taft. Bryce was also highly regarded for his measured historical writings and as an architect of the Anglo-American special relationship. Furthermore, he had spoken out against the Bulgarian atrocities and the genocide of the Armenians under Ottoman rule in 1915. Casement's attack on Bryce was therefore more than an attack on the government's manipulation of the truth for the purposes of war; it read as an attack on the politics of what might be cautiously termed the 'atrocity culture' and how the historical record was vulnerable to deliberate acts of management and manipulation for official purposes. The argument was most assertively developed in his essay *The Far-Extended Baleful Power of the Lie*, published in 1915.[32] Here the unequivocal accusation was made that Bryce had been co-opted to lead the commission in order to attach his name and reputation as a historian to a report which was based upon unsubstantiated evidence: 'by lending weight to an official campaign of slander, defamation and calumny conducted on a scale unparalleled in any war between civilized nations during the last three centuries'. It is a claim that was not lightly made and which Casement, as a former Foreign Office official and troubleshooter was in an informed position to make. This attack also made explicit reference to Casement's journey to the Western Front and his direct witnessing of German-occupied Belgium.

Unlike Lord Bryce I have been in Belgium since the war began. I was there within a few weeks of the passing of the great wave of invasion. I saw the wrecked and ruined houses; I passed through some of the stormed and battered cities Namur, Liège, Dinant; I conversed with Belgians in the streets of those terrorised towns and I formed a judgement of my own, not derived from hearsay in another land or the lips of fugitives afar, but from the scenes and spots and human wreckage I passed through … Wrongs were undoubtedly committed in Belgium, but they were not all committed by Germans upon Belgians.

The shadow of the war on truth entangled with the controversy over German atrocities and the fabrication of historical evidence might also be read into the secret history of Casement's trial. Professor J. H. Morgan, part of Casement's defence counsel and the *amicus curiae* during his trial and appeal, was deeply implicated in compiling testimony and statements about German atrocities in Belgium. For over a decade, Morgan had been personally known to Casement and, as a professor of constitutional law at the University of London, he had edited an important collection of essays on Irish Home Rule in 1912.[33] In the autumn of 1914, Morgan was appointed to the adjutant-general staff as Home Office representative with the British expeditionary force to inquire into the conduct of the German army in Belgium. Over the next two years, he published numerous articles, pamphlets and books on legal aspects of the war. In his co-authored study *War: Its Conduct and Legal Results*, he wrote on the Defence of the Realm Act and the question and meaning of treason in war time. His writings on German atrocities in Belgium were widely circulated through articles and various mass-circulation books. His most important publication was *German Atrocities: An Official Investigation*. His case exposing German war crimes was published in a more accessible version in *Germany's Dishonoured Army*,

31 NLI MS 33726 Roger Casement to Fräulein Meyer, 1 July 1915.

32 *Continental Times*, 3 November 1915. The essay was reproduced in *Roger Casement: The Crime against Europe* (Belfast, 2003).

33 J. H. Morgan, *The New Irish Constitution: An Exposition and Some Arguments* (London, 1912) This was published under the auspices of the Eighty Club, a London-based political club, closely aligned to the Liberal Party, and of particular consequence to the political careers of both H. H. Asquith and David Lloyd George. Morgan's introductory essay argued how a delegation of authority at the level of both the executive and legislative would make the imperial government stronger. Home Rule, he argued, was a way by which the Imperial parliament could reorganize and strengthen its own constitutional attachments through the establishment of an Irish parliament. Devolution, he believed, was not a step backwards but a step forward.

Dinant, Belgium, August 1914. Captured by the German Third Army under General Von Hausen, who ransacked the town and rounded up and shot 612 civilians (Photo by Popperfoto/Getty Images).

printed by the Parliamentary Recruiting Committee—the state agency responsible for issuing propaganda posters justifying the war and conscription. In 1917, he wrote *Gentlemen at Arms* under the pseudonym 'Centurion'—a series of sentimental short stories about the experience of war. Morgan was closely involved in the construction of an official narrative of the war, which dichotomized the public imagination between the brutal, scheming and dishonest 'Hun' and British heroism, fair play and sacrifice. His writings on German atrocities supplemented the official government report produced by the Bryce commission and helped to popularize parts of the evidence for popular consumption.

Whether Casement knew about Morgan's work for the Bryce commission is unknown. Nothing in his trial notes would suggest that he did know, and he maintained complete trust in Morgan to the bitter end. Likewise, Morgan persisted in his defence of Casement and wanted to take on unnamed government agencies over the use of the 'Diary' (acknowledged today as the Black Diaries) which helped railroad Casement to the gallows and have ever since dominated his public mythologizing and historical management. On 4 August 1916, the day after Casement's execution, Morgan wrote to the Home Secretary, Herbert Samuel:

> there is a very strong feeling abroad—*The Times* gives expression to it this morning that someone in authority 'inspired' a campaign of malignant and studied calumny against the prisoner which was not only necessary to the course of justice but calculated to pervert it.[34]

Morgan had inside knowledge on the use of the 'diary' to destabilize his defence and undermine the different petitions for clemency. Because of his close personal knowledge of Casement, he was also in a position to know whether the rumours about Casement were founded in truth. In the immediate aftermath of Casement's execution, Morgan contacted Casement's solicitor, George Gavan Duffy, seeking his views on a letter he wished to send to F. E. Smith, the arch-Unionist attorney general and founder of the Ulster Volunteer Force, who led the Crown's prosecution against

---

34 George Gavan Duffy Papers NLI MS 10763 (20)—J. H. Morgan to Home Secretary, Herbert Samuel, 4 August 1916.

Remember Belgium Poster by Ellsworth Young, 1918
© Swim Ink 2, LLC/CORBIS

Casement and was closely involved in First World War propaganda strategizing.

You [Smith] will remember that at the interview with you on July 14 you expressed some concern lest 'questions should be raised' as to the use of a certain diary attributed to Roger Casement and that at the subsequent interview of Mr Jones & myself with you on 29 July you—in reply to a representation—made by Mr Jones as to complaints on the part of Casement's friends that attempts had been made to prejudice the press and members of the public against him by revealing the contents of the said diary—assured us that there was 'not a word of truth' in these complaints.

I regret to inform you that information has since come to me from various quarters which, though not conclusive, raises grave doubts in my mind and those doubts are certainly not allayed by the remarkable protest in *The Times* of Friday last—a protest which practically amounts to an allegation of dishonourable conduct against some person in authority—and a protest which, I observe, has received no official contradiction. You will understand that I am now writing to you in my professional capacity and that my letter is in no sense to be taken as any reflection on the proceedings in the courts which proceedings indeed were in my humble opinion, worthy of the best traditions of English justice. I write merely as a public man who is anxious for the good name of his country and who is deeply concerned at the damaging statements which are being made in various quarters as to the conduct of someone in authority. But I do not suppose that anything can now be done and this letter needs no answer.[35]

Gavan Duffy advised Morgan that his desire to pursue a public inquiry would be pointless, as any appointed committee would be filled with men who would inevitably find in the government's favour—a result unhelpful to Casement's cause. However, the issue of this contested diary in Casement's trial underlines the importance of this genre of writing. It was obviously important to an inveterate keeper of diaries such as he was. Equally, it was also as an evidentiary source which can be readily characterized as a form of the most private kind of truth and 'sincerity', or as a source of unintended revelation or exposure and, fatally in this instance, as a genre given to all kinds of artifice and forgery, either by the author or by the 'authorities'. Casement had kept diaries to explain his thoughts and deeds with the intention 'that some day the truth may be known'. He did this in the Congo in 1903, in the Amazon in 1910 and 1911 and in Germany from 1914 to 1916. There is also evidence that he tried to keep a jail journal, although the prison authorities soon put an end to that. It is no wonder, therefore, that some should still question the sexualized narrative, referred to by Morgan in his letter to Smith, of such dubious provenance, originating in the dark recesses of the British security services and so persistently used to subvert Casement's moral authority and to obscure his place in Ireland's revolutionary history.

Understanding Casement's role in 1916 can open up what Lord Denning, when dismissing allegations of police brutality against the Birmingham Six, infamously called an 'appalling vista'. Casement's investigations of the excesses of European imperialism haunted his generation. The shadow of colonial violence darkened the European modernities, the famous 'Heart of Darkness' that Conrad too, in his glaring and subtle fiction, pondered and exposed. As in Africa, so in Europe—Casement's critique of the propaganda behind the German 'atrocities' in Belgium is another exemplary instance of the suspect nature of official evidence and of the vulnerability of the historical record to such typical acts of intellectual treason.

[35] George Gavan Duffy papers NLI MS 10763 (20)—Confidential draft of letter from J. H. Morgan to F. E. Smith.

Soldiers walk around puddles created by shelling on the wetlands near Gheluvelt, Belgium, during a World War I battle over Ypres, c. 1914–17
© CORBIS

1. Philipp von Berckheim (1883–1945) was a secretary at the German General Staff.
2. Mr Hammond was the name adopted by Casement after arriving in Berlin. During the course of his journey to the Western Front, his identity was kept secret from two of his three travelling companions.

Diary of Roger Casement

I.

My Journey to the German Headquarters at Charleville

Novr. 17 (Tuesday) from Berlin and back there (Friday) 20 Nov.

[Berlin] Monday 16 Nov. [1914]

I got a phone call from Baron von Berckheim[1] of the General Staff, at 8 Moltke Str. about 1 o'clock asking me, 'Mr. Hammond,' to go round there and see him between 3 and 4.[2]

I went accordingly, in a taxi, to the address given. It is across the big Königsplatz in front of the Reichstag—I was shown up by a young orderly soldier who said he could speak 'Italienische' but not 'Amerikansche'! After wandering through many corridors, going to various rooms (all wrong) he waylaid a very pretty girl (possibly a typist I imagined) in a hat as if to go out who spoke

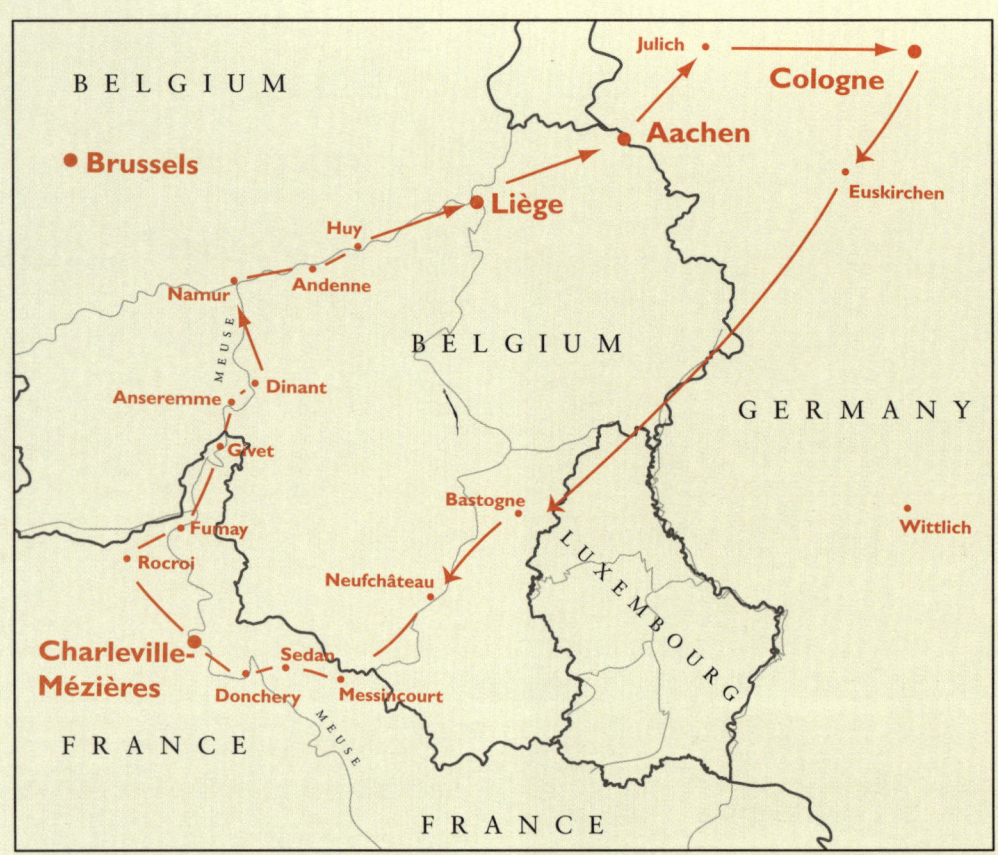

Roger Casement's route from Cologne to Charleville and back, 1914.

good English and she directed us to von Berckheim's room, No. 182. He came at length, a young officer with sword and spurs in a grey cavalry uniform with riding boots and greeted me kindly & in good English. He said he had heard about me from Kurt von Lersner[3], and that he too, had been at the Washington Embassy and hoped to return there later on. We found the 'waiting room' occupied, so he cleared two servant maids out of a dining room— and there we talked. He explained that the 'Headquarters' (at the French front) wished me to go there at once. Von Lersner who knew me already, had charge of the affair— was I ready to go? I said 'at once.' He said that arrangements would be made for my journey on the morrow, to leave Berlin by the night train for Cologne, where an automobile would meet me sent by Lersner to take me straight to Headquarters. I would be accompanied the whole way by an officer, a Graf something, whose name he forgot for the moment. Would my military passport be made out for me as Sir Roger Casement or as Mr. Hammond? I said better as Mr. Hammond, and he agreed.

He explained that the journey was to be kept quite secret and that the Count who took charge of me would only know me as Mr. H.—and knew nothing of the objects. I would be simply Mr. H., an American, going to the front in his charge. He explained that Headquarters wanted to talk with me about the Irish prisoners. We discussed this matter and a few other things. He explained further that there was a possibility that the motor car from Cologne might be full the next night and if so my departure wd. be for Wednesday night from Berlin but he would let me know at my hotel by noon next day (Tuesday) whether the departure would be for that night or Wednesday.

I left about 4.30 and walked back to the hotel thinking first to go [to] the Foreign

3   Kurt von Lersner (1883–1954), was a German diplomat and politician. He became close friends of Franklin D. Roosevelt when stationed at the German embassy in Washington in 1913/14. Casement met with von Lersner in New York before journeying to Germany and was one of the officials he met on his visit to the German Headquarters of the Foreign Office at Charleville. In 1919, von Lersner served as president of the German delegation to Versailles and along with Georges Clemenceau and David Lloyd George was one of the first signatories of the Treaty of Versailles. From 1920 to 1924 he sat as a deputy for Leipzig in the first parliament of the Weimar Republic. A close friend of Franz von Papen, he was sidelined by the Nazis because of his Jewish ancestry and sent as cultural attaché to Istanbul. Captured after the war by the US he was interrogated and released. For several years he worked closely in liaising between US diplomats in Germany and President de Gaulle in France.

4 Richard Meyer served as Casement's liaison officer with the German Foreign Office and was one of the few Jews on the permanent staff. Almost all communication to and from Casement during his time in Germany passed across Meyer's desk and the two co-operated closely on the formation of the Irish Brigade and the preparations for Casement's return to Ireland in April 1916. Meyer was involved in various covert operations on other fronts and went on to direct the Political Division of the Foreign Office. He was denied citizenship by Hitler in 1936; however, because of his many years of public service, he was allowed to 'escape' to Sweden in 1939.

5 Count George von Wedel (1862–1943) was one of the notable diplomats in the Kaiser's service. He had served as an attaché in Tokyo, Vienna, Cairo and Rome before taking on the direction of the English Department at the German Foreign Office (Auswärtiges Amt). Von Wedel arranged with the German secret police for Casement to be granted diplomatic immunity on his arrival in Berlin. He and Casement remained in close contact until the departure for Ireland in April 1916. NLI MS 43, 227 1-4.

Office and tell them there—but I decided to await Meyer at the hotel at 5 and tell him.[4]

He came about 5.30, and on hearing my news said he must go at once to the F.O. and tell them there of this sudden summons—and he hurried off in a taxi—returning later to say he would try to accompany me, if possible, to Headquarters and that I should call on von Wedel next evg at 5, to talk things over.[5]

I spent the evening alone, as usual, taking a walk in the Thiergarten after a light 'dinner' at Hoffmann's restaurant, as usual, where I am now a recognised habitué.

Saw several detachments of recruits going off today—some in uniform, with flowers in belts and bosoms—some in plain clothes, with packages in hand of all sorts and mostly just wrapped in paper—women and friends walking alongside. The men—all young mainly—looked happy and smiling—and many were smoking. The passers by stopped to look with kind eyes on the sons of the Fatherland marching sedately to the trenches of death.

A quiet, patient, obedient and sure-hearted people this, if ever Europe had one. There is an entire absence of jingoism—and yet today, confirmation came of rumours of a great victory over the Russians. This is the first outcome of the battle Professor Schiemann[6] told me of on Sunday. Von Berckheim gave me the assurance that the news in the evening papers was exact, and added that a much bigger event was expected—viz.—a decisive victory in the East. The German retreat towards Thorn was part of a plan with the Austrians—now the advance from Thorn to the Vistula, where fighting was on both banks, was part of this plan. It was hoped to drive the Russian centre southwest towards the Austrians at Cracow &c. and then for the German forces to close the rear and to capture or destroy a very large force. This engagement was now proceeding in part he explained—but nothing of it was given out to the press and he asked me to regard it as a 'secret.' The news actually announced,

however, is excellent for the German army. In two engagements, one at Soldau, and one on the Vistula at Wloclawek, the Russians have been defeated with a loss of 28,000 prisoners, 70 machine guns, one large gun, and several cannon.

The number of killed and wounded are not stated, or definitely known. The hotel manager (Klick) said '50,000 killed and wounded.' Meyer, when he called, later in evening said they were 'now believed to be 70,000.' Anyhow it is a considerable victory—and the evening news sheets are being sold rapidly.

[Berlin] Tuesday. 17 Nov.

Berlin is all beflagged today in honour of the Prussian victory. Von Hindenburg[7] the victor again! He is the hero of the Prussian heart—and rightly too—for this victory cannot fail to greatly aid the cause of Germany.

Today I sent Adler out to buy various things needed for my journey and arranged all details of his return to Moss on Saturday next (when his teeth are finished, poor boy!) With two faked letters and some pages of my 'Diary' he has 'stolen.'[8]

Von Berckheim called on me at noon to say all was arranged for my departure that evening at 9.45 in company with the Count, whose name is still uncertain—and that he would call on me about 7.30 p.m. that evg.

I had nothing to do but to get ready, as the tickets, passport &c. &c. would all be in the hands of the Count who would call for me about 9 p.m.

Meyer called and told me that I should call on von Wedel at 5 or 5.15 & that he would call for me then to take me to F.O.

I went with him at 5, to 76 Wilhelmstrasse[9] & was shown into the Saloon to wait for v. Wedel who was just collared by an earlier caller. In this room I found Professor Schiemann—who was delighted with my story of the 'Christiania incident' (I had written out on Monday) which he had in his hand to get typed at F.O. and a copy of it sent with a covering letter to the Emperor. Schiemann complimented me on the way I had written the 'story'—'un vrai roman'—but one that he believed the Emperor would be greatly interested in. He told me that Fräulein Meyer had received a letter from her brother Kuno from Rotterdam saying his 'coffre' had not arrived and that he was sailing without it.[10] Neither Schiemann nor the sister know if this referred to the box of papers or to some ordinary trunk of clothes. Schiemann was alarmed and I shared his alarm, if it should prove to be Kuno Meyer's box of damaging papers. I pointed out that if, by ill luck, the English got hold of this they would certainly arrest Meyer anywhere at sea—even just outside New York. Schiemann left me in the waiting room to go and see Zimmermann;[11] I waited on until 7, as Meyer came in twice to say that von Wedel was still kept by his urgent visitor. This waiting room of the German F.O. is interesting. It is furnished in crimson red, with claret coloured wall paper. There are two life sized portraits, one of the old Emperor William, the other of his father King Frederick William of Prussia. There are two busts (I don't know of whom) flanking the latter picture; and a photograph of the old royal castle of Goslar, Schiemann told me had been built by the Emperor Henry IV and is kept up and liked by the present Emperor.

Several visitors came and went while I was waiting for the call from von Wedel. At 7 Meyer came for me—and Wedel told he thought I should see von Jagow[12] and perhaps the Chancellor at the front.

He told me to tell Baron von Stumm,[13] the chief of the political department of the F.O. whom I should find there, 'everything.'

He then showed me the written copy of the interview and declaration—this the Declaration of Goodwill to Ireland—I had sent him on the 11th which had been sent to Headquarters and was now back amended and somewhat shortened.[14] The first two sentences have been struck out altogether and it begins with the general statement of goodwill towards Ireland, and ends with my words 'national prosperity and national freedom'.

In its amended form it contains all the essentials I desire—and is given a more emphatic character as the opening few lines now reads:

'In reply to this enquiry made to the Under Secretary of State the Imperial Chancellor has directed the following Official Declaration to be issued.'

The 'interview' part remains as I had penned it save that they prefix to my name 'the distinguished Irish nationalist' Sir Roger Casement. I protested and begged to have this struck out—in vain.

I got back the Christiania papers from von Wedel to show at the front, if necessary—and then I told him of the loss of Kuno Meyer's trunk and my fears that it might be his box of compromising papers. I pointed out that it might be as well to keep back the issue of the declaration until the truth was known, or even until we were sure that Kuno had reached New York safely. Von Wedel was anxious to issue the Declaration at once and told me he should like to give it out the next day. I agreed, provided they felt easy about the Professor's journey—admitting that I might be over anxious in this regard.

I left von Wedel about 7.30 with his final good wishes for my journey to the front, and his kindly face smiling after me as I turned down the stairs.

Meyer met me outside and told me it was settled that he should accompany me to the front, as there was room in the motor car. He would call for me at 9.30 at the Hotel.

At 9 p.m. von Berckheim came with my guide and guard the Graf von Lüttichau[15] —a baldish headed young Prussian nobleman. He was in uniform, that of the 'Volunteer Automobile Corps.' All the necessary papers were with him.

Meyer came, and all three came to my room, where we arranged for Adler's passport to be visé, so that he could leave

6   Professor Theodor von Schiemann (1847–1921) historian, archivist and policy expert on Germany's Eastern Front was a key intellectual ally of Casement and a close friend of the Kaiser. Schiemann was collaborating with anti-British elements in the Irish republican movement from as early as 1906. He visited Britain just before the outbreak of war to consider the deepening political crisis in Ireland. His report on the imminent outbreak of civil war in Ireland influenced Germany's urging Austria to go to war with Serbia, based on his view that internal conflict in Britain would prevent involvement in any European conflict. In 1915 he published *Die Achillesferse Englands* (England's Achilles Heel) containing his translation of Casement's essays published in *The Crime Against Ireland* (1914). After Casement's execution he wrote a foreword to Antonie Meyer, *Der Casement-Prozess und seine Ursachen / Sir Roger Casement: ein Irischer Märthrer* (Berlin, 1916). See NLI MS 22987 for Casement's letter to Schiemann discussing George Freeman.

7   Paul von Hindenburg (1847–1934), statesman and field marshal. Von Hindenburg's military victories in 1914 at the Battle of Tannenberg and the Battle of the Masurian Lakes were being celebrated.

8   Casement's decision to use faked letters and diary entries in his misinformation strategy against the British Foreign Office is questionable, to say the least, in the light of the campaign of counter-misinformation launched by the British secret services at the time of his trial.

9   Wilhelmstrasse is the street in central Berlin where the German Foreign Office was located along with other administrative organisations. The Reich Chancellery was located at No. 77.
10 Kuno Meyer (1858–1919), eminent Celtic philologist. He founded the School of Irish Learning in Dublin and edited the journal *Ériu*. Kuno Meyer was a key link in Casement's German network and a close friend of Theodore Schiemann. Casement met Meyer frequently in the weeks after his arrival in Berlin. In November Meyer left for the US and made a series of anti-British speeches mainly to Irish-American audiences. From this reference to Meyer in the conversation with Schiemann it appears that Meyer was involved in a conspiracy. See Seán Ó Lúing, *Kuno Meyer: A Biography* (Dublin, 1991) and Andreas Huether, 'In Politik verschieden, in Freundschaft wie immer': The German Celtic Scholar Kuno Meyer and the First World War', in Fred Bridgham (ed.), *The First World War as a Clash of Cultures* (London, 2006) 231–44.
11 Arthur Zimmermann (1864–1940) was Undersecretary of State at the German Foreign Office, succeeding Gottlieb von Jagow in November 1916. He met with Casement in early November 1914 to discuss the various aspects of his mission to Germany.
12 Gottlieb von Jagow (1863–1935) was German Minister for Foreign Affairs from 1913 to 1916.

for Moss on Saturday without danger of the 'papers' I was giving him for Mr. Findlay's benefit being seized at the Sassnitz frontier on his way out of Germany.[16]

Bidding poor old Adler (who nearly wept!) good-bye, 'Mr. Hammond', with his uniformed escort of the Baron and Count and his attaché Mr. Meyer, was bowed out of the hall by the manager and staff.

We walked round to the Friedrich Str Station and got our 'compartment' with some difficulty and delay. The train was crowded—and a great many soldiers and officers in it—and some wounded going back 'cured'—while stretchers were on the platform to have others carried off to the hospitals.

Finally we got off. The Count v. Lüttichau and I in one carriage, Meyer going into a sleeping car as far as Hanover where, he said, he would have to leave the sleeper and come and disturb us for a seat.

[Cologne to Charleville] Wednesday, 18 Novr. [1914]

We reached Cologne about 7.30 a.m. getting a fine view of the splendid, old city from the bridge over the (always) hurrying Rhine. The last time that I had seen the Rhine was at Coblenz in May 1912, with Dick Morten and Brab Lake! What changes! to all the world—and to me.[17]

At Cologne the motor car met us—a Herr Meckle, with a young chauffeur, in the corps uniform, being with it. We got our things in and went, at once, to the Dom Hotel on the square, looking out on the splendid cathedral. The cathedral is magnificent. Altho' so new it looks old—and it soars up to heaven as if inspired with all the past of this glorious old city of the Rhine.

We went inside and found the nave filled with the devout crowds of men and women kneeling and a priest I thought collecting—while far up in the lighted chancel one could see and hear the distant chant of the choristers. Cologne they tell me is probably 'four-fifths Roman Catholic'.

After a very hurried dejeuner—coffee and bread & butter—at the Dom Hotel—for which I paid m1.50—we left for Headquarters. Meyer sat next me in the body of the car—the chauffeur ('Stephan'—an East Prussian youth of 21 or so) on one of the two sliding chair seats—and von Lüttichau in front next to Meckle who drove the car. Two Mauser rifles (loaded) were fixed across the barrier in front of us, in a metal stand purposely made. It was bitterly cold—a hard white frost on all the roads. I was the only one without a fur coat. Meckle, von Lüttichau and the chauffeur had fur-lined leather coats—and Meyer a fine fur-lined tweed.

We went off at a great rate and kept this up throughout the whole run only stopping once to show the papers to a guard over a railway bridge; at the other military posts, and they were many, the driver was known and allowed to go thro'.

The route taken was over the Eifel region[18]—going high over the tops of that arid region, where snow lay in places, and through northern Luxembourg into southern Belgium by Bastogne, through Neufchâteau and out into France near Sedan and so to Charleville-Mézières where the Emperor and the Headquarters of the German army and imperial government are. The distance traversed they told me was 270 kilometres and as we did it in 6 hours and stopped (only for short spells to find the road or look at the wheels &c.) many times our speed must have been fully 50 kilometres (if not more) per hour.

Our route from Cologne lay first to Euskirchen and then through pretty little towns to the high blank ridges of the Eifel. South of us was Wittlich I had so delighted in with Dick Morten in May 1912—but none of that pleasant region could be seen from this line of country. The cold was intense and despite fur-lined gloves my fingers ached so much I had to take the gloves off & sit on my hands for nearly an hour to restore circulation.

I dare say our highest point was 600 metres. There were many farms on these bare, treeless uplands of the Eifel—but all were wrapped in winter haze and frost covered the ground and the sprouts of 'winter wheat' or rye more probably. We passed through small towns and villages to St Vith and soon were going across northern Luxembourg and out into Belgium at Bastogne. Here we first saw houses burnt, roofless and blackened with tumbled walls sometimes—from shellfire. But not many. At Neufchâteau, both on entering and leaving the town there were a few such ruined houses—but these were the sole traces of war, beyond the numerous German soldiers at times met on the way, or Red Cross motors, or forage motors, we came across. Such Belgian country people as we met, or saw in the towns were going about their business. It was a day of general prayer, and everywhere there had been numbers of people at early mass. In Neufchâteau the townspeople seemed resigned enough, and save for the half dozen or so ruined houses one could never have guessed that this was a conquered land and people. Boys were playing marbles busily in the square of Neufchâteau.

We entered France by a road thro' Messincourt-Messimpre and were soon in Sedan of many memories.

Here again were very few traces of war or conquest—save that most of the fine houses had the shutters up—the families fled. The poor people, who could not fly, were there as usual, as along the countryside we had passed through. It was only on leaving Sedan to cross the Meuse we came across the first striking sign of the war. The fine bridge over the river, I remembered from 1912, was in the river—a few French labourers under a guard were repairing it—two tugboats lay also sunk deep on the opposite shore.

At Donchery a few miles out from Sedan, however, we saw the dread evidence of the recent combat. Donchery lay across the Meuse, on our right hand. There was scarcely a house uninjured. The whole town lay there roofless, empty, a mass of ruins. The church in the midst was a shapeless mass. The bridge destroyed—but as at Sedan, a temporary wooden bridge served.

An old priest, who came from the town, passed us with bare head. I would have saluted him, had he looked, but he kept his eyes to the ground. At Charleville and Mézières, we found the town bridges all destroyed, but temporary structures had been run up alongside them.

Here, too, on the outskirts, were ruined and roofless houses—but in the two towns themselves—they are really one town divided by the winding Meuse—were but few traces of destruction. Soldiers were here in plenty, and motor cars go leór. We drove to the former Prefecture now the residence of the Headquarters staff of the great German armies. Somewhere near, I knew, must be the Emperor himself.

We were shown in first to a room where a Lt. Nicolai (I think) received us where after Graf von Lüttichau and Herr Meckle had retired, Meyer explained who I was. This officer, however, spoke no English. I gathered that the Baron Kurt von Lersner (whom I had last seen in the Ritz–Carlton in Madison Avenue!) would soon arrive— so as we were all of us starving we went to the former dining saloon of the Prefect, where an excellently simple luncheon was served by soldier servants. Other officers entered while we four took of the plentiful dish of stewed beef, macaroni and boiled potatoes, with a plain white wine—and then we adjourned to the absent Prefect's drawing-room—furnished in a yellow satin, poor Madame La Préfet—& had our coffee. Here von Lersner found us and after a brief delay Meyer & I went to his room upstairs where we discussed the matter of the 'Irish Brigade' which is that nearest the heart of the General Staff I can clearly see.[19]

Lersner told me of the steps being taken to collect the 'Irish Catholic soldiers,' who are prisoners of war, and to put them in one place where I could visit them. Nothing much has so far been done I gathered—

13 Wilhelm August von Stumm (1869–1935) was Director of the Political Department at the German Foreign Office, with tremendous influence at the highest level. In 1916 he became under-secretary of state for foreign affairs. Casement met von Stumm in Charleville and it is likely that von Stumm's approval was vital to the acceptance of Casement's plan.

14 The *Declaration of Goodwill* was a statement by the German Chancellor—drafted by Casement—intended to reassure Ireland of Germany's good intentions towards her. Contrary to the official newspeak circulated in the British press and through war propaganda outlets ... 'that a German victory would inflict great loss upon the Irish people ... The Imperial Government formally declared that under no circumstances would Germany invade Ireland with a view to its conquest or the overthrow of any native institution of that country'. See Doerries, 60–61. Some manuscript drafts of the declaration are held in NLI MS 13082 (7/ii).

15 A number of variant spellings were adopted by Casement to identify Count von Lüttichau—an old noble family from Messines in upper Saxony. Von Lüttichau facilitated Casement's journey to the German HQ at the Western Front and wore the uniform of the *Volunteer Automobile Corps* so as to be recognized at checkpoints along the way.

MY JOURNEY TO THE GERMAN HEADQUARTERS AT CHARLEVILLE

NCOs of Roger Casement's Irish Brigade, Zossen, Germany 1915. L–R: Corporal Peter Golden, Sergeant Major Keogh, Corporal O'Mahoney, Sergeant Daniel Julien Bailey (alias Beverley), Zerhussen (interpreter), Corporal Kavanagh, Corporal O'Callaghan, QMS H. Quinlisk. MS18081

16 The notorious Findlay affair or Christiania Incident—named after the British Minister in Christiania, Mansfeldt Findlay—whose efforts to have Casement 'bumped on the head' mushroomed into a very messy and unfortunate tangle of conspiracies, claims, counter-claims, forgeries and false allegations. The assassination plot ate like a worm into Casement's head and he referred to the incident repeatedly in his diary, correspondence and journalism. Several aspects of this government-inspired conspiracy still need to be satisfactorily explained and, though the plot failed, it foreshadowed the shoot-to-kill policies adopted by the British State during the Troubles. Casement's published diary contains a continuous commentary on the conspiracy.

their difficulty being largely that they don't know the difference between an Irishman and an Englishman! All are 'Englander' to them. However, after explaining things to von Lersner and discussing, too, the matter of the chaplain for the Irish prisoners, and even the possibility of sending one or two of the men, released, back to Ireland to try and get a good priest to come here—as well as to tell the Provisional Committee of the Volunteers what I am doing here—I left Lersner with the understanding that, as soon as a few score even, or some hundreds of Irish prisoners—authentic Irish—are collected they will let me know and I shall go to the camp to interview the men.

Leaving Lersner we found von Lüttichau and Meckle and after a quest for 'quarters' we got a 'billet' for the night in the Hôtel de Commerce of Charleville. This we found with some difficulty and found there only one manservant in charge. He was a Luxemburger named Joseph left in charge when the personnel of the hotel had fled at the German approach.

Joseph showed us very cold rooms and said there was no food, or hot water, or electric light even in the hotel. All had gone. He got his daily 'ration' from somewhere. He had only a few bits of candles & these he doled out to us. We next visited Meckle's quarters, which were in a private house. The family all save one lady had fled, like all the rest of the well-to-do Charleville population. Only the poor remained—and as Joseph explained to me they were better here, with the Germans, than starving homeless fugitives in the 'outlands.' They, the poor, had their passes and got their daily food somehow served out to them. For the rest they were in no danger as long as they stayed in their prescribed districts and had their proper papers. He showed me his military 'pass' which allowed him to be out till 11 p.m. if he liked. Meckle's landlady lived with some family that had not fled, but came daily to the house where he and some other officers were billeted and sat knitting, poor lady, in her empty salon! This we entered. She was away—but her knitting was on the table. A grand piano was there with a plentiful stock of music—Schubert, Mozart, Beethoven—as

I remarked to von Lüttichau 'nearly all German music'.

Finally I returned with Lüttichau to the Hotel de Commerce—for I was told I must go nowhere by myself. One of the gentlemen had to be always with me—for my own safety. Guards were everywhere through the streets, and patrols—and as my pass was with the General Staff and I could speak no German it was far too dangerous for me to be out alone.

At the Hotel, Meyer met me and said he had been to the 'Foreign Office'—in a fine building in the Avenue Delafare—where he had arranged for Baron von Stumm the head of the political department to see me at 9.30 a.m. on the morrow. It was decided that after this interview I should return to Berlin—and Lüttichau begged me to try and get thro' my interview with von Stumm by 10.30 a.m. so that we might return by Dinant, Namur and Liège. This, a much longer route back to Cologne would be far more interesting as we should pass thro' some of the most famous spots of the opening stages of the war. Meyer had got a pass for his dinner and mine at one of the officers' messes in some private house where his friend at the 'Foreign Office' told him to take me early as we should then find it 'nearly empty'.

On getting there about 6.30 we entered after showing our pass to the grounds of a sort of a large villa or even a Casino it seemed. Here were again military servants one of whom took us in hand and asked many questions about me. He deposited us finally at one of seven long tables—at which I counted in all 128 chairs. There were some 30 or 40 officers already at table—we bowed to them and they to us.

The servant brought a book in which Meyer wrote his name and mine, 'Mr. Hammond of New York.' I noticed Meyer getting more and more perturbed. At length the servant came and said something to him and he went out, leaving me alone to go on with some tough hard sausage and bread and red wine. In a minute Meyer returned and told me I was 'wanted to speak with someone' out in the hall.

Here I found an old officer in a grey frock coat with General's stripes on his shoulders.

He clicked his heels and bowed formally and I bowed without the heel 'klick'. He then asked me who I was, where I had come from, what I was doing at the General Staff and who had 'asked me to come' there. All this in slow, good English. I said I was Mr. H. of New York—that I had come from Berlin where Baron von Berckheim had called on me asking me to come to the General Staff and that I believed that I had come at the direct request and invitation of Baron von Lersner whom I knew in America. He then shook hands with me, said he hoped I should be interested and that he would see me again. We then returned to our places at the table, after more very courteous bows, and Meyer begged me to 'hurry up' and get away before any further contretemps arose.

So I left with no more than a bite of cold sausage and a piece of bread and when in the garden Meyer said he was really alarmed for me—and that I must get back to the hotel at once and stay there in my room till morning. He explained that all explanations <u>might</u> come too late! 'You might get arrested by any patrol, and speaking English and with no means of explaining yourself and no papers on you, you might very well be shot in a jiffy, before any of us would know.' So I was hurried back in the motor car at about 7.30 to the Hotel where I found Joseph in the dreary 'kitchen', a kitchen with no food! To Joseph I talked for ½ an hour, on the plea I was cold and wanted to get warm before going up to the icy bedroom. Joseph confirmed there was not even coffee in the hotel, and that in the morning, we should have to go to the 'Gare' to get our cup of coffee, that was the only place in all Charleville where one could <u>buy</u> a cup of coffee!

After exchanging condolences with Joseph until 8, when his wife and a friend came to give him his evening coffee I went

17 Casement toured through this region in May 1912 with his old friend Richard Morten in a car provided for by the German government. Given Casement's commitment to building up international networks sympathetic to both Ireland's cause and the subversion of British imperial power, it seems likely this was much more than a motoring holiday, but a carefully planned route through the region, interspersed with meetings, discreet intelligence gathering exercises and moments of historical and cultural contemplation. Their route took them through Strasbourg, Lake Constance, Nuremberg, Coblenz, Rottenburg, Wiesbaden, Heidelberg and Frankfurt. The identity of 'Brab Lake' has not been established.

18 Much of the Eifel region is now a national park in the south west of the federal state of North Rhine-Westfalia.

19 The raising of the Irish Brigade—or, Casement Brigade—became the nemesis of Casement's mission to Germany. For different accounts see Brian Maye's useful edition of Michael Keogh, *With Casement's Irish Brigade* (Drogheda, 2010), originally published in the *Catholic Bulletin*, January–December 1928. Michael Keogh, the author of this memoir, claimed to have first met Casement in New York in 1911/12. This was apparently during Casement's brief stop-over on his way to Washington to meet US President, William Taft about the Putumayo atrocities. Whether Casement had any intention to establish an Irish brigade this early is unclear.

20 Sir Edward Grey (1862–1933) British Foreign Secretary 1905-1916. Casement returned to foreign service in 1906 on a personal request from the new Liberal Foreign Secretary and the two co-operated closely on Congo reform and the revelation of the Putumayo atrocities. As Casement became more intolerant of the betrayal of Gladstonian Liberal ideals by the Liberal Imperialism of Grey, the respect between the two men declined. Casement never forgave Grey for taking Britain into the war. Their basic sense of a shared universal humanity disintegrated in the bitter ideological clash over *jus ad bellum*— Britain's justification for the war. In 1915 Casement wrote a blinding attack on Grey, published in *The Continental Times* (18/10/1915) and the *Gaelic American* (20/11/1915). Casement's letter to Grey respecting his knighthood in 1911 was used prominently by the prosecution at the trial to reveal the insincerity of his professed loyalty to the British Empire. Casement was executed in 1916 on the anniversary of Grey's epoch-making speech to the House of Commons on 3 August 1914.

21 Casement's guarantee of Irish independence was closely tied to his vision for a new Europe. His volume of essays *The Crime Against Europe* argued for a reconfiguration of the balance of power in Europe. He was deeply critical of the diplomacy of 'secret treaties' and advocated instead a more transparent and accountable foreign policy, where power and commerce were more evenly distributed. To those ends he saw a German victory in the war as essential to the long-term security of Europe. In contrast, he saw Britain's

to my bedroom. Fearing the very damp sheets of a very cold, uninhabited inn, I wrapped my woollen comforter round my neck and my Irish rug round my body and then got into bed thus well protected by thick layers of wool from contact with the cold touch of the sheets.

I slept on & off till 8 a.m.

[Charleville to Cologne] Thursday 19 Nov. [1914]

When von Lüttichau came in to call me from his room next door & take me off to the station to get our morning coffee.

We went on foot, and after a dose of truly abominable coffee in the buffet of the station where some officers were already at work too, we visited a barbers opposite at a small shop, sandwiched in between two wings of the Hotel du Nord. The barber boy was a young German in charge of the (fled) Frenchman's shop. He shaved v. Lüttichau while I bought chocolates and photos of the wrecked bridges over the Meuse at Mézières-Charleville.

At the Hotel I had to wait till nearly 10 for Meyer to come with the car and take me to the 'Foreign Office'. Here, after a brief delay I was shown into a fine, airy big writing room where a clean-shaven man of some 48 or 50, I judged, in a brown uniform & riding boots was standing. We bowed and shook hands and Meyer left us alone. The conversation that followed was of great interest. Baron von Stumm spoke perfect English and told me of more than one talk he had had with Sir E. Grey.[20] Of Grey's abilities he had a poor opinion—a mediocre intelligence, an inferior man, how is it that they think him so wonderful in England? I confessed I shared very largely his opinion of Grey's abilities, altho' I did not doubt his honesty, to which estimate the Baron subscribed.

Most of the talk was mine. He asked about the Christiania incident and I described it fully and he agreed with me that it was well worthwhile to try and get

Mr. Findlay 'caught in the act' through my man Adler—and then to make the whole story public and try and get him turned out of Norway.

We talked of the Volunteers in Ireland, of Redmond's recruiting dodges; of 'Home Rule' and of the prospects of keeping the Irish out of the army. I explained the Irish position to him clearly and closely. He admitted he knew nothing about it—that he had once been in Ireland (on a hunting trip I fancy) but that he knew nothing of the feeling of the people.

I told him of my larger hope—'a dream if you will'—of an independent Ireland emerging from this war and he at once said it would be to Germany's interest to have an independent Ireland.[21] I said 'Yes—to the interest of Europe at large.' As to the Volunteers and why we were not armed already I explained the situation in Ireland and how the British had 'closed the ports' as soon as the Irish Volunteers were started on 15th Nov. 1913—'just one year ago'.[22] I said that Germany had herself very largely to blame for the position in which she found herself today—and he agreed. I said 'Why did you not make friends before the war with those who had reason to oppose England?—why did you not think of Ireland?'

He replied 'that is the best proof of our innocence, of our sincerity towards England—we believed she could be kept neutral—while she was plotting against us. Had we known—had we acted as <u>she</u> did—we should have had agents in Ireland, in Egypt, in India'. As regards my 'larger hope' he talked frankly. Germany had no objection, on the contrary only the desire to do it, <u>if possible</u>, but that while he fully expected Germany would win the war against France and Russia, and so conclude a general and, for her, successful peace, he did not know how far she could prosper in her fight with England towards the point of '<u>imposing</u> conditions of peace there.' That was all uncertain. There was no immediate or even probable prospect of the German fleet gaining a great victory, so as to clear

World War I. Belgian civilians fleeing German Invasion (Photo by Keystone-France/ Gamma-Keystone via Getty Images)

the seas and render the transport of men and arms to Ireland possible. Were there, it would not be unlikely.

He believed the war <u>must</u> end soon—that none of the combatants, except England, could carry it on for a long period. France would go first—next Russia—perhaps both together.

And here a trenchant phrase was uttered. 'We will make peace with France—we pity them too—they and the Belgians will learn that England is responsible for their miseries—not Germany. <u>But what we hold we will keep</u>'!

It is this phrase that rings in my ears. The Baron expressed himself deliberately, and the prospect it offers is, indeed for Belgium and France a dreadful one. 'What we hold we will keep'! He was quite emphatic in declaring that the German armies could <u>not</u> be driven back. Where they were they stayed—and it was only a question of months, possibly weeks, when the French & Russian endurance—and materiél—would give out.

We shall see. I do not think he was over confident as to the powers of resistance, or of maintenance of the present lines of the German armies—but I think it is highly probable that to secure a just and binding peace in Europe and so leave Germany free to tackle England—the Sea Serpent—the Baron's chiefs would agree to give up what they hold. Otherwise the war <u>will</u> go on for years—despite his estimate of French weakness—for neither France nor Belgium will agree, one, to a dreadful dismemberment—the other to extinction.

I told him England would go on for years. He agreed she might, but asked 'What can she do to us? She can't get near Germany. Her fleet is become a laughing stock. Her empire will and must break up—her diplomacy has been childish—for she has risked everything, more than we—and in future any little state like Norway or Holland, with a fleet of submarines can bottle all the British navy up into ports. Thus while she may have been able to destroy our external trade she has not been able to use her fleet against ours or directly

22 Towards the end of 1913 Casement had lobbied publicly and networked tirelessly to have a German shipping line—the Hamburg-Amerika Line—stop at Queenstown (Cobh) on its transatlantic voyages to and from Boston. The plan was announced in the *Irish Times* (10/12/1913) and quite advanced plans were put in place early in 1914 for the arrival of the first steamship. But the plan was interfered with at the highest level in Westminster. This infuriated Casement and his measured explanation of 'the reversal of a business project, so full of promise and happy augury for Irish trade and intercourse with the outside world' was printed in his lengthy letter to the *Irish Independent*, (16/2/1914). Casement saw the reorientation of Irish trade towards both Europe and America as vital to the future of the balance of power in Europe.

intention in the war driven by imperial strategy, commercial interest, domestic difficulties and incompetent governance.

against our coasts. She cannot come near us. Her position has become ridiculous.'

I said that England counted on wearing Germany down 'as she did Napoleon' that she would not care for the destruction of France—she would always counsel France to continue, even a hopeless resistance, as she did the Belgians at Antwerp—and rely on her ability to beget fresh forces for Germany and to redress the injured balance of power in Europe by calling in Asia, Africa, America. I pointed out that I was sure England counted on getting the United States in the field against Germany in the end—certainly if the war should go on against England. Her steps to this end had already been taken and I was convinced that if, by chance, the German fleet won a considerable victory (he shrugged his shoulders) there would go up a preconcerted and organised howl throughout the American press on behalf of 'the Motherland'—of a threatened 'common civilisation' and that England would spare no effort, no money, no means to compelling the Washington administration to take sides on her threatened behalf. Further there was Japan, and the grave possibility of the Japanese being brought to Europe in the end. The danger to Germany was a 'war of years' as England predicted. Von Stumm agreed that Germany could not go on for years as England might, but that there was any possibility of France or Russia holding on, even as long as Germany, he did not agree. Germany must win so far as her land frontiers lay and land forces went—but he was by no means confident of her ability to get at England 'this time'.

If she did, 'my dream' might come true! It would accord with her policy and interests. We discussed briefly, I more than he, the Declaration his Government had made at my instance and which I said I presumed would be issued that very day—I pointed out that while it went far on the road of our wishes it did not say all we wanted—and the fullest fruits could not be hoped from it alone—but that I was not 'impossible' and did not want them today to go further than they felt was wise.

We were agreed in aim—as to the means to attain it I knew these lay on the lap of the gods—and I was content to go on with the hope that the fortune of war wd. more and more bring about the possible realisation of my larger hope.

Von Stumm was clearly interested in our talk, and it was I who rose to leave and end the interview after fully an hour. He would have even kept me—but I pulled out my watch—it was 11.15—and said I should not detain him longer. Meyer was waiting outside the door—and after a second farewell in the corridor to which he accompanied me I bade the Baron & the travelling Foreign Office adieu and hurried downstairs and back in the motor car to the Hotel de Commerce to get my things, to pay 'Joseph' a pourboire of 5 marks—instead of anything to the hotel for the night's lodging—& then to pick up Meckle and von Lüttichau at the rooms of the former.

When these were settled in the car and everything aboard it was nearly noon—and fully midday when altogether we steered out of Charleville on the road to Rocroi. The market place or grand place was showing a sprinkling of women & men with vegetables, carts and country produce—an attempt at a market. The women looked less downcast than the men. Small boys even begged from us smiling for 'einer pfennig!'—in bad German. An old woman with white hair came up to us while waiting outside Meckle's rooms and I heard her pleading voice and the words 'dans la misère.' I gave her 5 marks in spite of Meckle's protest that 'they all do this'. I said it might be so—but they were 'all in great trouble and misery' to which he & Lüttichau agreed. They remonstrated more at the amount than at the act—saying 50 pfennigs would have been enough.

(I had noticed during the hurried walks the previous evening to and from the officers' mess that townswomen were walking about with, or even waiting for, German soldiers! There was no doubt of it. I noticed more than one case—this to my mind gave convincing proof rather of 'misery' than of immorality. I did not tell my German friends of what I had noticed in this respect—for they would scarcely have understood my feeling I fancy.)

As we left Charleville—the ruined outskirts were often a new source of regret—the road to Rocroi lay northwards and upwards. The frost was strong and enduring, the fields and trees covered with it—and the air still and sharp. A few cabs came past—but as yesterday, the vast majority of vehicles met were either automobiles, like our own with men in uniform, or large wagon motors of Red Cross comforts or of provisions. Rarely with escorts, generally alone or in troops of cars—but once or twice we met horsemen going through a strip of wood as we neared Rocroi we met a telegraph party out putting up a new wire through the forest—some trees were felled or being felled—and the second line being stretched along the existing single line.

Rocroi lies high, fully 1,400 feet above the sea. We did not enter the village or the fortress. We skirted the outer dry moat of the grass fortifications, diamond pointed Vauban-constructed maybe—and went on through largely abandoned suburbs and damaged houses into the open hill country looking across the steep valley of the Meuse as it wound into the deep wooded hills of the Ardennes. The view here was splendid—despite mist and wintry gloom.

The steep cleft where the Meuse penetrates the Ardennes lay to our right the wooded hills on the far side being I judged close on 1000 feet above the gorge. Tufts of white mist clung to the sides of the hills & of the gorge itself. Every tree & shrub was like a fairy tree—each twig & branch a delicate branch of silver—and afar the frosted trees shone white on the darker ground.

Soon we came to the top of the ridge and the road stretched down before us, with great curves and sweeping angles into Fumay on the Meuse itself. We descended rapidly and ran thro' Fumay without pause. Here were many burnt houses—but the town was peopled again and shops open and people moving about their affairs. We were soon through this pretty little town and running along a fine smooth road that followed the left bank of the Meuse. The river about 100 yards broad, and deep brown. Every bridge was down. Some totally wrecked—others only partially injured. In some cases the piles alone had been blown up—& the iron superstructure had collapsed in the middle into the river, the two ends standing intact. In nearly all cases where a bridge had been thus destroyed by the retreating French, the invaders, (now the occupying tenants) had run up alongside, or in the near vicinity a wooden structure on piles that served all the immediate needs of road transport, but not of railway.

In several cases the wrecked bridges themselves had been already repaired—in one notable case, just before reaching Givet, the entire iron superstructure which had not been injured by the explosion that caused its collapse into the stream had been lifted again, well nigh intact, and as we passed it was being used in the ordinary way. Several of the (older) stone bridges of massive masonry had had only one or two arches blown up and in these cases the German engineers had already bridged the cavities with temporary ironwork and the bridges were again in use.

From Fumay we ran alongside the Meuse almost the whole way when the river made wide curves and the road took the short cut. Villages and little towns on both banks, nearly all showed traces of the havoc wrought no doubt so often by the retreating defenders as by the invading foe. What greatly struck me was that in several cases there were villages in close proximity, or little townships, one of which would be almost entirely destroyed, the burnt and shattered frameworks of roofless and wall-less houses alone marking the site, while

23   Casement spells them Hermiton and Anserem.
24   Uhlans were Polish light cavalry regiments used by the Germans.

less than 400 yards away a similar village would present an entirely undamaged front and its inhabitants were going about their business seemingly unconcerned.

At Givet we came across the first evidence of a shattered fortress. Here on the cliff top more than 150 feet above the river I should say—perhaps 200 feet, the ridge was crowned with the stone wall and turreted bastions of a type of fortification no longer erected I imagine. Fine to look upon but of little use against modern guns. This battlement showed pregnant gaps where the German guns, from the hills across the river had battered it. At its foot, and between the roadway and the river, a long stone building of three stories— fully 250 yards long—which had been the caserne of a considerable French fort, was riddled with shell fire. Not a window remained—the walls had holes in them a coach and four could have gone through— the floors had often collapsed, and a great part of the roof was piled up in the mounds of debris that choked the basement. Givet itself had not suffered so greatly—although we could not see much of it as our car sped through. It was necessary to hasten, as by this much longer route it would take us all our time to reach Cologne in time for the night train to Berlin.

Soon after leaving Givet we crossed the frontier into Belgium—the former customs notice at the barrier 'À la Douane' still held out its arm across the road – but we had no customs search to pass, for today there is no Belgium!

Several of the road inspection posts here at which we halted an instant were in charge of Saxon troops, for the green and white standard of Saxony was often visible. The river cliffs as we drew near Dinant were perfectly charming. Great crags and peaks and pinnacles of grey limestone (I think) often garbed thick with dark green ivy, and crowned with a forest of birch and hazel and aspen trees rose some hundreds of feet sharp from the banks of the Meuse.

We burst two tyres almost together when between Hermeton and Anseremme[23] and stopped just at a beautiful château that was built right on the roadway with gardens, stables, hothouses and a perfect little forest park at the back and sides. Von Lüttichau, who told me he was a landowner himself and farmed all his own lands, went in by the fine gateway to the courtyard. I followed—and he soon found out from some Uhlans[24] quartered there that the château belonged to a Belgian Baron 'quelconque' who was at the front (in France poor man!) with his King and the remnant of the Belgian army. While Mme. La Baronne still kept house at home for the Uhlans. These were certainly very well behaved. One young trooper came down to the river with a pail for water and von Lüttichau talked with him. He had been invalided home sick, and was not yet recovered but he had begged to be allowed to return to the front—and here he was with his troop again. We entered the gardens—they were in excellent state—and the hothouse was well heated, and some noble blooms of chrysanthemums in fine flower. Evidently Mme La Baronne had courteous and scrupulous guests.

At Dinant we saw the great fortress (on the right bank) similar to that at Givet, but with no visible signs of wreckage at all. Even the notices 'Entrée à la forteresse'— 'Hotel Lion d'Or' &c. &c. on the summit of the cliffs were quite undamaged. The cliff drops sheer, a wall of 250 or 300 feet from the centre of the fortress to the town, where at the foot a platform of land lies on which the old church or cathedral stood. It still stands, but it showed many traces of the heavy fire—and the houses in its immediate vicinity are only a shapeless mass of rubble—a pile of dead bricks and mortar. The bridge that connects the two banks, right in front of the Cathedral had been well blown up—but parties of Belgians—under guard—were repairing it slowly, while a wooden improvised bridge 60 or 70 yards upstream connected the two banks and was full of traffic as we passed. Meyer explained that all the gangs of French or Belgian workers we had seen at work on bridges or roadways were paid for their labour. In many cases I noticed houses that had been greatly damaged by shell fire already well on their way to recovery—floors, windows, roofs &c. &c. all being put in. The left bank of Dinant had suffered less than the right—and as we passed slowly on out of the town we passed many people. Some boys were playing see-saw—and we got courteous speech from any one we made enquiry of.

Through similar scenes of destruction tempered by clearest evidence of law and order erected on its base we passed always down the left bank of the Meuse, through many charming resorts, with châteaux old and new and pretty villas and well built villages and townlets to Namur. Here we stopped to lunch (at 3.20 p.m.) in a restaurant that was indicated to Meckle by the headquarters of the Automobile Volunteers Corps at which we first stopped.

The great stone fortress on the cliff or hill rather here for it was a grassy slope rather than a precipice as at Givet & Dinant—showed absolutely no trace of fire. Several bridges were down; but the chief bridge, an old one of stone over the Meuse, had been restored. This we were told was the 'oldest bridge in Belgium'—we crossed the Sambre too, in leaving the town by a different road with a Bavarian Catholic priest who besought a passage to Liège. (He was in the army I presume—a chaplain).

The City Hall and buildings near it were terribly shattered—and yet along side these piles of destruction shops were open, people moving about and no sign of war! Little boys were selling picture postcards—and I bought a batch of them from a nice little chap of ten or eleven with whom I talked in French outside the restaurant. Beggars too came—just as usual and besought alms or help from the enemy!

From Namur, we crossed the Meuse to the right bank, and with the priest explaining certain points of interest to the others we hurried on to Andenne. A good part of the destruction we saw was caused by Belgians themselves. Thus all the bridges for instance were their handiwork—and as artillery fire is mutual very much of the damage we saw was caused by the defenders. Thus the priest pointed out a ruined factory across the river which the Belgians themselves had destroyed. At Andenne, Meckle stopped the car to show me a gruesome sight and tell a horrible story.

First the story.

After the first passage of the German Army, when Andenne was already in German hands, a long column of German ammunition with a smallish escort was passing through Andenne on its way to the front. The town had already submitted and all the Belgian soldiers were scores of miles away.

At a signal, <u>given from the church</u>, the church bells ring out, and from all sides rifle fire was opened on the German column. Many men were killed—the punishment was not, as at Louvain, to destroy part of the town, but to seize a number of the men and shoot them then and there. Three hundred and fifty men were thus arrested, taken to the river front, lined up against a brick wall surrounding an empty yard and shot, and buried in two long graves between the wall of execution and the river. I was taken to this spot.

The wall showed many traces of where the bullets had spattered and broken the brick work. Dashes of lime I fancy on the wall itself and at the foot of it told their own story. The two graves lay a few yards out from the wall. The mound over them were perhaps a couple of feet high and were covered with flowers—chiefly chrysanthemums—some in pots even—and with wreaths while a bedding of lime told the same story of sanitary precaution that was written across the wall.

The flowers were accompanied by numberless cards and 'in memoriam' writings. Poor wives, sons, daughters, mothers! I nearly wept as I looked at these pitiable evidences of a sorrow that is now, perhaps, the chief national asset of the

25 Casement's 1904 report on the Administration of the Congo Free State initiated a diplomatic war over native policy and has been claimed recently as a pioneering human rights investigation of the modern era.

Belgian people. One card to 'notre cher époux et père' I bent over.

There were people there too—some of the mourners doubtless. Two workmen in corduroys were bending over the graves when we came up. They moved off—with averted faces. Some women and children, and a well dressed family were there too— but they slowly withdrew from the spot at the sight of the uniforms. How little these poor folk could have guessed that one man of that group was no German—but was the very 'British Consul' who had indicted their sovereign and his abominable Congolese system ten years before.[25]

Sometimes, I must confess, when the present 'agony of Belgium' confronts me— and it cannot well be minimised it is in truth a national agony—I feel that there may be in this awful lesson to the Belgian people a <u>repayment</u>. All that they now suffer and far more, they, or their king, his government and his officers wreaked on the well nigh defenceless people of the Congo basin. And with no such reason as the Germans. Germany offered Belgium fair terms—she asked only a 'right of way' to meet her foemen face to face on <u>French</u> soil. Belgium refused—at the instigation of England and preferred the arbitrament of arms. She relied on English promises and French support. Where are these today? Criminal as he was, Leopold II would never have landed his country in the awful plight this morally better King Albert has placed it in. Leopold before he opposed the German demand by force would have made England show her hand. He would have called her cards. He would have said—'Yes, that's all very well to defend my neutrality! But can I do it? What help can <u>you</u> give? Where is your army—where your guns that are going to ensure the inviolability of Belgium if I resist the Germans?'

And if that question had been put, as it should have been put by the ruler of these betrayed people, what answer could England have made? She could not defend 'Belgian neutrality' and she knew it right well. She deliberately for her own selfish ends, in order to hinder, damage and weaken the German forces, put Belgium into the fire. However blameable Germany may be from the standpoint of international morality in forcing her way through Belgium, England is infinitely more blameworthy. For England <u>knew</u> she could not help the Belgians. She knew her promises of support were worthless. She knew that if Belgium resisted the weight of an irresistible invasion must crush the Belgian people to the earth and lay waste their thriving and prosperous country. All this she knew and yet Sir E. Grey telegraphs to the Br. Minister in Brussels before war breaks out that he urgently begs the Belgian Govt to 'defend its neutrality' at all costs! What a crime! Here, these two graves at Andenne, and the looks in the faces of the population as we pass away from it— dejected, scowling, uneasy and with all the evil of latent ill-will in many glances— should be laid at the feet of the British Minister and I thought too of von Stumm's firm statement— 'We keep what we hold'!

God in Heaven! What will it mean to these poor conquered people in the end if that be the irrevocable intention of the German Government!

That phrase has been ringing in my ears all the morning since I left Charleville and the 'Foreign Office.'

There they are—the German legions stretching now from the north sea, almost, on the French frontier (at Nieuport) right down through some of the fairest parts of France, through the chief steel, coal, iron and textile manufacturing districts with a large part of the Champagne district in their power to the Vosges near Switzerland. All Belgium, save a tiny strip less in size than Middlesex perhaps, and probably a twelfth part of the area of France with a normal population of 3,500,000 or 4,000,000 of French men and women and that the centre of the principal French industries are now held by German troops. A ring of iron, trenched in blood and bones of a million dead and wounded Germans stretches now from the Channel to almost

Newspaper political cartoon depicting in humorous fashion Belgium's resistance to German incursion. (Photo by Time Life Pictures/Mansell/Time Life Pictures/Getty Images)

in sight of Paris, and holds in a hand of steel what France will die rather than give up! How will it end?

Of the German ability to 'stay where they are' I have little doubt. All French and British efforts to break that line of blood and iron I believe must fail. And as that line remains, or even perhaps advances, France shrinks. Even the stationary line means a shrinking France. For it is thus.

They say 15,000 square miles of France now held by Germany represents a very great proportion of French industrial production. The remainder of France, every day growing weaker in blood—and material too—is deprived of a part of its framework essential to national well-being. But not only is this rich region in German hands, and so aiding German effort against the rest of France by furnishing its products to German and not to French armies, but the many fugitives from this region are now a charge on the rest of France. Say 1,000,000 (at outside) of the 3 to 4 millions of this region fled at the approach of the Germans. How are they living? On what? At whose expense? They constitute an added burden the remaining 11/12ths of France has to bear in addition to the awful strain of bearing up against that solid wall of steel from Armentières to below Verdun that threatens every week to begin a further move south west. The break may come at any moment as all my German friends think and say. France, they assert—as von Stumm did—will not be able to support the strain for more than three months longer. Once the break begins, it enlarges—it increases. The break at the front will mean the break at the heart, and a point must be reached where France will be forced to say 'Enough'—England may intrigue, may plot, may beseech, may subsidise with gold and food and supplies but its men will win the fight.

That is the German gospel of this war. They are sure of their men; confident of their manhood and convinced that 'what we hold we can keep.' I thought of all this and much more as we hurried through the conquered lines of French and Belgian towns and villages. I seemed to see in the eyes of many of those we passed on the wayside a question—in France the dejection of face and bearing was more apparent than in Belgium. Their glance was afar. Their hearts, their souls were straining far south and west where by Rheims and Soissons, by Laon and Verdun—and westward by Arras and Amiens, the roar of French gave back shot for shot to German fire.

Will those guns ever draw nearer? will the boom of cannon come up from the south and west? Will France ever come back? That was the question I thought I saw in every eye—a haunting dreadful, fear that this present nightmare of today would prove to be reality and not a dream! That never again would Charleville or Mézières, or Rocroi or Givet see the red and blue of a French uniform but only the smoke grey coat of the new owner, that never again would French life, French speech, French mirth be in these streets—save as the badge of the conquered. 'Joseph' at the Hotel de Commerce I could see had something of this fear—altho' a Luxemburger. He put the blame on England! The education of the conquered goes quickly.

Surely this land I passed through today never saw a stranger sight than that I witnessed! As our car topped the western heights beyond Rocroi and we began the descent towards the great cleft in the wooded hills where I knew the Meuse was clearing its way through the Ardennes I looked out on a scene that Caesar and his legions must once have eyed with something of awe. The vast spread of forested hills was the same probably today as then—the same white-frosted trees, the same tufted break of cloud half hiding half showing where the Meuse flowed into the northern hills. Only the men had changed—and these not much in mind. In place of Caesar you have the Kaiser! And Gaul is still the quarry. The Belgae that that first of the Kaisers was then advancing against perhaps by this very gap through Fumay and Givet have heard the tramp of many legions since those of Rome crossed the Meuse.

But what were the wars of Rome, the legions of Caesar compared to those of Berlin, to the army corps of the Kaiser! Germany today, Major Lothes told me last week, has seven millions of men under arms! France, (poor France!) must have fully four millions. Austria Hungary must have from four to five millions now—to say nothing of the millions she has lost! While Russia, who can tell what millions of men she has gathered or is gathering for this world slaughter!

And England!

England that is chiefly responsible for the war, that stands to draw the surest profit from it and already counts the gains of the 'captured German trade'—what has England contributed of British flesh and blood to hold up the cause she was the chief instrument in erecting? What has the chief conspirator against Germany given of her own lifeblood to this vast conspiracy of murder directed against the mightiest of European peoples?

According to Mr. Asquith, in a recent speech, she has 'sent to the Continent' a force of less than 100,000 men!

It *is* incredible—and I do not believe it. But, at the outside she has certainly not offered her 'allies' more than 200,000 men and fully one third (or more) of them would be Irish and Scotch.

The best test of the sacrifices each party to this awful war has made lies in the mortality returns. The killed and wounded are the evidence that nothing controverts. How does England stand here? Of all the combatants engaged the 'British' losses are incredibly the least.

Mr. Asquith is reported in a recent London message to the Berlin press to have stated in Parliament that the total British losses since the outbreak of the war amounted to 57,000 men—killed, wounded and missing. Lord Newton,[26] I see, in a later speech, denies the accuracy of the Prime Minister's statement and puts the figure at 80,000 men.

But of these, how many are killed? I gather that the death list is well under 10,000 men (on land—the figures, I fancy, are not referable to the sea fight).

There are no published figures yet of Belgian losses—but we know that the Belgian dead alone must be <u>at least</u> three times, possibly five times the British. A recent German casualty list brought the total of Prussian losses up to 549,247 officers and men killed & wounded—this excluded the losses of the Bavarian, Saxon and Württemberg armies that are estimated at not less than 400,000 and these returns deal only with casualties notified up to the middle of October, while the British return was to date—say 12 November. A recent return (published in the Milan *Corriere de la Sera* of 19 Nov.) gives with precision the Austro-Hungarian losses 'during the first three months of the war.' Here they are.

<u>Killed</u>
Officers	4,612
Men	215,175	=	219,787

<u>Wounded</u>
Officers	12,111
Men	481,965	=	494,076

<u>Missing i.e. prisoners & dead</u>
Officers	2,252
Men	187,191	=	189,443

Grand total		=	903,306

The infamy of the English position could scarcely be more clearly defined than by contrasting British losses with the British share in provoking the war and the gains to be derived from it with the losses suffered by all the other combatants.

England is to secure the trade of the world, the destruction of the German navy and of the German mercantile marine, the crippling of German industries and the acquisition of German colonies at the loss of a few thousand of her poorer classes and these, be it noted, to be as carefully drawn from the 'Celtic fringe' as the gullibility of the 'Celtic' temperament will cheerfully permit. In fine, the 'sacrifices' England proposes making are to be mainly those of Irish boys and men—but the 'captured' trade will not go to Ireland! The case is so lucidly put by the English themselves that I need only quote from the *Liverpool Daily Post* of 12 September best to establish my argument from the mouth of the enemy himself:

Commenting on the then call for 500,000 soldiers made by Kitchener an editorial writer pointed out that they could not be raised in England without 'a derangement of its industry.' He therefore urged the 'signing of the Home Rule Bill' because then the King 'could make a

26 Lord Newton (1857–1942) served as British Paymaster-General during the First World War and as an assistant undersecretary at the Foreign Office dealing with foreign propaganda.

triumphal tour of Ireland north, south, east and west and in reply to his personal appeal there would be 300,000 Irishmen of all creeds and classes for the front in less than a week. In England the question becomes more and more important in the interests of the efficiencies of our trade whether we can spare any more skilled mechanics for the ranks of hate. The capture of the German trade is almost as vital to the existence of the Empire as the destruction of Prussian militarism and this can be done solely by maintaining our workshops and plant in the highest state of efficiency'.

Here we have the case put with that charming naiveté so characteristic of the English pickpocket when *chez soi*. Let an Irishman, a German, an 'enemy' accuse England of fighting this war for the sake of commercial profit and he is greeted with the figure of Sir Edward Grey assuring the world that England is inspired by a 'high moral purpose, to defend the Public Law of Europe and maintain the sanctity of treaties'—or of that even more contemptible character Asquith fulminating at Edinburgh on behalf of the 'small nations' a victorious Prussian militarism would crush beneath the heel of its jack boot. And while these fine speeches are being made, the Govt. making their plans, I believe, the biggest fraud ever yet worked off against that 'small nation' Ireland—by offering it a post obit 'a promissory note payable after death' as I truly called it in my appeal of 17 Sept to the young men of Ireland, in the shape of the Home Rule Bill 'placed on the Statute Book' in return for the life blood of all young Ireland.[27] A people who, as the same Government's official return shows, lost over 5,000 of its inhabitants last year (deaths & immigration exceeded the births in 1913 by 5,497—the figures were

1913	Births	100,094
	Deaths	74,894
	Emigrants	30,697

are to 'flock to the colours' in Lord Crewe's phrase because the British Govt. has kindly signed a piece of waste paper.

In return for a partial promise to allow Ireland to erect a debating society on the banks of the Liffey at some wholly unspecified future date, Irishmen today are to give 300,000 men to the shambles in France & Flanders in order that the Englishman, who is too valuable himself to be put in danger may 'capture the German trade.'

I rejoice mightily in my treason when I read these things—and think of those oleaginous scoundrels, like Haldane,[28] quivering masses of blubber—who are so busy killing the Kaiser with their mouth while trying to seduce my brave hearted countrymen to do the real killing—or be killed themselves.

If my treason does nothing else but save Ireland from this I shall have deserved well of my country. To keep our young men at home, for the future of our own country & for all her needs that is the counsel every true Irishman should give today. Thank God I came to Germany—and God be praised for the aid this people and their Government are giving Ireland today!

But this long digression leaves me between Andenne and Liège—in a hurrying motor car, with cold and darkness gathering in intensity.

We sped on through Huy past many factories, some silent, some at work until moments later we came to the outskirts of Liège—or Lüttich as my German friends call it.

We had some trouble in getting to the bridge, as the two that Meckle first steered for were down, and guarded—but we found a splendid bridge, with four columns of victory winged angels on top, two at each end—and over this we entered the busy part of Liège on the north bank of the Meuse. The river seems to be divided here into separate branches—so that more than one bridge is needed to cross it. The broad reach of the Meuse as we saw it from this big bridge was very fine, looking downstream,

---

27 This is a reference to Casement's *Open Letter to the Irish People* dated New York, 17 September 1914 arguing against Irish participation in the First World War.

28 Richard, Viscount Haldane (1856–1928). As both Secretary of State for War (1905–12) and Lord Chancellor (1912–15), operated in the Liberal Party's inner circles of legal and political power. From as early as 1906, he was closely tied to Edward Grey and Britain's secret preparations for an eventual European war.

with a blaze of light from the city and a shining well lit riverside walk. We left the Bavarian priest at what had been the City Hall I presume—an imposing building on the Grand Place. It is now the headquarters of the German military governor—& orderlies, autos, motors, soldiers were coming and going. The streets were full of life—the shops well lit and the tram cars running filled with people. In fact, from inside no one could possibly say this city had recently been carried by assault and was now in the hands of a 'horde of barbarians' —*vide* the Anglo-Saxon press of England and England's dutiful daughter the United States of North America. Of all the lies England has distributed in recent years throughout the world, by her admirable system called 'free trade', I guess this lie of German barbarism and 'German atrocities' is the most wilful, the most perverse and the most evil intentioned.

As we hurried out of Liège, through crowded streets, past well lit windows and also by pleasant squares and esplanades I thought of the picture of Liège I had formed in New York and Philadelphia when the Anglo-Saxon lies were walking the streets of those cities. I suppose there is no people in the world so gullible as the Americans. That is doubtless why they invented poker. But the original poker face must have come from England—and I am convinced it came in the 'Mayflower', with an extraordinary pedigree behind it too and a family bible printed on the backs of the cards.

Leaving Liège, the suburbs, again on the south bank of the Meuse, which we recrossed by another bridge lower down stream, we stopped to ask the way from a crowd of workmen. A gendarme officer, a Belgian gendarme bien entendu, replied and offered to guide us.

He jumped on the footboard & we invited him into the car, and he took us up about 2 miles of our way on the road to Aachen—Charlemagne's city of Aix. This gendarme—he was an officer too—explained that the people were 'quite tranquil' now, and no trouble threatened.

His talk was friendly enough and his manner too. The ordinary civil & criminal courts, Lüttichau and Meyer explained to me, were working as usual in Belgium and I noticed the ordinary gendarmes on duty in the streets—without arms or sidearms. The only armed men in Belgium today—east of Ypres and Dixmunde!—are German soldiers. After the treacheries of Louvain, Andenne, Termonde, Tirlemont &c. &c., it would indeed be madness for the army of the conqueror to leave arms in the hands of the population or their representatives. Meckle told me he had been shot at, in his car, at Tirlemont when going with despatches and that his earlier journeys thro' Belgium had been dangerous enough. Meckle speaks good and nice English. He told me he had been a good deal in the States. Meyer tells me he is a well known German automobilist and aviator too. Like many others of his class he is a volunteer. Germany has over a million volunteers under arms now—mostly youths. They, the volunteers, boys largely, carried Dixmunde the other day by assault singing 'Deutschland über alles' which the Anglo-Saxon press of America I see cites as another proof of German intentions against the freedom of the world! Asinine is scarcely the word to apply to the pranks of the so-called American newspapers since this war began. A semi-educated newsboy ought to know that the meaning of this is not that Germany is to be on top of all other countries, but that Germany is to be before all else to the German. But just as the Park Row style editors[29] beat the daily drum on the 'Kaiser's war' and the 'War Lord' instead of 'Commander in Chief' so they glory in the latest Anglo-Saxon fable, that Germany seeks to conquer the world! Seeing that England has now brought pretty well half the world to her side against the 67,000,000 of Teutons she feared to face alone it would indeed be true to say of England today

'England on top of Everybody.'

The disgrace of this war; the shame of it to Englishmen is to me overwhelming. Were

29 Park Row was New York's newspaper district.

[30] Casement here names three of the most notorious Belgian officers employed by the Congo Free State administration.

I English I should open my veins to let the blood out!

Not content with the 160,000,000 of Russians, the 40,000,000 of French, the 42,000,000 of Great Britons, the 3,000,000 of Servian & Montenegrin cut-throats, to pit against the 120,000,000 of Teuto-Hungarians, England has brought in the 52,000,000 of Japanese, the 300,000,000 Hindoos, the 12,000,000 or 15,000,000 of Canadians, Australians, New Zealanders &c. &c. of the Great Dominions, the millions of African Negroes of her own and the French protectorates—and now I see by the latest telegrams that some 'Genuine Red Indians' will form part of the next Canadian contingent; and that a regiment of Fiji Islanders is on the way to support the cause of the 'small nationalities.' It only remains for King Albert of Belgium, from his new seat of Government—Havre, I believe—today to command a corps d'armée of Congo cannibals to come to the rescue of the Lothaires, Fievezs, Fanquis[30] and other expatriated Belgian heroes who are now employing the methods of *la compagne Congolaise* against the German savage as they once employed them against the rubber runners of the heart of Africa.

For the Belgian people I have nothing but pity—for their King and Government hearty contempt. These sacrificed the interests, the life itself of their country, to the interest of England. Léopold deux, with all his criminal career on the Congo, was a far better King for this unhappy people than this good King Albert.

I doubt now if Germany will 'give back' Belgium. After von Stumm I doubt it very much. Von Lüttichau confided to me today while we were visiting the garden of the Baroness's château near Anseremme, that he was not in favour of retaining any of the conquered territory now held by German troops. His argument is right. He says 'What do we want with 7,000,000 of Belgians to hold down? We have enough foreign elements already in our midst—the Poles—the Jews! All we want is a united Germany, ensured against assault absolutely on her own national frontiers.'

This opinion certainly prevails among the Germans I talk with—but whether it will prevail with a victorious Germany seeking compensation for the terrible sacrifices in blood and treasure she has been put to by the wicked conspiracy of England, France and Russia is another matter—I doubt it. I guess the German official view may be something like this— 'We have lost, say, 2,000,000 of men' (if the war goes on for 6 months these losses may well be that); 'we have lost all our colonies; our foreign trade has been ruined; our shipping swept from the seas; our internal industries closed or killed—our losses actual and eventual are colossal.

'We need not only guarantees for the future peace of our frontiers and the peaceful development of our national and industrial life, but we need some great compensation for all you have wantonly destroyed of ours or deprived us of.'

It is true that if Germany beats down French defence she can impose on France a profitable peace—but to make France 'pay all' is well nigh impossible. And yet Germany will say 'disgorge—not only my stolen colonies, but my ships, my trade, my industries—<u>and</u> an indemnity on top.'

England will not be willing to disgorge anything—she entered the war for plunder and that chiefly—that & the destruction of the great rival's 'menace'—and Russia has nothing to disgorge and cannot be made to pay anything. Now when it comes to the point of France saying to England 'I must give in; I cannot hold out longer'—England will shrug her shoulders—wrap herself in the mantle of the seas and failing to get France to go altogether into the fire of defeat as she has put wretched Belgium she will retire from the conflict with all the German swag and an untroubled conscience—leaving her quondam 'ally' to her fate. For France to pay all will mean ruin—in one shape or another. That has come to her in any case. Even if the 'allies' win the war, France is done for. She can never regain the lifeblood lost, the cities destroyed, the lands depeopled that already three months of devastating horror have brought to her once fair fields.

Germany will either do as von Stumm assured me 'Keep what we hold' or release it only on such satisfaction as will reduce France to half a century of impotence. As for Belgium, if she is happy enough to get back her independence it will be a freedom qualified by more than one restraint. Belgium will become a larger Luxembourg. Her port, Antwerp, will surely be kept in German tutelage—her fortresses either dismantled or held in trust for the German army; her foreign relations controlled from Berlin; her customs possibly also; and in time, her national life subordinated to the dire needs of German future safety and the extension of German rights in the world. For there lies the true cause of the war. Germany claims, demands world rights.

It is this that England has secretly plotted against—it is this assertion of German world interests that is the unpardonable sin to Downing Street—and because it was clear to the intriguing spirits of the British governing classes that, left to herself, Germany must acquire power commensurate with her rights England decided to convert the Franco-Russian agreement from a negative policy of defence into an active policy of offence.

These and thoughts like them were in my mind all the way from Charleville through ruined Givet, and occupied Namur and Liège until in piercing cold and mist we crossed the German frontier and sped towards Aachen, Jülich and Cologne.

The suburbs of Liège, so far as one could see from our car lamplights in the darkness, were almost all destroyed. We passed through village after village, or suburb after suburb of empty shattered and dismantled houses. Whether by German or Belgian shellfire no one can say now—then came fields—miles of them—and our lamps showed the barbed wire entanglements (like grape vines on low trellises) the Belgians had set up to impede the German advance against the ceinture of forts. None of these forts was visible—it was dark—all we could see was the barbed wire, acre after acre of the most worthless crop ever sowed by the hand of men. The wires were lit by the hoar frost—white and clear—a laceworks of death. Meyer told me that the German troops had not crossed by the fields, but he came by the roads & so this wire had served little purpose—at any rate it was still there—intact and useless now. We went thro' Aachen without stopping, and thro' Jülich and reached Cologne at 8.50 p.m. The city seemed so peaceful, even gay and pleasant and clean and well lit—after the dark, barbed-wire fields around Liège.

From the hurried glimpse I have got of it I should think Cologne must be one of the pleasantest cities in Europe to live in. I liked it from the first—and on getting to the station at 9 p.m., cold, tired and hungry, I liked it better still. The station was full of life—people of all classes and soldiers innumerable going and coming.

We got a hurried dinner in the Speisesaal[31] and then bidding Meckle adieu with a hearty handshake, Meyer, Von Lüttichau and I settled in sleeping cars for the night. As we crossed the Rhine bridge leaving the city, all the lights in our train went out. Von Lüttichau explained that this was a precaution 'leaving the fortress' against possible air-raids. Two searchlights were sweeping the heavens constantly. Our train remained in darkness until we had got well clear of the city defences, and then the lights were turned on and I went to sleep.

Von Lüttichau & Meckle, I am sure, were told sometime during the day by Meyer who I really was. They had taken me at first for 'Mr. Hammond of New York', but after the long interview at Charleville with the Headquarters staff and the F.O. this pretence was not sustainable. Their manner had grown more interested and when we parted, with Meckle at Cologne and with von Lüttichau at Berlin at 8 a.m. on Friday morning our adieux were warm and friendly and almost intimate.

31   Dining room

II.

Roger Casement
A Last Page of my Diary

Angus Mitchell – Introduction

This second extract, from 17 March to 8 April 1916, briefly covers the months and, more specifically, the days leading up to Casement's departure for Ireland from Wilhelmshafen, aboard a German submarine. The reader is confronted with a very different man to the Casement of November 1914—one whose influence over events in Ireland has been diminished by the tyranny of distance and poor communications and whose standing with the German military authorities has become very stressed and bedevilled by suspicion.

One embedded view in the standard biographical interpretation of Casement is the suggestion that, as his plans for an Irish-German pact began to unravel and his hopes for the Irish Brigade floundered, he gradually descended into an unstable psychological state caused by a nervous breakdown and acute anxiety. This 'madness' derived from both his 'treason' and his long exposure to the tropics. As is evidenced by the two extracts presented here, there is an identifiable difference between the confident and buoyant Casement, who visited the German Foreign Office on the Western Front in November 1914, and the Casement of early 1916, dejected by Prussian militarism, outraged by the empty daily slaughter of the world war, despairing of the imminent prospect of a Rising in Ireland, and frustrated by his own gradual isolation by the main Irish revolutionary decision-making centres in the US and Ireland. He was also clearly unwell and in early 1916 spent significant amounts of time bed-bound in a sanatorium. Despite the setbacks and his disillusionment, Casement's natural authority and his clarity of vision were invigorated when confirmation of the Rising reached him in February. He revived his diary-writing routine in order to document his lengthy negotiations with officials from the German General Staff, the Foreign Office and the German Admiralty. *A Last Page*—as this diary was titled—attests to Casement's dogged determination to continue to shape events even though he had lost direct authority and was deeply tortured by doubt.

His description of his final weeks in Germany is extraordinarily candid and provides honest insight into what he justifiably considered to be an impossible situation. We see a man trapped by the motive force of history, at the mercy of a regime of military power that had largely lost sympathy with his cause. His sense of isolation and misgiving was deepened by his inability to communicate secretly and efficiently with the Irish revolutionary leadership in either the US or Ireland. His network of informers, sympathisers and comrades—that once stretched from Mar del Plata in Argentina to the Gaeltacht of Connemara—had been seriously disrupted and reduced. In February 1916, he tried to get word through to Devoy, in advance of the Irish Convention held in New York, and sent messengers in different directions to influence the revolutionary command centre. John McGoey was despatched to Ireland to contact Eoin MacNeill, the chief of staff of the Irish Volunteers, and convince him that without the right military support from Germany, the Rising would be little more than a sacrificial slaughter. But the fate of these various messengers is obscure. British intelligence was by now keeping abreast of events in Ireland through interception and deciphering of communications.

In this diary, Casement set down exactly why he objected to the Rising on military, political and moral grounds. Much of the argument proved highly prescient. But in adopting this oppositional line, he knew that he was himself open to accusations of 'treason' against the very independence struggle which he had worked so hard to initiate and organize. The failure of the Irish Brigade had left Casement in an extremely compromised position. The German military authorities had lost faith in his cause, quite possibly influenced by the Kaiser's lukewarm support for a rebellion in Ireland. Casement was convinced that both the German General Staff and Foreign Office were only supportive of the Rising in order to rid themselves of the Irish question and the Brigade. In his reckoning, their commitment to supplying a shipment of arms was little more than an empty gesture; without the right military support the rifles were worthless and the rebellion inevitably doomed. Even though Casement helped to negotiate the arms shipment, he had little belief in the success of the plan, which he felt was underprepared and unlikely to succeed. The energies of the rebels, he believed, would be more effectively deployed in properly organizing the rendezvous with the arms shipment and getting the guns into the right hands so that a sustained guerrilla war in the west of Ireland could be mounted.

The level of Casement's tactical influence might be measured by the fact that the G.G.S. and F.O. commissioned an internal report on Casement in the weeks before his departure to determine whether it was more strategically valuable to keep him in Germany, or to send him back to Ireland to meet his fate.[32] Casement was unwavering in his desire to go back to Ireland. But deep frictions began to open up in his negotiation with the different departments of war. His succession of meetings with the German spymaster, Rudolf Nadolny, director of the Abteilung IIIb, were particularly hostile and the diary entries diagnose the breakdown in trust as the fundamental reason for his deteriorating relationship with German military officials.

Casement's principal concern was to maintain the guarantees obtained in the treaty signed at the end of 1914 and ensure some level of security for the Irish Brigade after his departure. But the German government was trying to back away from the treaty; the low number of recruits to the Irish Brigade had, in its eyes, rendered it invalid. Casement had to argue hard to stop the G.G.S. from sending the brigade back aboard the arms ship, the *Aud*. In the last weeks Casement made various trips to Zossen in the company of Father Crotty to reassure the soldiers and prepare the men as best he could for the impact that his departure would have. Eventually he won his point by arguing that if the brigade was sent back to Ireland without the 'efficient military support' promised in the treaty, then this might result in a humiliating public relations disaster for Germany.

The most dramatic aspect of these last weeks was Casement's determination to persuade the G.G.S. to provide a submarine or U-boat for his return with Monteith. Nadolny and the G.G.S. appeared reluctant to send Casement back by submarine, because they believed there was little chance of the vessel arriving in time or breaking the naval blockade. Casement argued that he could supply valuable intelligence on the landing of the arms, an excuse used to conceal his real intention: to be put ashore on reaching Ireland and do his best to stop the Rising. At the last moment the decision of the G.G.S. was reversed through pressure from the Admiralty and various German officials who had Casement's interests at heart.

A Last Page of my Diary has survived in multiple copies. A manuscript version is held in NLI MS 5244 but there are several typed copies which circulated after the Rising in an effort to clarify what had actually happened. Interestingly, the diary has never been published in its entirety and in doing so should elucidate a number of lingering misconceptions about Casement's role in the Rising and the events leading up to his landing on Banna Strand on Good Friday 1916. If his narrative reveals a great sense of foreboding it also reaffirms Casement's underlying motivation—to serve the ultimate objective of Irish independence.

32 See *aan de Wiel*, 195, where he refers to an internal report by the German Government, minuted by Noegerrath and von Wedel, although not apparently written by them, analyzing the 'Casement factor' and whether he was more useful in Germany, working for the Irish cause on the Continent, or returning to Ireland.

33 Casement became friendly with the Baron and Baroness Nordenflycht during his years as consul general in Brazil.

34 The name of the resort town in southern Germany where Casement went to work and relax.

35 This is the diary held in NLI MSS 1689 & 1690 subsequently published as *Diaries of Sir Roger Casement: His Mission to Germany and the Findlay Affair* (Munich, 1922).

36 The list is not appended. A list is held in NLI MS 18081 (10) and is included as an appendix in the article by **Andreas Roth**, op. cit..

St. Patrick's Day, Berlin, March 17, 1916

I write this beginning of what I feel is a last chapter on Patrick's Day in Berlin this year of war 1916. Last year on Patrick's Day I was also in Berlin, ill in bed, in the house of the Baroness von Nordenflycht.[33]

Even then, hope had gone from me—for I realized then, already, that those I trusted here were little to be trusted and that their only interest in me lay in exploiting me, and the Irish cause in their own supposed interests.

Since then a hundred proofs have accumulated—and yesterday the climax came, and as now but little is left I begin, today, a hurried record of things that must be stated in order that some day the truth may be known.

In three weeks I shall probably be at sea in the maddest and most ill planned enterprise that the history of Irish revolutionary efforts offers. But it is not of my choosing, of my planning, or undertaken with my approval. I go because honour calls me to go—and because to stop it now (even if I could stop it) would involve others and perhaps bring greater grief. Moreover by going with the tiny band (12 men probably) that is to sail on 8 April I _may_ save them—and perhaps Ireland too from a dreadful fate. To stay here, in safety, while those others go would do no good to Ireland—and would leave me a prey to eternal regret.

Thus while I strongly disapprove what is being attempted, and so wretchedly attempted with a foregone assurance of failure, I _must_ lend it my countenance and accompany the forlorn hope.

And now to make a little daylight for the hereafter.

I will confine myself today to dealing with events only since the beginning of this year, trusting to the few days of quiet I hope still to get at Riederau am Ammersee[34] to put down earlier happenings, since I stopped keeping a regular diary at the beginning of February last year.[35]

I stopped that Diary when it became clear that I was being played with, fooled and used by a most selfish and unscrupulous government for its own petty interests. I did not wish to record the misery I felt or to say the things my heart prompted. But today it is my head compels me to this unwelcome task.

At the beginning of this year I was staying out at Zossen, the most wretched of men.

The small band of Irish soldiers who had volunteered in May last were there (see the list attached)[36] in uniform, but still kept practically as prisoners of war, and Lt. Monteith in command of them.[37] I had gone out to Zossen on 4th December 1915, to be near him and the men, to encourage and cheer them in their bitter disappointment—and always in the hope that our long-urged journey to the East, to get into action, might be sanctioned. The General Staff here had promised me repeatedly, in December 1915, that the 'Brigade' should be sent East.

Enver Pasha[38] had agreed and it only lay with the German ships in the East to accept the men. The final assurance was given me explicitly on 4 January 1916 (on return from a hurried run to Dresden) at the German General Staff [G.G.S.][39] that the corps would be sent to Syria, and that they would 'at once' be trained in the use of machine-guns. This promise, like all preceding promises—was not carried out.

Day by day I got worse. I had been ill for long—sick at heart and soul, with mind and nerves threatening a complete breakdown. No man was ever in a falser position. The truth I could not tell to my friends in America. I had no means of communicating with them, except by letter that had to pass through the hands of those I felt sure would read it—and to expose their perfidy thus would scarcely work.

Finally I broke down and acting on the advice of a great doctor I went to a 'nerve rest' at the Kuranstalt, Neuwittelsbach, Munich. This was on 19 January 1916.

---

37 Robert Monteith (1879–1956) was born in Newtownmountkennedy, Co Wicklow. He saw action in India and South Africa and served for 16 years in the British Army before throwing in his lot with James Connolly and the Irish Workers' movement. He was one of the first recruits to the Irish Volunteers in November 1913 and elected as Captain of A Company of the First Battalion of the Dublin Brigade, Irish Republican Army. He began to drill both Citizens Army and Volunteers openly in Dublin. After the outbreak of war he was forced to leave his house at 6 Palmerston Place and settled in Limerick to instruct the Volunteers. In October 1915 he left the US for Germany where, on Casement's insistence, he took over command of the Irish Brigade at the end of November 1915, although he felt he was not up to the job.

38 Enver Pasha (1881–1922) was on Ottoman military leader and leader of the Young Turk revolution. In December 1915 Casement intended visiting Constantinople in order to discuss the deployment of the Irish Brigade 'in the Eastern warfield with the object of assisting the Ottoman forces to expel the British from Egypt'. This plan was set out in a Memorandum by Casement written on 1 December 1915 and reproduced in Doerries 166–68.

Image of a Roger Casement plaque on a guest-house in Riederau, a small village on Lake Ammersee, Bavaria: The text translated reads:
Here resided in Summer 1915, Sir Roger Casement, a martyr for Ireland's freedom, a magnanimous friend of Germany in difficult times. He sealed the love of country with his blood.

I was very ill on arrival—but I gradually got better. Then, while there, came the return of my friend Gaffney from America.[40] He stayed in Berlin, but wrote me often, and imperatively begged me to go to Berlin, as there was a matter of 'great importance' to discuss with me.

After days of delay and doubt I came here to Berlin arriving on 16th February & coming to this Hotel Saxonia, Gaffney & Lt. Monteith meeting me at the station at midnight.

I was ill and unfit to travel—and got worse here.

I stayed here until 26th February, returning again to the Kuranstalt on 27th where I was ill in bed for some days on my return.

Gaffney had asked me to come to Berlin to discuss here the chances of my going over to the USA. His project was that by a steamer of the Norwegian Line—the 'Kristianasfjord'—I would probably be safe. A certain Mr. Schirmer, a Norwegian (of German descent) was constantly travelling by that vessel on 'missions' of the German Foreign Office & was entirely trustworthy.

If S. agreed and said the Captain of the 'K' agreed to take me, I might get over in safety. Mr. S. came to see me several times, but deprecated my going away with him at once on this journey. He was going over to USA by the 'Kristianasfjord' from Bergen on Feb. 23rd, to leave Berlin on Sunday 20 February. He said the best thing to do was to leave him to try and arrange the matter with the Captain of the 'K' for the following voyage. Gaffney & I agreed. Letters were given to Mr. S. to take over to

39 Casement abbreviates German General Staff in different ways. For the sake of clarity and consistency, G.G.S. has been used throughout.

Thomas St. John Gaffney (1864–1945).

40 Thomas St. John Gaffney (1864–1945). Born in Limerick, Gaffney was the US consul general in Dresden (1905–12) and then Munich (1914). His pro-German and pro-Irish sympathies eventually led to his dismissal by President Wilson. Gaffney was part of Casement's revolutionary circle in Germany. He enjoyed Casement's confidence most of the time and was entrusted with the care of the Irish Brigade in April 1916. His volume of memoirs—*Breaking the Silence: England, Ireland, Wilson and the War* (New York, 1930)—contained quite extensive chapters on Casement and revealed sensitive aspects of the vicious propaganda concerning the war on truth.

certain friends in New York pointing out the desirability of my making this attempt.

At the same time Gaffney had told me of the forthcoming Irish Convention[41] in New York on 4–5 March and urged me strongly to send over by Mr. Schirmer the original Findlay letter[42] of £5000 bribe for my capture & other papers with a bearing on that disgraceful incident. I was assured these papers would be absolutely safe with Mr. Schirmer. I gave them to him on Saturday evening 19 February, in this hotel, Gaffney being present—and he promised to deliver them in person to Judge Cohalan[43] along with a covering letter from myself.

At the same time, apart from this, I had seen Mary MacFadden and as she wanted to get back to America, I supplied her with the funds (Mks.1750.00) to allow of her sailing by the same boat.

Lt. Monteith helped to get all her things ready and she, too, left on Sunday morning—20 February—for Bergen and I hope and believe sailed by the 'Kristianasfjord' on the 23rd. She took only verbal messages, & our hope was that she might reach New York in time to be present at the Convention on 5 March. As matters turned out, the 'Kristianasfjord' was 'held up' at Kirkwall for two days and reached New York only on 7 March. It was reported here in the German press that 'her mails' had been taken off by the British authorities—and that is all we know. I do not know yet if the Findlay letters arrived safely or if the English got them.

Mr. Schirmer was to have cabled under the name of Newman to a friend here in Berlin, J. E. Noeggerath,[44] & if the cable had the word 'sold' in [it], I was to know that the matter of my going over to New York was agreed to. This cable was to arrive here, at latest, by 17 March. That day is here now—and no cable has been received. Mary Mac Fadden was also to cable on arrival to a friend here, but none has come. So as I write, I do not know whether the Findlay letters &c have got over safely or been seized at Kirkwall—and I do not know how my friends in America regard the proposal for my going over. However, in view of what occurred yesterday, I presume they disapproved and think I can be more useful here. They little know the true situation here.

After the departure of Mary MacFadden & Mr. S. I stayed on in Berlin until Saturday 26th being ill most of the time. I went back with Gaffney last night to Munich and to bed again at the Kuranstalt.

On Friday, 3 March, while in bed I got a letter from Lt. Monteith dated 1st March urging my immediate return to Berlin.[45] No reasons were given. I answered that I could not travel then & begged him to explain the reasons that called me back so hurriedly.

On 6th March a letter from him of the 4th came, telling me there was 'a move on' that he could not write, or tell to anyone save myself, and that he would come to Munich to see me, arriving the next morning. I was then much better and on the following day, Tuesday 7th March, he arrived and spent the forenoon with me.

The 'move' was this.

On the 1st March he had been asked by the G.G.S. to call where he had seen Lt. Frey. Frey said a 'telegram' had come from Devoy[46] asking for rifles &c. to be sent to Ireland, as 'something' would happen shortly of 'great importance'.[47]

The military here at G.G.S. were willing to give <u>'up to 200,000 rifles' with ammunition</u> Frey said; to land them in Ireland by a given date, probably in trawlers—and Monteith wanted my counsel and help as to what to do.

I said first—'My difficulty is that I don't trust these people in anything they promise—they lie always—they may or may not keep faith today—but I have no reason to believe that in anything they do they ever think of us, or of others—but only of themselves. If then they promise today to give just <u>200,000 rifles &c</u>. I am forced to seek their real reason. It is *not* to help us—rest assured of that. They have shown me, so repeatedly, that they cannot keep faith and that they have no feeling about Ireland at all, that in anything they promise now I seek only their real motive and what end of their own they are after.

However, as they offer us this large armament we should be fools not to take it if we can get it. Let us get what we can.'

I drew up a Memorandum for Monteith to take back with him that night & hand to them the next day in Berlin—promising to follow it, in person, in a few days.

Time was precious. Monteith said he gathered the 'something' in Ireland would occur in April—& the arms were to be there in good time. Devoy's telegram had been in a cipher arranged with Bernstorff[48] & said that a letter coming over by first mail would explain details. This letter was due to arrive, Monteith said, in the course of the present week—13 March

41 The third Irish Race Convention was held in New York 4–5 March 1916 and was the last significant gathering of Irish-American support before the Rising. The principal speakers were John Devoy, William Bourke Cockran and Judge Cohalan. The Convention demanded that 'in the name of liberty and of the small nationalities ... that Ireland may be cut off from England and restored to her rightful place among the nations of the earth'. The moment is above all significant for launching the Friends of Irish Freedom—an organization advocating Irish independence, with an executive committee dominated by Clan na Gael members.

42 The 'Findlay letter' refers to the efforts by the British Minister in Christiania (Oslo) Mansfeldt de Chardonnel Findlay (1861–1932) to bribe Casement's manservant to betray him. The letter, on British Legation paper, promised to pay Christensen £5,000 if his information led to the capture of Casement.

43 Judge Daniel Cohalan (1865–1946). Elected a Supreme Court Judge of New York State in 1912, Cohalan was one of the most influential Irish-Americans working behind the scenes in the U.S. and an open supporter of John Devoy, Clan na Gael and Casement's diplomatic mission to Germany. He was active in the founding of Friends of Irish Freedom.

44 J. E. Noegerrath (1877–1936), a German-American electrical engineer with extensive connections in Berlin. Noegerrath was closely involved with German secret services. In 1914, he published a brief *The Truth about the War* (Munich, 1914). He proved indispensable in early April 1916, helping Casement obtain the submarine.

45 These letters are held in the NYPL Maloney Papers IHP 2-1.

46 John Devoy (1842–1928). Born in Kill, Co. Kildare, after a brief spell in the French Foreign Legion, Devoy submerged himself in the Fenian movement. Exiled to the US, he earned a living from journalism. By 1914 Devoy was the most active Irish-American involved in revolutionary circles and with his own newspaper *The Gaelic American*. He communicated closely with the Germany embassy and supported Casement's diplomatic mission (with some reservations). However, the shared aspiration of Casement and Devoy for a united and independent Ireland was compromised by their different views on how that end might be achieved. By early 1916, Devoy had apparently lost confidence in Casement and was particularly concerned about indiscreet talk and those he was prepared to allow into his confidence.

47 The telegram referred to is reproduced in Doerries, 185.

48 Count Johann Heinrich von Bernstorff (1862–1939), served as German ambassador in Washington 1908–17 and clandestinely in an intelligence capacity. Politically, he was considered a moderate, although his support for the antics of his military attaché, Franz von Papen and his knowledge of subversive activities carried out by German diplomatic staff on US territory alienated his support. A photograph of Bernstorff wearing a swimming costume with his arm around two similarly clad women was strategically used by the British Secret Intelligence Service to cast moral aspersions on his suitability for the post.

to 18 March—and he begged me to try & come to Berlin in good time. I agreed. My Memorandum of 7 March (a copy is attached).[49] (Note Monteith kept copies, but burned them for safety here in Berlin he tells me now—I will try to get copies from G.G.S—8.4.16) pointed out that it was essential to send over, <u>before the shipment of arms</u>, certain intelligence to our friends *in Ireland*, so that the landing place or places, might be definitely fixed, the dates &c. & all arrangements made in concert. I pointed out the vital necessity of this step & showed how it could be done by submarine landing me and two of the Irish soldiers I should pick out, on the coast near Dublin. The submarine to wait and bring back the messenger I should send back.

At the same time Devoy could be told by telegraph, in his code, of what was being done.

Monteith took the 7 March 1916 Memorandum back with him that night to Berlin.

He wrote me next day that he had given it next day to the G.G.S. & they were 'pleased' with it—I wrote him that I should leave for Berlin on Tuesday or Wednesday of this week.

I left the Kuranstalt on Monday, 13th March—& went to Riederau am Ammersee. Next day I tried to see Dr. Curry[50] but missed him & had to wait over till Wednesday 15th—when he hurried back to Munich to see me. That evening while on my way to the station with Dr. C[urry]—I got the telegram from Monteith (attached) begging me to hurry to Berlin.[51] I arrived here yesterday morning at 8.40 a.m., being met by Monteith at the station and he told me he had arranged with Captain Nadolny (Abteilung IIIb)[52] to receive me at 10a.m.at the G.G.S.. We went together to the Staff & spent over an hour with Nadolny and two other (junior) officers, Hauptmann v. Huelson[53] and Graf von Haugwitz[54] (Ausbacher Cuirassiers).

The proposals *now* made were the following:-

1st. The Admiralty refused to send me or anyone ahead on the submarine. Their reason was that it was 'too dangerous'! Too dangerous for our project. The Irish coast was so closely watched the submarine would be seen & thus the whole project 'blown open'. I pointed out that this by no means followed. Submarines had often been seen off the Irish coast & nothing followed & it was absurd to say that if one *were*, by chance, seen it would reveal our plan. But if my advice were followed, she could not be seen & no risk incurred for her—only for us who landed & that was our affair. Moreover if the watch was so close that a submarine could be seen then how did they hope to land arms from a big steamer?

All the arguments were brushed aside with the statement that the German Admiralty <u>would not agree & there was an end of it</u>.

So then we advanced to the 'project' itself. It was this:

The G.G.S. would load up twenty thousand rifles (not 200,000!) with 10 machine guns & 5,000,000 cartridges in trawlers or 'on a steamer' & dispatch them, with our Irish handful at Zossen by 8th April at latest. The 'rising' in Ireland was arranged for Easter Sunday & the guns were to be 'in hand' before that date. They reckoned here to allow ten days for the journey—so that this armament should reach the appointed spot (wherever that might be!) by say 18th April.

Devoy would be informed by wireless & he would have to make the connection with Ireland, to arrange from New York, all details with the Revolutionary Committee in Ireland for reception of the rifles & guns. <u>No prior word could be sent from this & nothing done from here save inform Devoy in this way</u>. I pointed out all the grave objections to such a very limited, uncertain and roundabout way of arranging with the men in Ireland—but all in vain.

Nadolny[55] suggested that *all* the 55 Irish soldiers at Zossen should go, but I said that all could not be trusted, and the selection must be left to Lt.Monteith to pick out the men he believed in. These, I said, must *at once*, without an hour's delay, be trained in machine gun practice, so that on landing they could use the guns (or some of them) if needed to ward off police attack or rifle fire. As the proposals developed I saw how hopeless and inadequate they were—and I saw how false were all the professions accompanying them. Nadolny said that with this 'help' we should surely be in a position to dictate our terms to the British government and secure '<u>at least autonomy</u>'!

The 'war' in Ireland would compel England to 'surrender' to us!! Was there ever such a Mind in the World! If sincere & he believed what he said, he was a bigger fool than any I had yet met—& if not sincere he must have taken me for that man.

I could not say what I thought of it all. I listened, smiled and looked at Monteith across the table. I even pretended to concur in these manifestations of lunacy, or at least I did not say ' you are an ass or a rogue'. What else could I do? The guns were of service. If we could get them to Ireland they would be a reinforcement to the armed men there who had already with such inadequate weapons, compelled Great Britain to exclude Ireland from the Conscription Act.

Twenty thousand more armed men & 5,000,000 cartridges would be an added security to keeping Ireland out of the war— all I was now hoping for. Besides I saw it was <u>all</u> we were to get. If I refused this offer—& pointed out all the absurdities of the plan and the grave risks, I should rob Devoy & the Irish in America and my Volunteers in Ireland of the <u>only</u> chance of external help that would ever come from Germany.

The Germans would throw the refusal on me—the Irish in America & at home would do the same. The facts, as I knew them, could never be known—all that would be said or seen would be that this government had offered 'generous help' in response to our request & I had stood in the way & opposed. So I was bound to seem to agree to what was patently the most despicable offer. I asked for the documents they had got from Devoy to see what he had actually asked for. They produced <u>at length</u>, a typed copy of a letter dated '*16/2/16*' & signed by him as secretary.[56]

This letter stated what he believed to be the situation in Ireland both as regards the Government forces available, & the number of Volunteers to be counted on. The former were put at 40,000 men (30,000 troops & 10,000 police), the troops inferior men with little artillery.

The Volunteers were put at *10,000* already armed, but with only some 200 cartridges per rifle, and many thousands available if arms could be supplied. Devoy asked for these, saying that if <u>100,000 rifles and artillery and German officers</u> and artillery men could be landed, there was no doubt of our ability to defeat the British forces.

He suggested Limerick as the best place for landing—and said that the 'rising' would take place on <u>Easter Sunday</u>. The final paragraph of the letter was a request that I should remain in Germany as the accredited representative till the end of the war of the Irish Revolutionary Body!!! Poor, good, brave old man—& it is to get rid of me, him, Ireland, the Treaty[57] and all their commitments they now send out this shipment.

I pointed out to Nadolny that Devoy laid stress on the presence of German officers & some trained artillerymen, & that they were not sending any but only Lt. Monteith and some 20 men of ours at outside <u>not trained</u> in gun practice.

I said no more. I added that the final paragraph it was my obvious duty to disregard and that I should have to accompany the men. He said '<u>of course, it is impossible</u> for you to remain behind. You must be there with them. Everything forces you to go'.

I again urged the dire importance of first sending messengers from here to let the 'Supreme Council' in Ireland know exactly what was going to be done.

He refused, and put it all on the Admiralty—pointing out that if we

This was another example of using sexual innuendo as a way of undermining the moral standing of the enemy.

49 The memorandum has not yet been traced. It referred to Casement's intention to have a U-boat put at his disposal so that he could return to Ireland and organise the landing of the arms and try and call off the Rising.

50 Charles Curry became a critical figure in Casement's last weeks in Berlin and was left detailed instructions by Casement as to the dispersal and publication of his papers, including his diaries and the original copy of the treaty, known as the 'Irish Verses'. A detailed statement of 26 March 1916 held in NLI MS 17026—'A Last Word for my True Friend'—is addressed to Curry and comprises nine numbered double-sided foolscap pages and a supplementary document setting out instructions for the distribution of his papers after the war. 'All this "raw material" should, with the letters & copies of my letters in the various trunks, allow a fairly complete history of my stay in Germany be put together … The best person to edit all would be Professor Kuno Meyer, the Celtic Scholar.' Casement also mentioned E. D. Morel, William Cadbury and A. S. Green as possible collaborators in this publishing venture.

51 Copy held in NYPL Maloney Papers IHP Box 2.

52 Abteilung IIIb is the name of the German military intelligence division of the G.G.S., formed in 1889 and directed from 1913 to 1918 by Colonel Walther Nicolai. See Markus Pöhlmann, 'German Intelligence at War, 1914–1918,' *The Journal of Intelligence History* 5, (Winter 2005), 25–54.

53 Casement spells the name Huelson, but this appears to be Ernst von Hülsen.

54 Count Curt Ludvig Heinrich Georg Max Erdman Haugwitz-Hardenberg-Reventlow (1885–1963). Haugwitz was a member of the Politik-Berlin of the German General Staff and worked as a liaison officer between the German F.O. and the Emperor's Military HQ. He was in charge of organizing the shipment of arms for Ireland. He wrote a brief account of Casement's time in Germany and the unrealized plan of returning with Casement to Ireland in a brief memoir presented to Eamon de Valera in 1947. It is held in NLI MS 13774.

55 Rudolf Nadolny (1873–1953). Born in Poland. After holding various diplomatic posts in Russia, Persia, Albania he was given a post in Abteilung IIIb where he created an independent political operation known as 'P' (Politik) and became a spymaster, directing covert support for various anti-government groups in Russia, Ireland and elsewhere. Nadolny's negotiations with Casement turned increasingly bitter. After the war, Nadolny became a singular advocate of the German-Soviet alliance.

56 See Doerries, 181–84.

57 This is a reference to the Treaty signed between Casement and the Imperial German Government on 23 December 1914 that guaranteed German support for the Irish independence struggle. Casement believed that in his last weeks the German General Staff was manoeuvering to ditch its commitment to the treaty, to Ireland and to him.

raised difficulties on this score they might refuse the ships &c. & the whole enterprise collapse.

The trawlers would be accompanied by a submarine—that was all! He would cable Devoy & he, Devoy, would have to arrange everything with the men in Ireland. Meantime he would go the General at the War Department and get the men Lt. Monteith should pick out <u>at once trained</u> in machine-gun exercise. I pointed out this would take some days—to get the permission &c. &c. &c. that the training could not begin for perhaps a week. He agreed. So that the invasion of Ireland in 1916 is to be with 12 or 20 men (who are not to be told in advance a word!) & who are to have perhaps a week's practice with a machine gun at Zossen!

We are all to go on the trawlers (dressed as soldiers in English-made clothes, got from some of the interned British prisoners in Germany—(this was my idea)—'accompanied by a submarine', round by way of Norway &c. &c. to the West coast of Ireland—Or possibly in 'a steamer'. What a fine party! Was there ever seriously put forward by a great military power in the world such a proposal!

And if I point out its stupendous idiocy, its fundamental falsity, its foredoomed failure, I shall be held to all ages in Irish history, as a 'traitor', as the man who, at the moment of destiny, failed his country's cause & prevented the great German empire from extending 'military help' to revolutionary Ireland. My God! Was ever sane man in such a position!

I left the G.G.S. with Monteith at about 12.10 and walked back with him across the Tiergarten by the pond, behind the hideous and appalling Hohenzollerns of the Sieges Allée!—How I loathe that Allée—How I abhor these grotesque & ponderous monstrosities in marble—fitting types of the line of coarse and selfish heads of this Prussian abortion.

I told Monteith all my fears—but how I saw clearly I <u>had</u> to go. He agreed that I could not stay behind. He also agreed with me that in any case, without a German army corps, any 'rising' in Ireland by ourselves alone is hopeless—worse than hopeless.

But to attempt it with this meagre 'help', under such conditions is madness and criminal. He agrees to it & sees the hopelessness, but feels with me it is our duty to try & get the rifles into Ireland. We have no right to stand in the way of that attempt. I explained to him that my only hope in going is to arrive in time to dissuade the leaders at home from the attempt. That if I can only get ashore a little ahead of the rifles I may be able to stop the 'rising' and arrange only for the safe delivery of the rifles. If this can be done <u>then</u> (& then only) would the thing prove useful. Otherwise it is an awful danger. Of course the chances are that we shall never get near the shores of Ireland. If it is too 'dangerous' for a submarine to go off that coast, how do they expect 'the steamer' or the trawlers loaded up with rifles &c. to escape observation? The thing is worse than mad—it is dishonest.

The more I think of it, the more do I believe it to be an act of dishonesty. It is to get rid of us—'the Brigade', me, the Treaty with Ireland, & all their responsibilities to us, founded on their past dealings with me and with the Clan in the USA—on the cheapest possible terms to themselves, under the pretense of complying with our request and furnishing us with the very aid we asked for.

In any case, <u>they</u> stand to lose nothing. The 20,000 rifles &c. will be captured—Russian guns, probably—so, too, the machine guns—probably English machine guns captured in Flanders. The handful of German sailors who will navigate the 'steamer' or the trawlers, I fully expect will be instructed to take to their boats at the first sight of capture & get off in the 'accompanying submarine'! We should be left to our fate,

That is, probably, why she accompanies us, with the added hope that possibly she may succeed in torpedoing the English cruiser, or war vessel that overhauls us. Should we be captured, well & good—Germany has 'done her part'. She tried, sincerely, to help us 'to the best of her ability' under the naval conditions prevailing, and the failure was a chance of war. At any rate, she <u>tried</u> to fulfill her pledge.

The Irish in America would be assured of this—we should be dead, or in jail & the alliance in the USA would continue to strengthen Bernstorff & impede Wilson & the pro-Britons.

If, on the other hand, we arrive in Ireland (by a miracle), then the subsequent events don't concern Germany at all. Our hideous failure—a 'rebellion' whiffed out in a few discharges of constabulary rifles, or at best of machine guns—would be our failure—not theirs.

No German officer or man would be in it—and even proof that the arms came from Germany would be wanting—or at least no publicity would attach—as the English government would hush up, for naval reasons, the successful landing, if we succeeded in landing.

The only object <u>this</u> Government (the German Govt) has in <u>now</u> offering us this meagre & belated help is to continue the fooling of the Irish in America & a possibly far-off hope that we may create some little complication for England in Ireland. They know <u>nothing</u> about Ireland—& not much about England. They are incapable of understanding the minds of other men—or of dealing with free men. They have no conception of personal freedom or of how men used to free action & free thought think. Their sole method of dealing with other people is to apply the methods used at home to their too obedient, servile, drilled and disciplined population.[58]

Certainly from the point of view of foreign government, Germany does not deserve to win this war. Her people do deserve to win—for they are innocent and victims—and England is certainly attacking them not because of Prussian militarism but because of German commercialism. Still, the Emperor and the gang around him are a hard nut for the world to deal with.

In some ways I have acquired sympathy for the English standpoint when I contrast the individual candour, truthfulness and straightforwardness of the Englishman with the absence of these qualities in the governing classes here—or indeed in almost any section of the people. Collectively a great nation—individually an undesirable one.

Here comes Gaffney—so I must stop for the present. I have written all the morning nearly—and shall try to go on here & at Munich between this and the 4th or 5th April when I must return to this horrible city to go to my doom. I don't mind that, if only I could feel there was some way out for Ireland & those at home, who are so misled into believing that 'help will come from Germany'.

I see no way out. There is nothing for it but to go to what I know leads only to ghastly failure. I am making an attempt at 3 today, through Captain Heydell[59] of the Admiralty, to still try & get off ahead on the submarine or if that cannot be arranged then to try and send John McGoey[60] over to Ireland to warn them clearly of the limited character of the help & the entire absence of real German support.

Munich, Monday 27 March, 1916

It is ten days since I began my 'final page' at Berlin on 17th March. That afternoon, at 3pm, I went to the Reichsmarine Amt[61] & saw Captain Heydell & two other Captains in Room 763 who had charge of the project. Captain Stültzer is the chief officer in charge of the business.

<u>I learned much more</u>. First, I renewed the appeal for the submarine to take me & two men ahead. They rejected it—peremptorily. I pointed out the grave importance of this step—they met it with alleged naval reasons, the chief being that the Irish coast was very closely watched &

58 Casement added a note on 8.4.16: ('I was wrong here—they had & have a far worse object—viz, bloodshed in Ireland. The guns are to be a real gift of death. I have seen for days now that no action of mine can stop the guns. They are determined to send them as they have arranged for bloodshed as their price.')

59 Captain Eberhard Heydell of the German admiralty. Casement wrote a letter to Heydell from the U-19 the day before the landing in Kerry. Thanking him for his efforts organizing the submarine and suggesting that submarines would be the only means of landing further guns if the cargo from the Aud was landed safely. See NLI MS 22987.

60 John McGoey (1883–1924), remains something of a mystery. Scottish-born to Irish parents, he emigrated to Canada and US in 1903. In late 1915, he was sent by McGarrity to assist Casement and joined the Irish Brigade at Zossen. Different rumours surround McGoey's fate after his despatch to Ireland. Casement believed he was captured in Kirkwall and possibly executed. Allegations that he was a British spy are made in Aodogán O'Rahilly, *Winding the Clock* (Dublin, 1991). His movements after bidding Casement goodbye are unclear. More recent research suggests that he survived the war and returned to the US where he died in an accident on a building site in Chicago.

61 The Imperial Naval Office.
62 Captain Walther Isendahl was one of the directors of 'N' the intelligence department of the Imperial German Navy (Nachrichten-Abteilung)

the submarine would be <u>caught</u>. How then about the steamer or steamers with the guns? And they said the shipment would be in a 'small steamer of 1,000 tonnes under the Norwegian flag'. She would have false papers of course. <u>She would not be accompanied or convoyed by a submarine</u>. I insisted on this, but Heydell said it would give the thing away. The submarine to keep up with the steamer would have to steam on the surface & then the British cruisers &c. on look out would see the smoke of the submarine alongside & that would damn the steamer & draw close attention to her. Nothing I could say would change their obstinate refusal to either send anyone ahead by a submarine, or to convoy the gunship by a submarine! This being so I said I should then rely on trying to get a messenger sent over ahead, & I asked them if they would pass John McGoey over the frontier for me. They sent for Captain Isendahl[62] (of last 1915 February reminiscences!) who at once agreed to get McGoey off whenever I brought him in. I said I should have him there at the Admiralty next afternoon—18th March. They had a chart (an English Admiralty chart) of the coast of Kerry & pointed out to me where they proposed to land the rifles.

It was to be at Tralee Bay, at Fenit Pier. The steamer with the rifles would come to 'Inishtooskert' (the N.W. of the 'Seven Hags' Rocks north of Rough Point), between 20-23 April—& we (the Irish) were to have a pilot there to bring her into Fenit. The pilot boat to show 2 green lights (after dark) only for a short time. This information they said had been cabled over to John Devoy and his reply 'All right' <u>dated 14 March</u> was shown me!

Now, the previous day, Nadolny of the G.G.S. pretended they had been waiting for me to come to telegraph Devoy because when I said 'you will then cable fully to Devoy' he said 'of course, of course'—and yet it is now clear they arranged everything long before I came—for if Devoy's reply is of 14 March, when was their cable to him sent? There is a growing mystery in the whole thing—or, rather I see clearer & clearer the game they are playing.

It was on 1st <u>March</u> they first told Monteith & wrote to me the curt letter asking me to go to Berlin at once. They did not tell Monteith immediately they got Devoy's telegram. That is certain. It would be discussed all round. When did Devoy telegraph? His letter of details was dated 16 February 1916—this followed the telegram. Probably the telegram was sent about the same date as the letter. So that about 18th February or so they had the request for the rifles. Why did they all at once change their studied refusal to supply us with the arms into this gift? Let me think.

Say they got the telegram on 18th February, it would be discussed by the G.G.S. [and] with the Foreign Office. Both are equally anxious to get out of their Irish obligations. The Foreign Office bitterly regret the Treaty; the General Staff 'The Irish Brigade'. Here was a chance of killing two birds with one stone!

They might ship the Brigade to Ireland with a load of rifles—& as they knew me quite well enough they knew I would go too—& then there would be an end to the whole engagement to help Ireland. I feel more and more convinced this was the scheme (it was only part of it—a minor part, the real thing was the 'Irish rising' 8/4/16).

Why else did Mr. Meyer send me on 29th February '<u>in these times</u>' Robert Emmet's Dying Speech?[63] When I got Assessor Meyer's letter & that typed copy of the Death Speech I was ill in bed at the Kuranstalt. I could not imagine why it was sent me.

Here it is—<u>just as received</u>.

The idea of the German Foreign Office typing Robert Emmet's last speech for me whom they have so often ignored and derided, & after their attempt to evict Father C[rotty][64] in January & February too—(his letters herewith too) made me wonder at the time, as to their motive.

Now I see it. Certainly, then, by 29 February the Foreign Office and the G.G.S. were agreed that the request of Clan-na-Gael for rifles was an admirable chance of shipping off the whole Brigade and myself—and getting rid of the galling obligation they had so 'chivalrously' assumed of 'good will to Ireland'. The Robert Emmet letter to me on 29 February was to prepare my mind.

Then, when all was decided on & the Admiralty agreed to furnish ships &c. &c. they sent for Monteith on 1 March & tell him of the telegram, of the expected letter of details from Devoy, and of their willingness to supply 'up to 200,000 rifles'. Liars!

Another point—Monteith told me Nadolny had urged him 'on no account' to worry me 'lest I might not be well enough to go'! (See Monteith letter). Nadolny's impudent pretence that with these guns I should dictate terms to the British Government was really the last straw. The whole thing is dastardly. They are, I verily believe, rather hoping we shall all be caught and hanged or jailed for life.

Captain Heydell said they thought it likely the steamer might be stopped by a British auxiliary cruiser & a prize crew put on board to take her into a British port—in that event he said ' your only chance will be to throw the prize crew overboard' & go on with the ship. I said we would go one better. We would try & capture the prize crew & bind them, not kill them, & take their uniforms for the Irish boys who would then become the prize crew!

I left the Admiralty even more hopeless than the G.G.S. the day before. The thing gets plainer and plainer. It is a regular plot to get rid of their Irish obligations on the very cheapest terms to themselves, with the least risk and least publicity.

And what will the Clan be doing? They have been told that there will be a ship at Fenit on a certain date (20–23 April) but have they been told she will have only 20,000 rifles & 10 machine guns & <u>no</u> German officers or artillerymen?

I feel sure not. They have been led to believe that Devoy's letter is being favourably considered & the 'goods' supplied—while, in truth, they are avoiding the fundamental issues raised by Devoy—our lack of officers in Ireland & of trained artillery men &c. &c.

I went back to the Saxonia Hotel, in a very despondent mood and sent for John McGoey to be brought in next day.

Here again, in this case the military have behaved with their usual disregard of promise or politeness. I had applied for his release on 28 February & no reply had been received—see the accompanying correspondence attached here. John McGoey had come over from the US as a Volunteer, to help me in any way, with strong recommendations from J. McGarrity.[65] As I could do nothing else with him at the time, I sent him out to Zossen to the 'Brigade' on the conditions prescribed in the undertaking he signed on 2 December 1915 which provided for him 'immediate' release whenever I should need him for other service. In February I wished to send him back to US to warn our friends there of the double dealing & faithlessness of this government—& how little reliance we could place in anything they said.

Now, as the letter for his release had been ignored, I told Monteith just to bring him in to me without anyone being asked good, bad or indifferent. I would arrange for the War Office being told once I got him out of the country.

McGoey was brought in next day—I explained all the situation to him very fully and pointed out the imperative need of trying to get some one into Ireland to warn them there of the wholly inadequate help being given & to say that I strongly urged no 'rising'. He (like Monteith) was with me here. McGoey said it would be criminal & that he had long suspected the Germans of playing a double game. He would do anything I asked him to. I told him it was necessary for me, to keep silent as to my real opinions before the G.G.S. and that

63 Casement was very familiar with Robert Emmet's speech from the dock along with the litany of speeches from the dock made by those who resisted British rule in Ireland over the generations. Casement's reply to Meyer is in Doerries, 187, where Casement admits to giving copies to 'some young Indian students in Dublin & one of them ... learned it by heart so that, as he said, on his trial he might recite the dead Irishman's words for the benefit of his fellow countrymen'. For a perceptive comparison of the two speeches from the dock, see T. P. Dolan, 'Irish Oratory from Emmet to Casement', *Irish University Review,* 6:2, Autumn 1976, 151–163.

64 Father Thomas Crotty (1867–1930). Born in New Ross to a family with a prosperous bakery business in Kilkenny; he joined the Dominicans in 1884. In November 1914, he was sent by the Vatican to Germany and began to work as a special envoy to Irish POWs, first in Limburg and then Zossen. He developed a strong bond with Casement and appears to have influenced Casement's own spiritual shift towards Catholicism. The correspondence between Crotty and Casement is held in NLI MS 13085/20. My thanks to John Kirwan for information on the Crotty family connection with Kilkenny

when I took him to the Admiralty he must do the same.

We went at 11.30 o'clock and found the three Captains again—all was explained to John McGoey. He is to go as an added string to our bow (in addition to the telegram to Devoy) to tell the Dublin Council to have the pilot boat ready at Inishtooskert, &c. &c. but he goes really to get the heads in Ireland to call off the rising & merely try to land the arms safely & distribute these.

My view, sent by John McGoey, was that we should try to get the arms &c. landed—and once distributed among 20,000 fresh Volunteers, we are so much stronger as against the Coalition government & then we might perhaps find means of getting off further rifles &c. from Germany. Make them keep Frey's offer of 200,000 rifles!

Captain Isendahl said a police agent would come for McGoey at my hotel that evening, to identify him, & that he would go next morning 19th via Warnemünde—with no papers or passports & be put over into Denmark—I agreed—& that night I gave John McGoey full instructions. The police agent came at 7 & was to return at 7.30 a.m.

The chief satisfaction I have is to think that I am successfully getting John McGoey out of the country over the heads of the War Office & the others—who have been so ill-mannered. If he gets safely through to Dublin he is to seek out Tom Clarke,[66] & through him B. Hobson[67] & try to 'call off' the rising & get them to concentrate only on the successful landing of the guns.

The name of the steamer not yet known. They could tell me on Tuesday, but I said it was more important to get John McGoey off <u>at once</u> than keep him two or three days just to learn the name.

He left Sunday morning 7.30 with the Detective—and I can only pray and hope he got across the frontier all right & that he may be able to get a ship at Copenhagen to Scotland. I gave him (against his will) 300 marks in Danish money—the hotel porter got it changed for me—and then 30 marks in German money—I saw him off at 7.30 on the stairs of the hotel with a last blessing & greeting in Irish.

The chance of any steamer getting there has been enormously lessened by the Mowen's exploit.[68] The English have a ring of patrol boats right across from the Orkneys to Norway & I don't think there is the ghost of a chance of our getting thro'.

The more one considers the whole thing, the more certain it is that the chief aim of this Govt. is to 'cut their losses' & shuffle out of all dealing with Ireland.

The Emperor had doubtless again changed his mind—or those round him. Just as he once played with President Kruger—so he is now trying to do with Ireland—blowing hot & cold. But this is more than the abandonment of Kruger—because this *is* the <u>betrayal</u> of me into the hands of the English.

They know well we shall be taken—& they know the fate that means for me surely & perhaps for the poor young soldier boys.

The only thing I can see is that by going with them I may save them—as the English will be content with catching me & putting the blame all on my shoulders. But I can not imagine a more cowardly proceeding by any Govt. than this one arranged by three Departments of State to get rid of a handful of poor men they have deceived & of an obligation that has become hurtful to them.

If I live to make all clear—someday—but there is no chance of that. And yet it is only right that the truth should be known and told—for history is history, however Govts and rulers change their minds—& it is historic fact that the German Govt. made a Treaty with Ireland & promised recognition of complete independence following on the attempt they were pledged to of conveying military aid. And this is the way to try to fulfill their pledge! To invade a great Kingdom with 12 men!—dressed as sailors. Was ever such a thing seriously put forward! They are really beneath contempt.

---

65 Joseph McGarrity (1874–1940), born Co. Tyrone, came from a strong Irish nationalist tradition. He emigrated to the US in 1892 and became leading figure in Clan na Gael. He provided support for many causes in the build up to 1916 including Casement's fund-raising tour among Irish-American sympathizers. Casement stayed with him during his trip to the US in 1914 and the two conspired on various fronts. He was deeply implicated in the Hindu-German conspiracy and organized and paid for the *Annie Larsen* arms purchase. He steadfastly opposed the Treaty of 1921. He spent considerable time and money trying to salvage Casement's reputation from the propaganda conflict of the post-war years. Unlike Devoy, his belief in Casement never wavered. The IRA signed all statements 'J. J. McGarrity' until the split in 1969. See Marie V. Tarpey, 'Joseph McGarrity, Fighter for Irish Freedom', *Studia Hibernica* 11 (Dublin, 1971), 164–80 and Sean Cronin, *The McGarrity Papers: Revelations of the Irish revolutionary movement in Ireland and America 1900–1940* (Tralee, 1972).

66 Tom Clarke (1858–1916), Irish revolutionary and a signatory of the Declaration of the Republic, who was executed in 1916 for his leading role in the Rising. He assumed leadership of the insurrection in face of opposition from Casement, MacNeill and others. Clarke had dedicated his life to Irish liberation, was imprisoned for long spells and worked in the shadows of republican organization through his newsagents shop in central Dublin. He was the main advocate for sending Monteith to Germany.

I told Gaffney who was constantly with me that John McGoey was going back to Philadelphia to J. McGarrity.

That Sunday afternoon (19 March) Gaffney and I went out to Zossen to attend the funeral of poor Holohan,[69] the first member of the Brigade to die. He died on Patrick's Eve—& the priest Monteith had got down to confess the men on Patrick's Day arrived 20 minutes before his death—God be praised.

All the poor lads fell on their knees & recited the rosary when they heard of Holohan's death.

Today the funeral was well done, & the priest who had been in Ireland, preached a fine sermon over the grave. Some of the boys cried. Then Gaffney, Monteith and I went out to the camp and Gaffney sang a stanza of 'The Boys of Wexford'.

We returned at 7 to Berlin.

Of course Gaffney knows nothing. Nadolny impressed (on 16th March) on Monteith & myself the absolute necessity of 'secrecy'—and here is the second part of the proposal. As soon as we are gone with our party, the rest of the Brigade are to be locked up—'in prison' Nadolny said, until it is known we are safely across. A fine fate! And who will ever see them out of prison? I said, in answer to this proposal that of course they remembered they were committed to sending the men to America and he said 'of course, of course'. It is all 'of course' of a course with much else that I have found at their hands.

How can I go on with it? What am I to do? Whatever way I turn, misery, failure, degradation & no way out. I know not what to do. I have told Monteith the acute fear I have—not physical or for myself, but for Ireland & our national cause. We are being put in an abject position—and this by this great almighty power.

I left Berlin again on 22 March for Munich intending to spend some quiet days and write my Diary up at Riederau—but I cannot!

I went to Riederau on 24th & stayed over to 25th walking in to Diessen. I returned on Saturday 25th to Munich & decided to go to Berlin on Sunday 26th. Took tickets & packed & at 8.45—when about to leave the hotel, a feverish attack came on. I knew it would get worse in night—so at last moment I decided to stay. No use arriving at Zossen ill, with high temperature to go to bed. My last week in Berlin will be a very busy one. So here I am in bed this Monday—better & determined to go in morning by first train.

I shall be in Berlin tomorrow night 7pm & go to 'Saxonia' & talk things over with Monteith. He only got the machine gun to begin to practice on 25th March—nine days after Nadolny spoke of getting it. They will have a little over a week's training—and it is <u>ten months</u> since they were taken from Limburg with the promise to be 'at once' trained & equipped.

I am getting more & more disposed, as I lie in bed here in Munich (with 6 grams of aspirin in me) to put my foot down & call off the whole thing—so far as I can.

Unless they agree to send a submarine with us—then all might be different. I shall talk it over with Monteith tomorrow night.

Berlin, Wednesday 29 March 1916,

I arrived here last night at 6.50 from Munich. Monteith came. He agreed with my view that the thing is worse than mad. 'Dastardly' is his expression, mine too.

He is training the whole 38 men at the machine gun in Zossen but says only about 12 'at outside' can be counted on. I told him my last idea, arrived at yesterday while lying ill in Munich waiting for the doctor—viz.—to point out the grave wrong (and risk to Germany too) of sending the men. That to do so is a break of faith of the kind to them & a flagrant breach of the agreement of 28 December 1914.[70] Moreover, it means that once we are captured the men would naturally & rightly point out the falsehood and the trick played on them by the German Govt. & recount too, many

67 Bulmer Hobson (1883–1969). The relationship between Roger Casement and Bulmer Hobson was vital to preparations for the 1916 Rising. Hobson was a tireless grassroots activist and organized various republican initiatives including the Dungannon Clubs, Na Fianna Éireann and edited newspapers such as *The Irish Peasant* and *Irish Freedom*. He was instrumental in the pick up of guns from Howth harbour in July 1914. In the days before the Rising, Hobson did his best to call off manoeuvres and implement Eoin MacNeill's countermanding order. To prevent this, he was held in a house in Phibsboro until military action was too far advanced. See Marnie Hay, *Bulmer Hobson and the Nationalist Movement in Twentieth-Century Ireland* (Manchester, 2009).

68 Casement here has tipped in a brief clipping from the *Augsburger Zeitung*, 24 March 1916 about the sinking of the *Greife* in the North Atlantic, and adding '(Since the above, the '*Greife*' has been sunk by the English.)'

69 Patrick Holohan died in Zossen and was the first casualty in the ranks of the Irish Brigade.

70 This refers to the agreement or treaty signed between Casement and the German Government determining the agenda of the Irish Brigade.

71 Casement was instrumental in the first successful running of guns into Ireland at Howth in July 1914.

breaches of faith perpetrated on them. The English Government would be pleased, perhaps, to pardon the men to make the perfidy of the German Govt stronger & plainer. As to the 'rising' itself in Ireland I am & have been always hopeless on that point, or rather absolutely convinced that without serious foreign aid, say 5,000 men <u>at least</u> & plenty of guns &c. &c. it would be worse than a disaster. To attempt it with <u>this</u> help—well [it] is a masterpiece of idiocy that admits of only one explanation. That explanation is clear. The German Government want to bury the 'folly' of the Brigade, the Treaty & all their coquetting with 'Irish rebellion' in this paltry gift of 20,000 rifles, leaving us to bear the shock & pay the piper and they want bloodshed in Ireland.

My view is still we should try & get the guns across. If we don't do that we run counter to the strong wish of those at home and in America who are counting on this at least. The guns, if landed, are an asset & to merely land them need not necessarily involve any bloodshed, or serious trouble, if the men in Ireland can act well.

Having sent as I hope John McGoey to Ireland to explain the meagre help coming & the dire need of *not* rising, I feel we should still try & get the guns over <u>but not at the cost of the lives of these poor chaps at Zossen</u>—the attempt at any rate. This in no wise requires the presence of the 12 boys from Zossen. That part of the proposal is so manifestly a put up game between the G.G.S. and the Foreign Office to get rid of the embarrassment of the 'Irish Brigade' that it does not really fall into the affair at all.

Devoy asked on 16 February for 100,000 rifles, trained artillery-men, officers and plenty of cannon & suggested Limerick as place of landing. They replied to that request (I have never been shown their reply yet 8/4/16) saying a ship, or ships, would be at Fenit by 20–23 April to which on 14 March he is said to have answered 'all right'. I arrived on 16 March in Berlin and saw the G.G.S. at 10.30 am. I was not told that they had already telegraphed Devoy & got his reply, but I was led to believe that they <u>would</u> telegraph to him now that I 'approved' the plan.

My 'approval' consisted of pointing out that I was willing and anxious to help my countrymen, being worse than useless here, & for the rest that what they were sending did not tally at all with what Devoy had asked for.

The whole thing was sprung on me & the only clear thought I had was that those making it were false-hearted scoundrels & if I could get out of their clutches soonest this risk I'd go & try to stop the whole thing. Then came the interview at the Admiralty next day, 17 March & following day 18th, with John McGoey & John McGoey's departure on 19th. No news from him yet. I have waited these days, pondering it all, day & night & hoping to get a card from John McGoey saying he was off. Once I am sure he is clear & away I shall feel more free to deal with the situation here. (He was to send a card to 'Mr. Hammond' at Auswärtiges Amt when sure of getting away from Denmark to England. None come yet 8/4/16).

Now today 29/3/16 I am sending a note to Captain Heydell to say I wish to see him & I shall go round & tell them there, first, that I object to the soldiers going at all—but am willing to go myself. That I regard the thing as quite hopeless & wish to limit the number of victims to myself.

I will draw up a Memo giving all the overmastering reasons & send it to the Admiralty once I have discussed it with them.

They are much franker & straighter than the G.G.S. or Foreign Office & are far more likely to speak the truth. They are merely innocent agents in the matter, carrying out as well as they can the wishes of the German Government as represented by the G.G.S. & Foreign Office—whose object is to get rid of us all under pretence of complying with Devoy's request—& above all to ensure bloodshed in Ireland.

I shall not say anything of this to the Admiralty—but merely express my personal objections to sacrificing the men who trusted in me and the Treaty of 28 December 1914.

Monteith agrees entirely. He would go further & stop the rifles too—as likely to provoke bloodshed in Ireland, even if successfully landed.

I reply to that, that we are ignorant of all the plans & methods in USA & Ireland & it is not right to rob them of this tiny offer of help which would not <u>necessarily</u> involve more bloodshed than Howth if the parties to get the guns do their duty.[71] At any rate, as things are I <u>dare</u> not accept the responsibility of stopping the guns (even if I could do so!) & leaving the men in Ireland in the lurch.

I am sending this note to Heydell.

29 March 1916

Dear Captain Heydell,

I arrived last night (having been detained two days by a return of the influenza attack) & shall be very glad to see you today whenever convenient to you.

There are some things of importance to discuss and I will call at any hour you name.

Yours sincerely,
Roger Casement

The things I jot down for this interview are the following:-

1. To show me the *exact* text of the cablegram they sent to Devoy to which he replied on 14 March 'all right'.

<u>What</u> was the exact offer they made? I know his demand—what have they told him they are doing?

2. To point out the grave risk of sending Lt. Monteith & the men—how it may fatally compromise German honour before the world—& how it is really in direct contradiction with the solemn promise of the German Govt. in the Treaty.

If the men are captured, as is almost inevitable, they would be regarded as victims of German duplicity & the case against Germany would be overwhelming. I shall not *say* all this out brutally—but let them see the danger—I shall insist that I go with my eyes wide open, knowing I go to a dreadful fate & that I don't intend to have my innocent young countrymen risk their necks too so hopelessly.

I shall tell them, too, I mean to have poison with me—& that I go really so that they here in Germany shall not say I was a coward.

3. To get the name of the steamer, the port she goes from, the date and hour of departure—& when I must go and be on board, if it is still decided that I go after I put my foot down on the shipping of the men.

It is probable, highly probable, I think, when the G.G.S. & Foreign Office learn that I am resisting the shipping off of the 'Irish Brigade' they will recall the whole thing and give up the attempt even to land the arms—putting the 'blame' for the abandonment on my shoulders. (I was nearly right there! R.C. 8/4/16)

4. I will ask to be allowed to communicate by wireless with John Devoy. (I did not know until Monteith told me in Munich on 7 March) that J. D. had any means of communications with German in cipher or they with him. Another proof of their double dealing! They never told me they could send messages for me to him in cipher & never once offered—& from the first day I landed they have always had some card up their sleeve and have never been frank or straightforward. It is a vicious bureaucracy indeed!

At the Admiralty I was sent to Captain Stültzer. Heydell came & brought in the chief naval officer Captain [???] in charge of the details of the shipment and the Captain of the steamer. Latter young, tall & frank—a fine young fellow.

I told them then that I feared to take any of the Irish soldiers—on political

72 Franz von Papen (1879–1969), diplomat and German Chancellor. As the German military attaché in Washington in 1914, von Papen collaborated closely with Casement and other Irish revolutionaries to destabilize the Anglo-American alliance. Important communications between von Papen and the IRB were stolen by agents working for the US Department of Justice, from a German embassy office on Wall Street, which contained important information about international aspects of Irish revolutionary activity. Von Papen later wrote the foreword to the second edition of Monteith's *Casement's Last Adventure* (Dublin, 1953).

73 The letter from Devoy to Count von Bernstorff is reproduced in Doerries, 181–84.

74 Major F. von Baerle of the German War Office accompanied Casement and Monteith on various visits to the Irish prisoners at Limburg and Zossen towards the end of 1915. Casement had little time for him.

grounds—that if captured they would surely turn 'King's evidence' & rightly & the blame would be on the German Government. They saw the gravity & said I'd better go to the G.G.S. at once. The whole scheme was controlled & directed from there. The Captain said he would come with me. We rang up Nadolny & went on in Captain [???]'s motor car—a govt. one.

At the Abteilung BIII of the G.G.S. I found Nadolny and his two aides—von Hülsen and Haugwitz. The Captain explained my fears about taking the men, & I added some remarks. Nadolny became very angry & exceedingly rude—& Von Hülsen glared at me with bleary eyes and whispered to the Naval Captain. The only one who behaved well & is a gentleman is the young Count von Haugwitz. It was a most unseemly exhibition of German military culture.

I gave back as much as I got & insisted on the whispering stopping & the conversation being conducted in a language I understood, either English or French. The chief cause of the fury was my having sent John McGoey to Ireland! I nearly laughed in Nadolny's face. He said it was a gross breach of faith. I told him he was a liar. He said he would cable to J. Devoy & say that owing to my action the German Government now refused the rifles. I said he might do so if he pleased—but that his statement would be an obvious falsehood.

I asserted my absolute right to send a messenger to Ireland—that McGoey had come for this very purpose—sent by the Clan—& that unless I was to assume, which, with a shrug I said I clearly was—I had entire freedom to communicate with my countrymen in Ireland or America.

If Nadolny cabled I presumed I should be permitted the same action. 'No,' he roared—'I will tell your countrymen it is you have robbed them of the guns they asked for.' The Naval Captain, having had his ears filled by Hülsen, got up & scarcely looking at me, went out. I stayed on & talked more with Haugwitz than the others.

Nadolny went and came—so did Hülsen—Haugwitz stayed by me—a gentleman. Their fear was that I had sent John McGoey to stop the rising! They asked again & again if I had given him instructions to that effect. I said I was not the master of the Irish Revolutionary body & whatever I might say would only be advice or suggestion. I avowed that John McGoey himself was dead against a rising, & the fury was uncontrolled. How had I dared to send such a man to Ireland without letting them know!

I saw in a clear sharp light, the whole devilish game—Devoy was being fooled too—had been fooled I felt convinced by the ass Von Papen.[72] Devoy, an old man of passionate feeling against England, burning for one brave fight before he dies, had been assured of the entire good will of Germany & of strong military aid. His letter of 16/2/16 showed what he expected at least, and asked for.[73]

These people wanted only bloodshed in Ireland for their own ends—& the fatal steamer was to be the price of the rising. I was being shipped by her, merely to get me out of the scene, tear up the Treaty, & having had their 'rising' in Ireland, for what it might be worth to them, then they could wash their hands of all further connection or contact with 'the Irish'. I had, possibly, spoiled the game by sending John McGoey across, & at any rate gravely imperilled the 'rising' coming off—or 'the War in Ireland' as Nadolny termed it!

I saw this clearer and clearer—the 'rising' was the thing—the only thing they were really after, & it was only for this the ship was going & the rifles. Shipping me on her, (& the men at Zossen) was but a sideshow. They were relieved of the embarrassment of our presence & of the pretence of keeping faith where no faith was. I explained to Haugwitz my entire right to send McGoey—turning my back on Nadolny—& showed how the 'breach of faith' was on the side of the War Office and Foreign Office, who tried, I said, 'to play battledore and shuttlecock with

Count Kurt Ludvig Heinrich Georg Max Erdman Haugwitz-Hardenberg-Reventlow (1885–1963). Haugwitz was a member of the Politik-Berlin of the German General Staff and worked as a liaison officer between the German F.O. and the Emperor's Military HQ. He was in charge of organizing the shipment of arms for Ireland.

me' when I asked for his being put at my disposal in February, as they were bound to do in virtue of the Declaration he signed on 2 December last on entering the camp at Zossen.

They had ignored those repeated requests—mine to F.O. and Monteith's to von Baerle.[74] When Monteith had gone to F.O. with my request of 19 February for John McGoey's release, Assessor Meyer had asked first: 'Why does Sir Roger want him?'. Monteith said he knew nothing—only my orders. Then Meyer said the matter concerned the War Office & if they released McGoey then the Foreign would give him a pass to cross the frontier. I told Von Haugwitz he should get my letters on the subject from the War Office & I added with a laugh 'I taught them and your F.O. a lesson in politeness'. He blushed.

Finally—it was two hours or more I had been there—Nadolny who had been going

& coming to his other rooms, came and sat down and said, 'Well, Sir Roger Casement, you must promise to do nothing—to move no hand or finger in this matter & communicate with no one—we shall decide what course we'll take.' I said 'I <u>can</u> tell no one—you take good care of that—you have me here virtually a prisoner.' He laid stress on my not communicating '<u>with America</u>.' I said 'How can I? You hold all the channels of communication with America & anything I send there is read by your people. Let us talk sense. I shall certainly communicate as I choose with Lt. Monteith—my officer.'

He started & I saw a look in his eyes—'How can you forbid me to do that? He is here in command of my men, with the sanction & recognition of your government under my orders—& I shall tell him anything I choose. The only thing I regret is I have not twenty faithful John McGoeys!'

He gulped with rage. 'Very well,' he said, 'tomorrow we shall decide what we shall do and act as we think fit.'

I said, 'No one can prevent you.'

Coming back from this revelation of depravity and cowardice & of worse—of attempted blackmail—I met Gaffney & he said Noegerrath wanted to see me, so we went together. There—in great distress of mind, I made both promise to keep silent & told them all. I did it to enlist Noeggerath's action with F.O. to see if pressure could not be exercised there to see that I got a fair deal and above all that the men at Zossen were spared the ordeal I had to go thro'!

Noeggerath promised to act at once & telephoned there & then to Under Secretary Zimmermann to seek an appointment for tomorrow. Z. gave it by phone while I was there for the morrow 'between 12 and 1' in the Reichstag 'to come by the Tiergarten entrance'.

I told him what I wanted—to impress on Z. the grave danger of taking the men on board the ship—since they would assuredly be bound to give the German government away under question and expose how it had not kept faith with them. My true reason is to get the men saved as Monteith implores me to do.

They came back to dinner with me at Saxonia & we talked till late.

[Berlin] Thursday 30 March [1916]

I did not sleep all last night. I had fever & tossed in misery on my bed.

At 10.00 a.m. or so I got a call from Nadolny asking me to go to see him soon—I said at 3, as I was to see Noegerrath before he went to Z. Nadolny replied that would be too late as he would have to decide by 12. Then I said 10.30 & tore off to Noegerrath's office. He came fortunately while I was there. I told him I had to see Nadolny at once. He said, 'Try to gain time and play for that.'

I went on to the G.G.S. at 10.30 am & found Nadolny alone. He said as follows:

'The plan of aiding your countrymen in Ireland was proposed to us from your friends in America. We had & have no responsibility in it, beyond trying to the best of our ability to comply with <u>their</u> request. It is not our plan. Your countrymen in Ireland are determined, they assert, to rise on a given day—your friends in USA appeal to us for help. We knew nothing of it before Mr. Devoy's telegram came & all our subsequent action has been based on that. You know our proposals & we have sent them to Mr. Devoy. He agrees.

He said much more. He said, 'We have no idealistic interest in Ireland and no revolution, no rifles. If it were not that we hope for a military diversion there we should not give the rifles.'

I said I could guarantee no revolution and that I sincerely hoped there would be none! I was profoundly against it unless there was great military support & they were giving none—practically three men in a boat to invade a kingdom. The thing was an insult to my intelligence & either he was a fool or thought I was one to speak to me as he had about 'autonomy'. But as things were, I was forced to try & get the rifles to Ireland since they had so planned things that the 'rising' seemed certain through their promises & these promises I did not know but could guess.

'You oppose the project—or you are hindering it. The soldiers are an essential part to its success. The naval men say so. The machine guns must be ready to come into action as soon as their steamer arrives. We have no other men to send. If they don't go the whole thing may collapse. I shall cable Mr. Devoy and say owing to your action we are compelled to withdraw from the matter at the eleventh hour, & leave your countrymen in Ireland in the lurch—and all the responsibility falls on your shoulders.'

I protested this was gravely unfair—that they were not, to begin with, complying with Mr. Devoy's request at all—in sending a far smaller consignment of arms than he had asked for & no officers on which he laid such vital stress. He had never asked, either, for me or for the Irish soldiers. I personally had to go—that was evident and required no further word. I had to stand beside my friends in their resistance whatever it might be & take all the consequences, since I was so largely responsible for the whole situation, although not for this wholly unexpected development. As to the men I felt a peculiar personal responsibility for their not being captured by the British Govt. That was my objection today. As to the ship, she must go at all costs—I would go alone—but he insisted on the men.

I left him in despair & saw Noegerrath after his interview with Z. He said that Z. had listened very attentively & would act. Also submarine essential.

Monteith had come in to see me before I went to the G.G.S.. I told him to do so, by 'phone, by telegram & by special letter. He reported Haugwitz had been out there at 9.30 a.m. ostensibly to see how the men were shooting—really to try & get him, Monteith to take the men to Ireland over my head. Monteith said it was a clear 'try on'. He even offered money in shape of 'funds for propaganda'. Monteith replied he was here absolutely & solely under the orders of Sir Roger Casement. It was on finding out that they could not capture Monteith (they would then have ignored me completely) that Nadolny 'phoned me. Haugwitz had come back from Zossen with Monteith—& turned up at the G.G.S. after Nadolny had tried to compel me to assent by his (repeated) threats to denounce me to the Irish in USA as the man who had stopped the guns and robbed my poor battling countrymen in their hour of need of the only help offered.

I had apparently submitted to this threat and left the G.G.S. in complete despair—and I returned to the hotel & saw Noeggerath again, before he went to Zimmermann at the Reichstag. Noeggerath returned at 2 saying he had seen Zimmermann who was interested and said he would look into the matter and do something.

I was in despair—and my fever on me worse than ever. That evening before Monteith returned to Zossen we talked things over. I told him that I should play a last card & write Count Georg Wedel, one of the few men here I had any regard for and tell him just how I saw it all. This with a view to save the men at all costs—that idea was growing firmer and firmer—that they at any rate could not be taken. Monteith begged me to do this—that he thought it infamous to take the men—in any case & especially with the absurd training of only 2 or 3 days already at the machine guns.

He urged me to haste—& I said I'd write that night. I lay awake for hours in despair and at 1 a.m. or 2 a.m. got up and wrote a rough draft of a long letter to Wedel— I did not lie down again until near 5 a.m. and was awake again at 6.30 a.m.

Von Haugwitz on his return from Zossen apologised to me for going there—saying he had not wished to do anything behind my back.

I absolved him.

75 Captain Hans W. L. Boehm (1873–1959) was assigned by the G.G.S. to assist Casement. He was arrested in British waters off Falmouth in 1917 and interned. The correspondence between Casement and Boehm is held in the UCD archives.

76 This letter, which survives in multiple forms, was a précis of the diary for the last few weeks and sought to explain to von Wedel the impossible situation in which Casement found himself. See Doerries, 192–203. For a draft of the original see NLI MS 43,227 (1–4).

77 Edwin Emerson (1869–1959), journalist, secret agent and a graduate of Harvard University. Emerson served as Theodore Roosevelt's clerk during the Spanish-American war. Later, he worked as a mercenary in South America and as a journalist for various US publications. Sympathetic to Germany on outbreak of war in 1914, he was involved in editing the English language propaganda newspaper *The Continental Times* to which Casement regularly contributed during 1915. After the war he was expelled from various countries for subversive activities, before setting up in 1933 the *Society of American Friends of Germany*.

78 Franz Fromme (1880–1960), linguist and author. Fromme translated many of Casement's essays into German, published in *Sir Roger Casement: Irland, Deutschland & Die Freiheit der Meere & Andere Aufsätze* (Munich, 1916). He later wrote on Ireland's independence struggle in the light of the rise of Nazism in *Irlands Kampf um die Freiheit*, 1933.

He is the only decent man I have met at the G.G.S. the rest are all cads, scoundrels or cowards—& invariable liars.

I have detected Nadolny often, (v. Lübben once!) Boehm[75] more than once, Herwarth v. B. &c. &c. There is not one I'd trust out of my sight on <u>anything</u>.

[Berlin] Friday 31 March [1916]

I was ill in bed all day with the Doctor—congestion of lungs threatening—I finished as well as I could the long letter to Wedel.[76] I emphasized so much—and repeatedly the danger of capture to myself because I wanted to excite their fears for themselves. If they could be brought to see that my capture by the British government would reflect on their honour, possibly they would begin to appreciate the importance of my request for the submarine & if I could get that and land in Ireland before this d--d ship & her guns arrive I may stop the whole dreadful thing.

It is for this I still play, but I am so sick and utterly wretched beyond expression. Doctor told me to stay in bed and prescribed usual stuff.

Berlin, Saturday 1 April [1916]

Finished my letter to Wedel—softening down some of the rougher passages. Gaffney came & I read it to him & Lt. Monteith took it (after hearing it) up to Wedel & gave it to him in person. He saw Wedel who said it should have his 'immediate attention.'

I was in bed till afternoon when on Drs advice I went out for a very short walk in blazing sun to Tiergarten & then to tea at the Esplanade Hotel with Emerson[77] & my translator Fromme.[78]

The Zerhusens[79] came—she a dear, kind-eyed Irish woman—Gaffney dined with us.

I wrote Wedel again today—a short letter pointing out the <u>sole</u> justification I could see for any armed attempt in Ireland[80]—and I was told he had 'gone on leave of absence till Thursday.'

I thought he might have gone to the Hauptquartier to intervene and call off the whole thing.

[Berlin] Sunday. 2 April, [1916]

Spent day mostly with Gaffney—writing & hoping that Wedel had taken action of some kind. At near 7 p.m. a phone call from Assessor Meyer to say that Wedel had left my letter to him to read—& they reported that they could do nothing in the matter. It did not concern them—but only the G.G.S. and the Irish in U.S.A. and referred me to the G.G.S. I said that was quite useless—as I always had spoken very plainly there & I saw no object in continuing such uninteresting conversations with those from whom I disagreed so profoundly. He then asked if I would go to the F.O. I said 'what is the use of that—if one of you runs away & you have no power in the matter—I shall do nothing. My mind is made up and the men shall not go.'

Walked a little bit with Gaffney & dined with him in evening.

<u>Berlin Sunday – 2 April 1916. 6.35 p.m.</u>

This morning I sent a letter (No. 2)[81] to Count Wedel following on that sent yesterday morning (No. 1 of 30 M'ch)—see both.

The messenger reported that Count Wedel had gone away on 'Urlaüb'[82] until Thursday next. Gaffney was with me at the time. We both hope that this meant he had gone to the Hauptquartier to try and arrange things as I decided.

I decided to stay here all day, instead of going to Zossen, and now at 6.35 p.m. I get a telephone call from the Auswärtiges Amt from Assessor Meyer. I record it instantly. He said:

'Count Wedel left yesterday for some days leave of absence, and before going he handed me your letter. He reports he can not do anything in the matter. This has been arranged entirely between the Gr. Staff and the Irish organization in America and we cannot interfere or bring any pressure to bear on them. You must arrange everything with the G.G.S. and I suggest you seeing Captain Nadolny.' I said—'I have written very plainly my standpoint and I must abide by it—I cannot and will not be forced into a false position by Captain Nadolny or the G.G.S. and do what I feel to be wrong.'

Mr Meyer said. 'We cannot discuss the matter in detail over the telephone'—I agreed—and went on 'perhaps you will come here tomorrow and see me?'—I said 'What use is there in that, if you, the Foreign Office, cannot interfere?'

I then asked if he had seen the letter I had written to Count Wedel today—and he said 'No—that must be the one lying on his table—I will read it—and then, perhaps I may ring you up tomorrow, but in any case the matter must be settled between you and Captain Nadolny.'

I said again that 'I am not going to be forced into a wrong position by the G.G.S. and my last word, or at least my last fixed opinion is expressed in the letter sent to Count Wedel.'

So there it stands.

This is the climax of their cowardice and infamy!

The whole thing, so far as they are concerned, is a put up murder plot (in which I am to be one of the victims) and Ireland the chief. Anything more atrocious is hard to conceive.

The war party here—who are supreme, evidently think they had a chance of reaping some military profit from bloodshed in Ireland—and at a very cheap price! (Twelve men in a boat!) — '£200.000' as Nadolny priced it!

The 'Irish Brigade' is to be got rid of—& the Treaty with me buried.

The Germans are to have their pound of Irish flesh at all costs.

A more infamous form of blackmail it is hard to conceive.

Wedel runs away on purpose till Thursday! Knowing that by Thursday I shall be 'dealt with'. What <u>shall</u> I do?

If I go and take the men as the Staff wants me to do—shall <u>we</u> seize the ship and give ourselves up? That is one thought. Anything to punish <u>these</u> scoundrels and ruffians and base, dastardly cowards.

I must see Monteith and talk things over with him tonight.

It <u>is</u> the most damnable position a man was ever put in—and <u>this</u> is the Great German Govt!

My God! What curs and cowards and infamous scoundrels—and <u>these</u> are the ruffians I thought might help Ireland. English rule in Ireland has indeed been a curse—but the English man is a truthful man and a gentleman & his word is sure—and here no one of these men is a gentleman. They don't know the meaning of the name.

11.30 p.m. I saw Monteith & kept him till 1.28 train when he went out to Zossen. We don't know where we are—but we agree that under no circumstances am I to consent to the men going—that M. will accompany me—but we go alone. That is all I can decide.

Tomorrow Meyer will 'ring' me up again & say I must see Nadolny &c. I shall decline—& say that they must come to me—that my mind is made up & I go forward on <u>my</u> terms alone—& part of those are that they come to me to discuss the minor details left. Or if I go to the G. Staff that then I take a witness with me! One or the other. But <u>in no circumstances</u> shall I take any of the soldiers or allow them to go. On that M. & I are fully agreed & beyond that I can dictate nothing. I am already a 'dead man'—but not yet a wholly

79 Joseph Zerhusen (1880–?) worked in the timber trade before the war and was located in Liverpool, where he was briefly a partner of the West African Mahogany Syndicate. He married Ellen Hand in 1914. In 1915 he was assigned to serve as one of the translators of the Irish Brigade. NLI MS 43 570/1–2 contains a 98-page typescript of Zerhusen's recollections about the Irish Brigade from 1915–18, with a particularly good description of the camp at Zossen.
80 See Doerries, 204.
81 See Doerries, 204–05.
82 'Urlaüb' is leave.

83 The 'certain lady' was Princess Blücher (née Evelyn Stapleton-Bretherton). Her husband Count Gebhard Blücher was the great-great grandson of Marshal Blücher, the saviour of Wellington at the battle of Waterloo. Casement's friendship with the Blüchers extended back to Africa days and they kept in contact over the years. Princess Blücher later wrote a memoir *An English Wife in Berlin: A Private Memoir of Events, Politics and Daily Life in Germany Throughout the War and the Social Revolution of 1918* (New York, 1920). This was widely translated and included quite a substantial and not altogether flattering description of this last meeting with Casement, 130–31. The Casement-Blücher correspondence relevant to 1914–16 is held in Clare County Archives. See Róisin Berry, *Casement in Germany: A Guide to the Roger Casement papers in Clare County Archives* (Ennis, Clare County Council, 2005). After the war, Princess Blücher passed Casement's letters to British intelligence. For a critique of the strategic and distorting treatment of Casement by the countess, see G. Barry Gifford's essay 'Princess & Patriot' in NLI MS 13091.

84 Erich von Falkenhayn (1861–1922), chief of the German General Staff during the First World War. After taking over as chief of the General Staff in 1914, Falkenhayn responded positively to Casement's plan.

85 The information concerning Christensen had been relayed to Casement in a letter from Devoy dated 19 December 1915 (see NLI MS 13,073/44/viii). Devoy described how Christensen had been trying to swindle money from Devoy in order to support his wife and newborn baby.

dishonoured one, despite all my mistakes. God knows they were not for self. R.C.

[Berlin] Monday, 3 April 1916

A very bad night. After M. left for Zossen, poor chap, at 11.28 I tried to sleep & did. This morning I wrote a letter more and decided to see a certain lady in whom I could trust. I met her early & told her enough—not anything of the inside matter, merely my awful doubts and the hopeless position in which I was and the use they were trying to make of 'the others'. I did not say who the others were, and she does not know or guess—but I said I had made up my mind not to budge from my position on that point—and I asked her to keep the two letters (copies) of 30 March & 2 April to W.[edel] I handed her these & she promised faithfully to keep them until the end & then to hand them over to the person whose name I gave her & wrote on the cover.[83]

Also I am going to leave my 'Diary' as far as it goes with G[ebhard]. I may be arrested, I think, at any moment! The lady said that the Emperor himself was powerless today—he was in the toils too—and was being accused of being 'pro-English'—that the whole power of the land was in the hands of Falkenhayn[84] & a small clique and everyone trembled before them. That Falkenhayn *was a* scoundrel and swayed by 'finance'—whatever that means!

She agrees with me that this curse of Prussian militarism is an internal evil that must be fought by the German people themselves & broken from within.

I then saw G[ebhard]. at his quarters—& told him I wanted him to keep papers for me until he could get them in a safe place—if such be in this land today. Everyone is spied on. That is certain. They have had spies on me ever since I came here. She told me of some of the stories circulated against me! She doesn't know half of them.

She does not know the situation I am in—poor lady.

I got at 12 a telephone from Count von Haugwitz begging me to come to the G.G. Staff at 3 p.m. this afternoon.

I demurred & asked him to come here. He said he could not leave the place—someone was away & it was very desirable we should meet and Captain von Hülsen was not there. I think he said not there. This Captain V.H. is a bleary-eyed pig who has the papers in hand & the whole business is his particular show. Nadolny is the presiding chief of the whole 'Political' Department—which is really the Spy Department of the G.G.S.—as things are going and as the time is so short now, I have consented to go at 3 but I feel it is a mistake—yet what can I do? At any rate I must at all costs stick to my guns and help the soldiers here.

Today settles their fate sure—or rather as far as I am concerned that is settled. It settles mine—for ever.

I arrived at 3 & found him & von Hülsen there. The first thing they did was to show me a typed paper with the names cut out signed John Devoy recording Christensen's perfidy in U.S.A. dated 20 Decr. 1915.[85] It had been brought by von Papen they said. I nearly laughed—and asked why they had not shown it earlier. What their idea was in now showing me this paper I can scarcely conceive, except that they stupidly thought it would intimidate me to see that Christensen, the man I had trusted & sent to America had turned into a ruffian & was found out by Devoy. I read the paper smiling & told them I was already perfectly aware of the whole of the facts there recorded. This preliminary settled, they began telling me of the plans made and what had already been done in the way of getting the rifles, ammunition &c. ready.

Finally there was a lull and it came my turn to say that I had made up my mind not to take the men. From the way they received it I could see that they were perfectly aware of my letter to Wedel & knew well my whole point of view. They argued & expostulated civilly & nicely, pointing out the need of the men until about 4 p.m. Nadolny came in. They explained to him my 'new departure' over the men, and immediately the issue was joined. Nadolny began by disputing entirely my right to regard the men as in any way under my power, and said he quite refused to recognise my right to interfere as the Agreement was 'dead'!

The conversation this afternoon on Nadolny's part was even more infamous than before. He insisted first—that the Agreement of 23–28 December 1914 was now null and void—and he declined to recognize my right to interfere in any way in regard to the Irish soldiers at Zossen. The 'Irish Brigade' had not materialized and therefore the agreement had not come into existence! He could do as he pleased with the soldiers at Zossen and send them to Ireland if he chose and they agreed.

I said laconically 'try it'.

I pointed out that while the purpose of the Agreement had not been attained the pledge to the men certainly held good, if the German govt. regarded its honour.

He called the agreement a contract— very well, a contract between two parties. One party could not interpret it as he pleased. I had as much right as the German govt. in the matter to put my interpretation on it—and this was clear that the pledge of the German govt. applied as fully to <u>one</u> Irish soldier who had come at my call, on faith of that agreement, as to 500 or 5,000. If the Agreement were dead, non-existent, I asked him what then was the status of these men at Zossen?

'Oh!' he said—'Deserters!' 'Deserters!' I exclaimed—'and <u>who</u> made them desert, you? I?—did the Imperial German govt. actually descend to tempting men to desert? and does it now propose to despatch deserters to Ireland against their will—or with their will for that matter?'

'And if they are 'deserters' —<u>what</u> is Lt. Monteith the officer in command, with the sanction of your war office?'

I had the cad there. He blushed, looked down & stopped.

'Oh well' he said: 'Let us view it this way—those men are Irish patriots, they wish to fight for their country, we offer them a chance, we are sending help to Ireland & they are <u>vitally</u> necessary to the success of the undertaking to have the machine guns ready for instant use on landing. You are not a soldier. You oppose this vital military requirement on a theory, a doctrine—we shall appeal to the men direct over your head and ask them if they are willing to go to Ireland under these circumstances.'

I said I could not prevent him doing so if he insisted, since I was so obviously a prisoner here in Germany (I did not say in the coils of a serpent!) but that I could and should still prevent him getting the men, unless he took them by force & as prisoners on board.

He said '<u>How?</u>'

I said 'because you do not understand the minds of free men! The men will respond to your appeal to fight for Ireland with alacrity, I know—& then they will ask—the first question—what about Sir Roger Casement and Lt. Monteith, our officer—<u>Where are they? Are they not coming?</u>

And if you do that, and try by this method to entrap these men against my will, then I don't go—and Lt. Monteith does not go—and once the men know our view, *they* will not go—unless you kidnap them.'

He glared, & bit his lips—'Then,' he said, 'I shall telegraph to the Irish Committee in America and ask them if they will require the men to go?' I said again— 'You may do so—but I should demand the right to telegraph too & put my views forward.' 'No,' he said—'you shall not telegraph.'

'Very well,' I said 'try that course if you like but don't think it will succeed either

86 Franz Hugo Krebs was a Boston lawyer of German extraction. Krebs worked as a pro-German journalist during the war for the *New York Times*, among other newspapers.

87 The third man on the return to Ireland Julian Bailey / Beverley was a member of the Irish Brigade who was held in high regarded by Monteith, which is why he was chosen to be on the mission. After his capture on 21 April 1916, he was deliberately placed in the dock beside Casement and deployed carefully by the prosecution. He was found not guilty in return for turning king's evidence.

for you will surely find that in anything you try to do with these men you will have to come back to me, and my mind is made up. Nothing you can say or do will alter it, or budge me one inch. You may take me out there and shoot me,' & I pointed to the Spree bank outside the window of Zimmer 178III—'but I'll never agree to those young men going. They trusted in my honour & good faith—as I in yours—or that of the German govt.—and while I am not responsible for your point of view, I am for mine.'

The only gentleman on their side was young von Haugwitz. He agreed with me on all points except that the military necessity of the case required the men as gunners.

I said I should let no plea of military necessity or any other necessity override my sense of honour. They said—collectively—'you argue for a theory—a principle—we, as soldiers for a vital military need. Do you wish the thing to succeed or fail?'

I said I should not wish for any success founded on a dishonourable and cowardly act and that I feared we had 'been brought up in two different schools of thought.'

I said this to Nadolny. It was impossible to agree I knew—and our respective views were grounded in a wholly different personal regard for certain things and different estimation of their value.

The fight had been long and exhausting but I saw I had won. Nadolny wound up (about 6 p.m.) by saying: 'Well, we will settle it tomorrow, we will refer the matter to Lt. Monteith on military grounds—he is the expert there & you are not—& will abide by his decision—& then if he agrees with you, you & he must sign a paper absolving us from all blame on military grounds, for the non-despatch of the men.'

That night at 11 p.m., I got a wire from Fr. Crotty he would arrive at 8.44 a.m. on Friday at Friederickshaven.

Berlin, April 4, Tuesday [1916]

Fr Strasse 8.44 to meet Fr. Crotty from Limburg. Missed him there but found him at Potsdamer Station 9.33 train for Zossen—stopped him & brought him back to hotel—gave him bath & breakfast and then told him all. He was horrified and we talked long as to best course. I told him of my idea of using Krebs[86] perhaps to go over & try to stop the thing. I later took Krebs into our confidence—but he was not able (& rightly I think) to carry out the half thought I had had. But he remains a witness.

Fr. Crotty went on to see a certain lady and then to his Dominicans—& returned at 6.30 or 7—& I kept him here getting him a good room.

Monteith & I went on to G.G.S. in afternoon & got all details for departure on probably Friday night from v. Haugwitz after it had been settled that only Beverley[87] goes with us. The gun men at Zossen go on with their target practice so as not to excite suspicion if it were suddenly stopped with us both gone away.

V.[on]H.[augwitz] promised me to get poison for us. I begged him to do so—& he agreed.

We will take £100 in gold—paying German money for it – v. Haugwitz gets it for us from bank.

We are all there to go to G.G.S. at 6 or so on Friday night—I shave there—we change clothes & emerge by another door & exit (the orderlies all sent away in meantime from the corridors) to the quay by Lehrter Station & take the train to Hamburg in a reserved carriage.

Such is the plan.

Back & dinner with Fr. Crotty—& then Gaffney came and talked till 11 nearly in my room—& talked me asleep. Fr. Crotty enjoyed the change greatly I think, God bless him.

[Berlin] Wednesday, 5 April 1916

Out to Zossen with Fr. Crotty. He confessed most of the men, and then I gave a short address, telling them I had to go away with Lt. Monteith for a time and begging them to go on with everything just the same. It was dreadful. I could not tell them the truth—and I had the vision before me all the time of the dreadful deception being practiced on them—and of the callous treatment they would have once we were gone and all pretence of an 'Irish Brigade' finished—God forgive me—and God protect these poor boys. I am writing the Chancellor direct about them. We (Lt. M[onteith], Fr. Crotty & I) came back to Berlin at 5.30 & I met Krebs there. He has a copy of my letter to Wedel of 30 March and a few other things—for use <u>after the war only</u>—& only then if I am dead.

Fr. Crotty left for Limburg at 9.17 p.m. & I came back and wrote the long 'Exposé' that follows. This I did after talk with Fr. C.[rotty]. He said to make another effort to impress the serious character of the thing on the German Govt.—& I wrote this 'Exposé' specifically for <u>their</u> eye. It will go to Noeggerath in morning.

'Exposé'

Another day gone, and another last page to my Diary! Today I went to Zossen, ostensibly with the Priest who confessed the men, really to bid them goodbye. At least I have saved them! The whole thing appalls me as a piece of the most ghastly folly—or rather one of the most criminal attempts ever perpetrated. And I am debarred from saying so and taking the needed steps to prevent it by fear of incurring a personal reproach of cowardice (already grossly implied by some of those who are handling the matter at the G.G. Staff). Or worse still or perhaps, <u>not</u> preventing it but only depriving them of the arms at the critical moment.

Am I not, perhaps, a greater coward in fearing to incur this reproach, or any reproach rather than take the wholly courageous step of protesting in the highest quarter against a scheme that has been considered, I fear, only by underlings and is being rushed to certain failure by men of inferior intelligence at the best, and in this particular matter (Ireland) of no understanding.

How can a scheme so launched and by <u>such</u> methods as those I have had witness of the last week succeed?

On all grounds by which we may consider it, it is a scheme that can only bring failure—and probably something far worse than failure—disaster. Let us—let me put down these grounds as I perceive them. This is a record of my mind and understanding—and I want it to live after me.

1. Military

On military grounds the project is beneath contempt. To begin with it is <u>not</u> a military enterprise at all—but a piece of gun-running.

It has no military element about it, except poor Lt. Monteith! He, I, (and perhaps one young soldier) disguised as sailors, (each with a bottle of poison kindly supplied us!) are to invade a Kingdom—bringing with us 20,000 rifles and some cartridges.

As a gun-running enterprise or effort, it might pass if attempted say by Walford & Co. of Antwerp, or some other notorious firms of that character who make a living by supplying arms to <u>irate</u> savages and semi-civilized South American republics. But for the G.G.S. of the greatest military power in the world it is an astounding adventure—and as an episode in this world war it will surely be without parallel. I say nothing of the Navy because I am convinced they are doing the thing as well as it can be done and that from the naval point of view, as a 'job' entrusted to them for execution they will do everything they can to carry it through successfully.

But on all other grounds of a military character is has not been properly approached and none of the essentials to success are even being applied. I will not discuss here, tonight, these shortcomings—they must be apparent to any soldier who is given the rudiments of the proposal to consider.

On military grounds I am convinced, I could damn it before any staff college in the world. The dangers I foresee are far less from the obvious military shortcomings than due to the absence of political intelligence.

Let us consider it on political grounds.

2. Political

On political grounds (even if the scheme were susceptible of sound military handling) it involves the gravest dangers to Germany—perhaps far greater than to Ireland.

I see dangers enough to Ireland in it at the best. The only reason that justifies it at all on Irish grounds is the argument put forward by John Devoy in his speech on 4–5 March in New York—viz. that the Irish Volunteers were going to resist disbandment by force, and this being so their friends in America should help them. That a fight would come in any case—only a scuffle really—and it would be only chivalrous to help them to put up a better fight.

But the political dangers are so tremendous, when I put aside the natural sentiment of desire to help these young men if they do fight, that I think they far outweigh the possible gain that might come from a successful street scuffle that deferred or hindered greatly the possible recruitment of these young men.

Here are a few of those dangers. The vast bulk of Irishmen are law abiding and peace loving. They will bitterly resent bloodshed and civil strife in Ireland—forced on them as will then seem apparent by a filibustering expedition launched from Germany for that purpose. And in truth that is just what it is being sent for. Nadolny confessed quite frankly to me that what the German Staff wanted was bloodshed in Ireland—a 'diversion' there that might help Germany. The diversion may indeed come! But it will not help Germany I fancy. It may be a last straw the other way.

Once it becomes clear—as it surely will become clear—that Germany tried to incite a revolt or 'rising' in Ireland by a paltry gift of second hand rifles put in the hand of excitable young men, all that is solid and respectable in Ireland will be moved to the deepest resentment—'Pro-German' feeling of today will be changed into wrath and contempt.

The object of Asquith's visit to Rome, I believe, (or one of the objects) was to get the Pope to move the Irish clergy to an anti-German attitude. He failed I feel sure, but this 'anti-Irish attempt' of the German Govt. to embroil Irishmen on their own soil, so that Germany might reap some trifling military advantage from bloodshed in Ireland can redound only to the extreme discredit of Germany, and may easily secure from the Irish Bishops a Declaration that Mr. Asquith failed to obtain from an appeal to the Holy See.

Once the Bishops (who, with the exception of the Archbishop of Tuam, have been very fair and just) are moved to denounce a 'German plot' against the internal peace of Ireland, then we may find public feeling in Ireland change to the complete detriment of Germany and leave her with no shred of Irish goodwill. The British Recruiting Sergeant will get the reward—not the German military machine.

And certainly that machine does not deserve to get anything but a kick for the way it has tackled this problem.

The political results will not be confined to a mere increase of ill feeling in Ireland against Germany—they would I feel confident, in the end, be of a far more widespread character and would probably cross the Atlantic and sway Irish feeling in America just in the opposite way to that hoped for.

The <u>inadequacy</u>, the hopeless inadequacy of the means employed and the absence of any prior precautions to ensure success will convince all thinking Irishmen that the project was not inspired by goodwill to Ireland at all, but sprang solely from a desire to secure profit from <u>any</u> sort of blood-letting in Ireland. Anger, contempt and resentment would be aroused once the <u>facts</u> of the attempt became known, and we may trust the British government for making these very widely known with a colouring and a 'colour scheme' all their own.

Not even the 'rape' of Belgium was exploited as this attempt to stir up strife, and secure a massacre of half-armed boys in peaceful Ireland will be exploited. And the moral will be a plain one. German 'good-will' is as dangerous as that of a mad dog—it bites the friendly hand as impartially as that of its enemy. *Timeo Danaos et dona ferentes.*[88]

If all the facts connected with the ill considered and half thought out enterprise become known—and they will become known within a very few weeks at the latest—then the fair name of Germany, or at least of the German government is tarnished before all neutral countries and chiefly in the United States. Only success could justify an enterprise of this kind—and all the elements to ensure success are wanting so far as I can see—have not, indeed, ever been invoked at all.

If my diary is ever published—as some day it may be—what a figure all these military minds or political minds of this great Empire will cut!

The excuses put forward to me that it is being undertaken solely at the request of Irishmen themselves and without the moral responsibility of the German government being involved at all will not hold for a moment. I, even I here, with my hands tied (as it were) and my means of communicating with my friends in Ireland or America cut off can see that this statement is only very partially true. The very methods employed to enforce my acquiescence in a project I have expressed my disapproval of convince me that these assurances are wholly insincere.

I am given no chance of a free decision—and when I seek to express the opinion of an honest man I am threatened with a wholly devilish (I can call it nothing else) charge that the blame for failure will be put entirely on me.

3. Moral

On moral grounds the thing does not bear inspection at all. As Monteith said to me, referring to how the issue effects myself—'it is dastardly.'

How can a scheme of 'helping Ireland' that evokes such comment from a wholly unselfish and chivalrous Irishman produce happy results?

Let us look at it on 'Moral' grounds. These are closely associated with the political aspects of the affair—they cannot be dissociated from the political.

On moral grounds I think nothing <u>can</u> be said for the thing, <u>as it is being worked</u>.

Advantage is certainly being taken of me in a wholly unfair and even cowardly way—and if (the inevitable!) I am captured by the British this will be made clear.

It must be made clear.

Nothing I may do, or abstain from doing, can then save the character of the German Govt. Most men will charge them with putting me in a dreadful position—with running me into the hands of my enemies—some even, with deliberately handing me over to the British Government!

All the circumstances connected with the agreement the German Govt. made concerning the ill-fated 'Irish Brigade' will come to light. They are, already, fairly well known in England—and while it suits the English government <u>today</u> to vilify me as a 'traitor'—it will suit them far better, once I am safe in their hands, to vilify the German government for having actually betrayed me

88 Virgil, *Æneid* II. 49: 'I fear the Greeks, even those bearing gifts.'

89 Nurse Edith Cavell was shot for treason by the Germans in October 1915 after helping some 200 British troops escape into the Netherlands from Belgium in violation of German military law. She became an iconic propaganda figure and her death was used to amplify German barbarism.

90 This refers to the decisive defeat of the King of France, Francis I, at the battle of Pavia in 1525. In his letter to his mother after the battle Francis wrote: '... all is lost to me save honour and life ...'

as they will say, their poor dupe, into the very hands of the Government I had defied with the concurrence and support of the German Govt.

Whatever wrong I, the individual Irish rebel, may have attempted will be swallowed up in the far graver charge of treachery the British Govt. (through its press) will bring against Germany. 'Why' —they will say—'they couldn't be loyal even to the wretched man who had sold himself to them!'

And the world will support the charge. I, the 'traitor' of today will become the 'sacrificed dupe' of tomorrow.

The more the question, thus posed, is inspected, the more pitiable my case will be made out—the more contemptible that of the people who launched me on the road to doom.

No one will seriously assert for a moment that the German government really believed that by sending me on a ship to Ireland, with no support, no help, no possible means of escape, even they were doing a chivalrous thing.

The 'murder of Nurse Cavell'[89] will not be in it with the 'betrayal of Sir Roger Casement.'

The English are quite capable of shutting me up in a lunatic asylum and asking the world what it thinks of the people who handled the lunatic thus!

And the world will give only one answer. My madness may be pardoned— but the cowardice of those who first took advantage of it where they thought they saw some gain, and then flung the madman to destruction, when they had no longer any use for him, will echo through the world as a possibly crowning example of 'Hun' methods.

I should not like to be von Falkenhayn when the British Govt., having dealt with Sir Roger Casement, turn upon those who planned this 'military aid' to Ireland!

(I much prefer to be myself in any case— with all my faults and mistakes. At least no man, or people, or country can say I sold them or gave a friend away.)

This aspect of the affair does not concern me personally—my honour and my courage cannot be questioned, however my intellect may be arraigned. I have not shirked the ordeal—and when, if ever, the facts become public of how I have been forced to act against my judgment in the matter then, indeed, most men will forgive me while they will despise those who put me in the fire.

I am not free here in Germany, forced by ignorance, by the dire necessities of the case (as it is presented to me) to go blindly on, to dictate or prescribe the necessary steps that should be taken if the attempt is to be regarded seriously.

I see what should be done—and I have said so. My clear statement in the two Memoranda I gave the General Staff has not been acted on. I am told it cannot be— for 'technical reasons.' If technical reasons prohibit the preliminary steps that are essential, from being taken then the thing should not be attempted at all. That is clear.

But I was told it must go on in spite of the absence of these essential precautions; and I am forced to assent or incur a shameful reproach. I go on—because I am fool enough, or brave enough, or coward enough—I know not which—while I know it is hopeless.

Like Francis I, I say 'all is lost but honour'.[90] The right thing to do even now is to stop the whole thing—to delay it, until we are quite sure of the condition of things in Ireland, of the means at the disposal of our friends there, both for resistance and for the immediate landing of arms—and until adequate steps had been taken at this end to afford sufficient help.

That is the right thing to do—obviously. I ought to insist on that. And yet I dare not. If I do—God only knows what may be the result. I am so completely in the dark as to what is really being planned in Ireland, in America, that I dare not accept the responsibility. And no one here will accept any responsibility. They put it all on me. And threaten me in an infamous way with the responsibility of betraying my friends,

Rudolf Nadolny (1873–1953). Born in Poland. After holding various diplomatic posts in Russia, Persia and Albania he was given a post in Abteilung IIIb where he created an independent political operation known as 'P' (Politik) and became a spymaster, directing covert support for various anti-government groups in Russia, Ireland and elsewhere.

if I can't fully accept what I know is a half-digested project.

I must swallow it at all costs. All I have been able to do has been to save the poor Irish lads at Zossen—and still leave even these to their fate. For, it is clear from what Nadolny said yesterday afternoon, that they are going to be treated again as prisoners of war and sent to some detention camp.

That is a gross violation of the pledge of the German Govt.—Nadolny even called them 'deserters' to my face! No wonder the English Govt. charge me with being a 'traitor'! My God—it is the most abominable position a man was ever put in. Whatever I do is wrong—is hopeless. The thing <u>cannot</u> work well, conceived in such a spirit as this—planned with a total disregard of the first essentials of

MY JOURNEY TO THE GERMAN HEADQUARTERS AT CHARLEVILLE

91 A newspaper clipping has been tipped in.

military efficiency and launched with a callous indifference to the most obvious considerations of honour and sincerity it can only produce evil—of that I feel sure.

And the evil will fall on the heads of those who planned it and persisted in carrying it through in violation of all they <u>must</u> know to be right.

Whatever happens to me is a small thing—But what may happen in Ireland is a big thing—and since it <u>can</u> only be evil I feel that the evil after all, will not fall on Ireland, but on those who have ensured it.

This absurd expedition may—who knows?—produce incalculable consequences. It is Germany, I feel certain, will reap them in the end—and they will prove a sorry harvest. It may well be the turning point, with a vengeance, of German relations with America, and all the Chancellor's wise efforts to retain friendly relations with America may be wholly brought to ruin by this half thought-out scheme of soldiers who know as much of Ireland as they do of America.

From a telegram in tonight's papers I see the British fleet is 'very busy' on the Norwegian coast these last few days. Here it is.[91]

That is perhaps the most hopeful sign in the whole business as it now stands! Our chances of escaping capture are daily diminishing—and to be captured may be the only way out! Who knows?

Well, I can do nothing. The madness is not of my choosing, planning or design—I have done my best to preach sanity and to enforce reason and I am insulted for the effort. Fate may be using me in some inscrutable way to end the war! I sometimes think it. But how?

I who have tried to save Ireland from the horrors of the war and to be the friend of Germany may now, by the very act of the German Government become the very instrument to launch Irishmen into the war—and possibly with them the Americans too.

The whole thing is appalling—and as Saturday approaches and the irreparable step is taken, I fell like a man <u>already</u> damned. All <u>I</u> can hope for is that, later on, my part will be made clear and it will be seen how great a victim I was.

Pray God, that Germany be not the far greater victims for the sins of her military counsellors. They have usurped the place of her political advisors, in this matter at all events—and I think she will pay bitterly for the exchange.

I have no time for more than these crude fears tonight—tomorrow is already here—it is 1 a.m.—and I have much to write.

I must write Zimmerman or the Chancellor maybe on the fate of the Irish soldiers left behind at Zossen and insist that, as Wedel promised me formally in writing last June, apart from the clear terms of the agreement itself, they shall not be the victims of the G.G.S.—even as I am—but that the promises of the German Government shall be strictly and honourably filled in their regard, after I am gone. This morning when I spoke to them and pretended I was just going ahead of them on a journey to clear the way for their deployment in the East, as they think, I could scarcely refrain from crying. I felt that I was leaving them to deception and misery—they who have already sacrificed so much—to be treated as 'Deserters'—or disgraced 'prisoners of war'.

It is time I died—for if I looked them in the face again I could not say what I wrote just now—'all is lost but honour'. I feel that <u>all</u> is indeed lost and the sooner my life is taken from me the better.

NOTE I showed this part of my Diary to Noegerrath. He saw the vital gist of the thing & went to Zimmermann who authorized him to go to G.G.S and Admiralty. I said no use going to G.G.S. but perhaps to Admiralty for submarine. He went with the result that in the end they gave the submarine—not because it ensured my safety en route so much as their own reputation. It was only that argument appealed to them! Chivalrous! But the German Admiralty is the best part of all this show—a long way the best. 8.4.16.

[Berlin] Thursday, 6 April, 1916

On getting up I sent for Gaffney, read him my Diary of last night with every word of which he agrees. I expressed my ever-growing anxiety as to the consequences in Ireland. He went up to Noeggerath who came down to se me; having read the Diary he went to Zimmermann, the Under Secretary of State (after having come to me) & returned to say that Zimmermann could not go to the Chancellor, who has to speak again today in Reichstag, but authorized him (Noeg.) to go to G.G.S. they were hopeless and Nadolny a low-minded intriguer but that he might go to the Admiralty.

Georg v. Haugwitz called in forenoon to say that the arrangements were as follows:

Certain articles of clothing still to be purchased by me, he supplying the rest G.G.S. [£100]? in gold ready (I to give him a cheque). Monteith to come in tomorrow to go to G.G.S. & also to see some more explosives. Sgt B[everley] (who goes with us after all) not to be told until tomorrow night, say 6 p.m., & v. Haugwitz will come too. Finally, we are all three to 'change' at G.G.S. on Saturday afternoon—when I shall change & shave (the last time was in the Hotel Prince George, coming to Germany Oct. 17. 1914!) & go off to the Station 'disguised' as sailors & in charge of the Captain of Marine who is running the show. The man I already met at Admiralty who went with me to G.G.S.

Noegerrath with me several times today—and dear old Krebs the faithful one. Krebs is full of fight. Monteith brought Beverley in at 11.30 or so & he went out to see the town. Noegerrath went to the Admiralty, he told me, & explained the standpoint, political standpoint—throwing a 'bombshell' in, he said. They were greatly impressed and said that they 'might have to reconsider the whole thing'.

Noeg.'s idea is that they had given no consideration to it at all—treating Ireland as a thing of no account—only a childish incident. The Chief of the Admiralty Staff was away but was to be consulted & Noeg. was told he would be informed later of the decision come to. What Noeg. chiefly impressed on them was that I should be sent to Ireland before by submarine—that it was a fearful risk for them as well as for me to send me by the steamer & they had no right to incur that risk for themselves—if they did not regard mine. Of course personal risks are not considered & cannot be in war—all go out to die—but in this case there were possible consequences (to Germany) on the lines of my Diary of last night that they had to consider and then the grave risk of being 'tarred' with responsibility for the whole thing.

This point, viz. German responsibility they had none of them considered—so my Bombshell has hit the mark.

Each of the parties I have had anything to do with disclaims responsibility!

1st. The G.G.S. are 'only complying with the request of Irishmen themselves and have no responsibility in the matter—in which they were not consulted' &c. &c.

2nd. The Admiralty are 'only carrying out the work entrusted to them by the G.G.S. & have no power of decision on any point of policy' (This is all right and I agree with this—they are the only innocent parties in the business.)

3rd. The German F.O. have 'no responsibility of any kind'!—they 'know nothing of it as it was all arranged between the G.G.S. & 'my friends' in America!' Everyone is clean handed. And yet on 29 February Assessor Meyer is kind enough to send me Robert Emmet's dying speech 'in those times'. It is quite clear they had made up their minds that although they had 'no responsibility', & all was between G.G.S. & America—& that America had asked to keep me out—they had decided to bring me in. My mind was to be 'prepared' by R. Emmet's speech for the proposals coming after. Now it is absurd to think that Germany had no responsibility in a matter of this supreme importance—viz.—equipping (quite inadequately) a rebellion in Ireland—which is made contingent really

92 'A friend of James Malcolm' was Count George Noble Plunkett, the father of Joseph Mary Plunkett, who had travelled out to Germany the previous year to negotiate for arms and officers and had agreed with Casement to use the name 'James Malcolm' in future communiqués. See Honor Ó Brolcháin, *16 Lives: Jospeh Plunkett* (Dublin, 2012). Count Plunkett was in Berne to finalize plans before the Rising and various messages were exchanged through the German ambassador in Berne, Gisbert von Romberg, regarding the final preparations for the Rising. Count Plunkett remained in Berne until 11 April before continuing on his way to Rome to inform Pope Benedict XV of the Rising and to seek his blessing for the republican cause. See correspondence in Doerries, 206–09.

93 See Doerries, 207–08.

on the arrival of arms! For it is clear 'no revolution, no rifles' is the maxim of the whole crowd here—& their fury against me is due to the fact that I am pressing home this argument & <u>compelling</u> them to shoulder some of their responsibility, & that I sent J. McG. out of the country & they fear he may call off the whole thing.

After Noegerrath had come & gone—I was in my room very unhappy until 4 p.m. when I went down to go out for a few minutes—& got in the hall an urgent letter from Wedel of Foreign Office. It was dated today (see it) and forwarded a letter from Berne of 5 April—signed by 'a friend of James Malcolm',[92] with the signs agreed on last June with J.[oseph] P.[lunkett]. This letter said that the writer was sent from Dublin <u>with the urgent message</u> from Ireland—

1st. The rising fixed for Easter Sunday night.—

2nd. The steamer with the 'large contingent' was to come to Tralee Bay not later than dawn of Easter Monday.—

3rd. German officers vitally needed. '<u>This is imperative</u>'—

4th. A submarine to be in Dublin Bay.

I wrote instantly to Noeggerath to come here before 6 & then went to the Admiralty—saw Heydell who took the letter to Chief of Staff (he said) & after 20 minutes returned to say <u>they would not give a submarine</u>. This was final! For all the other matters I was referred to the G.G.S. I said that was useless for I had the measure of their intelligence always and we saw very little in common, or eye to eye.

I said even more—for I was angry—not with Heydell, but with the whole of the soulless thing.

I told Heydell some of the things I had written in my Diary as to the danger to Germany from an act of this kind—'treachery' I called it and I wound up by saying that I had no opinion of the political intelligence of the G.G.S. and if that was the thing going to rule Germany '<u>it would send it straight to Hell!</u>' I don't know what

Heydell thought of me—probably mad. I was for the moment & bitterly angry when I thought of Ireland, of those poor boys on Easter Sunday & Easter Monday waiting for the steamer—the 'rising' already accomplished!—& their one hope the ship with rifles and the officers—who will not be there. The utter callousness & indifference here—only seeking bloodshed in Ireland—the 'rising' is their one hope!

The guns are so timed to arrive as to ensure that the rising must precede them—'<u>no blood, no rifles</u>'.

I came back to the hotel a horrified man & telephoned at once to von Haugwitz to come & see me urgent[ly]. I wrote Wedel a brief note of thanks & said I'd reply to the Berne message tonight—<u>see my reply to Wedel</u>.[93]

Then Noeggerath called & I showed him the letter—& Monteith who came in—& they were reading it when Von Haugwitz was announced. I had to prevent him seeing Noeggerath and Monteith cleverly stopped him in nick of time & got him up to my bedroom where I showed him the letter. He said '<u>the officers were impossible</u>'. That I knew already—his reasons on military grounds, I admit at once. German officers could not go without <u>some</u> German soldiers—& to command Irish Volunteers [with] different discipline &c. &c.—I agreed on all these grounds but I pointed out then the lamentable state of the 'rising'. Here they were, some thousands of brave boys, armed very indifferently, without true cohesion, commissariat, baggage and <u>No Officers</u>, going to commit an irreparable act, & be swept down in hundreds—or perhaps thousands—& the world will always hold me responsible for the whole thing—whereas in every single particular my advice has been scorned—& I have not been consulted until too late & these wholly imperfect 'arrangements made'.

One of the things I predicted on 16 March when I was dealing with the gun running aspect of the matter alone has now come to pass—a check at the eleventh hour—all of us working in the dark—no coherent plan and no communication kept up.

How could a scheme so engineered with the essential preliminaries neglected be successful?

Poor young von Haugwitz, he is a gentleman—one of the very few I have met here. Heydell too, I like at the Admiralty—but the whole thing is a brazen serpent, lifted up in a wilderness of worshippers—worshippers from fear at bottom. This Prussian system is a curse. I see it clearly. It represses all the higher sentiments of humanity—they dare not exist beside it—it is the embodiment of 'soulless efficiency', in mere military things only, dominating a great people. Here in my case it is absolutely soulless—& not efficient either—because while these poor asses think they are dealing with a military problem it is a political problem of the very highest order they are assailing with such rude hands. An abortive rising in Ireland, inadequately armed & supported by them, yet encouraged & urged on by their promise of support—let them say what they will—is a crime they will pay for bitterly. I have now said it so plainly to them all they must be beginning to tremble. To von H.[augwitz] I said 'the ship must go—nothing can stop her: she is bound to go—you are pledged to that—& I go too. That is all'. As regards the man at Berne I tell him that no officers & no submarine can be given—& I will send the letter by Wedel. He said it was absolutely certain no officers could go—& if I was equally sure from the Admiralty that no submarine could go, then he agreed I might write the letter to Berne at once. I sat down and drafted what I was going to send to Berne.

Noeggerath came again & I kept him to dinner alone. We talked very much. Krebs came & squatted for a spell.

N[oeggerath] said (when Krebs was gone) that he was quite sure there were 'very serious' talks going on over the whole thing. That he hoped still for the submarine. I said yes—but they would not send me in her! 'Why?' he said.

'You know,' I answered, 'they fear my intelligence. They know how profoundly I disapprove the rising & they want it—& they fear if I get to Ireland, I may be able to stop it. It's that that they are afraid of. Their fury over my dispatch of John McGoey shows me that they meant to keep me from all communication with my friends to launch me out in the dark, & let all responsibility fall on me and others.'

There is one ray of hope—that John McGoey arrived in time & that they may listen to him. He knows the true character of German good-will to Ireland now. He saw how they kept their promises to the poor betrayed handful of men at Zossen & how they treated himself! No uniforms & refusal to release him when I demanded it in February. He told me that he had sized up German militarism & he is heart and soul against it even as I am!

Later in the evening I told Noeg. that I felt an absolute conviction that the British would seize the ship & that I was praying for it, as probably the best way to avoid the greater evil. If the ship is arrested & the English Govt. publish the fact that they had collared a ship with rifles & Sir R.C. on board, then the mere fact of that publication will stop 'the rising' in Ireland. That is clear. Knowing that the steamer is in the enemy's hands & no relief can come they will never go on with it. So I pray God in His mercy to have this the solution. Anyone that saves the situation in Ireland—and saves our young people from being made the victims of this callous conspiracy. Poor Ireland! God save her indeed—only He can.

Von Haugwitz said he would bring me back the Berne letter tonight—but he did not come by midnight. That all shows that there is a very animated fight going on somewhere. Noeg. said the Admiralty people, while profoundly impressed with the gravity of the situation revealed by his views (mine of yesterday's Diary), were 'raging' at my having told him.

He said he thought they all mistrusted me—& I said I felt sure of it—and I repaid them all the compliment with a vey clear comprehension of how much they deserved my mistrust.

Even Noeg. Now agrees that I <u>must</u> go with the arms—that I <u>could</u> not, in honour, stay here & let the guns go, feeling as I do—but that the infamy of the thing is that the German Government does not send me in a submarine. He still hopes. So he said. I don't. He begged me not to send any reply to Berne about the submarine until he sees me again tomorrow as the naval men will let him know—I agreed.

We talked of other things till late and he left me worn out and I fell asleep at once. Here I am again.[94]

[Berlin] Friday morning, 7 April [1916]

Tomorrow is the last day. Today there will be a last fight for the submarine. I know it is futile. Then clothes to buy—a long letter to the Chancellor about the fate of the Irish soldiers at Zossen—to see that Nadolny's infamous intentions are not executed.[95] I can only plead. I dare not threaten—it is not fair to the Chancellor either—yet I know that the machine (he hates it too I fancy) responds only to pressure and fear.

Last night among other things Noeggerath said he was convinced that S[chirmer]. (who took the Findlay letters &c. over on 'Kristianisfjord' in February) has been captured!

The letters were to be in Captain's safe—I expect the British got them too! All Gaffney's doing. When I was ill to urge me as he did to send them to the Irish Convention in New York. No word from S.[chirmer] or Mary MacFadden since they sailed. They both left Berlin on Sunday 20 Feb. & were to sail on *K'fjord* on Wednesday 23rd.

The ship was held up two days (or more) we know in Kirkwall—& arrived in New York on 7th—two days after the Convention. Mary had letters to (Nina)[96] from me & S. to Cohalan—but nothing of moment save to ask them if I should try & come over as G.[affney] suggested—that I was useless here & ill & it would be far better to try and get to them.

No answer of any kind has come.

I had returned to Munich after this with G. on Sunday 27 February with fever & was in bed for a week nearly & then came Monteith on 7th & this project & everything else has paled into insignificance.

<u>What</u> a laugh! There in America they want me to stay here as their 'representative', thinking there is an Irish policy here & that I can influence these people—little knowing that they insult me, lie to me, break faith—& would now, for their own ends, [let me be] hanged, if it served them.

Emerson told me on 1 April when I had tea with him at Esplanade that the Turks were now completely disillusioned as to the character of German 'goodwill' to Turkey. He said when I told him of my opinion of the G.G.S. *apropos* something else—he said 'You should hear the Turks on them!'

Today is really my last day—& I shall be haunted and riven all day. It is still early.

I told that faithful splendid Monteith last night that I should be glad to go even to death on the scaffold—to an English jail to get away from Germany & these people I despise so much. He said, 'Indeed, I think I would too.' He & B[everley]. slept here last night. Latter in an old suit of mine.

If my papers survive and above all the Treaty and some kind friend of former years (say E. D. M.) should edit them there may yet be told a strange chapter of Irish history. In any case it will be shown that I was only a fool—to trust German honour or goodwill—& never a rogue.

The picture of me in *Graphic* of February 26, 'The Voice of the <u>Traitor</u>' Fr. Crotty tells me was sent to many of the soldiers in Limburg.[97] The Kommandantur there asked the N.C.O.s to state on oath that it was false. They refused—although Fr. Crotty says everyone knows it to be a

---

[94] NLI MS17027 contains a further statement written on 6 April by Casement to Curry concerning his papers. He comments, 'I am giving Gaffney a big bundle of papers &c., here—collected by Monteith & myself. They are important because a lot of them are my closing pages of my diary here now.' He speaks at length about forwarding the documents to Alice Stopford Green after the war. He also predicted how 'By assailing me and my character they will hope to blacken my cause too—at any rate to gravely weaken it.'

[95] A draft copy of this letter to Bethmann-Hollweg is held in NLI MS 13085 9/ix.

[96] Casement's sister, Agnes Newman.

[97] *The Graphic* waged the most vociferous campaign against Casement, who eventually opened legal proceedings against the publication. On their front page of 26 February 1916 they published a full-page pencil drawing, by William Hatherell, the Edwardian newspaper illustrator, of Casement addressing Irish soldiers in Limburg camp.

lie. He said the young Nussing (Brother Canethus Warren) is now a Nationalist & said it was a horrid lie against me.

Of course, we all know that Fr. Crotty promised to contradict it in writing. I hope he may, dear soul.

I must get ready for the ordeal of this last awful day. God keep me straight and help me to go right for Ireland's sake. That is all now I can hope to do.

Monteith went out to Zossen to pay the poor boys & clear all out from bank there. He returned at 6 or so, with the balance of cash to credit of Brigade Fund—Mks 3878.30—& handed it to me. I then told him the matter was delayed—& that the Admiralty had promised me a submarine to take him, Beverley and myself over to Ireland in time to take part in 'operations'.

At 10 I got a message from v. Haugwitz asking me to go to G.G.S. I went and found a trio—Von Hülsen, Nadolny and the young Count—he was always nice and sincere.

N. produced the letter of the Delegate from Berne and we discussed it. They seemed suspicious at first—as usual—but I was able to assure them it came from the right quarter.

I telegraphed from G.G.S. as follows:— When did you leave Dublin? (2) Steamer with so much ammunition & rifles (stating quantities) will be off Inishtooshkert rock, N.W. on Easter Monday dawn. (3) No officers can be sent (4) No submarine going (5) When can you return to Dublin?

I gave v. Haugwitz a long letter to follow by special courier leaving today for Berne. (I append it here). It was brought back at 7.45 (in the evening).

Then V.H. brought me back to hotel in his car after deciding all about our departure tomorrow night. We three are to go to the G.G.S. in afternoon—change there into other (sailor things). I get shaved & then we go off to Hamburg (I fancy) in a special coupé.

Nadolny was very cheery. He said it was impossible to get a submarine & he was sure this way was all right. He asked after Noeggerath, putting many questions, saying I had sent him to Z. & the Admiralty & latter were very angry & charged them (G.G.S.) with breach of faith. I said put it all on me. 'I am responsible for telling Noeg. and involving his aid to try & get a submarine since all other means had failed. I explained how Noeg. was a confidential agent of the Foreign Office & entirely in their confidence & they might rest assured there was no danger from his being brought into my confidence.

I added I had told Gaffney a little only as I was leaving him to look after the interests of the Irish soldiers at Zossen & that I was writing to the Chancellor on that subject. They were very anxious to know if I had told anyone else—but I evaded that by talking on Gaffney's share. I was sorry to deceive them, but could not help it.

Noeggerath came to Hotel on my return. He had no news from Admiralty or F.O. & asked if I had—I had none. Very soon after I got a phone call from Assessor Meyer asking the name of the marine officer I had seen at the Admiralty. I said Heydell and he said 'all right'.

Soon after I got a phone call from Heydell asking me to go round to the Admiralty at 4 adding it was 'over the submarine'. I went & he left me with a junior nice, young Korvettenkaptain— where I stayed until 6.30 reading back numbers of English papers.

Then came Heydell in great excitement to say they had a full dress debate & the thing was settled. I was to go by submarine. Details would be arranged later. I said 'but you must promise to land me in time for any fight in good time' and he promised. Captain Stoelzel came breathless from running upstairs & told me it was settled—& repeated the positive assurance I should be landed in good time—I was to return at 1 p.m. tomorrow. I left feeling another victory!

Noeggerath I had seen going into the Admiralty just before I did—but we did not greet each other.

When I got to the hotel I told Monteith in a whisper—& then came Noeg. He had been present all through the debate & it was his arguments had swayed them—but they had not told him the decision come to. He learned it only from me & was delighted. While we were talking young von Haugwitz came bringing me back my letters to the Delegate at Berne saying it was no use sending it now & he had stopped it. The telegram had gone he assured me.

I discussed what to do with the Delegate & said I'd like to get him here—or if not to send him back to Dublin post haste—but he demurred & said it was better to wait—until tomorrow at any rate. He congratulated me warmly on the change of plan & said he had been very unhappy about the steamer & that he was delighted I had got the submarine. He added 'I will bring the poison all the same.' He begged me to keep out of danger in Ireland & said many things.

Gaffney came—many times during the day—I told him only that there was a delay—no more—& that we should have more time to arrange things & talk over the proper line for him to take about the affairs of the men at Zossen after I was gone & that I was naming him in my letter to the Chancellor as my representative in their regard.

I dined with Frau Remy Barsch[98] & Krebs and turned in at 10 p.m.

Monteith I forgot to say had been sent for to F.O. by Meyer today at 8 p.m., who asked him many questions about the 'rising' & what prospect of success there might be. M. had replied that he regarded it as quite hopeless and impossible of success.

I am in further distress about the man at Berne. It may be J.P. but I think now I know the writing—but cannot remember its owner at the moment. It is <u>perhaps</u> T. MacDonagh. Were these people or this Govt inspired by any sense of decency, fair play or gentleness of soul they would at once have brought him here—or permit me to communicate frankly with him. They do neither—but carefully keep us apart—at this crisis in our country's affairs!—and it is doubtful if he will be told anything for sure at all—or if he will be told I have gone away to Erin.

[Berlin] Saturday, 8 April 1916

I was to have left today—disguised as a sailor at 3 p.m. or 4 with M.[onteith] & Beverley from the G.G.S.—but yesterday's debate at the Admiralty has changed that. Now I await the fresh developments from the Admiralty at 1 p.m.

Gaffney called at 10. Showed me this![99]

This is awful! I don't know what they may do now. Surely there *is* a fate that hurls things on. How Liebknecht got a hold of this goodness only knows. Monteith came at my request and Zerhusen who is here to translate it. Z. has two copies he says of the Treaty; so has Hahn[100] And the soldiers had it for months—& the 'Times' long ago brought out a very <u>fair rendering</u> of it.

Noeggerath just 'phoned to say he was leaving town for a few days and wished to see me—and I told him to come at once. He is coming. He came at 12.30 to bid me goodbye & to ask me to give him a letter of authority to recover the Findlay letter from the Captain of the 'Kristianiafjord'. He thinks Schirmer was arrested at Kirkwall on the outward voyage of the 'K', say 25–26 February.

S., it seems, was not on the passenger list! S. was to have handed the Findlay letter to the Captain to keep in his safe. Noeggerath thinks this was probably done & that the letter may be there, safe & sound, but the Captain does not know what to do with it, as it would have been in an unaddressed envelope. Schirmer was to have given it to D[aniel].C[ohalan]. in New York—as no word has come, we presume that S. was taken off the boat.

I have written a letter authorising Noeggerath to get the letter back from the Captain, if it still is in his possession and have given N. a letter of introduction to D[aniel].C[ohalan]., J[ohn]. D[evoy]., and J. MacG[arrity]. in America.

I then went on at 1 to the Admiralty and saw Captain Stoelzel the chief of the affair & one of his under Captains. No word had yet come. Heydell had gone to Wilhelmshaven to see about the submarine—but the matter had not been settled at 1 o'clock. I was asked to call again at 3. I have just been there & saw Stoelzel & the message was there just coming by phone as I sat on this sofa. It was that a 'U Boat' would be at my service from Emden on 12 April. I was to call on Heydell on Monday 10th in the forenoon and get details of departure.

98 Frau Barsch also resided in the Hotel Saxonia. She was an Egyptian married to an Austrian and became a close friend of Casement.

99 In a side note Casement has written 'All the papers have it. The *Preussiche Zeitung* puts asterisks for the name and omits in same way some of Herr L.'s remarks. *B. Tageblatt* and *Lokalanzeiger* has it in full. R. C.' The relevant cutting from the newspaper is no longer attached but the articles referred to a speech made by Karl Liebknecht, the leader of the German socialist party, who had attacked Casement in the Reichstag the previous day when he read out the Treaty.

100 Hahn was the name of the other translator attached to the Irish Brigade with Zerhusen.

We shall probably leave this for Emden on 11th April (Tuesday) night.

Monteith & Beverley are here. Latter knows nothing yet—but Monteith says he will surely go & with joy. I think M.'s real reason for taking Beverley's was this. M. was in a fearful state over my going by the steamer (I still don't know her name!) and would have done anything to save me. Seeing it was impossible to get a submarine (as we thought) & that I must go I think he meant to 'capture' me at the last moment down at Kiel or wherever the port was—with Beverley's help & tie me up and leave me behind or else, perhaps, as we were coming along the Norwegian coast (in territorial waters all the time) a chance might come to do this & put me on shore.

Old K[rebs]. put the idea before me! He said M[onteith]. was capable of anything to save me and that I must get on board that ship 'alive or dead'. I agreed with K[rebs] & laughed. Now since yesterday evening this 'possibility' has gone.

Zerhusen is here & buying things for Beverly 'for the journey to the East'. Z[erhusen].'s a fine chap—and his wife a good Irishwoman still. If I live I hope to see them again—but there is not much chance in this world.

Anyhow now there are three days more.

My chief trouble now is the man at Berne. They clearly want me <u>not to</u> see him or communicate with him—& I don't know what to do. I am powerless—in their hands.

The once thriving rural village of Lungundo, one of many habitations destroyed under King Leopold II's terror regime to make way for new rubber plantations. Congo Free State (Democratic Republic of Congo), c. 1904. (Photo by Images of Empire/Universal Images Group via Getty Images)

1   Ciaran Brady (ed.), *Interpreting Irish History: The Debate on Historical Revisionism* (Dublin, 2004).

'Phases of a dishonourable phantasy'

Angus Mitchell

Everything is metamorphosed into its inverse in order to be perpetuated in its purged form. Every form of power, every situation speaks of itself by denial, in order to attempt to escape, by simulation of death, its real agony.

> Jean Baudrillard, *Simulacra and Simulations* (1998)

The role assigned to Roger Casement in the various commemorations of the 1916 Rising has varied greatly. In 1991, the 75th anniversary, his name was conspicuously absent. The principal historiographic collection analyzing Irish revisionism *Interpreting Irish History,* contained not a single reference to him.[1] Yet, interest in his life and legacy revived again in the years leading up to the ninetieth anniversary in 2006, and has continued since.

The swerve of Casement's career from imperial servant to scourging critic of empire disoriented those who defended the increasingly indefensible system that he exposed. It was one of the internal shocks that contributed to the strange death of Liberal England in the decade before 1914. In those years, Casement carried out two landmark official investigations into crimes against humanity in sub-Saharan Africa and the Amazon. These investigations, which unsettled widely held views of the supposed advance of progress, modernity and civilization, won for him a tremendous international prestige. But in the propaganda battle during and after the First World War, there was a concerted effort by the British to discredit Casement and his support for the Irish revolution against the Empire. Recent histories of the British intelligence services have revealed how a ruthless and covert war was waged against any threat to the imperial order and how Casement was identified as a particularly dangerous subversive because of his familiarity with its inner workings and because of his international moral stature.

Executed for high treason, Casement survived as a famously troublesome ghost. His shadow loomed over the signing of the Anglo-Irish treaty settlement, to which both his chief prosecutor, the Lord Chancellor, F. E. Smith, and his defence solicitor, George Gavan Duffy, were signatories. The return of his body to Ireland in 1965 temporarily calmed the bitter controversy that had raged over his life and death for the preceding half century. However, release of state papers in the National Archives (UK) between 1994 and 2006 and the National Archives of Ireland in the 1990s, brought Casement back into public consciousness. The debate over the last two decades has restored this unwelcome apparition to the moveable feast of British-Irish relationships.

Casement was acutely aware of the role his ghost might play in explaining unofficial truths. In a letter to his friend Dick Morten, written just a few days before he was hanged, he imagined one such haunting:

By the way, you remember the day I wrote a certain polite letter—and how long I hesitated? Don't you? Well *don't* forget it. You know the truth about that and some day my ghost may call on you, and demand the recollection.[2]

This was one cryptic comment in a sequence of predictions about how his truth would emerge, once the fog of confusion had lifted. Casement's close friend, the poet and activist Alice Milligan, believed that his trial and execution had been foreseen and foretold and that the eventual revelation of his story would 'have an immense effect in restoring union and in uniting Ulster.'[3] Such an outcome remains to be seen. The durable ghost trope was invoked in the first public controversy fought over his reputation in W. B. Yeats's poem *The Ghost of Roger Casement* and Alfred Noyes's *The Accusing Ghost: Justice for Casement*. Repeated acts of exorcism since have failed to drive it away. In Derridean terms, Casement's ghost is a reminder of an alternative history or ontology. This counter-history remains in a state of irreconcilable conflict with the officially shared versions of events and incites questions about the underlying practice of the historical discipline and the archive upon which interpretation of the past depends.

* * * * *

In his long and distinguished life as a British consular officer, Roger Casement had stood close to the inner core of imperial power. After working for seven years in various capacities as colonial officer, civil missionary and labour recruiter in the Congo Free State, he was engaged in 1892 to work as a customs official and

2 National Library of Ireland (NLI) MS 31724, Roger McHugh Papers, Roger Casement to Richard Morten, Pentonville, 28 July 1916. (Typed copy)

3 Catherine Morris, *Alice Milligan and the Irish Cultural Revival* (Four Courts Press, 2012), 51.

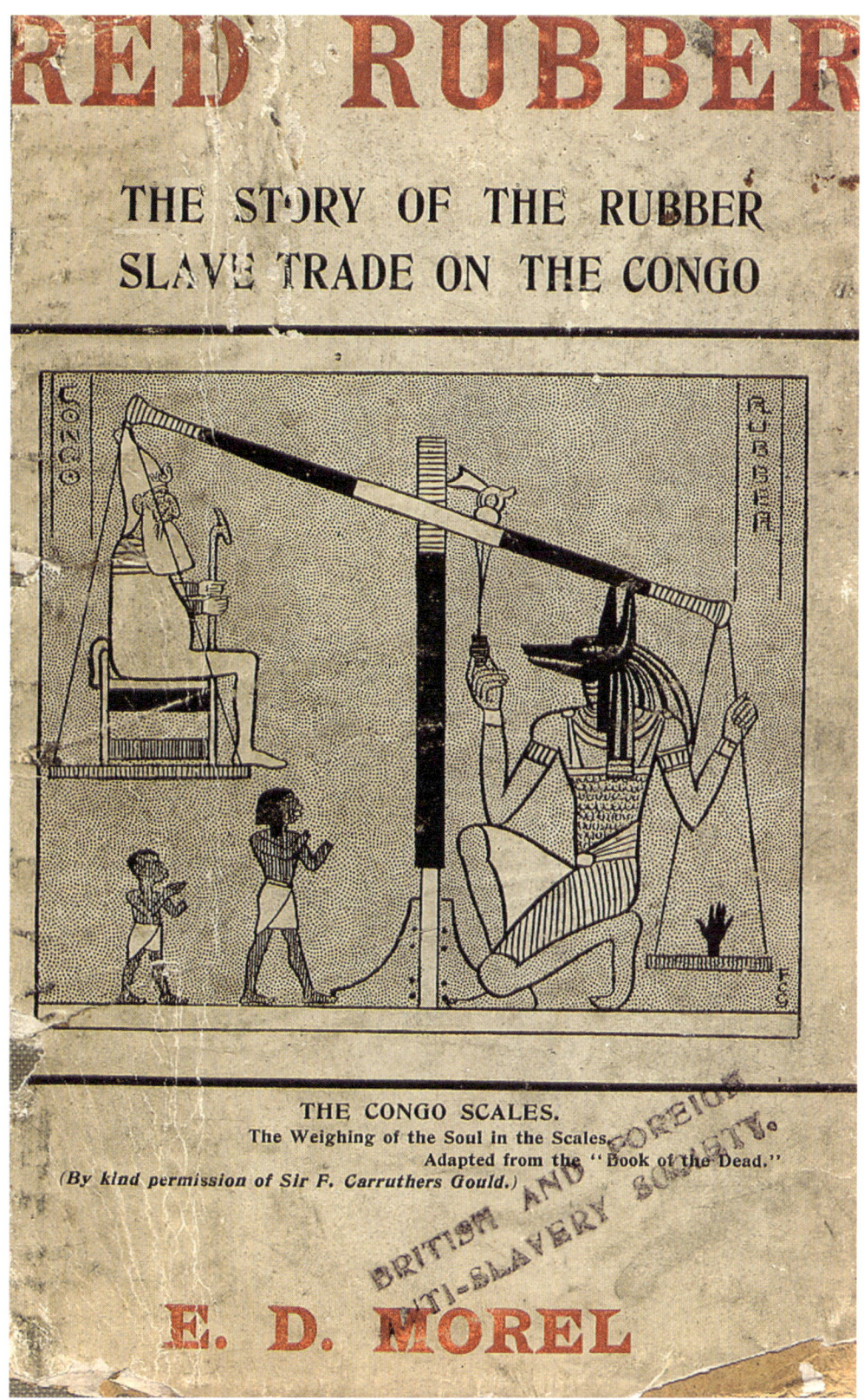

The book jacket of *Red Rubber*, a publication written by Edmund Dene Morel, exposing the atrocities of the rubber slave trade in the Congo Free State. *c.* 1906. (Photo by Images of Empire/Universal Images Group via Getty Images)

survey officer in the emerging British administrative district of the Oil Rivers Protectorate (Niger Coast Protectorate). Over the following years he enjoyed the confidence of British foreign secretaries, including Lord Salisbury, Lord Lansdowne and Sir Edward Grey. His ties with the world of British intelligence and its secret service agencies, as they emerged after the Boer War, are still hidden. It is apparent, however, that he was operating at the highest level in the great game of European power in Africa and served as a troubleshooter for the Foreign Office. In 1904, the publication of his official report on the administration of the Congo Free State sparked a diplomatic war. It also heightened the realization that, in the wake of the abolition of slavery in the US, Brazil, Cuba and elsewhere in the Americas, new slaveries, based primarily on debt peonage, had emerged. Casement and a number of other activists—the journalist, H. W. Nevinson; the historian, Alice Stopford Green; and the activist, E. D. Morel—collaborated tirelessly to expose these. In time, their investigations helped to create the idea (or ideal) of an ethical foreign policy, distinct from the missionary-driven antislavery activism of the nineteenth century and based on that more secular sense of human rights which informs—at least in principle—the conduct of international relations today.[4]

Casement, disillusioned by the inability of the Foreign Office to improve the situation and chafed by the restrictions of his official position, became, along with the journalist E. D. Morel, one of the founders of the Congo Reform Association. Through it he was able to challenge the imperial system as such, advocating a more ethical foreign policy in Britain, and fostering support for various advanced cultural nationalist initiatives in Ireland. But the crisis in the English Liberal Party, evident in the deepening divide between the fading idealism of Gladstonian Liberals and the hawkish intentions of Liberal Imperialists, sharpened the political and ethical conflict between the clamant imperialism of the latter and its rejection by the movement for Irish national independence to which he became wholly committed.

His experience of the African and South American frontiers seemed to change Casement's view on European empires and colonial relations. He came to see Ireland's relationship with Britain as a colonial one of commercial and cultural domination, and not as a political union founded upon shared democratic principles. His intellectual and financial support for numerous initiatives promoting the Irish cultural revival gradually expanded into a full-scale political commitment. He worked tirelessly in the weeks before and after the founding of the Irish Volunteers and became a leading voice in recruitment drives across the four provinces. In May 1914, with the support of his intellectual mentor, Alice Stopford Green, he organized gunrunning into Ireland and thereafter was involved in a network of various anti-British conspiracies. On the outbreak of war in August 1914, the British Foreign Office and its associated intelligence services took a special interest in the renegade Irishman, closely monitoring his movements during his eighteen months in Germany, from November 1914 to April 1916, and setting in motion a plan to have him assassinated. On his return to Ireland, he was arrested near Banna Strand, spirited off to London, placed in solitary confinement in the Tower of London, until the insurrection in Ireland had been suppressed and the leaders executed following secret military courts martial.

Casement's trial, at the height of the First World War, reveals a great deal about the efficacy of the intelligence services and their skill in managing public perceptions. Recent accounts of MI5 have shown how Casement became the target for a coordinated counter-subversion strategy from the outset of war, led by two closely linked intelligence chiefs: the director of

4   For two recent studies on the new slaveries, see Kevin Grant, *A Civilised Savagery: Britain and the New Slaveries in Africa, 1884–1926* (Oxford, 2005) and Lowell J. Satre, *Chocolate on Trial: Slavery, Politics & the Ethics of Business* (Ohio, 2005).

5. See Christopher Andrew, *The Defence of the Realm: The Authorized History of MI5* (London, 2009) where Casement is clearly shown to have been a priority security risk for different agencies.
6. Brian Harris, *State Trials from Socrates to Nuremberg* (Stroud, 2006).
7. See Elizabeth Jaeger. 'Roger Casement: How Effective Was the British Government's Smear Campaign Exposing the Homosexual "Black Diaries"?', *Éire-Ireland* 46: 3 & 4 (2011), 132–69.
8. The National Archives (TNA)(UK) HO 144/1636/311643/52&53 Cabinet Memorandum.
9. National Archives of Ireland (NAI), Department of Taoiseach (DT) S 9606A. The file contains a copy of Eamon Duggan's account, written on Dáil Éireann paper, describing the authentication.

the Criminal Investigation Department of Special Branch, Basil Thomson, and Admiral Reginald 'Blinker' Hall, the architect of Naval Intelligence (Room 40).[5] Their intricate plans to capture Casement included the chartering of a yacht to patrol the west coast of Ireland in anticipation of Casement's return. The critical paradox of his trial is that while many high-ranking figures in the British state were determined to kill Casement, he was himself in pursuit of the martyr's crown. Martyrdom can make a mockery of the law. For Casement, the hangman's noose was a noble end to a life secretly dedicated to the cause of Irish independence. The trial is now considered to be one of the great state trials of world history—comparable to the trials of Socrates, Joan of Arc or Sir Thomas More.[6] For both the British state and the accused it was a performative moment—sacred drama—and a deliberate act of history-making. Beyond its contribution to the argument that justified Ireland's right to rebellion, his speech from the dock became a model for anti-colonial revolutionary leaders around the world.

Beyond its significance in redefining and updating the meaning of treason, the trial was also an important exercise in public propaganda. It became a theatre for opposing ideologies and competing systems of power and belief. The conspiratorial relationship between the press, the prosecution and several senior politicians is so redolent of a Stalinist show trial that it unwittingly undermines the intended exemplary display of a specifically British justice. This is the context for the discovery and deployment by Basil Thomson and Admiral Hall of the Black Diaries as the instrument by which a long and convoluted process of managing Casement's guilt and martyrdom was initiated and sustained. Knowledge about the sexually explicit diaries began as rumour and hearsay. Selected pages were shown to newspaper editors, statesmen and foreign dignitaries. Brief items appeared in mass circulation newspapers.[7] On an immediate level the idea that Casement had for years been 'addicted to sodomitical practices'[8] disorientated his defence counsel and the various campaigns for clemency. It also distorted his message and clouded public understanding of his revolutionary trajectory. The suggestion that his political activism was underpinned by a predatory sexuality, his figuration as an imperial adventurer exploiting unequal power relationships, threw his life's work into disrepute.

Casement went to the gallows in Pentonville on 3 August 1916. The climate of intrigue, secrecy and suspicion surrounding the trial and execution set the scene for decades of controversy. It allowed for the political and humanitarian message of Casement's work to be elided and horribly transfigured. Over the years, a process of manipulative leaking resulted in the conspiratorial acceptance of the Black Diaries as genuine, without the appropriate searching questions being asked and answered about the probability of their veracity or any critical examination of their provenance. But in death Casement proved even more tricky and problematic than he had in life. As the last of the sixteen executed leaders of 1916, his memory was elevated to a level of devotion among the generation of Irish republicans who fought the War of Independence. In February 1922, in a peculiar moment of shared history, Michael Collins visited the House of Lords with Casement's prosecutor the Lord Chancellor, Lord Birkenhead, F. E. Smith, to authenticate the Black Diaries. On his return to Ireland, he opened a file in the Taoiseach's office on 'Alleged Casement Diaries'.[9] The implication of these actions is that, at the foundation of the Irish Free State, Collins officially accepted the authenticity of the Black Diaries and that this acceptance was part of a secret deal struck in the diplomatic shadows of the negotiations. This would explain why the Irish government remained so ambiguous about the authenticity of the diaries for many decades afterwards. This ambiguity is evident in the statement made by de Valera that 'a further period of time must elapse before the full extent of Casement's sacrifice can be understood'.[10] It might also explain why all discussion of the Black Diaries was closed down in 1965 at an official level in Ireland on the return of Casement's remains and his televised state funeral.

But the intrigue surrounding Casement's life and death has only added to his mystique. To date, there are around thirty biographical studies of different kinds documenting his life. In the early 1930s, full-length biographies appeared in English, German and Italian, indicative of Casement's interest to a European audience.[11] In the late 1930s, the first major dispute began following the publication of William Maloney's *The Forged Casement Diaries*. Maloney's forensic work examined British counter-subversion during the First World War and was one of the earliest studies to forensically deconstruct the unknown world of the British secret service. W. B. Yeats, G. B. Shaw and other prominent public intellectuals involved themselves in the dispute.[12]

The outbreak of the Second World War brought this phase of the controversy to a close. But a new one began in 1953 with the opening up of the G.A.A.'s Casement Park in West Belfast and de Valera's unscheduled visit to north Antrim to inspect the Old IRA at Murlough Bay, where Casement had asked to be buried. From 1953 to 1965, Casement's name was hardly ever out of the newspapers; the controversy over the return of his body from Pentonville prison to Ireland was blended with the persisting controversy over the Black Diaries, the existence of which the British Home Secretary was still refusing to acknowledge. Several volumes of memoirs appeared with direct references to Casement and comments were often strategically included to endorse the distortions created by the propaganda offensive. Roger McHugh, a UCD lecturer, a member of the republican party Córas na Poblachta, and an Irish senator from 1954 to 1957, became one of several academics intent on shining more light on the issue. But confusion and division continued to dominate the debate.

In Britain, part of the enduring strategy against Casement was discreetly orchestrated by the newspaper tycoon, Lord Beaverbrook. Beaverbrook's mass circulation newspapers had been partly responsible for disseminating the earliest rumours about the Black Diaries back in 1916. In spite of his Canadian background, Beaverbrook stood close to the nexus of Unionist power in Britain, including Winston Churchill, Andrew Bonar Law and David Lloyd George. Towards the end of the First World War, he was appointed Minister of Information. In the mid 1950s, it was one of Beaverbrook's favoured journalists, René MacColl, who fired the next salvo in the Casement controversy. MacColl published a controversial and deeply hostile biography *Roger Casement: A New Judgment*, which inaugurated a long and bitter exchange in the letters page of the *Irish Times*. His interpretation placed unsubstantiated myths at the very heart of the biography and used the unsympathetic testimony of Casement's senior counsel, A. M. Sullivan, to verify Casement's renegade sexuality, even though the existence of the Black Diaries was still denied by the British Home Office.

If MacColl's biography aggravated tensions, it also firmly embedded a demonic view of Casement and undermined a dwindling cohort of Casement supporters in Britain. The critical intervention in the debate came with the publication in 1958 of *The Accusing Ghost: Justice for Casement* by the English poet, Alfred Noyes. In 1916, while he was working for Britain's Ministry of Information in the US, Noyes had been used to authenticate the Black Diaries. He had stood by his belief in their veracity in his spat with Yeats in the 1930s, but in the post-war period serious doubts started to emerge in Noyes' understanding of his role in the story. In *The Accusing Ghost* he summarized the contradictions implicit in the argument supporting the authenticity

10 Roger Sawyer (ed.), *Roger Casement's Diaries 1910: The Black and the White* (London, 1997), 12.

11 Denis Gwyn's biography was translated into French by Jean-Henry Morin and published by Libraire Gallimard in Paris and went through several editions. The respected journalist and anti-fascist intellectual, Mario Borsa wrote an original biography *La Tragedia Impresa di Sir Roger Casement (1916)* (Rome, 1932). Another biography was published in Germany by Balder Olden, *Pardiese des Teufels: das leben Sir Roger Casements* (Berlin, 1933). Olden's book, which took a strongly anti-colonial position, was placed on the list of banned books by the Nazi Party and Olden was one of the thousands of intellectuals exiled from Germany in 1933.

12 This is the part of the controversy to have received most academic study. See W. J. McCormack, *Roger Casement in Death or Haunting the Free State* (Dublin, 2002). Lucy McDiarmid has also mapped aspects of the debate in 'The Afterlife of Roger Casement', in *The Irish Art of Controversy* (Dublin, 2005).

of the Diaries and explained why his views had reversed and why he now understood the Diaries as forgeries.

In 1959, the greater part of the Black Diaries narrative was finally published in a clandestine edition by the Paris-based Olympia Press. This was a lavish publication, limited to a first edition of 1,500; it contained over eighty black-and-white photographs and endpaper maps of Dublin during the Easter Rising. This deliberate blending of the Black Diaries with Casement's biography and a history of the struggle for Irish independence might be read as a purposeful effort to destabilize not merely Casement's meaning but to cast aspersions over the intellectual legitimacy of the entire struggle for Irish freedom. The frontispiece photograph of F. E. Smith was perhaps a veiled reference to an undisclosed aspect of the story. The author-editors of the volume were Peter Singleton-Gates, a shadowy newspaperman, and Maurice Girodias, a maverick and unscrupulous publisher, famed for not paying his authors. Since the 1930s, Girodias had built up a controversial reputation as a publisher of avant-garde authors including Henry Miller and Samuel Beckett. He encouraged his writers to script pornographic literature because it sold. Among the works that made Olympia Press famous were J. P. Donleavy's *The Ginger Man* and Vladimir Nabokov's *Lolita*. The British government had persistently tried to close down the Olympia Press, but without success. According to the historian of the Olympia Press, Girodias himself took immense interest in the Black Diaries project and wrote significant parts of the text himself.[13]

Whatever the merits of or issues with the edition, the publication of the larger part of the Black Diaries helped the process of authentication. In 1959, the Home Office finally released the Black Diaries into the Public Record Office. Permission to access them was required from the Home Secretary and was restricted to researchers who could prove they had worthy and scholarly reasons for analyzing the documents. The public debate continued to rage between London and Dublin, with the line now clearly drawn in the sand.

In the early 1960s, the hand of British intelligence was again evident in the intervention of the Unionist MP, H. H. Montgomery Hyde. Montgomery Hyde had served as a secret intelligence agent during the Second World War and throughout the 1950s was in regular contact with Lord Beaverbrook, with whom he dined privately on several occasions.[14] He was also chiefly responsible for raising the issue of the Black Diaries in the House of Commons and emerged as the principal authenticator of the Diaries in the public sphere. In 1960, Penguin Books published his account of the Casement trial and included an appendix with passages from the most explicit diary that dealt with Casement's voyage up the Amazon in 1911 and that had not made it into the Olympia Press edition.[15] At the time of their publication these passages were possibly the most explicit descriptions of homosexuality ever to appear in a mainstream publication in Britain. As the sexual revolution of the 1960s took off, Casement was to assume a peculiar role, not as Irish but rather as sexual liberator. But this prospect did not amuse nationalist sentiment in Dublin and, with the 50th commemoration of the 1916 Rising on the horizon, feelings intensified.

After years of diplomatic negotiation and popular protest, the decision to allow Casement's remains to return to Ireland was taken at a private meeting between Irish Minister of External Affairs, Frank Aiken, and British Prime Minister, Harold Wilson, on the day of Winston Churchill's state funeral in January 1965. A few weeks later and following his disinterment, statements were made simultaneously in the House of Commons and the Dáil as a plane took the coffin containing Casement's bones across the Irish Sea to Baldonnell airport—later renamed Casement Aerodrome. After the lying in state in Arbour Hill, tens of thousands lined the streets on a stormy March day as the coffin

---

13 For the views of the Black Diaries held by Girodias, see John de St Jorre, *Venus Bound: The Erotic Voyage of the Olympia Press and its Writers* (New York, 1994) 264–67. Samuel Beckett was also intrigued and influenced by the Diaries, as argued by Patrick Bixby, 'The ethico-politics of homo ness: Beckett's *How It Is* and Casement's *Black Diaries*', *Irish Studies Review*, 20(3), 2012, 243–61.

14 The Lord Beaverbrook papers held in the Parliamentary Archives, House of Commons Library, has significant material detailing the link between Montgomery Hyde and Beaverbrook. The main subjects of their conversations were Sir Edward Carson and Andrew Bonar Law, both intimate friends of Beaverbrook, but it is likely that Casement figured in their discussion. A letter held in BBK/h/186/K-W 1956 from Beaverbrook to MacColl, 3 May 1956, refers to Beaverbrook sending a copy of MacColl's Casement biography to the University of New Brunswick.

15 H. Montgomery Hyde, *Famous Trials 9: Roger Casement* (London, 1964)

was paraded past the General Post Office to Glasnevin cemetery in Ireland's first televised state funeral.[16] The return of the body helped to improve relations between England and Ireland, but Casement's ghost still had many 'cunning passages, contrived corridors,/ And issues' to haunt.

From 1965 to 1985 Casement's reputation underwent a process of biographical revisionism as the narrative of the Black Diaries was stitched, in a variety of patterns, into the fabric of his life. At the height of the conflict in Northern Ireland, two popular biographies appeared. One was written by the Irish historian turned television journalist, Brian Inglis, a former editor of *The Spectator*. Another was penned by the American literary historian, Benjamin Reid. Both books adopted simplified psychoanalytical theories to argue that the Black Diaries fitted well with the psychological profile of Casement as a disaffected consul with tendencies to psychosis and erotomania. The medico-psychiatric vocabulary masqueraded as a form of analysis, and it remained as a favoured element of the new propaganda offensive against Irish republicanism and nationalism in Northern Ireland, an obsessive determination by people, who were usually woefully undereducated, to identify nationalism as a pathology. These biographies were widely reviewed in both academic and mainstream journals as part of a strategy of depoliticizing and criminalizing the broader republican movement. In terms of their interpretative trajectory, the Black Diaries comply with what Kevin Whelan has defined as the second and third phases of Irish revisionism from the late 1950s to the 1990s.[17] Revisionist historiography in Ireland, which developed in tandem with Ireland's modernizing programme, served as a supplement to the political crisis of a divided nation and the Black Diaries, the denials about them, the endless hissings of and about conspiracies, were all seized upon as illustrations of the 'toxic' and 'aberrant' features of Irish Republicanism

and Northern Irish Nationalism. In their resourceful anxiety to expose a racial malady in their chosen targets, the revisionists displayed a ruthlessly obsessive disturbance. Revisionism is the disease for which it professes to be the cure (apologies to Karl Kraus). No historical figure, with the possible exception of Padraig Pearse, illuminates and exacerbates this condition more than Casement.

However, by the 1990s attitudes to sexuality in Ireland had undergone a dramatic change. The combined effect of that, along with the opening of the Casement archive in Britain and the prospect of a peace process in the North was to increase even further the fissiparous energies of the Casement controversy. New divisions emerged in the two decades between the release of the last significant tranche of Casement papers in the 1990s and the creation in 2010 of a 'global' Casement, following the publication of a semi-fictionalized biography by the Peruvian author and Nobel Laureate, Mario Vargas Llosa.

Understanding the alterations and altercations in the interpretation of Casement can help to explain what we may call the politics of knowledge and the ongoing difficulties in the construal of 1916 as both 'narrative' and 'event'. A persistent reluctance to tackle the uncomfortable issues raised by official secrecy, is a notable feature of the dispute over Casement and the Black Diaries. One of these issues is the avowed requirement to control archival knowledge in the name of 'national security'. And in the vexed politics of the writing of Irish history, the Casement dispute raises important general questions about the production and diffusion of history as both a discipline and myth.

The Archival Turn

The death of the journalist-historian Brian Inglis in 1993 coincided with the republication of his 1973 biography, *Roger*

16 Chris Reeves, 'The penultimate Irish problem: Britain, Ireland and the exhumation of Roger Casement', *Irish Studies in International Affairs*, 12, 2001, 151–78; Kevin Grant, 'Bones of Contention: the repatriation of the remains of Roger Casement', *Journal of British Studies* 41 (July 2002), 329–53.

17 Kevin Whelan, 'The revisionist debate in Ireland', *boundary 2* (31: 1 (2004), 179–205.

'PHASES OF A DISHONOURABLE PHANTASY'

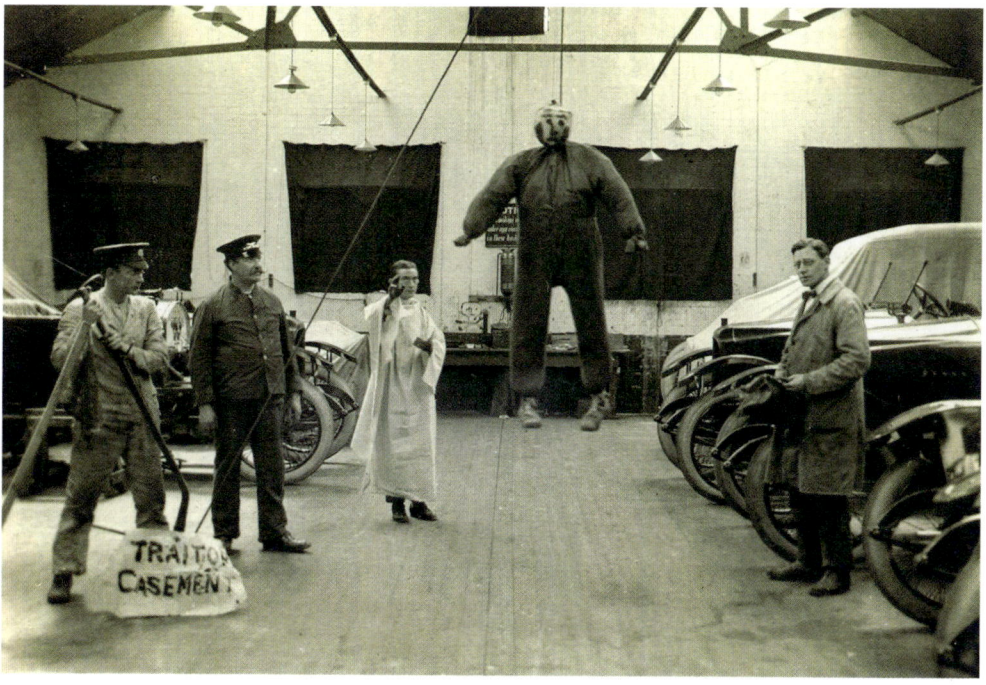

'Traitor Casement'. British soldiers stage a mock execution of Roger Casement. Date and location unknown.

Casement, in which he claimed to have established the veracity of the Diaries. The book was widely regarded as the most authoritative historical appraisal of Casement. Inglis bridged the divide between television media and the writing of history with more ease than any other figure of his generation—A. J. P. Taylor excepted. His televisual appeal confirmed his argument about the diaries; his was the view accepted by academics and journalists as 'balanced'.[18] With scant regard to methodology, Inglis argued for an approach based on reason rather than either forensic analysis or scholarly judgment:

> Nevertheless, the case against the forgery theory remains unshaken. No person or persons, in their right mind, would have gone to so much trouble and expense to damn a traitor, when a single diary would have sufficed. To ask the forger to fake the other two diaries and the cash register (and if one was forged, all of them were) would have been simply to ask for detection, because a single mistake in any of them would have destroyed the whole ugly enterprise. Besides, where could the money have been found? Government servants may sometimes be unscrupulous, but they are always tight-fisted. Why should they pay a forger to do more than was strictly necessary for the immediate requirements?[19]

There are a number of assumptions here. First of them is that there is no need 'to damn a traitor', because, by the law of the State, there is indeed no worse criminal. But the telling phrase assumes the guilt and denies the need to prove it. Second, it is assumed that there could be no rationale for forgery beyond its immediate purpose, to undermine the powerful support for Casement. Inglis ignored all consideration of the relevance of the Diaries as documents of historical record, or of how they had shaped public understanding of Casement. For him, the value of the diaries was what they revealed about their author's sexuality, not what they were intended to reveal about the crimes against humanity under investigation. Apparently Inglis was not struck by the fact that the diaries coincided precisely with Casement's official

---

18 Inglis had been involved in the Casement controversy since the 1950s and over two decades had established himself as an 'authority'. No one did more to build both public consensus and the discursive conventions about the Diaries, especially through the new medium of television. In 1961 Inglis was chosen to offer an afterword to the television documentary produced by Peter Wildeblood, *The Trial of Roger Casement*. Wildeblood was imprisoned in the 1950s for his part in the notorious homosexual scandal known as the Montagu case.

19 Brian Inglis, *Roger Casement* (London, 1973), 381.

investigations of crimes against humanity in the Congo and Amazon; he avoided all reference to the larger question of the representation of atrocities.

Instead, Inglis promoted the view that to suggest or even to think the diaries were forged was to be irrationally recalcitrant, politically motivated and anti-modern. The preface to the 1993 edition of his biography argued that forensic testing 'would be superfluous, so strong is the evidence of Casement's homosexuality'.[20] In other words, to deny the authenticity of the diaries was to deny Casement's homosexuality. Despite its contradictions, the Inglis view was accepted and recycled unchallenged for over twenty years.[21] Most problematically, the argument sustaining the authenticity of the diaries was not based on recognized scholarly methodology, or on a comparative reading of inconsistencies within the archival material. Instead, it was sustained on undisclosed opinions on the handwriting, on the testimony of those who claimed they were 'in the know', and on the conviction that the British secret services would not undertake such an unnecessary and expensive conspiracy.

The republication of the Inglis biography coincided with the decision in Britain to release the diaries under the Open Government Initiative. By the early 1990s almost all resistance to the Black Diaries had disappeared. Ireland was also in the process of modernizing its legislation on sexual offences and legalizing homosexuality. In advance of the release, a document examination was carried out and a BBC radio documentary produced to solve what was pitched as 'one of the riddles of 20th century politics'.[22] The focus of the programme was a forensic examination of the documents by a former British Home Office employee, David Baxendale, who pronounced them 'authentic'. Six months later, on 28 March 1994, the Black Diaries were finally released to a brief salvo of press reports. The journalist and historian of Ireland, Robert Kee, involved in the story since 1956, gave an informed résumé of the controversy and, having accepted their authenticity, tried to answer 'why were successive governments so secretive?'[23] Other newspapers also cashed in on this unusual meeting of history and current affairs.[24] In Ireland the story allowed the mainstream press to try out a new sexual vocabulary not normally associated with daily newspaper stories. The consensus built after the publication of the Inglis biography was now embedded as firmly among academics as it was among the general public. Dissent had been reduced to a cranky few.

Release of the diaries coincided with various political and cultural changes in Ireland. A new era in Anglo-Irish relations dawned and with it the promotion of 'transparency' in government. On 31 August 1994 the Provisional IRA announced a complete cessation of military operations and negotiations opened between Westminster, Leinster House and the Sinn Féin leadership; these led to the Good Friday Agreement. In October 1995, a further 200 closed Casement files were declassified. The bulk of this release included Home Office documentation dealing with Casement from the moment of his capture on 21 April 1916 up to 1959, when the diaries were finally released into the public domain; another 28 Prison Commission files concerned his imprisonment and burial in Pentonville prison. To the dozen or so journalists who attended the press day, the files were well ordered and their descriptions formed a tidy narrative about Casement's capture, trial, execution and afterlife. Various documents had been photocopied and were distributed to the press. These included a transcript of Casement's first interrogation and an array of documents containing new evidence about his alleged homosexuality, including signed affidavits by witnesses to an extremely indiscreet sexual relationship with his Norwegian co-conspiritor, Adler Christensen. There was no obvious reference to the tradition of historians, public intellectuals, poets and

20 Brian Inglis, *Roger Casement* (Belfast, 1993), 10.
21 Back in 1974, most historians and reviewers rowed in behind Inglis; the most circumspect voice was F. S. L. Lyons reviewing in the *Irish Times*, 12 May 1973.
22 The show was *Document: The Casement Diaries*, 23 Sept. 1993, BBC Radio 4. *The Independent* ran a piece on the programme on 16 September 1993 and *The Times* on 24 September 1993 by the journalist Stephen Ward.
23 *Times*, 26 March 1994. Robert Kee's involvement can be traced back to the 1950s in correspondence held in The National Archives (UK).
24 In British newspapers the best article was written by David Pallister in *The Guardian* (G2) 29 March 1994, 'Sex, lies and red tape'. In the *Sunday Times*, on 3 April, Paul Bew compared the Casement diaries unfavourably with Alan Clark's 'recent classic'. *The Irish Times,* on 29 March 1994, published an article by the 18th-century historian, Ian MacBride. The wittiest opinion was by Declan Kiberd in *The Sunday Press*, 3 April 1994, 'Is Ireland ready for a gay patriot?'

politicians who had denounced the Black Diaries as forged, or to the coordinated propaganda assault on Casement's character unleashed by the Ministry of Information. Intriguingly, two sub-files and fourteen documents were held back under section 3(4) of the Public Record Act 1958 on the grounds of national security. The implication was clear: there were still reputations to be protected.

The declassification singled out Casement as the most actively dangerous revolutionary leader involved in the Easter Rising. From the scribbled minutes written on the covers of several files, the principal preoccupation of the authorities in 1916 was to prevent Casement 'attaining martyrdom'. The British government realized that Casement wished to wear the martyr's crown—the word 'martyr' crops up frequently in the inter-departmental minutes, and in the correspondence between the leading Home Office officials involved, notably Ernley Blackwell and Basil Thomson. Together, Blackwell and Thomson went to great lengths to control information about the prisoner and suppress anything potentially revelatory or damaging to the government. The files might be read as a perfect example of the Foucauldian description (in *Discipline and Punish*) of how the state takes control of the criminal's body, his reputation and his meaning. During the months of Casement's imprisonment, from late April to early August 1916, there are several references to the censorship of his mail, the strict control of access and contact with his legal advisers, friends and relatives. After his execution, the strategic management of information about Casement continued and there is a significant reference to the deliberate destruction of Casement papers on 16 August 1916.[25]

Beyond the matter of censorship, the release of files displayed a very specific intention in 1916 to present Casement as mentally sick, aberrant and sexually perverted. Documentation on the question of Casement's sexuality originated in Basil Thomson's Central Intelligence Department at Special Branch, the same department to initially 'discover' the diaries soon after his arrest in April 1916. Another file contained a single letter dealing with the post-mortem digital probe of Casement's anus and the discovery of incontrovertible and expert proof of his sexual preferences.[26] Further correspondence, from various professionals, tried to establish Casement's 'insanity' and 'madness'. A letter from Rev. Richard de Bary (late Chaplain of Belfast Castle) recalled how Casement had 'become the subject of singular illusions' and was apt to suddenly believe he was 'in the midst of the '98 era'. Casement, he felt, had been 'touched by sunstroke or some other physical influence', which had resulted in a kind of 'amnesia inducing specific illusions'.[27]

In stark contrast, the surviving manuscript material in Casement's hand is completely at odds with this official presentation of the prisoner as mad, bad and dangerous to know. For historians of the 1916 Rising, the most valuable part of the 1995 declassification was the file containing early drafts of his speech from the dock and other fragments from his prison writing.[28] The tone is one of relentless defiance and aggressive opposition towards the British Empire and the powers who wished to divide Ireland along sectarian lines. Casement's profound understanding of British power had alerted him to the strategy of divide and rule. His knowledge of the motive force of history and his deliberate identification with the radical revolutionary tradition is articulated in his essays on 'Wolfe Tone and his Modern Admirers' and '"High Treason"—Why Ireland is Poor'. The logic behind his decision to go to Germany is explained in 'Why I appealed to Irish Soldiers in Germany to Fight for Ireland'. He deliberately connects himself to a legitimate tradition of national resistance in his scribblings on 'Garibaldi as a "Traitor"—his "treachery" and "treason" were the beginnings of his "Patriotism"',

25 TNA (UK) HO 144/1637/311643/176.
26 TNA (UK) HO 144/1637/311643/141 Dr. Percy Mander, Medical Officer of Pentonville Prison to Sir Herbert Smalley, Medical Commissioner of Prisons. On the question of Casement's anus see letter to editor of *Times Literary Supplement*, No. 5624, 14 January 2011.
27 TNA (UK) HO 144/1636/311643/32.
28 TNA (UK) HO 144/1636/311643/32A

and 'Patriotism by "Treachery": Louis Kossuth seducing Hungarian Soldiers from their Allegiance'. Perhaps, most threatening to the authorities was Casement's clearly stated desire to die for Ireland and thereby to be included in a genealogy of revolutionary sacrifice dating back to the eighteenth century.

When placed beside the voluminous trial notes held at the National Library of Ireland among the George Gavan Duffy papers, these essays suggest that Casement was still completely in control of his critical faculties during his final months. The official narrative, evident from the Home Office files, also contradicts his own diary narrative describing his time in Germany. Part of a series of covert strategies to control Casement included a campaign to associate his treason and support for revolutionary politics with loss of sanity. Arthur Conan Doyle, along with other public intellectuals, tried to make the case that years in the tropics had somehow unhinged Casement's thinking. In the extract from his German diary published in this issue, Casement admitted suffering from nervous exhaustion, but there is nothing 'mad' or unreasoned in his behaviour. The logic and motives of his actions are clearly explained. There is no evidence in either his trial notes, or in his speech from the dock to suggest that he had in any way lost his mind. The narrative of the British state archive aims to present Casement's politics and the organizations he supported as in some sense 'aberrant', like his sexuality. But the clear conflict between his extant prison writings and the accusations of madness and of sexual indiscretion—all sourced in anecdote—remains unexplained, not even addressed. The focus is on the normality and legitimacy of the state and the abnormality and illegitimacy of any individual or group that challenges it.

His prison writings and police files yield other essential information about the labyrinthine paper trail left behind after his execution. They reveal an unusual determination on the part of the authorities to follow this trail wherever it might lead them. From his first official posting to the Oil Rivers Protectorate in 1892 to his resignation from the Foreign Office in 1913 as Consul General of Brazil, Casement had systematically bombarded the Foreign Office with letters, memos and reports from his different African and South American postings. In the last two years of his life, as his revolutionary commitment and treasonable acts deepened, the scale of his official and unofficial archive became an acute problem both for him and for the British authorities.[29] In one key respect Casement was the perfect imperial servant, fastidious about the value of the written word and the sacrosanct nature of the official record. With his revolutionary turn he became conscious of the imperative need to take control of his own record as a way of taking charge of his historical legacy—his diaries contain frequent references to this.

Before leaving Germany, he had left careful instructions with Dr Charles Curry 'regarding his diaries and their publication upon the close of war'.[30] His instructions to his solicitor George Gavan Duffy contain several references to the safety of his papers.[31] The historian Alice Stopford Green had also endeavoured to sort out his paper trail. Interest in Casement's recorded legacy continued beyond his execution. His sister Agnes had complained in 1927 how several letters from her brother, and others from Michael Collins and Lady Lavery had been confiscated at Harwich, when her trunks were in transit.[32]

The Black Diaries have been deployed very effectively to manage information about Casement by miring public discussion and academic discourse in an interminable debate about his sexuality. While they were used in the first instance to confuse his defence and discourage the petitions for clemency, they were useful in the longer term in making the sexual issues prevail over and pollute the political.

29 On Casement's pseudonymous writings see my article 'John Bull's other empire: Roger Casement and the press, 1898–1916', in Simon Potter (ed.), *Newspapers and Empire in Ireland and Britain: reporting the British Empire* c. 1857–1921 (Dublin, 2004).

30 C. Curry (ed.), *Diaries of Sir Roger Casement: his Mission to Germany and the Findlay Affair* (Munich, 1922).

31 See NLI MS 10764 (11) 'A Private Note for my solicitor'. After his trial Eva Gore-Booth wrote to Gavan Duffy asking if he thought it 'a good plan to get questions asked in Parliament about R.C.'s papers'. (NLI MS 10763 (20). Gavan Duffy's correspondence with Home Office is held in NLI MS 10763 (24) and TNA (UK) HO 144/1637/311643/176. Also see TNA (UK) PCOM 9/2326.

32 TNA (UK), HO 144/23429/311643/211

33 TNA (UK), HO 144/23481/311643/281, 23 September 1958.

34 See correspondence in TNA (UK) LCO 2/7951.

The state papers released in the 1990s also revealed a startling degree of confusion over the repression and then the release of the Black Diaries. The actions of Ernley Blackwell, the legal adviser to the Home Office, who can be said to have helped to shoehorn the Diaries into the official record, ultimately confused and mystified successive home secretaries. Thus in 1958, as the Diaries controversy reached another acrimonious crescendo, the Home Secretary R. A. B. Butler set up a 'Working Party'. That action in itself indicated departmental confusion about the conspiracy of official silence that had surrounded the Black Diaries from the moment of their discovery after Casement's capture to their partial release in 1959. On 23 September 1958, the British Ambassador in Dublin, Sir Alexander Clutterbuck, wrote to John Chadwick at the Commonwealth Relations Office to suggest that a 'waiting policy' was best:

> I am not so unrealistic to believe that, when the documents are made available to scholars, we shall not be faced with some difficulties, but we can only hope, perhaps optimistically, that with the passage of time some small measure of bitterness will have been removed from this particular controversy and that, in any event, the verdicts of the scholars will at least cancel one another out.[33]

This is a strange comment; is it an example of what is now called 'spin' for slow learners? If the Diaries had initially been part of a policy of warping the public view of Casement, then Clutterbuck's attitude seems to be that, although this had indeed been the aim, the disgrace of that policy might fade with time as the scholars predictably quarrelled over the facts. A long-term strategy might allow it all to simmer down. Obviously, admission of the Diaries into the historical record system was risky—but their continued suppression was hardly an option. Precisely because they had been suppressed in the first place, then leaked, the government had no option but to release them. Official hands were tied after their clandestine publication.

There were certainly concerns about the receipt of the Diaries into the custody of the Public Record Office in 1959 and whether they could or should be considered as public records.[34] Access to the Diaries was initially restricted. Permission to consult them had to be granted by the Home Secretary and the Home Office continued to refuse access to the documents well into the 1990s until their unfettered release under the Open Government Initiative.

Another disquieting connection exposed by the release of the papers was that between the journalist Peter Singleton-Gates, responsible for publishing the Diaries in 1959, and the head of Special Branch, Basil Thomson, a competent, Oxford-educated historian who found the Diaries. Thomson, who briefly served as Director of Intelligence at the Home Office after the war was retired from his senior job as Assistant Commissioner in Special Branch in circumstances that remain murky, and after 'committing an act in violation of public decency'. A letter from the Commissioner of the Metropolitan Police, Brigadier-General Horwood to the Permanent Under-Secretary at the Home Office, John Anderson in 1925 indicated the rancour surrounding Thomson's dismissal:

> [He] took away copies of every important document, photographs of every important personage, and transcripts of all shorthand records of every investigation and interrogation conducted by him during his official life as head of the Criminal Investigation Department and the Special Branch, which might be likely to be of interest and productive of financial gain to him as a journalist ... Every document disappeared.[35]

Every photograph published in Thomson's *Queer People,* the letter went on to explain, was 'filched from the official records', and Horwood had no doubt that Thomson was behind the efforts to get the Black Diaries published in 1925 'knowing that it would be a bit too hot to publish this book in his own name, he is in consequence utilising the services of Mr Gates, a newspaper man who calls here daily for information from the Press Bureau'. Between 1925 and his death in 1939, Thomson became an embittered and capricious publicist. He gave at least five conflicting and factually contradictory statements about the Black Diaries, their provenance and their physical appearance. The anger and irritation felt by the authorities for Thomson's actions can be understood from Anderson's reply to Horwood's letter, where he expressed a desire 'to have his [Thomson's] blood'. Thomson had held onto the Diaries while he remained in office, and while Anderson reassured Horwood that the original was in 'absolute safe custody' he commented that 'a good many copies were made at the beginning and pretty widely circulated'.

Revelation of the collusion between Thomson and Singleton-Gates enabled a radically alternative reading of the process of 'discovery', 'rumour', 'silence' and 'publication' surrounding the official version of how the Black Diaries were so conveniently conjured in 1916 and as quickly disappeared. The view endorsed by various biographers, most notably Roger Sawyer, of Singleton-Gates' 'trustworthiness' as a journalist was placed in serious doubt by this disclosure. Singleton-Gates was clearly 'embedded', and the Olympia Press publication in 1959 was not a neutral act by an independent journalist and a sympathetic publisher. Rather, it was part of a deliberate long-term strategy to confound both politicians, public and biographers about Casement's transformation from imperialist to rebel and revolutionary. The peculiar, almost mocking idiosyncrasies evident in the Olympia Press edition of the Black Diaries, notably the frontispiece photograph of Casement's nemesis, F. E. Smith, and another image of Ernley Blackwell, make sense in the light of this revelation. Singleton-Gates had remained Thomson's man and had carried their secret through to this outcome.

Media reaction to the declassification of files at the Public Record Office in the mid-1990s once again followed the 'official' line issuing from Whitehall: 'Home Office papers reveal smear against Casement' boomed the headlines.[36] Anyone who had followed the story since the late 50s knew the government had admitted this long ago. Once again Casement's 'voracious' sexploits were held up against his achievement exposing crimes against humanity—but in the popular view, the sexual stigma still overshadowed the political achievement of his work in Africa or South America. The only dissenting voice was mine. In an article in the *Irish Times*, I drew attention to the collusion between Thomson and Singleton-Gates and offered other reasons for doubting both the official narrative promoted by the archive and the traditions authenticating the Diaries.[37]

The release of the Diaries and the declassification of the Home Office files at the National Archives at Kew demonstrated the tremendous power of archives in structuring the public understanding of history. Journalists were once again privileged over professional historians to pronounce their verdict on the past. Casement remained a news story rather than an object of historical study. However, the treatment of his archive and the strategic use of the Diaries displayed ever more clearly the essential role of archives in the shaping of specific narratives and in giving priority to chosen points of view.

Too often, archives are promoted as neutral spaces where facts and history are discovered. This view has undergone serious revision in recent years; the agency of archives as instruments of power has been subjected to scrutiny and question. Ann Laura Stoler has argued that colonial archives are 'cross-sections of contested

35 This letter is held in TNA(UK) HO 144/23425 and is dated 21 January 1925. Thomson's dismissal and subsequent decline has never been satisfactorily explained, although it is clear from this letter that he was inclined to take the law into his own hands.

36 *Times* and *Guardian*, 19 October 1995.

37 *Irish Times*, 21 October 1995, 'New files fuel theory of a plot against Casement'. Letters appeared in *Irish Times* in response to the article; E. Neeson, 27 Oct.; A. Mitchell, 7 Nov.; J. Kilbracken, 15 Nov.

38 Ann Laura Stoler, 'Colonial archives and the arts of governance', *Archival Science* 2 (1–2): 2002, 87–109 (87).
39 TNA (UK) FO 743/22, 7 October 1908.

knowledge' which are themselves sites of power and 'intricate technologies of rule'.[38] Casement was an exemplary instance of an official acutely alert to the function and value of recording material. Part of the reason he rose so quickly within the diplomatic system was that he was highly conscious of the value of the written word and of the creation of records. With almost every new posting Casement reported at length on the state of the consular archive he had inherited. After arriving in Belem do Pará at the mouth of the Amazon, in October 1908, he sent a memo to the Foreign Office:

> The method of keeping confidential papers at this consulate has been a very loose one. Despatches marked separate and secret have been invariably included in the ordinary *dossier* of the series to which they may belong … I think that a separate register for all 'separate and secret' and confidential correspondence should be required by the Secretary of State to be kept at each official consulate … I have already reported the state of the 'archives' to the Foreign Office.'[39]

Casement's recommendations for the re-ordering of all consulate archives indicated how well he understood the archive as a component of the memory of the state. His writings define and redefine the boundaries between private and public, open and secret. Documents become central to legitimating the practices of the state and in shaping identity, memory and history. Casement's definitive act of subversion was to place on the official record a narrative which would forever condemn European colonialism. Furthermore, he deployed the archive for his own revolutionary purpose of bringing about the constitutional break up of the Union. For these reasons, the archive remains haunted by the spectre of one of its builders. The response to Casement's presence within the official memory of the state was various—destruction of documentation, manipulative leaking, selective access, forgery—all of them archival operations.

The Diaries Controversy

In October 1997, two years after the opening up of the Home Office files, there appeared in Dublin bookshops, on the same day, different versions of Casement diary material for 1910. Casement's biographer, Roger Sawyer, published *Roger Casement's Diaries 1910: the black and the white*. The other volume, *The Amazon Journal of Roger Casement* was edited by me. Both editions contained different versions of the diary material associated with Casement in 1910. I had originally been commissioned to collaborate with Sawyer on a comprehensive edition of the Black Diaries, and, although I had initially accepted the Inglis line on the authenticity question, the discovery of two diaries for 1910 with parallel entries for a seventy-five day period, led me to re-examine my earlier assumptions and to delve more deeply into the archive and into the political and cultural background to the forgery controversy. My underpinning research question was straightforward: how had the orthodoxy of authenticity been established and what methodology had been adopted to verify the diaries? Quite quickly I realised how dubious logic and questionable analytical reasoning had been used. As a consequence of this research, I was obliged to sever my collaboration with Sawyer, as my suspicions rose about why and how the biographers, in failing to apply a rigorous methodology to establish authenticity, had contributed to a consensus which had not in any genuine sense emerged but had been from the outset, with a degree of stealth, imposed.[40]

These suspicions can be broadly sketched. The first peculiarity was the existence of parallel diaries for 1910: two diaries recording the same daily events at a time when Casement was in extreme danger

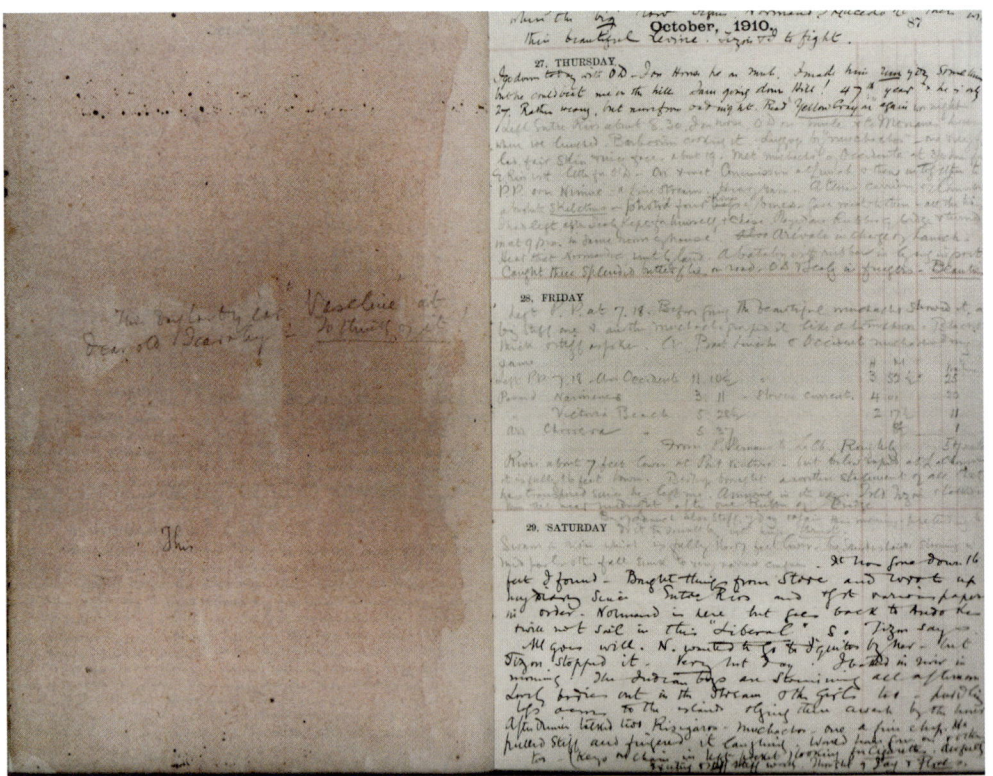

A page from the 1910 Dollards Black Diary for 27 to 29 October 1910. The mystery of the textual relationship between the parallel diaries covering the same 75-day period in 1910, detailing Casement's investigation of atrocities in the northwest Amazon, persists as the defining issue determining the authenticity of the Black Diaries. Independent comparative analysis of the inks and graphite used in the writing of these documents would contribute towards satisfying the lingering concerns about forgery.

and suffering from an acute eye complaint. Why had Casement's biographers so deliberately overlooked the longer journal in favour of the sexualized version, and why were they reluctant to even make reference to the journal which, to my mind, was the most significant piece of sustained writing by Casement surviving from his official career? Sawyer's explanation of a 'black' and a 'white' diary—one version containing pornographic references and another 'cleaned up' account—was an unlikely scenario. His view that the sexualized diary was an initial draft, aide memoire, or field notebook, from which the longer account was derived, failed to stand up to scrutiny. Further doubts arose from circumstantial concerns, textual inconsistencies and probability issues. In this comparative analysis, it is the case that the devil is in the detail and for that detail it is necessary to read *The Amazon Journal* with a forensic eye.

Additional suspicions about the Diaries' provenance, and conflicting accounts of how they were so conveniently discovered only compounded the misgivings raised by the contradictory physical descriptions given earlier by Basil Thomson. With no verifiable corroborating evidence for them, the purpose and authenticity of the diaries became for me a pressing issue, especially as their continuing propaganda value in keeping the interpretation of Casement hopelessly enmeshed in the speculations about his sexuality was so obvious. My deep comparative reading of the texts had revealed significant inconsistencies between the parallel entries and led me to the reasoned conclusion that there is a measured and coherent argument supporting the idea that the Diaries are skilled forgeries.

Further compounding my suspicions was the fact that three of the four Diaries dealt with the years 1910–11 when Casement made his two voyages up the Amazon to investigate the atrocities. Most of the alleged sexual antics occur on the Amazon, in circumstances when

40 Articles describing the contrary positions taken on the diaries were published in the *Irish Times*, 14 Oct. 1997. It inspired vigorous correspondence in the letters page. See Harriet O'Donovan Sheehy, 18 Oct.; W. J. McCormack, 20 Oct.; R. Sawyer and John McGuigan, 21 Oct.; A. Mitchell, 31 Oct.; John Garton, 1 Nov.; Séamas Ó'Síocháin, 18 Nov.; R. Sawyer, 19 Nov. & 2 Dec.; A. Mitchell, 5 Dec.; J. McGuiggan, 15 Dec.; R. Sawyer, 20 Dec.

'PHASES OF A DISHONOURABLE PHANTASY'

This 1916 cartoon showing Casement being rudely booted from a German U-Boat indicates that the British press were well aware of the strained relations between Casement and the German General Staff in the weeks before his departure from Berlin.

SIR JONAH: A CARTOON BY AN IRISHMAN

It is understood that the German submarine got orders before leaving Kiel that, whatever happened, Sir Roger Casement was not to be brought back to Germany.

Casement's movements were under constant surveillance by parties who wished him dead. The Diaries as historical documents had really very little to do with Irish history per se; they belonged to Atlantic, African and South American history. Their location within Irish history was a mere obstruction to understanding Casement's revolutionary significance. If forged, they had been deployed, successfully, to manage Casement's historical meaning. A large number of general historical studies treated the Diaries as the defining source in their interpretation of Casement. In this regard, the Diaries had deflected discussions of Casement's historical importance. His critique of empire was downplayed or ignored; for the press and the academy he provided an opportunity for voyeurism, amateur theorizing about decadence and nationalism and much scholarly posing about inks, handwriting and paper. Yet, simply by lifting one's eyes to the uncontested writings by Casement during those years, one saw more starkly by the comparison just how problematic the narrative of the Black Diairies was.

The spat with Sawyer led to some fierce reactions in the press.[41] My stated view that the forged diaries were more appropriately interpreted as homophobic documents, which located homosexuality inside a world of alienation, corruption and marginality, bereft of real emotion, provoked some strong reactions. Accepting the diaries as genuine was not to make a strike for sexual freedom but rather betrayed a foolish readiness to accept homosexuality as characteristically involved with a cruelly exploitative imperialism. I did not preclude the possibility that Casement was homosexual, but I did insist, as others had done before me, on the incompatibility of the character that emerges from the Black Diaries (akin to a predatory sex tourist who debases and objectifies the native) with the humanitarian revolutionary who fought to liberate the oppressed and whose investigative narrative was focussed on the figure of the native victim.

The renowned novelist and literary critic, Colm Tóibín, a champion of gay rights in Ireland, entered the fray and appeared to have accepted the authenticity of the diaries largely because he wished them to be true. Tóibín, like many public intellectuals associated with a 'revisionist' view of the Irish past, made Casement's sexuality the core of his significance. In his rush to proclaim a gay patriot, he overrode all methodological, archival and historiographical concerns. Later, he compared the forgery theory to a form of modern 'heresy'. In his review of the two editions of the diaries, he stressed the emancipatory potential of the Black Diaries rather than their function in constraining Casement's revolutionary legitimacy:

> The Black Diaries should be published in full so that everyone's prejudices can have a great big outing. I admire Casement more because of his Diaries. I admire the quality of his desire, his passion, his erotic complexity, his openness, his doubleness, his sexual energy.

In this comment he associated the publication of the Diaries with the liberation of the gay consciousness and as an opportunity to challenge residual (and open) prejudice within Irish society towards gay men; however, he ignored the historical context of the diaries. Homosexuality was then a crime. In 1903, the year of the earliest sexualized diary, the trial and conviction of Oscar Wilde was still fresh in the public memory, as was his flaunted association with *fin-de-siècle* decadence. Indeed, Casement's trial in 1916 has interesting parallels and connections with the Wilde trial and the Black Diaries contain specific words and expressions used in the underground world of metropolitan homosexuality at the time. Tóibín ignored how the diaries had been used to execute Casement, to humiliate his supporters and discredit his investigations of the abuse of human rights.

Tóibín's account rested uncomfortably with that of others who maintained the veracity of the diaries. Roger Sawyer revealed his own sexual politics in the *Irish Times* stating, 'I do not dislike homosexuals, but I detest buggery ... that goes for homosexual buggery too—the good Lord didn't provide

41 For reviews of the books see Colm Tóibín, 'A whale of a time', *London Review of Books*, 2 Oct. 1997; Pauric Travers, 'Not so black and white', *Tribune Magazine*, 26 Oct. 1997; Padraic O'Farrell, 'Casement's Amazon tale', *Examiner*, 15 November 1997; Mark Bostridge, 'The hanged archangel', *Independent on Sunday*, 16 November 1997; Raymond Carr, 'All put down in Black and White', *Spectator*, 22 Nov. 1997; Gerry Dukes, 'Heroic Fight against Slavery', *Irish Independent*, 6 Dec. 1997; Roy Foster, 'Forgeries or not? Never a black and white case', *Times* (London), 11 Dec. 1997; Charles Nicholl, 'Into the Dark Heart', *TLS*, 9 January 1998; Ann Sinnott, 'Did the Secret Service conspire to send an Irish Hero to his Death?', *Camden New Journal*, 5 Feb. 1998; Deirdre McMahon, 'Black Days on the Putumayo', *Irish Times*, 11 February 1998; Lucy McDiarmid, 'Martyr for Many Causes', *New York Times Book Review*, 8 February 1998; Nigel Jones, 'The Killing of Roger Casement', *Guardian*, 28 February 1998; Kieran Francis Kennedy, 'Official Secrets, Unauthorized Acts' *Irish Literary Supplement*, Spring 1998; Simon Edge 'How jolly was Roger?', *Gay Times*, April 1998; Peter Costello, *Studies: an Irish quarterly review*, Summer 1998, vol. 87: 346, 209–11; Martin Green, 'Rubber Diarist', *London Magazine*, January 1999.

Peruvian novelist, Mario Vargas Llosa made journeys to the Amazon, Congo and Ireland in order to research his fictionalised biography of Casement, *The Dream of the Celt*. Here he stands beside the monument at the iron age ring fort, known locally as McKenna's Fort, Co. Kerry, where Casement was captured by the RIC on Good Friday 1916. Photo: A. Mitchell, 27 September 2009.

for the consummation of that lust.'[42] Tóibín and Sawyer formed an unlikely alliance on the issue of authenticity. Reviewing Tóibín, Adam Mars-Jones hit the nail on the head when he commented that without the diaries 'much of what Tóibín admires in Casement would disappear'. He suggested that the continuing uncertainty around the issue of authenticity allowed entertainment of the idea that the forgery was 'inventively evil rather than merely unscrupulous—an attractive thought'.[43]

But contradictions also bedevilled the forgery school. Since Casement's execution, in the absence of the Black Diaries themselves, various theories had been developed about them. The intervention of W. J. Maloney, *The Forged Casement Diaries* (1936), endorsed various myths which had lingered for decades. Most notable of these was that the Black Diaries were actually the diaries of Armando Normand, the most criminal of all the chiefs of section employed by the Peruvian Amazon Company. In the next fifty years the forgery theory changed in shape and size through a fog of misinformation. By the early 1990s those who held on to the forgery theory were dismissed as recalcitrant, homophobic republicans and conspiracy theorists, motivated by anti-statism and historical delusions. Conversely, those who embraced the Black Diary Casement were the agents of the modern, sexually liberated, confident, historically amnesiac Ireland of the Celtic Tiger. Both accounts suffered from a spectacular disdain for the facts. Unapologetic ignorance and misinformation have always been features of the controversy.

Since the publication of the diaries in 1959, a more complex forgery theory had evolved, based upon direct analysis of them. This began with Roger McHugh's essay, the first to engage with the archival question and a prescient response to the controversy.[44] The most hardened crusader on the Casement trail during the 1950s and 60s, Herbert Mackey, produced a short pamphlet *The Truth about the Forged Diaries* (1966) shortly before his death. This sought to analyze the linguistic patterns and inconsistencies in the Black Diaries, but the analysis was rudimentary and the tone was partisan. Mackey's approach was continued by Eoin Ó'Máille, a carpenter by trade, who devoted forty years of his life to challenging the authenticity of the diaries. Ó'Máille developed a personal and vernacular methodology derived from his own interpretation based upon advances in document examination, linguistic fingerprinting and forensic discourse analysis. By the late 1990s and following the publication of the two 1910 diaries, Ó'Máille had developed a technique for deep textual analysis of the two parallel diaries for 1910. He demonstrated, in a somewhat idiosyncratic way, how warped the Black Diary narrative was.[45] He showed, for instance, how some seventy key words in *The Amazon Journal* were missing from the parallel Black Diary narrative for 1910, suggesting that the beautiful, concise and clear style of English used by Casement in his private and official writings was disfigured and mutilated into a discordant and unintelligible mess by the forger. Ó Máille is sporadically convincing, but his approach was summarily dismissed because it failed to comply with the conventions and standards of Western academic writing and was clearly influenced by the author's deep Catholic devotion. Ó'Máille's approach was also open to accusations of homophobia and his intention to 'clear Casement's name' proved impossible. Every interpretation of Casement would inescapably have a sexual dimension, often composed in unequal parts of fascination and bewilderment.

Another important intervention was made by Mairéad Wilson, a long-serving Irish civil servant in the Ministry of Agriculture who for many years had spent her lunch breaks and evenings reading through the extensive collection of Casement papers at the National Library of Ireland. In a concise argument published in pamphlet form,[46] Wilson exposed the blatant discrepancies in the diaries.

So discomfiting was her persistence that the British Home Secretary refused her access to the Black Diaries at the Public Record Office in 1990. Although Ó'Máille and Wilson did not follow academic conventions in their work, their arguments were cogent.

Support for the work of Ó'Máille and Wilson was championed by the Roger Casement Foundation, established by two Dublin-based actors, Jack Moylett and Alison Mullen, with a background in community theatre. During the 1990s they organized an annual symposium at Buswells Hotel and produced an annual newsletter summarizing shifts in the debate. The symposium became a focus for different views on Casement. Among those who regularly attended the symposium were the actor and film-maker Kenneth Griffith[47], the Irish peer Lord Kilbracken, and the gay activist and Unionist spokesperson, Jeff Dudgeon. By the end of the 1990s the re-emergence of the Black Diaries controversy, following the publication of the parallel diaries for 1910, and the new forum for public discussion about Casement's role as both Irish rebel and human rights activist had restored to him once more a role in the public imagination.

Those who had known Casement, including those who had always denied the authenticity of the diaries because they knew he was not homosexual, were by now a distant generation. After them came the generations who knew him primarily as the disputed author of the incriminating Diaries. But in the 1990s a political transformation in Anglo-Irish relationships in turn transformed the image of Casement and the issues surrounding the Black Diaries.

42 *Irish Times*, 14 Oct. 1997, Medb Ruane, 'Who owns Casement?'
43 Adam Mars-Jones, 'Wouldn't it be nice to find a gay icon who isn't a martyr', *The Observer*, 10 March 2002.
44 Roger McHugh, 'Casement: The Public Record Office Manuscripts', *Threshold*, 4: 1, Spring Summer 1960, 28–57.
45 Eoin Ó Máille, *Roger Casement: The Forged Diaries Exposed* (Dublin, 1993). For a critique of how academic writing is constructed and legitimized see A. Suresh Canagarajah, *A Geopolitics of Academic Writing* (Pittsburgh, 2002).

Political Appropriation

The Good Friday agreement was a momentous event that instantly began to commemorate itself in a Northern Ireland where the act of commemoration had always been both an act of provocation and of preservation of inherited political attitudes. The bicentenary of the 1798 rebellion, the 150th anniversary of the Irish famine and the study of Ireland's role in both the British Empire and the First World War provided a peculiar climate in which people began to sense that they were at last beginning to commemorate a future in which the past had been settled. On 25 April 1999, in a speech at the Fianna Fáil Arbour Hill commemoration, Bertie Ahern addressed the question of the Black Diaries. He was voicing on this occasion the interest of his special adviser, Martin Mansergh, a leading political architect of the peace process. Ahern stated that

> there is now a compelling *prima facie* case for a new and vigorous enquiry into the provenance and genuineness of the so-called 'Black Diaries'. The issue is not one of interpretation but of fact. The truth ought to be possible to determine, using modern forensic and analytical techniques.[48]

Responsibility for this 'new and vigorous inquiry' fell on the Royal Irish Academy (RIA). In May 2000, it hosted a lavish symposium at its elegant premises in central Dublin. Casement was discussed in relation to different realms—Africa, South America, British Empire, Ireland— and to his different incarnations, by academics, activists and interested parties. Most significantly, the event provided the first proper discussion of Casement's complicated relationship with the British intelligence services. Intelligence files released in the 1990s indicated how, on the outbreak of war, they made Casement a priority and mounted intensive surveillance operations to capture or kill him. These files demonstrated what could now be identified as a hitherto unacknowledged obsession with their treacherous consul. The doyenne of the sub-discipline of intelligence history, Christopher Andrew, and the chief historian of the Foreign Office, Gill Bennett, both talked about Casement's prickly presence in Whitehall. The most sensational moment was the naming by Owen Dudley Edwards of a possible forger, Frank E. Adcock, professor of ancient history at King's College Cambridge, and a former high-ranking member in British intelligence and devoted colleague of Admiral Hall, the spymaster and chief of Naval Intelligence.[49]

From an academic perspective, the occasion revealed considerable methodological divisions between literary critics and historians and a continuing concern for the political implications. However, despite such differences and reservations, it was a genuinely inclusive event. In summing up, Declan Kiberd applauded the 'friendly and warm atmosphere in which potentially serious differences of opinion had been negotiated amicably'.[50] Proceedings were filmed by Alan Gilsenan working on an RTÉ documentary. But the congeniality was short-lived. The RIA Symposium was followed by a lull. Martin Mansergh had made a request for the publication of further material before committing to any forensic examination. He believed it necessary to take a scholarly and holistic approach to the history of Casement's history, and to contextualize the diaries within a wider body of surviving material and draw out more work on the subject before embarking on document examination of papers, inks, etc. It was a reasonable request from a trained Cambridge historian, but one hardly likely to appease a media hungry for both spectacle and closure.

The literary historian, W. J. McCormack, filled the vacuum. In 1998, he had organized a colloquium at Goldsmiths College in London to test the water, and he

---

46 Mairéad Wilson, *Roger Casement: A Reassessment of the Diaries Controversy* (Belfast, 2005).

47 Kenneth Griffith had produced, directed and starred in a dramatized documentary on Casement, 'Roger Casement—Heart of Darkness' for BBC *Timewatch*, broadcast on 28 October 1992. The film inspired W. G. Sebald to write his chapter on Casement and Conrad in *The Rings of Saturn*.

48 Speech by the Taoiseach Bertie Ahern T.D. at the annual Fianna Fáil Arbour Hill Commemoration, Sunday 25 April 1999 at 12.45. *History Ireland* reported the section of the speech relevant to Casement in its Autumn 1999 edition. For an example of editorial opinion, after 'mature reflection', see *Sunday Business Post*, 8 August 1999.

brought forty or so academics together to discuss the subject.⁵¹ Following the RIA symposium, McCormack attempted to maintain academic support while seeking a way of financing a forensic examination. He organized a second colloquium at the Public Record Office where he laid out plans to bring all Casement scholars under his wing.⁵² He took the opportunity to unveil an ambitious project entitled 'The Diaries Associated with Roger Casement', an initiative which, he claimed, would begin with a forensic examination, to be followed by the 'imaging of the five diaries preparatory to their reproduction in facsimile' and a state-of-the-art publication of the documents. When questioned on whether or not such an expensive and ambitious project would go ahead if the Diaries were in the first stage exposed as forgeries, he replied 'the documents do not lack anything in their value for the historical community whichever way the forensic matter falls'. Once forensic tests had established their authenticity, he intended to publish copies of the Diaries.⁵³ One of the principal concerns from the floor was whether such an approach would satisfy the extremes of opinion and it was agreed that a panel of international experts, rather than one particular forensic firm, should be given the onus of analysis.

McCormack's proposal was refused funding from the UK's Arts and Humanities Research Board and, to keep his project afloat, he had rapidly to start compromising his initial plan by financing the forensic examination through two television production companies. A BBC–supported Casement documentary had started production to challenge Alan Gilsenan's RTÉ–sponsored film. The two production companies, representing the state broadcasters, then entered negotiations to agree on how to co-finance limited forensic testing. Between the spring and autumn of 2001, McCormack came out in print with various articles, but rather than laying out a coherent methodology of how more informed conclusions might be reached through document examination, he had by now adopted an agenda-driven position, assuming an aggressive malignancy towards the tradition advocating forgery, while affecting a position of calculated neutrality. He contended that the 'Casement Wars' was a case of 'faith versus reason'. His approach was not to try and settle the issue but rather maintain the controversy inside its old dichotomies and appoint himself as some kind of fair-minded mediator with the power to declare winners and losers. What made McCormack's intervention glaringly problematic was that well in advance of the results of the forensic examination, he had started to publish material which clearly showed he had already made up his own mind about the outcome, based partly on personal political interests.⁵⁴

McCormack's appointment of a steering committee to oversee the forensic testing was no less problematic. His declared intention to avoid 'experts' and depend instead on those who had no apparent professional interest failed to stand up to scrutiny. One member of the committee, Siobhan Kilfeather had written a critical article on the Casement diaries several years earlier.⁵⁵ Mary E. Daly was overseeing my own work for the Irish Manuscripts Commission, and had taken on the responsibility of editing the proceedings of the conference held at the RIA. Other members were either archivists or document examiners picked from the professional bodies with most to lose in the case of an adverse result. On 6 February 2002, McCormack gave a lecture in Senate House, at the University of London in the same building as the Institute of Historical Research, where the founders of the profession of Irish historical studies had served their apprenticeship in the 1920s and 1930s. Once again, he tried to argue for an open-minded approach to the diaries, but his partiality this time was even more overtly expressed. He adopted a contemptuous stance towards the 'forgery theorists', making ad hominem attacks

49 For a memoir of F. E. Adcock see, Patrick Wilkinson, *Frank Ezra Adcock Kt., O.B.E., Litt. D., F.B.A. 1886–1968* (Privately printed for King's College, Cambridge, 1969).

50 Various reports appeared in the press, *Sunday Times*, 7 May 2000; *Sunday Independent*, 7 May 2000; *Sunday Tribune*, 7 May 2000; *Sunday Business Post*, 7 May 2000; *Irish Times*, 8 May 2000; *Guardian*, 8 May 2000; *Times* (London) 8 May 2000; 23 May 2000, *BBC History Magazine*, 1: 3, July 2000; *Irish Democrat*, August/September 2000. RTÉ radio, *Any other business*, 9–30 July 2000.

51 The Colloquium took place at Goldsmiths College on 28 February 1998. Speakers included Lucy McDiarmid, Gerard O'Brien, Roger Sawyer, Angus Mitchell, Andrew Gray, David Rose, Steve Wilson.

52 The second Goldsmiths College Colloquium entitled 'The Presence of Roger Casement' was held at the PRO on 1 December 2000. The Keeper of Public Records, Sarah Tyacke, opened the event and was followed by papers from Clair Wills, Reinhard Doerries and Jeff Dudgeon.

53 For my commentary, see *History Ireland* vol 9:2, (Summer 2001), 42–45.

both on individuals and on their family members. Any enlightened or transparent discussion on either Casement or the Diaries issue was closed down.

The following month, McCormack assembled a few members of the press and television cameras in central London to make a public announcement about the forensic tests and to distribute various statements supporting his conclusions.[56] Among those prepared to appear on the stage with him was the Warden of Goldsmiths College, the political biographer, Ben Pimlott, a close adviser to Tony Blair. In the full glare of the cameras, McCormack confidently pronounced his conclusion based on the document examination carried out by the former Metropolitan Police forensics expert, Audrey Giles:

> The unequivocal and confident conclusion which the Giles Document laboratory has reached is that each of the five documents collectively known as the Black Diaries is exclusively the work of Roger Casement's hand, without any reason to suspect either forgery or interpolation by any other hand. The diaries are genuine throughout and in each instance.

The *actual* findings of the Giles report, however, were significantly different. The only 'unequivocal' finding was the 'positive similarity and the absence of difference' in the handwriting comparisons. The most revealing aspect of the Giles report was the comment on the analysis of ink:

> Certainly preliminary examination of ink entries in these documents showed an enormous variation in the appearance of the ink deposits. I have therefore noted the physical differences of appearance and differences between inks as appropriate, leaving the question of possible further destructive analysis to be considered further.[57]

Despite the fact that no data about the inks was made available, McCormack ignored significant discrepancies in the conclusions, which demanded cautious conjecture rather than categorical public pronouncement.[58] Once peer reviewed, the report proved insubstantial and superficial on a series of levels. Methods used to examine the Diaries were rudimentary and supported by generalities, assertions and empirically unfounded conclusions. There was no identification of the range of handwritings adopted by Casement and the significant discrepancies in style and writing implements between the different populations of script in the Diaries. The approach also failed to provide a sufficient framework of standards for proving or disproving simulation. To those like myself who had kept a close eye on McCormack's intervention, the only transparent aspect of his project was his partiality.

The somewhat Orwellian ring to his proclamation was supplemented by the total dehistoricization of Casement. Beneath the flimsy absolutism of the unequivocal pronouncement lurked a host of uncertainties and unanswered questions. The emerging academic concerns regarding probability, provenance, propaganda, or the role of the archive in structuring historical memory and managing revolutionary history, were all ignored outright. Methodological complexity and historical nuance were ultimately diminished by the emulators of the television format, and the spectacle of the documentary 'special investigation' genre. There was no effort to satisfactorily explain the presence of two parallel diaries and the relationship between those specific entries. A headline-focussed press swallowed the story whole.[59] Truth was reduced to television soundbites. Once again those who argued for forgery were dismissed as atavistic republicans out of touch with the times. In the week before St Patrick's Day 2002, both documentaries screened: *The Ghost of Roger Casement* directed by Alan Gilsenan proved a critically superior film to the overtly

---

54 See W. J. McCormack, 'The Casement Diaries: a suitable case for treatment', *Hallmark: The Research Newsletter of Goldsmiths College, University of London*, Issue 8, Spring 2001, 3. In *Times Change*, Autumn/Winter 2001, 6–8. McCormack attempted to section all 'forgery theories' under the same umbrella and dismissed them collectively as 'vindicators' adding that 'vindication is an abrogation of history, a rejection of verifiable knowledge, a very Irish instance of fideism'. This article in particular showed McCormack as having a very definite agenda with regard to the outcome of the forensic examination. In the summer of 2001, he privately distributed for comment and feedback a typescript—*Ghosting*—an early draft of his monograph published by UCD in 2003.

55 Siobhan Kilfeather, 'Remembering pleasure and pain: Roger Casement's diaries', *Perversions: The international journal of gay and lesbian studies* (2: 1994), 5–22.

56 The press release was titled 'Casement diaries genuine: forensic tests end 80 year controversy'.

titillating format adopted by Paul Tilsey, the director of *The Secret of the Black Diaries*, one of the selected documentaries to launch the new worldwide digital channel, BBC Four. Tilsey's film, however, was repeatedly screened over the next eight years and proved a highly effective vehicle for broadcasting the story of the Black Diaries around the world and building global consensus on the issue of authenticity. Both documentaries concluded with McCormack's conclusive statement about the Diaries.

McCormack's methodology might have been enough to capture press attention but a healthy scepticism lingered in the air among those who were following the story at close quarters. Almost immediately matters began to unravel. The director of the RTÉ documentary, Alan Gilsenan, who was privy to the backstage antics of McCormack's steering group, commented that 'one of the unfortunate things about the forensic investigation is that it wasn't as conclusive as it might have been'.[60] However, after the heat of the controversy had abated, the startling, over-confident press headlines remained. It was not merely the flimsy nature of the Giles report, but the very choice of the document examiner herself that was now brought into question. Audrey Giles, it transpired, was a former employee of the Metropolitan Police and had worked for thirteen years for the very same organization that had discovered the Black Diaries so conveniently in the first place. That the McCormack Steering Committee had decided to place exclusive forensic control in the hands of a British forensic examiner from the very organization under investigation seemed to be more than a careless oversight.

The following month, in an effort to explore the conclusions, McCormack convened his third colloquium: 'Roger Casement: Science and Scholarship'. Several key speakers involved in the debate decided to back out, and McCormack delivered the plenary address himself.[61] While pleading that he had no preference for the outcome of the forensic tests, he did not attempt to disguise his own preconceptions and partiality, which had structured his approach from the start. His talk began by considering the scenario and political implications if the diaries had been exposed as forged. This, McCormack claimed, would have produced 'outrage in Northern Ireland' and given a huge boost to the work of Sinn Féin. He went on to attack Mr Blair and Mr Ahern who had seriously jeopardised the peace process 'by their tacit approval of opening an enquiry' and went on to link the forgery theory with militant republicanism and the IRA atrocity at Enniskillen. McCormack's suggestion was clear: Casement still constituted a threat to the present and a more informed understanding of his relevance was to be ignored; this was hardly the attitude to be expected from an academic confident in his scientific methodology.

But it was McCormack's desire to have the Giles Report peer-reviewed that caused him the greatest embarrassment. John J. Horan was an experienced document examiner with many years of practice in the New York Police Department. He had contributed a paper at the RIA symposium, where he had set out a viable road map for a comprehensive, state-of-the-art, forensic testing. In the light of the Giles report, McCormack had asked Horan to peer review her findings and asked if they would be acceptable in a US court of law. The response was decidedly negative. While expressing admiration for her professionalism, Horan strongly criticized the Giles report for failing to supply 'back up material' and the necessary data required to make it consistent with forensic evidence in US courts. Moreover, he censured her for her failure to determine the validity of the known writing and for failing to establish a proper and thorough sample from the 'known writing'. He was equally critical of the ink analysis, and pointed out that since the 1910 diaries were written in the same time periods then 'one would expect that the same ink

57 *Report of Dr Audrey Giles*, February 2002, 12. Reproduced in Mary E. Daly (ed.), *Roger Casement in Irish and World History* (Dublin, 2005) 209–10.

58 See 'Forgery or Genuine Document', *History Today*, March 2001, 16–18 for why historians should be concerned about document examination.

59 *Irish Times*, 13 March 2002; *Irish Independent* 13 March 2002; *Daily Telegraph*, 13 March 2002; *Times*, 13 March 2002; *Guardian*, 13 March 2002; *Irish News*, 13 March 2002; *Independent*, 13 March 2002; *Weekend Herald*, 16 March 2002; Irish Times, 16 March 2002; *Sunday Independent*, 17 March 2002; *Sunday Times*, 17 March 2002; *Sunday Tribune*, 17 March 2002; *Irish Times*, 21 March 2002; *The Week*, 23 March 2002; *BBC History Magazine*, April 2002. In the aftermath the *Irish Times* published letters from S. Brennan, 19 March; J. Moylett, 21 March; W. J. McCormack, 22 March; J. Kilbracken & J. Newman, 26 March; B. Keneghan & J. Moylett, 27 March.

60 *Irish Times*, 13 March 2002. Gilsenan, in an interview with Hugh Linehan, objected to the choice of the forensic examiner, Audrey Giles. Even MI5 official historian, Chris Andrew, had suggested an international panel to oversee any forensic examination.

and pencils would be used.' Horan had suggested the use of a software package 'Write On' to compare large collections of written material. Instead the conclusions had been based predominantly on subjective comparison of populations of handwriting by Giles. Horan concluded by saying that he would reject the report for publication in the leading journals in the field of document examination, 'because it lacks necessary details to show what was examined and how it was done'.[62] In short, Horan dismissed the Giles report as something of a simulation: enough to have generated dramatic news headlines, but utterly lacking in the professional standards and academic legitimacy expected of practised document examiners. Coming as it did several months after the dust had settled and the television documentaries had broadcast McCormack's 'unequivocal' conclusion, Horan's comments were ignored by the media. Other forensic responses revealed similar concerns.[63]

Towards the end of the year appeared McCormack's book, *Roger Casement in Death or Haunting the Free State* (2002).[64] A fundamental premise of his Lacanian reading of the controversy claimed that the accusations of forgery did not emerge until the 1930s and were a product of an Irish fascist mentality. This was purely and simply wrong. Accusations of forgery started as soon as the rumours were first circulated at the time of Casement's trial. Casement's devoted cousin, Gertrude Bannister, wrote several letters after 1916 suggesting dirty-tricks and a black propaganda campaign based upon doctored diaries. McCormack ignored all such early interventions and tried instead to sustain the argument that the forgery theory was a manifestation of the intellectual dishonesty surrounding the polarization of politics in the 1930s. He linked the Irish nationalist coterie of Casement supporters such as Bulmer Hobson and Joe McGarrity with the latent fascism of the interwar years and insisted on locking the controversy into old and discredited paradigms. His intervention neglected to either ask or answer the direct questions about both the diaries and Casement's involvement in various intersecting propaganda wars and his location within the shadow of British intelligence history. Moreover, the spitefully engineered subtext of McCormack's book confirmed him as an utterly unsuitable arbiter of the document examination. Nevertheless, his intervention was now strategically used to try and deliver closure on the issue.

In one of the few reviews, Keith Jeffrey, soon to be appointed the official historian of MI6, argued that McCormack's 'methodical investigation of Casement … ought to be the last word on the topic'.[65] Another specialist on intelligence history, Eunan O'Halpin, condemned the forgery theory as 'essentially an article of belief, not susceptible to conventional historical analysis'.[66] He stuck to the Inglis line of reasoning: why would forgers have gone to such 'fantastic lengths' when 'a single incriminating letter' would have done the trick. George Boyce, author of the Casement entry in the new *Dictionary of National Biography* argued that the McCormack-Giles report was 'surely final … proof that the diaries are genuine.'[67] Colm Tóibín suggested that 'in the light of Dr. Giles's examination, the greatest heresy is to believe that the diaries are still not genuine'.[68] Such emphatic statements, while seeking to shut down further discussion on the issue, also veiled anxieties that perhaps there was more to the forgery theory than most were prepared to admit, but did anyone need to know?

The political intervention by the Taoiseach, the symposium hosted by the Royal Irish Academy, and the competing television documentaries had helped reclaim Casement from relative obscurity and reposition him as both integral to the emergence of modern Ireland and as a critical anti-colonial voice, whose revolutionary turn had serious implications for British imperial history. The controversy had now started to unravel in a number

---

61 Events became particularly acrimonious on the second day when Professor Eunan O'Halpin refused to deliver his paper and Professor McCormack absented himself from the conference to take Professor Mary Daly to the airport. They left behind such an acrimonious and chaotic scene that Professor Katie Wales left the colloquium in disgust.

62 Two published versions of Horan's response appeared. The first was published in the *British Association for Irish Studies Newsletter*, No. 31, July 2002. A modified version appeared in Mary E. Daly, *Roger Casement in Irish & World History*, 238–42.

63 Marcel Matley, a forensic examiner from California, was hired by Kevin Mannerings to carry out an examination of the Giles Report. His paper, 'The "Black Diaries" attributed to Sir Roger Casement', was also critical of both the approach and conclusions.

64 Launched in Newman House by Ruairi Quinn, at that time leader of the Labour Party. The most scathing attacks on McCormack erupted from the desk of the Belfast pamphleteer, Brendan Clifford: 'Roger Casement: a new controversy', *Irish Political Review*, vol. 17: 10, Oct. 2002; 'Casement: A postscript on Fascism', *Irish Political Review*, vol. 17: 11; An Ulsterish Miscellany', *Irish Political Review*, Vol 18: 1.

of different directions as the floodgates of interest about Casement opened once again, as in the 1930s, 1950s and 1970s. A stream of writing about his life helped to build interdisciplinary connections between new sub-disciplines in the humanities. The acreage of print now dedicated to unpicking his meaning seemed to expand by the week and was pulled in multiple directions. Critical studies appeared on the politics surrounding his repatriation;[69] his significance to postcolonial radicalism;[70] his bearing on the archive;[71] queer readings of his gender and sexuality;[72] and his place within prison history.[73] Almost all these critical interpretations revealed the prevalent and dominant acceptance of the Black Diaries as authentic.

Among the many Casement publications to appear during this period, the most deliberately provocative was by the stalwart voice of gay activism in Northern Ireland, Jeff Dudgeon. As a devout Unionist and professed Irish non-nationalist and both veteran and architect of Northern Ireland's gay rights movement, Dudgeon took apparent pleasure in antagonizing and enflaming nationalist feeling on the Casement issue. His new version of the Black Diaries, published privately in the spring of 2002, gained academic approval following a launch by Professor Paul (Lord) Bew of Queen's University Belfast. This somewhat eccentric publication, which included extensive passages from all the disputed diaries, along with fresh interpolations and thoughtful omissions, amounted to little more than an updated and camped-up version of the 1959 Olympia Press edition, with a few original insights into Casement's early years in Antrim. Dudgeon upheld the diaries as the heart and soul of Casement's biography and used them provocatively as a means of destabilising (or queering) the martial spirit of Northern Irish Protestant nationalism and representing it as some deviant youth movement. The book baffled academics, and was as unashamedly political as it was scholastically unsound.[74]

The most searing critique of Dudgeon's book appeared in the *Irish Literary Supplement* (March 2004). The reviewer, Cóilín Owens, while once again adhering to the Inglis line on the authenticity of the diaries, found disturbing contradictions with a Casement who, on one hand, was excoriating Belgians, British and Peruvians for colonial looting while, on the other, taking advantage of local men and boys. In Owens's view the diaries condemn Casement as a pioneer of sex tourism. He also dismissed the diaries as 'repetitive, dull, almost entirely without originality … boring, tasteless, pathetic, pathological.'[75] He did not comment, however, on how the Black Diary narrative compared with entries in *The Amazon Journal* which, in contrast, are humane, innovative and critically aware, and develop in-depth characters and themes, thereby lending both authority and gravity to the narrative. Owens also criticized Dudgeon's publication for 'reinforcing the very stereotypes of the gay lifestyle that has been with us for so long: of the emotionally unstable, predatory, sadomasochistic, and promiscuous homosexual'. More problematically, he condemned Dudgeon for throwing 'a mantle of righteousness over pederasty and the sexual abuse of minors'.

Soon after McCormack's intervention in 2000, and acting on the advice of several senior Irish academics, I had decided to remove myself from the controversy rather than engage with every new polemical development. I reviewed the McCormack and Dudgeon books together, which educed an irate published response from the former.[76] Throughout this period, I concentrated on navigating a companion volume to *The Amazon Journal* through the committee stages of the Irish Manuscripts Commission. The work had been exhaustively checked for accuracy and academic honesty. At every turn there had been long and frustrating delays. The volume, *Sir Roger Casement's Heart of Darkness: the 1911 Documents*,

65 *Times Literary Supplement*, 15 November 2002.
66 *Irish Times*, 12 October 2002.
67 Boyce was also attacked from the fringes by Brendan Clifford, who published a pamphlet *The Casement Diary Dogmatists* (Belfast, 2004), a collection of essays on Casement.
68 Colm Tóibín, 'The Tragedy of Roger Casement', *New York Review of Books*, Vol. LI: 9, 27 May 2004, 53–57. W. J. McCormack responded to Tóibín in *NYRB*, Vol. LI: 14, 23 September 2004. For a critique of Tóibín's review see Barra Ó Séaghdha, 'Reviewing Casement', *Irish Review* 33 (2005), 85–95.
69 Deirdre McMahon, 'Sir Roger Casement: an account from the archives of his reinterment in Ireland', *Journal of the Irish Society for Archives*, Spring 1996 vol 3: 1, 3–12. Wesley Hutchinson, 'Roger Casement et les reliques de la république,' *Études Irlandaises*, 26–1, printemps 2001, 117–29.
70 Richard Kirkland, 'Rhetoric and (Mis) recognitions Reading Casement', *Irish Studies Review*, Vol 7: 2, 1999, 163–72. 'Frantz Fanon, Roger Casement and Colonial Commitment', in Glenn Hooper and Colin Graham (eds), *Ireland and Postcolonial Writing: History, Theory, Practice* (Basingstoke, 2002), 49–65. Luke Gibbons, 'Guests of the Nation: Ireland, Immigration, and Post-Colonial Solidarity', in *Traces 2: A Multilingual Series of Cultural Theory and Translation* (Hong Kong, 2002), 79–102.
71 Gerard O'Brien, *Irish Governments and the Guardianship of Historical Records, 1922–72* (Dublin, 2004).

endeavoured to collate as much of the surviving documentation relevant to 1911 in order to allow for an informed reading of the encrypted language of the two Black Diaries covering that year.[77] The year most closely covered by contested diary material is 1911, and, for a variety of reasons, is the key moment in Casement's final transgression from apparently loyal Foreign Office official to revolutionary Irish activist. It was the year of his knighthood and also the year when he made a return voyage to the Amazon—his most perilous and secret voyage on behalf of the Foreign Office—which was partly undertaken to prepare the extensive British interests in the region for the imminent collapse of the extractive rubber industry. Even though this book was deliberately intended to shift the contextual optic of the 1911 Black Diary narrative, its value was never deemed relevant to McCormack's test, although it might have made a valuable contribution.

The Casement story was now starting to shift beyond the antagonisms evident in the interpretation of British-Irish history. In 1998, the publication of Adam Hochschild's best-selling *King Leopold's Ghost* had reawakened public understanding of the crimes against humanity committed by the Congo Free State and had led to a flurry of reactions, which demonstrated that the issue was controversial and sensitive at an intellectual, public and diplomatic level.[78] Hochschild's account was derived from his reading of a number of scholars in Belgium, such as the former Belgian ambassador in the Congo, Jules Marchal, a debunker of long-held myths about the overly positive image of Belgium's colonial enterprise in Africa. A new generation of Belgian historians had identified an official policy to manage and mollify the memory of difficult colonial episodes.[79] The deliberate destruction of the archive by King Leopold II before his Congo territories were annexed to the Belgian state in 1908 was a well-known episode in a longer strategy to contain inconvenient truths, and a final act in a strategic policy of deception and misinformation used to manipulate public understanding of his colony.

The controversy erupted again after the screening of Peter Bate's 2003 docudrama *White King, Red Rubber, Black Death*—the reconstruction of an imaginary trial of King Leopold II.[80] What some Belgian historians were in the process of unmasking, partly influenced by recent interventions in postcolonial theory, was the extent of historical control imposed through diplomatic circles, press and educational institutions. The confusion caused by the remembering of colonial crimes and the pragmatic need to build global economic bridges between former colonial centres and frontiers caused peculiar moments of commemorative indecision. History seemed to interfere with a European intent to re-connect with Africa. While this re-engagement was driven by a wish to pacify the long and tragic civil war that had broken out after the indescribable events in Rwanda in 1994, it was fuelled by the global economic demand for the immense natural resources lying in the recesses of the African interior. Signs of the confused upshot of the meeting of postcolonial trauma, historical amnesia and economic determinism were not hard to identify. A large bronze statue of King Leopold II on horseback, erected in 1887, had lain in Kinshasa, in an open-air graveyard full of colonial statues after its removal from public display was ordered by President Mobutu Sese Seko in 1967. In 2005, efforts were made to re-erect the statue in front of the central railway station in Kinshasa. Christophe Muzungu, the Congo's Culture Minister, claimed that the people should see the positive aspects of the king, claiming that '[a] people without history is a people without a soul'. Others were not so sure. The statue was removed a few hours after being re-erected.[81] Belgium had no such anxieties. A new monument was dedicated to King Leopold II in the grounds of Tervuren Palace, his Versailles-like bastion on the outskirts of Brussels,

---

72 Kieran Kennedy, 'Who framed Roger Casement?: An Irish hero leaves a legacy of intrigue', *Linguafranca*, 10: 8, Nov. 2000, 44–53; Kathryn Conrad, 'Queer Treasons: Homosexuality and Irish National Identity', *Cultural Studies* 15: 1 (2001), 124–37; Patrick Mullen, 'Roger Casement's Global English: from Human Rights to the Homoerotic', *Public Culture* 15 (3) 559–78; Brian Lewis, 'The Queer Life and Afterlife of Roger Casement', *Journal of the History of Sexuality*, 14: 4 (October 2005), 363–82.

73 Conor Gearty, 'The Casement treason trial in its legal context', *The Irish Jurist*, vol. xxxvi (2001) 32–42; Seán McConville, *Irish Political Prisoners, 1848–1922* (London, 2003).

74 Dudgeon's book was reviewed favourably by his long-time associate in the gay rights movement David Norris in the *Irish Times*, 18 January 2003; John Bruton, *Daily Telegraph*, 28 December 2002; Christopher Andrew, *Sunday Telegraph*, 5 January 2003, republished in *Independent*, 11 January 2003.

75 Cóilín Owens, 'Queer Eye from the Irish Guy', *Irish Literary Supplement [ILS]*, March 2004. Dudgeon's response was published in the *ILS*, September 2004.

76 The review appeared in *Irish Economic and Social History*, Vol. XXX 2003, 191–92. McCormack's response was published in the *Newsletter of Economic and Social History Society of Ireland*, No.15, Spring/Summer 2004, 1–4.

77 Reviewed by Frank Callanan *Irish Times*, 31 May 2003; *Irish Independent*, 14 June 2003.

to mark the centenary of the founding of the building.

Similar disquiet underscored the Casement controversy. While there was a progressively valid, if complex, counter-argument for accepting the Black Diaries as part of the decolonization of imperial history, there was a desire not to interpret them as such. Turning a postcolonial blind eye was evident in an edited volume of documents containing the 1903 Black Diary and Casement's 1904 report, edited by the anthropologist Séamas Ó Síocháin and Michael O'Sullivan.[82] While the lengthy introduction set out a number of new insights, the work avoided reference to the disappeared diary maintained by Casement during his Congo investigation. More problematic was how the editorial line elided any discussion of the bitter war of representation that erupted when Casement's official report was published and how it was met by a sustained counterblast of pro–Leopold II sponsored propaganda that was kept alive for many decades afterwards. Support for the book offered by fellow anthropologist, Daniel Vangroenweghe, an authority on colonial Congo, further exposed a widening gulf between the approach of the anthropologist and the historian to primary sources.[83]

This gulf was rendered even more explicit by the publication of the proceedings from the conference held in 2000 by the Royal Irish Academy.[84] Edited by Mary E. Daly, a key member of McCormack's steering committee and the supervisor of my own work for the Irish Manuscripts Commission, her introduction took an ambivalent stance to the Black Diaries, an approach indicative of a continuing confusion within Irish academia about the status of the Diaries and an emerging inclination, in line with current political considerations, to maintain two traditions in confused harmony. The editor's decision to include the Giles forensic report as an appendix along with Horan's critical response was supplemented by a new report analyzing the paper (not inks) in the diaries, written by Peter Bower and 'relating to the Examination and Analysis of those diaries of Sir Robert [sic] Casement 1864–1916'. Daly's introduction opened with a reference to the American cultural critic Lucy McDiarmid and tried to tease out the different conflicting views into a contradictory whole. But much of the scholarship had been overridden by five years of debate which had elapsed since the symposium. The volume also excluded an overtly gay voice. From the 1950s, the Black Diaries had helped catalyze discussion around sexuality and whatever their historical status they would always hold a place in the cultural history of homosexuality.

But after a decade of heated debate, Ireland was suffering from Casement fatigue. As the ninetieth anniversary of 1916 opened, Casement was once more separated from mainstream historical discussion. The long delay in the publication of the RIA volume, the lack of a convincing, impartial methodology in the approach to the document examination, and the imaginative failure to engage with new postcolonial approaches to the archive and the instrumental power of history had helped to entrench an aura of stasis and confusion. Casement was now acceptable as both rebel and homosexual, but readings of his sexuality as revealed by the Black Diaries was itself undergoing a process of revision and re-evaluation. The amendments in the status of homosexuals in Ireland in 1993 had granted Casement a new legitimacy. But this was about to change. Casement's sexuality was being rebranded. He would emerge by 2005 not as acceptable homosexual, but as unacceptable pederast and/or paedophile. Once again the diaries were usefully deployed to bring about this transformation.

A memorandum circulated within the Public Record Office shortly after the release of the diaries in 1994 had referred to Casement as a 'practising paederast'.[85] At the RIA gathering in 2000, there

78 Hochschild's book was republished in 2006 and contained a personal afterword (309–18), where he described the controversy resulting from the publication of the first edition of his work in 1998.

79 See in particular Guy Vanthemsche, 'The historiography of Belgian Colonialism in the Congo', in Csaba Lévai (ed.) *Europe and the World in European Historiography* (Pisa, 2006).

80 *White King, Red Rubber, Black Death* dir. Peter Bate (2004) was also a BBC Four production. The film was reviewed in the *Times* (T2), 23 February 2004. On 24 February 2004, the documentary was broadcast back to back with *The Secret of the Black Diaries*.

81 BBC News April 14 2005.

82 S. Ó Síocháin and M. O'Sullivan, *The eyes of another race: Roger Casement's Congo Report and the 1903 diary* (Dublin, 2004).

83 Daniel Vangroenweghe published a response to the controversy 'Casement's Congo Diary, one of the so-called Black Diaries, was not a forgery,' *Revue Belge D'Histoire Contemporaine*, 2002 XXXII: 3: 4, 321–50.

84 Mary E. Daly, *Roger Casement in Irish and World History* (Dublin, 2005). The title of the volume was the same as the pamphlet produced to accompany the symposium and which contained original writings by Casement.

'PHASES OF A DISHONOURABLE PHANTASY'

85 Reader Services Department, Memorandum No 44. Compiled by B. M. Derrick. December 1994.

86 Christopher Andrew, 'Casement and British Intelligence'. Andrew made this comment at the RIA symposium in May 2000 but omitted it from his published paper included in the proceedings in Mary E. Daly (ed.) op. cit.

87 *Irish Times*, 18 August 2004. Browne also made a comment in *Irish Times*, 11 August. Browne's comments drew long responses in the letters pages of the *Irish Times* from Jeff Dudgeon, 25 August and W. J. McCormack, 2 September. In *The Village*, 10 August 2006, Browne went further calling Casement a 'paranoid, solitary, depressive and a hypochondriac. He was probably a paedophile.'

was a discernible division in his sexual interpretation. Consensual acceptance of Casement as a regular homosexual man, argued by both Brian Inglis and Roger Sawyer, was queried. Instead a new vocabulary was adopted to describe the actions apparent in the diary entries. The official historian of the British secret services and MI5, Christopher Andrew made the point:

> If the Black Diaries are genuine what we are dealing with is not simply sex between consenting adults, but sex with under age adolescents and if we operate on the assumption that the Black Diaries are not forged then there is something for which it would seem to me, despite Casement's undoubted heroism, something which we would not condone in any hero or any colleague, but of course, that depends on the view that we take of the diaries.[86]

It was Ireland's opinion-forming journalist and publisher, Vincent Browne, who emerged as the principal public intellectual prepared to make the case:

> I think it unfair to write off someone because of a perversity, however malign. I cited the case of Roger Casement. Almost certainly he sexually abused young boys. Does the fact that he abused children (or probably did so) obliterate the good he did? ... Why should recognition of the good he did imply a 'sympathy' for his abuse of young boys?'[87]

Jeff Dudgeon responded to Browne by saying that while it was more correct to use the word 'pederast' rather than 'paedophile' to describe the activities described in the Diaries was it really right to 'categorise' his behaviour in the first place?[88] Browne's view was repeated by other arbiters of public opinion. In early 2008 the condemnation of the Irish language poet, Cathal Ó Searcaigh, caused widespread public outrage when he was represented in a documentary as transgressing publicly acceptable boundaries of sexual behaviour.[89] A leader in the *Irish Times* defending Ó Searcaigh asked if those politicians and intellectuals who had suggested that Ó Searcaigh's poetry should be removed from the Irish Leaving Certificate would also 'expunge from syllabuses the study of the contributions to our history and artistic life of such famous pederasts as Roger Casement, Oscar Wilde and Mícheál Mac Liammóir.'[90] In the wake of the Ryan report, Mary Kenny—a devoted champion of the Black Diaries over the years—argued how the 'Roger Casement story shows that a good man can also be a paedophile'.[91] As Casement's name had been unintentionally used in the post-war period to help educate the public towards a more favourable attitude to homosexuality, it now seemed as if Irish journalists were in danger of becoming unwitting apologists for pederasty and paedophilia.[92] This was largely due to the failure to critically engage with the ethical issues and contradictions resulting from contemporary readings of the Black Diaries.

The confused fusion of 'black' and 'white' readings of contradictory diary material reached its apotheosis in the encyclopaedic biography on Casement by Séamas Ó'Síocháin.[93] Ó'Síocháin followed firmly in the Casement biographical tradition. Like Singleton-Gates and Girodias, Inglis, Reid, Sawyer and Dudgeon before him, he attempted once more to weave the diary narrative into the total chronology of the life. But the clouds of paedophilia and pederasty were disturbing and discomforting developments that had to be confronted by anyone entering the field. During the public debate over Casement's sexuality, which raged in the public domain between 1994 and 2005, Ó Síocháin had remained conspicuously silent and was quite clearly uneasy about discussing the matter. He went on record back in 1995 saying, 'whenever the issue of the diaries is raised it only detracts from his [Casement's] true contribution to humanity'.⁹⁴ This might well be the case, but the sexual issues raised by the controversy required, nevertheless, a mature interrogation of the sexual contradictions and not the polarized positions of either blind denial or blind acceptance, which had largely defined attitudes for over fifty years.

In a lengthy appendix to his biography, Ó Síocháin set out his case in defence of the Black Diaries. He adopted a position maintained by the former MI6 officer, Adrian Weale, and historians Christopher Andrew and Ruth Dudley Edwards, which deliberately conflated the forgery theorists with a morally conservative Catholicism that traditionally underpinned mainstream Republicanism'.⁹⁵ Those who argued for forgery were once more associated with an Irish republican tradition dismissed as recalcitrant, anti-modern and morally intolerant. He then apportioned a significant amount of space to attacking both Roger McHugh and myself for using a language about the diaries, which Ó Síocháin considered, in my case, to be 'intemperate', and in a footnote he wondered whether the employment of such language raised 'the question of the moral responsibility of the scholar in employing such language'. Presumably, this attack derived from my argument that the Black Diaries are themselves homophobic in that they associate homosexuality with insanity, illness, treason and now, paedophilia and pederasty.

Ó Síocháin's argument was partly derivative of Dudgeon's outlook that because 'the sexual life depicted in the Black Diaries is of a recognisable type'⁹⁶ then this should convince us of their authenticity. Because homosexuals were punishable under law in the early twentieth century then this could explain why none of his closest friends 'knew' and everyone was 'shocked' when the sexual truth was so sensationally publicized at the time of his trial. Of course, this line of argument was largely extraneous to the real textual issues and also allowed for avoidance of the deeper moral interrogation required of the sexualized aspects of the Diaries. It also ignored the critical context of the Diaries that configured with the moments when Casement was compiling a very definite case against colonial systems and imperial structures, and exposing them for the violence, exploitation and injustice they promote. Ó Síocháin found nothing wrong in accommodating the contradiction that while a man is carrying out a highly confidential and sensitive investigation into crimes against humanity he is able to exploit the very people he wishes to protect by divorcing principles from practice. In adopting this argument, Ó Síocháin shunned any judgment of the documents and the acts they describe. Instead, he suggested that those who have actually entered the moral minefield of the Black Diaries and dismissed them as 'homophobic documents' were building an interpretation which is simply 'in the eyes of the beholder'.⁹⁷ In this, he suffered from what Tom Inglis had perceptively diagnosed as avoidance amongst Irish historians and academics to deal with sex and sexuality directly.⁹⁸

Whatever they might have done to liberate Irish attitudes towards same sex relationships, the Black Diaries were still being used largely by the press in a disparaging, exaggerated and demeaning way to unhinge Casement's moral centre, and to serve as the prism through which the 'truths' and 'facts' extending from his life and death were refracted. This is evident, for example, in the review of Ó Síocháin's biography penned by the doyen of the Irish revisionist agenda, Roy Foster.⁹⁹ Although Ó Síocháin was quite restrained in his deployment of sexual references, Foster framed his lead review predominantly in terms of Casement's sexuality and the Black Diaries. The first third of the review dealt with a somewhat lurid examination of the controversy. His reading of the remainder of his life was punctuated with references and asides which sought to vitiate his achievements and by proxy

88 *Irish Times*, 25 August 2004.
89 Ó Searcaigh, the poet who claimed to have put the 'Gay back into Gaelic,' grew up in the area of Donegal where Casement visited for extended periods when attending the Irish college. Ó Searcaigh's own sexual formation during the 1960s had been affected by the Black Diaries and Casement was the subject of some early poems. The scandal over his sexuality erupted following the public broadcasting of the documentary film *Fairytale of Kathmandu* by Neasa Ní Chianáin in February 2008.
90 *Irish Times*, 23 February 2008.
91 *Irish Independent*, 25 May 2009.
92 The agents provocateurs of this were the opinion-formers and polemicists, Eoghan Harris and Kevin Myers writing in the *Irish Independent* on 10 February and 28 February 2008, respectively.
93 Séamas Ó Síocháin, *Roger Casement: Imperialist, Rebel, Revolutionary* (Dublin, 2007).
94 *Irish Times*, 21 October 1995.
95 See Adrian Weale, *Patriot Traitors: Roger Casement, John Amery and the Real Meaning of Treason* (London, 2001).
96 Ó Síocháin, 487.

97 Ó Síocháin, 488.
98 Tom Inglis, 'Origins and Legacies of Irish Prudery: Sexuality and Social Control in Modern Ireland,' *Éire-Ireland* 40: 3 & 4 Fall/Winter 2005.
99 *TLS*, 26 September 2008, and reply to Foster in *TLS*, 17 October 2008.
100 Ó Síocháin, 489.
101 See my article, 'The Casement "Black Diaries" Debate: the story so far', *History Ireland* Vol. 9: 2 Summer 2001, 42–45.

condemn Northern Irish nationalism, using an unnecessarily contemptuous and mocking tone. He dismissed '[t]he endless and often otiose discussion devoted to the provenance, analysis and manipulation of the Diaries', apparently failing to realize that such concerns for the authenticity of primary sources was a critical question for the discipline he both practised and professed. His review illustrated how the Black Diaries powered the engine of interpretative violence based in often crude psychoanalytical speculation. Both Ó Síocháin and Foster made clear their reliance and support for the work of Jeff Dudgeon, whose perplexing edition of the Black Diaries did much to reinstate belief in their authority, at a moment when their legitimacy was starting to collapse under the weight of unsustainable internal contradictions.

Over the years, general acceptance of the Black Diaries as the indispensable source in comprehending Casement's life had required not only an acquiescent recognition by journalists, biographers and a succession of historians and academics, but also a prolonged and negotiated insertion of the documents into the public domain. In response to the role of the British state archive in shaping Casement's biographical meaning, Ó Síocháin readily admitted how the 'import of the gradual release of fresh documentary evidence has been to strengthen the case for authenticity substantially'.[100] However, this appeal to 'fresh documentary evidence' referred exclusively to the release of British intelligence files in the National Archives (UK)—the repository where the largest number of Casement documents reside.[101] The declassification of files between 1995 and 2005 by various intelligence agencies mixed up in his surveillance, capture and interrogation had helped tidy up awkward and lingering issues to do with the provenance of the Diaries and their physical condition. The UK release also helped to re-confirm the view of Casement's unbalanced psychological state. But were these documents to be trusted? They may have helped make the history of the Black Diaries internally consistent within the UK's National Archive, but how did that consistency measure against other testimonies and other archives? Furthermore, as most of this secondary material was generated by the same department which discovered and clandestinely revealed the Black Diaries in the first place, is it reasonable to suppose that if a secret government agency was able to forge a set of diaries, then they would also be prepared to falsify a few supplementary documents to help authenticate that forgery?

The next significant intervention in this enduring saga came from Jordan Goodman, a respected British historian, with no apparent axe to grind. At the outset of his research in 2005, Goodman visited Ireland and conducted extensive interviews with me, bordering at times on cross-examination. His research adopted an open-minded approach, which could never be reproached for harbouring any hidden Irish Republican agenda. After four years of research and extensive visits to the state archives in Washington DC, the UK and Ireland, Goodman published a popular yet rigorously researched narrative account of Casement's investigation of the atrocities in the Putumayo—*The Devil and Mr Casement: One Man's Struggle for Human Rights in South America's Heart of Darkness*.[102] This located Casement's Amazon investigation at the birth of contemporary human rights history. Even though the largest part of the Black Diary narrative—the diaries covering 1910 and 1911—might have been deployed to structure Goodman's account, he chose to ignore them, and disregarded any reference to Casement's sexual double-life until a very brief reference in a paragraph at the very end of the book. 'Now that homosexuality is generally legal and acceptable, it is easier to see how irrelevant Casement's sexual orientation was to this story'. This brief statement was the excuse

Goodman made for avoiding any direct engagement with the authenticity issue or the intractable confusion surrounding his sexuality. However, a Casement stripped bare of his sexuality was a Casement few people wished to recognize.

Goodman's book was met by a blanket silence in the British press. Not a single significant review appeared in any mainstream newspaper or journal. The American edition fared little better.[103] In Ireland, Mary E. Daly contributed a lukewarm review in the *Irish Times*.[104] Ó Síocháin, Dudgeon and McCormack sat on their hands.[105] Reading between the lines of both Goodman's treatment of the Black Diaries and the combined silence of the British press and the three principal advocates of authenticity, it was apparent that Goodman's narrative had confounded expectations. When questioned about the authenticity issue following a lecture in August 2010, at the University of São Paulo, Goodman admitted that he found the whole presence of the diaries 'suspicious' and he had deliberately avoided using them in his narrative, as he felt they 'could not be trusted as sources'. It was an honest response to a vexing issue.

Goodman's retrieval of Casement into human rights history was part of an encroaching re-evaluation of Casement's writing and its relevance to the formation of a series of contingent protests which targeted both colonial labour systems and venture capitalism and was foundational to the surfacing of an international solidarity in defence of social justice. Casement's investigations and the work of the Congo Reform Association were now increasingly associated with a rising interest in the history of human rights and international humanitarian law.[106] In an analysis of the relationship between travel writing and atrocities, Robert Burroughs claimed that *The Amazon Journal* 'represents the outermost limit of antislavery travellers' embrace of political radicalism in its period: the representation of the traveller, pained and angered by the atrocities that he witnessed, and willing to trace those atrocities, and that anger, to their bases in British venture capitalism in colonised territories'.[107] Casement, E. D. Morel and the journalist H. W. Nevinson were seen as three pioneers of a new form of investigative writing of crimes against humanity, which was prepared to stand up to the excesses of the pre–First World War age and might be claimed as formative to the structuring of an ethical foreign policy later in the century.

Casement's reports and journals now appeared in new translations. His Congo Report (1904) was translated into Spanish and Italian.[108] His *Amazon Journal* and the 1912 Blue Book appeared in Spanish and Portuguese.[109] During 2010 and 2011 the vibrant Irish Studies programme in Brazil, based at the University of São Paulo, organized an exhibition and conference on Casement at the Federal University of the Amazon in Manaus and a semester-long cycle of seminars and lectures at the Centro Maria Antonia, a cultural hub in downtown São Paulo.[110] Another conference composed mainly of anthropologists was held at the University of Bogotá in Colombia. Unbridgeable differences remained in locating Casement within the multifaceted readings of empire. Robert J. C. Young opened his compelling historical overview of postcolonialism with Casement exiting the Amazon in 1910; interpreting this as a defining flashpoint in anti-colonial struggles of the twentieth century.[111] In contrast, Lesley Wylie argued that Casement's decision to return to England from that same voyage with an Amazindian man and boy was enough to suggest that 'his views on race and empire remained more or less consistent with British imperial ideology.'[112] Somewhat exceptionally for an academic article, Wylie's analysis aroused enough mainstream interest to warrant a substantial, if mildly absurd, article in the *Sunday Times* with the somewhat preposterous title 'Casement was no humanitarian'.[113] Séamas Ó Síocháin

102 In proof copy, the book was subtitled 'A Crime against Humanity'. It was published in 2009 by Verso in the UK and Farrar, Strauss and Giroux in the US
103 Greg Grandin wrote the most noteworthy review of Goodman's book in the US in the *New York Times*, 14 February 2010. His review ended with the somewhat enigmatic comment: 'Yet the devil continues to get the better of Mr. Casement.' In the same month Grandin published *Fordlandia: The Rise and Fall of Henry Ford's Forgotten Jungle City* (New York, 2009) the story of the Brazilian extractive rubber industry and Henry Ford's efforts to tame a vast region of the Amazon rainforest to use for plantation rubber. The book contained one peculiarly reductive comment about Casement.
104 *Irish Times*, 17 October 2009.
105 See my online review 'Against the Demon', *Dublin Review of Books*, Winter 2009/10.

responded with a paper defending the coherency of Casement's anti-colonial and anti-imperial thinking.[114] Insignificant though this polemic might have appeared to most people, it proved that Casement was still newsworthy a century on from the events in which he was so intimately involved.

The final word in this latest phase of Casement's historical interpretation, however, was not to be verified in the labyrinth of archival facts, but rather on the libertarian frontiers of drama and fiction.[115] Even during his own lifetime fiction was at play within Casement's interpretation. Joseph Conrad's *Heart of Darkness*, Arthur Conan Doyle's *The Lost World* and Erskine Childers's *The Riddle of the Sands*—three critical late Victorian/Edwardian novels—each connected in different ways to the real life tragedies of Casement's being. The Conrad-Casement connection became a particularly fruitful subject for academic interest and in 1995 linked Casement's name with one of the literary masterpieces of the late twentieth century, W. G. Sebald's *The Rings of Saturn*. Casement's name was embedded even more firmly in the global literary consciousness following the publication of the Peruvian novelist and essayist, Mario Vargas Llosa's semi-fictionalized biography *El sueño del celta*. Published in November 2010, a month after Vargas Llosa was awarded the Nobel Prize for Literature, the work elicited international curiosity in Casement and generated something of a publishing sensation.[116] While the novel was not elevated by the critics to the heights of Vargas Llosa's other works of historical fiction, notably *The War of the End of the World* or *The Feast of the Goat* it gained more concentrated publicity than any previous novel. Certainly, the prize helped to guarantee worldwide sales. Some 750,000 copies of the book were distributed across Spanish-speaking territories within eighteen months of publication. Translations appeared in Portuguese, German, English and other major world languages. The English translation by Edith Grossman was launched at the end of May 2012. Reviews appeared in the UK press during the week of the Diamond Jubilee of Queen Elizabeth II celebrated in Britain and throughout the British Commonwealth; however, the potentially unsettling juxtaposition between the global performance of imperial grandeur and the returning spectre of Casement was missed in the spectacle of the occasion.

The telling of Casement's story by a recognized master storyteller added a new twist to an already very twisted tale. During three years of research, Vargas Llosa visited the Amazon, Congo and Ireland: the three principal locations for the action in his novel along with the prison cell in Pentonville. While the author publicly professed to admire Casement's anti-colonial nationalism and his achievement as an initiator of human rights' investigative practices, the book was a somewhat heavy-handed effort to assimilate the glaring contradictions in Casement's life. It became a biographical pastiche: turning fact into fiction and fiction into fact. Inevitably, it placed a somewhat maladroit sexuality at the core of the story.

Vargas Llosa's reading of Casement configured, however, with the orthodox consensus developed since 1916. In a series of slightly inconsistent views about the Black Diaries in the build up to the launch, Vargas Llosa ultimately defended his acutely sexualized interpretation of Casement based on his right as a novelist. The Black Diaries frame the book. Their discovery is revealed to Casement in the opening few pages by an imaginary legal assistant. The Irish rebel emerges as a man of priapic stamina with a tendency to fantasize and exaggerate. Significantly perhaps, this interpretation mirrored the views of the police chief, Basil Thomson. Thomson, the discoverer of the diaries and the first champion of their authenticity, wrote in 1922:

---

106 Laura Izarra (ed.), *ABEI: The Brazilian Journal of Irish Studies* 12 (November 2010) dedicated an entire issue to Casement, including contributions from Jordan Goodman, Juan Álvaro Echeverri and Maureen Murphy; Dean Pavlakis, 'The Development of British Overseas Humanitarianism and the Congo Reform Campaign', *Journal of Colonialism and Colonial History* 11: 1 (Spring 2010); Ben Kiernan, 'From Irish Famine to Congo Reform: Nineteenth Century Roots of International Human Rights Law and Activism', in R. Provost, P. Akhavan (eds.), *Confronting Genocide, Ius Gentium: Comparative Perspectives on Law and Justice 7 (2011)*, 13–43; Matthew Norton, 'Narrative Structure and Emotional Mobilization in Humanitarian Representations: The Case of the Congo Reform Movement, 1903–1912', *Journal of Human Rights*, 10 (2011), 311–38; Marouf Hasian, 'Colonial hermeneutics of suspicion, the spectacular rhetorics of the Casement Report, and the British Policing of Belgian Imperialism', *Critical Studies in Media Communication*, 3, 2012, 1–17.

107 Robert M. Burroughs, *Travel Writing and Atrocities: Eyewitness Accounts of Colonialism in the Congo, Angola, and the Putumayo* (London, 2011), 132. For another insight into Casement's Putumayo investigation see Carlos Guillermo Páramo Bonilla, '"Un Monstro Absoluto": Armando Norman y la Sublimidad del Mal', *Maguaré* 22, 2008, 43–91.

108 G. W. Williams, Roger Casement, Arthur Conan Doyle y Mark Twain, *La Tragedia del Congo* (La Coruña, 2010); *Il Rapporto sul Congo*, translated by Mario Scotognella (Monterotondo, 2011).

Prison governor, Metropolitan Police Deputy Commissioner and head of the Special Branch from 1918, Sir Basil Thomson (1861–1939). Photo c. 1925. (Photo by General Photographic Agency/Hulton Archive/Getty Images)

I have often wondered since how much exaggeration there was in his [Casement's] revelations about the Congo and Putumayo. Colleagues who served with him in his official days have told me that they never took his statements quite literally. They always allowed for an imaginative colouring.[117]

Vargas Llosa's own take on the Diaries was derived from a similar position. In the epilogue to his book, while offering some passing credence to the forgery theory, he wrote: 'My own impression—that of the novelist—is that Roger Casement wrote the famous diaries but did not live them, at least not integrally, that there is in them a good deal of exaggeration and fiction, that he wrote certain things because he would have liked to live them but couldn't.'[118] If the fiction of the Black Diaries was deployed before and after Casement's death to subvert the authority of his historical legacy and the empirical weight of his investigations, fiction was now being redeployed to authenticate the simulation. Vargas Llosa, like others before him, seemed to avoid the irreconcilable

109 *Diario de la Amazonía*, translated by Sonia Fernández Ordás (La Coruña, 2011); *Libro Azul Británico: Informes de Roger Casement y otros cartas sobre las atrocidades en el Putumayo* (Lima, 2012).

contradiction that Casement's credibility as a witness to crimes against humanity and his revolutionary transfiguration was instituted upon his occupying the moral high-ground and in a fastidious determination to avoid all possible counter-accusations of hyperbole, ambiguity and imaginary invention. The art of fiction had now transformed Casement into the very antithesis of everything he had stood for in life.

'Good novels convince us that their lies are truth', Vargas Llosa had commented in his essay *The Truth of Lies*, tracking the centrality of fiction and lies in the mythologizing processes and structures of South American history. However, in this instance, the fiction did not facilitate access to the historical Casement, but merely re-inscribed a somewhat closeted understanding derived from the interpretive violence inaugurated with René MacColl's 1956 biography, and thereafter upheld in most mainstream biographical readings. Casement 'seems to be a character whose natural environment is a very great novel, not the real world.'[119] This was how the author avoided the polemic that he did not wish to face head on, and politely excused himself by invoking his status as a novelist. 'In fiction you are not limited by real facts. You can manipulate reality, you can invent without being disloyal to the essence of history.'[120] But the idea that his reading of Casement was in any way a hagiographic portrait was, to say the least, problematic. The Casement described by Vargas Llosa is not merely sexually deviant but prone to bouts of psychosis and delusional dreaming.

In the main, it has been historians with an Irish revisionist perspective, rather than literary critics, who have reviewed the book, and their judgments have been harsh, lacking the respect for Vargas Llosa evident in most Spanish and Latin American reviews.[121] Roy Foster dismissed the novel for 'over-burdened detail and a style hovering between A Child's History of the Congo and a Mills and Boon romance'.[122] Ruth Dudley Edwards felt that Vargas Llosa had 'got out of his depth when it came to Ireland and has fallen, as Casement did, for Romantic Irish Nationalism'.[123] She was indignant that a non-Irish person should so much as attempt to write about someone involved in a struggle that only Irish people like she could understand. In one candid moment she admitted that the principal reason Casement had been such an embarrassment to so many people in Ireland for so long was because of 'the secret diaries', although this did not make her doubt for an instance their veracity. Paul Bew took the well-seasoned approach and targeted the two stress points in the Casement interpretative edifice: paedophilia and pro-Germanism.[124] Diarmaid Ferriter, the author of a recent social history of Irish sexuality—*Occasions of Sin*—had blamed the contradictions evident in the interpretation of Casement's life as the fault of the man rather than his interpreters.[125] The historians agreed: Casement's story is an indecipherable palimpsest composed of infinite layers of reinterpreted opinion and myth masking a massive body of impenetrable fact.

In a more substantial review, Colm Tóibín expanded on the basic tenet of Roy Foster's analysis that this was a remarkably cliché-ridden book. He compared the style in places to the historical novels of Jean Plaidy and Georgette Heyer.[126] In analysing Casement, Tóibín's customary signifiers were there: the 'man of no mind', a 'mercurial … dreamy fanatic' and 'mad' German supporter. All these descriptive tags were subordinate to Casement's sexual energy and 'compulsion'—integral to all his thinking and action. Ó Síocháin was cited exclusively as the definitive and presiding authority on the question of the Diaries' authenticity. Any reference to the voices of dissent, those heretics still contesting the legitimacy of the official narrative, was emphatically silenced. Tóibín, however, took great exception to Vargas Llosa's revised Basil Thomson reading that Casement wrote the entries 'but did not live them, at least not integrally, that there

---

110 *Irish Times*, 4 September 2010. Separate English and Portuguese versions of the catalogue were produced for the exhibition *Roger Casement in Brazil: Rubber, the Amazon and the Atlantic World 1884–1916* (São Paulo, 2011).
111 Robert J. C. Young, *Postcolonialism: An Historical Introduction* (Oxford, 2001).
112 Lesley Wylie 'Rare Models: Roger Casement, the Amazon, and the ethnographic picturesque', *Irish Studies Review*, 18: 3, 2010, 315–30.
113 *Sunday Times*, 26 December 2010.
114 Séamas Ó Síocháin, '"More power to the Indians": Roger Casement, the Putumayo, and Indigenous rights', *Irish Journal of Anthropology* 14 (2) 2011, 5–12.
115 See for instance, Michael Laubscher, *Who is Roger Casement? A new perspective* (Dublin, 2010); Michael Carson, *The Knight of the Flaming Heart* (London, 2005); and Andrew Williams, *The Poison Tide* (London, 2012).
116 On the reception of *El sueño del celta*, see my essay, 'Peruvian Seanchaí: Mario Vargas Llosa and the Global reach of *El sueño del celta*', in Munira H. Mutran, Laura P. Z. Izarra and Beatriz Kopschitz X. Bastos (eds), *A Garland of Words for Maureen O'Rourke Murphy* (São Paulo, 2010)
117 Basil Thomson, *Queer People* (London, 1922), 91–92.
118 Mario Vargas Llosa, *The Dream of the Celt* (London, 2012), 399.
119 'An Interview with Mario Vargas Llosa', *Migration Studies in Latin America* 7: 2, July 2009, 137–43.
120 *Guardian*, 15 June 2012.

High Treason, Court of Criminal Appeal: the Trial of Sir Roger Casement 1916, by Sir John Lavery, oil on canvas, Honorable Society of King's Inns, Dublin.

is in them a good deal of exaggeration and fiction.' According to Tóibín, such a position threatened the very authenticity of Casement's sexuality, which conformed to a recognizable and recognized type of sexual behaviour among gay men and had made Casement attractive to both the literary and historical imagination in the first place. Tóibín's evaluation hints at the deepening confusion over the issue of the authenticity of both Casement and the Diaries, caught as they were in this twilight world where fact and fiction, moral purpose and amoral intent were inseparable and indecipherable.

Another literary luminary to intervene was the novelist John Banville. A decade earlier, Banville had developed a script with the director Neil Jordan for a proposed Casement film, but the project was never realised. Banville believed Casement to be the 'great disregarded hero of Irish history' and had long held a fascination for both the man and his entangled legacy.[127] On the question of the forgery, Banville demonstrated the conflicted thinking that now informed the debate. When asked about where he stood on the issue of the forgeries he claimed that 'it would have been impossible. You would have needed a team of the world's greatest novelists to put those Black Diaries together.' His comment implied that the Diaries were themselves a work of great literary merit. In making the claim against forgery, he recycled once more the old Inglis shibboleth about the lack of time to manufacture them. This widely held opinion ignored the critical fact that the extracts shown around in 1916 were physically completely at odds with the documents eventually released in 1959. The authorities actually had 43 years to perfect the look of the Black Diaries, which might also explain why Basil Thomson made so many contradictory public statements about the physical nature of the contested documents in advance of their release. Banville's argument underestimated the intellectual capabilities of the British intelligence services which, in 1914, included several distinguished men of letters and historians well able to plan and execute such a forgery in defence of the

121 The first review in English appeared in the *TLS*, 15 December 2010. Peter Kemp, *Sunday Times*, 27 May 2012; Billy O'Callaghan, *Irish Examiner*, 2 June 2012; Giles Foden, *Guardian*, 9 June 2012; Maurice Walsh, *New Statesman*, 13 June 2012; Paul Bailey, *Literary Review*, 399, June 2012; Liesl Schillinger, *New York Times*, 22 June 2012.
122 *Times*, 26 May 2012.
123 BBC World Service, *The Strand*, 31 May 2012.
124 *The Spectator*, 2/9 June 2012.
125 *Independent*, 2 June 2012.
126 *London Review of Books*, 34: 17, 13 September 2012.
127 These comments by John Banville are taken from a radio interview with Chris Donoghue on *Newstalk*, 9 July 2012. His review appeared in *New York Review of Books*, Oct. 25–Nov 7 2012, LIX: 16, 35–37.

'PHASES OF A DISHONOURABLE PHANTASY'

Sir Roger Casement (1864–1916) is escorted to the gallows of Pentonville Prison, London, 3 August 1916 (Photo by Hulton Archive/ Getty Images).

crown. Finally, in supporting Vargas Llosa's view that 'the Black Diaries are largely fantasy' Banville ignored the deeper ethical implications of what this fantasizing meant for his investigations.

Vargas Llosa's ambiguous comments about the authenticity of the Diaries and his somewhat ambivalent defence of their imagined veracity, when placed beside the academic defensiveness and public confusion, which in many ways defined the

Dublin, 1965: President de Valera attends the funeral of Roger Casement whose remains were removed from England and reburied in Glasnevin Cemetery. (Photo by McMahon/Getty Images).

debate over the last decade, were symptoms of a disintegrating secret. What the various conflicting interventions now entertained was the validity of two very distinct and opposing views of Casement and the Black Diaries associated with his name. Each view had merit. For the majority of people who believed in the supremacy and infallibility of the British state archive, the Black Diary narrative remained absolute: a self-authored conspiracy written by a misguided, indiscreet and, in the final analysis, mad, official. This view had deliberately reigned in the international, anti-colonial dimension of the Irish revolution and prevented Casement from achieving martyrdom by turning him into a sexual curio. But there was a secret history—clandestine and unofficial—revealing an alternative scenario for the Black Diaries. Partly, it must be said, to counter his own revolutionary and subversive conspiracies—which extended far beyond Ireland into transnational realms of revolutionary incitement in India, Egypt and the US—a process was set in motion in 1916 to shut Casement down through a dangerous act of historical necromancy conjured up at one of the most threatening moments in the history of the English-speaking peoples. This conspiracy was then shared at the birth of the Irish Free State and awkwardly carried through subsequent decades in the sensitive and at times shadowy negotiation of diplomatic relations between the Republic of Ireland and the United Kingdom & Northern Ireland.

This process of reining Casement in and reducing him to silence is manifest in

128 *The Irish Democrat*, August 1975, 'Roger Casement: The man they had to kill.'

John Lavery's history painting depicting the last act of Casement's trial, *The Court of Criminal Appeal*. The traitor's phantasmic face is at the vanishing point, suffocated by benches of lawyers and judges staring from beneath parapets of legal books and documents. A clock above the head of the accused is fixed ominously at the Faustian hour, five to twelve. Lavery has captured the agonizingly oppressive atmosphere of British imperial authority present in the court. From both a cultural and political perspective, the execution of Casement on the scaffold in London, on the second anniversary of Sir Edward Grey's speech committing Britain to war in August 1914, was the most symbolically-charged death of the First World War. But this was neither apparent nor comprehensible at the time. The logic of his revolutionary turn and his ignominious hanging were ruthlessly buried beneath a barrage of propaganda and public contempt. It has taken many years for different questions to be asked of his life and death.

In 1975, *The Irish Democrat* published a feature under the name 'Feicreanach', a pseudonym used by the historian C. Desmond Greaves. In a critical response to the Inglis biography, Greaves pondered: 'is it possible that we are all underestimating Casement's importance and the part he played on the stage of history?' and then speculated whether there was a more complex motive for forging the Black Diaries.[128] Greaves appeared to be alluding to the hidden histories connected to Casement: those forms of fugitive history that shadow and destabilize versions traditionally favoured by the state and disallowed by academic factions. In her classic study *Ghostly Matters*, Avery S. Gordon comments how a 'marginal discourse, the story of how the real story has emerged, consistently shadows and threatens to subvert the very authority that establishes disciplinary order.'[129] Is this why Casement remains so persistently disruptive, because he moves between so many different histories; some fugitive and secret, others transnational and authorized?

From 1904, Casement consciously fused the Irish cultural nationalist project to wider spheres of international solidarity concerned with social justice, rights and anti-colonial agitation. His reports on the extractive rubber industry investigated the hugely profitable resource critical to the triangulated nexus of Unionist power linking Belfast, Liverpool and Glasgow to the centres of capital in London and New York. The centrality of rubber in the rise of global interconnectedness has been recently reassessed in studies on the role of botanical gardens in the building of colonial space and the value of rubber to the growth of industrial mass production.[130] His official reports also disrupted diplomatic alliances and prompted new questions to be asked of colonial relations. If the Congo Reform Association bridged nineteenth-century anti-slavery humanitarianism with contemporary human rights, it also provided the last intellectual outpost for the ethical concerns of Gladstonian Liberalism, before the Liberal Party disintegrated into permanent opposition. The work of Casement and Morel in the Congo and their later stand against secret diplomacy might eventually be reclaimed as a relevant chapter in the early history of British socialism. Among those prepared to openly rally to Casement's side in the summer of 1916 were several intellectuals associated with the new Left. These included Fabians such as G. Bernard Shaw and Beatrice Webb as well as the trade union leader, Ben Tillett.

Casement's fate symbolized the crisis in the identity of Western civilization at the start of the 20th century—a crisis certainly precipitated by his revelations of slavery and atrocity, and amplified by the barbaric horrors of the Western Front. *The Crime against Europe*, his collection of essays challenging Ireland's involvement in any imperial conflict, and questioning the legality of Britain's declaration of war in 1914 was for many years dismissed as Sinn Féin propaganda. Read in the light of a century of historical interpretation, his analysis endures as an articulate and penetrating critique of the causes of the First World War, of the damaging effects of secrecy and an unregulated arms industry, and of the importance of Ireland to the political reconfiguration of European power. The arguments are rooted in a deep sense of history and the transtemporal trajectory of empires from the days of Carthage to the impending disintegration of the old imperial orders in which his own fate was ultimately entangled. Intriguingly, the essays also draw attention to the bitter history wars fought over the representation of Ireland by England. And as long as Casement's interpretation could be contained within the binaries of British-Irish history then his meaning could be hedged by the political anxieties restraining the writing of Ireland's revolutionary past. Ultimately, it proved to be Casement's internationalism that liberated him from the nightmare of Irish history.

For all the acreage of text produced, the Casement wars of 1991–2012 exposed the tenacity of his ghost. Once relocated into a transnational context rooted in the politics of rights and justice, Casement's spirit revived. As an inspirational voice among a chorus of anti-imperialist, Irish radicals his name will always be associated with James Connolly, Hanna Sheehy Skeffington, Jack White and Alice Stopford Green. His memory circulated for many years among British intellectuals sympathetic with Irish independence such as, E. D. Morel, H. W. Nevinson and C. P. Scott. Most controversially was his enduring influence upon world revolutionaries such as Leon Trotsky, Rosa Luxemburg, W. E. B. Du Bois, and Virendranath Chattopadhyaya. Casement's unifying achievement was how he had unmasked the networks of power, privilege and corruption that connected mass misery in sub-Saharan Africa, South America and Ireland to market forces, economic interests and the inequalities deriving from colonial administration. He ran guns into Ireland to arm the Irish Volunteers not as an act of brutish aggression, but to provide agency for Irish men and women to defend their rights to and hopes for self-government. His dream for Ireland was one of independence, peace and unity: a nation detached from the interests defining the deteriorating power games of European empires.

In his speech from the dock, delivered just hours before the outbreak of the Battle of the Somme—that formative flashpoint burned into the mythopoeic memory of modern Ulster—Casement challenged the motivation of Irishmen caught in the crossfire:

> We are told that if Irishmen go by the thousand to die, not for Ireland, but for Flanders, for Belgium, for a patch of sand on the deserts of Mesopotamia, or a rocky trench on the heights of Gallipoli, they are winning self-government for Ireland. But if they lay down their lives on their native soil, if they dare to dream even that freedom can be won only at home by men resolved to fight for it there, then they are traitors to their country, and their dream and their deaths alike are phases of a dishonourable phantasy.[131]

The dishonourable phantasy most often associated with his name was one he might never have imagined; others would dream it for him.

129 Avery F. Gordon, *Ghostly Matters: Haunting and the Sociological Imagination* (Minneapolis, 1997).

130 Valuable recent studies include John Tully, *The Devil's Milk; A Social History of Rubber* (New York, 2011); Joe Jackson, *The Thief at the End of the World: Rubber, Power and the Seeds of Empire* (New York, 2008); and Wade Davis, *One River: Science, Adventure and Hallucinogenics in the Amazon River* (London, 1997).

131 TNA HO 144/1636/311643/33 Rex v. Sir Roger Casement, 226.

Roger Casement on a visit to New York, 1914.

FIELD DAY REVIEW

Martimere and Brasyer Sikhs at Lucknow, 11 January 1858, where 2,000 rebel sepoys were slaughtered by the 93rd Highlanders and the 4th Punjab Regiment in Sir Colin Campbell's second attack. (Photo by Felice Beato/Getty Images)

1. John O'Leary, *Recollections of Fenians and Fenianism*, 2 vols. ([London, 1896] Shannon, 1969), I, 57.

Representing the 'Indian Revolution' of 1857: Towards a Genealogy of Irish Internationalist Anticolonialism

Amy E. Martin

In his 1896 account of his memories of the early years of Fenianism, John O'Leary describes the period between 1852 and 1858 as a fallow time in the history of nationalism and republicanism in Ireland. He writes, 'The period between the collapse of the Tenant League and the rise of Fenianism was the "deadest" time in Irish politics within my memory, and perhaps within the memory of any man now living.'[1] Indeed many historians and cultural critics would agree with O'Leary that the years between the Young Ireland movement and the

A group of Sikh sappers (combat engineers) of the Indian Army, 1858. (Photo by Felice Beato/Hulton Archive/Getty Images)

founding of the Irish Republican Brotherhood (and its North American counterpart, the Fenian Brotherhood) yielded little of interest in terms of anti-colonialism and nothing resembling the insurgency and cultural nationalism of ensuing decades. In Owen McGee's recent study of the Irish Republican Brotherhood (IRB), he identifies the 1850s as a kind of crucible for the emergence of Fenianism, even though the IRB constituted itself in 1858 against a stagnant political scene, one marked by the domination of an elitist, constitutional nationalist, anti-republican, largely bourgeois, intensely Catholic political establishment.

O'Leary, however, calls attention to an exception, a notable source of 'excitement' during this period. After dismissing the Crimean War as an event which did not engage 'the masses' in Ireland in a sustained or significant way, he explains:

> But in the next difficulty of England there was no such complication of feeling. Our feeling—that is the feelings of the great mass of Irishmen—were entirely on the side of India during the mutiny. We were altogether untouched by the thrilling stories of Indian cruelty, knowing but too well, from our own history, that England was quite sure to give as good as she got; and all subsequent and authentic accounts of the suppression of the mutiny show that we were quite right in preserving our equanimity, and that England in every sense showed herself quite worthy of her ancient fame, on this occasion.[2]

In this passage, he makes several important suggestions. To begin, he identifies the dominant British representations of the Sepoy Rebellion,[3] here 'the mutiny', as constituting what Ranajit Guha calls 'the prose of counter-insurgency', a form of historiography in which 'an insurgent is not a subject of understanding or interpretation but of extermination, and the discourse of history, far from being neutral, serves directly to instigate official violence'.[4] Therefore, O'Leary suggests a subversive practice of reading for colonial subjects, one that implies the emergence of a larger internationalist anti-imperial critique.

Just as interesting is O'Leary's further assertion that the Sepoy Rebellion stood as a model moment, a kind of potentiality for resistance to empire, even for an international solidarity between colonies. He also figures it as an event that played a significant role in the establishment of the IRB the following year. He writes:

> Here were opportunities—especially in the case of the Indian Mutiny, when Ireland was nearly denuded of troops—if only we could avail ourselves of them. But, alas! we could not. The country had not yet recovered from the physical collapse of '48, or what may be called the moral collapse of '55. She was without organization, or even the thought of organization, and so such an opportunity as we had not had for a long time before, have not had since, nor are likely to have soon again, passed away, leaving us no nearer freedom. *If Fenianism had been then, things might have been far different now; but the idea still lay more or less dormant in the brain of James Stephens, to wake up into activity, however, very soon after.*[5]

O'Leary mentions here the specific opportunity presented by the siphoning of British troops off to India during the rebellion, but we can see from his account of Irish skepticism about British propaganda that there was a general climate of anti-colonial resistance. The example of insurrection set by the Indian people could have, in more favourable conditions in Ireland, led to the creation of at least a solidarity in purpose between Indian and Irish insurgents. O'Leary argues that had a militant nationalist organization like the IRB then existed, the Union might have been overthrown and that this possibility figured in the anti-colonial republican vision of James Stephens that led to the founding of Fenianism in 1858. O'Leary's account of the significance of the Sepoy Rebellion compels a reconsideration of those years that he describes as 'dead'.

In the past decade, scholars have shown the significant attention paid to India by Irish politicians and writers of the nineteenth and twentieth centuries. For example, Sean Ryder calls attention to Irish nationalist writings in the 1830s and 1840s that engage in Irish-Indian cross-cultural comparisons. These are not only to be understood as an example of 'Irish Orientalism', but also as early ventures in the creation of an idea of

---

2 O'Leary, I, 58. This account of the importance of the Indian Mutiny is supported by historian John Newsinger who asserts that James Stephens's revolutionary strategy involved allying with the labour movement in Britain and taking advantage of England's weakness during foreign wars and insurgency within the Empire. See *Fenianism in Mid-Victorian Britain* (London, 1994), 25.

3 See several important histories of what is called alternately the Indian Mutiny, Sepoy Rebellion, or Sepoy Uprising of 1857: Thomas Metcalf, *The Aftermath of Revolt: India 1857–1870* (Princeton, 1964); Eric Stokes, *The Peasant Armed: The Indian Revolt of 1857*, C. A. Bayly (Oxford, 1986); Rudrahngshu Mukherjee. *Awadh in Revolt 1857–1858: A Study in Resistance*, rev. ed. (Wimbledon, 2002). For a collection of primary documents on the rebellion, see *Beseiged: Voices from Delhi 1857*, ed. and trans., Mahmood Farooqui (New York, 2010). In his introduction, Farooqui provides a most useful overview of the various forms of knowledge production about the uprising both in and outside of the academy. I am grateful to Kavita Datla for her advice on the historiography of 1857 and for calling my attention to these studies.

4 *Selected Subaltern Studies*, eds. Ranajit Guha and Gayatri Chakravorty Spivak (New York, 1988), 64.

5 O'Leary, *Recollections of Fenians and Fenianism*, I, 59 (my emphasis).

'The Hindoo Mother Engraved', by E. J. Portbury after H. Melville title page from *The History of the Indian Mutiny*, published in 1858. (Photo by Universal History Archive/Getty Images)

6 'Ireland, India and popular nationalism in the early nineteenth century' in Tadhg Foley and Maureen O'Connor, eds., *Ireland and India: Colonies, Culture and Empire* (Dublin, 2006), 12–25.

7 *Edmund Burke and Ireland: Aesthetics, Politics, and the Colonial Sublime* (Cambridge, 2003), 235–36.

8 See, for example, Gauri Viswanathan, 'Ireland, India, and the Poetics of Internationalism', *Journal of World History*, 15.1 (March 2004), 7–30, and Joseph Lennon. *Irish Orientalism: A Literary and Intellectual History* (Syracuse, 2004), 324–70.

political solidarity founded on the shared experience of colonial oppression, an anti-colonialism that goes beyond the specific Irish experience to embark upon a critique of empire as such.[6] Ryder focuses primarily on the Young Ireland movement and shows how indebted it was to Edmund Burke whose own writings on India, as Luke Gibbons's study of Burke suggests, 'trac[e] the lineaments of what might be seen in contemporary debates as a post-colonial ethics, one that relates to the universalism of human rights ... by means of a shared solidarity and a history of oppression, however variegated'.[7] A large body of work has by now established the serious engagements by the Cousins,[8] Alfred Webb,[9] writers of the literary revival,[10] and nationalists throughout the late nineteenth and early twentieth centuries[11] with Indian anticolonialism. Historians, most notably S. B. Cook, have documented how British authorities drew on colonial policy and practice in Ireland as a source of policy and tactics for colonial rule in India.[12] Equally, Ireland's role in colonialism in India has also been explored.[13] The struggle for Indian freedom was studied by Sinn Fein and the early Free State, although India also learned from Irish revolutionary organization,[14] especially from James Connolly's radical integration of socialist and anti-colonial thinking.[15] However, the period in question—the 1850s—remains relatively underexplored. On foot of O'Leary's assertion about the importance of 1857 to Fenianism, this essay examines Irish nationalist writing on the Sepoy Rebellion in Ireland.

From May 1857, the weekly *Nation* newspaper published a series of articles and editorials on events in India. At this time, the *Nation* was owned by the Sullivan family with A. M. Sullivan as its editor-in-chief. This proprietorship shifted the newspaper away from the anti-sectarian, republican politics and the advocacy of 'physical force' of the Young Irelanders who founded it in 1842, and moved it into the distinctly Catholic, mainstream nationalism typified by the Sullivan family itself.[16] Members of the IRB found this 'moderate' politics so abhorrent that in 1863 they established the *Irish People* as a rival organ, one that rejected explicitly the elitist, constitutional, and sectarian politics of the *Nation*.[17]

Despite this editorial shift by Sullivan, what we find in the pages of the *Nation* in 1857, on the outbreak of the Sepoy Rebellion, is a startling critique of empire. There are instances of the usual stereotypes of orientalist discourse about Indian insurgents, but they are infrequent.[18] Instead, these writings engage in an exploration of the problematics of writing the history of anti-colonial insurgency, using Irish history to illuminate events in India and to express the hope that the rebellion might serve as the first decisive blow in the fall of the British Empire. Therefore, O'Leary's brief invocation of the importance of the 'mutiny', as he calls it, to anti-colonial nationalism rightly indicates the formation of a distinct anticolonial politics in this period, a kind of prelude to the more fully developed internationalism and anti-imperialism of the Fenian movement.[19] James Stephens attacked and discredited moderate nationalists such as A. M. Sullivan, describing them as 'felon-setters', and argued that their constitutional politics was the enemy of the IRB.[20] Yet, however forthrightly the Fenians set their politics against the kind of nationalism found in the *Nation* at this time, the story is in fact more complicated than such an outright contrast would allow. The Fenian John Devoy documents the role of the Sullivans of the *Nation* in establishing a Fenian organization in Dublin. In fact, in describing their founding of the National Petition Movement to demand a plebiscite in Ireland to allow the Irish people to choose their own rulers, he asserts that 'this organization became the real foundation of Fenianism in Dublin ... [as] nearly all the members were later sworn into the Fenian Movement'.[21] Accounts such as Devoy's indicate that, despite the

9   See Jennifer Regan-Lefebvre, *Cosmopolitan Nationalism in the Victorian Empire: Ireland, India and the politics of Alfred Webb* (New York, 2009).
10 Lennon, 247–89.
11 See H. V. Brasted, *The Irish Connection: The Irish Outlook on Indian Nationalism 1870–1906* (London, 1981), and Michael Silvestri, *Ireland and India: Nationalism, Empire and Memory* (New York, 2009).
12 *Imperial Affinities: Nineteenth Century Analogies and Exchanges between India and Ireland* (New Delhi and London, 1993).
13 For a useful review of this work, see Lennon, 169.
14 Again, for a most recent example, see Silvestri.
15 For a brief and very useful discussion of Connolly's thought on internationalism, anti-imperialism and violence, see Robert Young, *Postcolonialism: An Historical Introduction* (Oxford, 2001), 293–307.
16 Owen McGee, *The IRB: The Irish Republican Brotherhood from the Land League to Sinn Fein* (Dublin, 2005), 25.
17 For a brief account, see McGee, 24–27.
18 For a history of Orientalism in Ireland, see Lennon.
19 On the international dimensions of Fenianism's anticolonialism, see Patrick Quinlivan and Paul Rose, *The Fenians in England: 1865–1872* (London, 1982), 6.
20 Newsinger, 26.
21 *Recollections of an Irish Rebel* (Shannon, 1969), 20–21.

significant differences between nationalists, as typified by the editors of the *Nation* and the founders of the IRB, there was significant overlap in their membership, institutions, and politics. This is affirmed by the fact that the *Nation* newspaper, with the widest circulation of any nationalist weekly in Ireland at this time, reached 'the great mass of Irishmen' who (O'Leary claimed) not only sympathized with the Indian insurgents but also understood them in the light of Irish history and experience.[22] Certainly many future Fenians were reading the *Nation* rather than the more moderate *Freeman's Journal* during this period. Therefore, this archive of writings on the Sepoy Rebellion occupies an important role in a genealogy of the nineteenth century critiques of empire and anti-colonialism that led to the kind of sustained internationalism[23] of the IRB and of late nineteenth and early twentieth century Irish radicals.

At times, I draw parallels between these narratives of the Sepoy Rebellion and the writings of theorists, historians, and revolutionaries working in postcolonial studies. This inevitably claims that these nationalist journalists are engaged in a kind of prolepsis, anticipating some of the central goals, concerns, and frameworks of postcolonialism. In his indispensable consideration of Ireland's colonial status and the relationship between Irish Studies and Postcolonial Studies, Joe Cleary writes: 'The kinds of scholarship referred to here clearly suggest that connections between Ireland and other colonial sites were a reasonably consistent feature of both British administrative and Irish oppositional discourses. What is still much less well established, though, is the extent to which discursive identifications between the Irish and other colonial situations remained scattered, opportunistic, and unsystematic or to what degree, or at what moments especially, they acquired systematic force.'[24] These writings in the *Nation*, I suggest, constitute one of the moments in which, under the pressure of the intense historical events in India during a six months period, comparative understandings of Ireland and India gain a kind of 'systematic force'. They do so, first, because of the influence that widely disseminated representations of a military insurrection by a peasant population would have had on Irish nationalists. (Challenging R. V. Comerford's analysis of Fenianism as a kind of leisure activity,[25] Toby Joyce identifies 1857, the year before the founding of the IRB, as a time of general military enthusiasm in Britain, an enthusiasm which in part fed into Fenianism.[26] The *Nation* articles demonstrate that a more likely source of military inspiration was the Sepoy Rebellion, which is described repeatedly in its pages as an inspiration to oppressed peoples around the globe.) Second—and my reading of this archive suggests that the question of whether postcolonial studies apply to Ireland may need to be reframed, or even set aside as irrelevant—what we can see in these writings is an understanding of colonial capitalism in the 1850s that stands as a prescient form of political knowledge, one that predates what we now call postcolonialism. My attention to this archive is in no way meant to suggest that its politics or analyses are universal or even typical. As Joseph Lennon reminds us, '[a] crosshatch of divided loyalties permeated Irish culture and its representations of the Orient'.[27] However, these writings are a significant part of the history of anti-colonialism in Ireland and they also allow us to think differently about how nineteenth-century nationalists in the period between Young Ireland and the IRB understood empire and the possibility of international resistance to it. While the writings were produced and published over only six months, their extraordinary force consists in their remarkably compelling vision of the place of Ireland and India in a world dominated by empire and capital, of violence in the process of decolonization, and the problem of writing the history of the colonized and of the non-modern, debates that remain at the center of Irish

22 In order to investigate the nationalist critique of empire that emerges in Ireland in 1857, I am restricting my archive to the *Nation*. However, these writings are part of a much wider debate in the Irish press about the Sepoy Rebellion. Jill Bender places the articles in the *Nation* in 1857 in the wider context of Unionist and conservative publications, arguing that, 'The Indian Mutiny provided an opportunity for the Irish—of all political and religious sympathies, at home and abroad—to voice their opinions regarding Ireland's position in the Empire … debate about the supposed savagery of the sepoys was adapted to suit the different agendas of nationalists and unionists', 'Mutiny or Freedom Fight? The 1857 Indian Mutiny and the Irish Press' in *Newspapers and Empire in Ireland and Britain: Reporting the British Empire, c. 1857–1921* (Dublin, 2004), 107. For a brief account of the *Nation* newspaper writings that similarly situates them as exceptional, see Silvestri, 16–17.

23 When I describe the internationalism of Fenianism, I refer to the movement's organization throughout the Atlantic basin and around the globe, its larger critique of empire, its attempts to support the liberation struggle of other colonized peoples, and its role in the radical politics of the First International.

24 'Irish Studies, Colonial Questions: Locating Ireland in the Colonial World', in *Outrageous Fortune: Capital and Culture in Modern Ireland* (Dublin, 2006), 28–29.

25 *The Fenians in Context: Politics and Society 1848–82* (Dublin, 1985).

26 "'Ireland's trained and marshalled manhood": the Fenians in the mid-1860s', in *Gender Perspectives in 19th century Ireland: Public and Private Spheres* (Dublin, 1997), 70–80, 72
27 Lennon, 167.
28 A similar debate occurred among various nationalist and unionist newspapers about the use of the term 'sepoy'. Unionist newspapers used the term to describe nationalists, and in response 'Irish sepoy' was at times employed by nationalists as a gesture of solidarity, and at other times used, in an attempt to undo the British claim to civilization, in a derogatory manner to describe imperialist 'barbarism'. For a brief account of the uses of this term in the 1857 Irish press, see *Bender*, 104–06.
29 For a consideration of the relationship between Irish nationalism and working class radicalism in the 1840s, see Amy Martin, 'Blood Transfusions: Constructions of Irish Racial Difference, the English Working-Class, and Revolutionary Possibility in the work of Carlyle and Engels', *Victorian Literature and Culture* 32 (1) (2004), 83–102. Dorothy Thompson provides a compelling account of the role of the Irish in Chartist politics in 'Ireland and the Irish in English Radicalism before 1850', in *Outsiders: Class, Gender, Nation* (London, 1993), 103–33. See also John Belchem's account of British reactionary response to the role of the Irish in Chartism in *Popular Radicalism in Nineteenth-Century Britain* (New York, 1996), 90–93, and John Saville, *1848: The British State and the Chartist Movement* (Cambridge, 1987).

Studies and Postcolonial Studies today. A re-examination of the response of the *Nation* to the 'Indian Mutiny' demonstrates what can be gained from turning back to those periods consigned to deadness and looking for emerging theorizations of a world and of a politics that have since become more fully realized.

The Battle Over Language, Representation, and History

The first mention of the Indian rebellion in the pages of the *Nation* occurred on 13 June 1857 in a lead column titled 'Military Revolution in India'. This article sets up some of the major critiques of the British press and debates about language, representation and the writing of history that would persist and be developed throughout the coming months. In a decision to foreground the politics of language in documentation and historiography,[28] the writer here rejects the mainstream British press's primary use of the term 'mutiny' and instead employs 'revolution' and 'revolutionary' throughout the account and analysis. The descriptor 'revolution' is notable in that it yokes together several historical discourses to describe and to categorize the earliest phase of Sepoy insurgency. It places Indian insurgency in a continuum of European revolution that begins with the French Revolution and continues through other revolutionary underground organizations on the Continent, particularly in France and Italy. At the same time, it links this 'military revolution' to the history of revolutionary and republican politics in Ireland and perhaps to the working-class radicalism that had played such a significant role in Britain (with important links to Irish nationalism) during the previous decade.[29] This is not to assimilate subaltern anti-colonial resistance in India to narratives of European modernity and nationalism. A sustained examination of these writings in the *Nation* suggests

that there are other important stakes in this choice. The insistence on the term 'revolution' indicates an awareness of the crucial nature of language, and especially of nomination, in anti-colonial discourse, and of the concept of representation in both its senses, textual and political. At the same time, as we will see, its deliberate use supports the sustained analysis of the relationship between empire and capital in which the *Nation* identifies the Indian revolution as one instance in a wider network of resistance to the global formation of the British Empire. Finally, this strategic description of Indian resistance serves as the foundation for a policy of violent anti-colonial insurgency as a rational political and legitimate response to the brutality of colonial domination. This last assertion of the logic of resistance to force was the warrant for the shift to 'physical force' and militaristic nationalism that we see in 1858 with the founding of the IRB.

The articles in the *Nation* refer variously to 'revolution', 'rebellion', and 'revolt', but there is a deliberate effort to avoid the term 'mutiny'. For example, on 8 August 1857, in a column simply titled 'Delhi', about the Siege of Delhi in June and July of that year, the writer analyzes the tendency of the British press to minimize and to dismiss the insurgency by describing it as 'mutiny':

> Meantime the English journals make believe that the business is by no means so bad. While their real opinion is a perfect panic, the journals, the *Times* especially, all pretend that the insurrection does not really signify … This week, able argument is exhausted to prove that the revolt is only a military mutiny … Supposing it to be a mere military mutiny! Is the mutiny of an army larger than all the Queen of England's British forces a spark to be stamped out by Colin Campbell's heel? It would be about as reasonable to characterise a French Revolution, with the National Guard in possession

of Paris, as a military mutiny. If in the year 1798, (wherof who fears to speak?) the Irish Militia had, as they proposed to do, seized Dublin in the name of the United Irish Directory—that would have been a military mutiny, too, we suppose ... In a national revolution, where the national army goes against the people, the people must extemporise an army— but where the army revolts at their head, they only do what the population of India are undoubtedly doing.[30]

This excerpt makes clear what is at stake in the description of even the earliest events of 1857. The terms chosen imply profound assumptions or govern instrumental narratives about insurgency and anti-colonial nationalism. The writer places this episode of Indian insurgency high on an ascending scale of revolutionary action—republican, radical, and anti-colonial—that discounts the view that it is a 'mere military mutiny' but is rather a radical event with the potential for a social and political transformation. The insistence on 'revolution' and 'revolt' in this series initiates what became an enduring refusal of those imperial narratives that, by categorizing the event as a 'mutiny', already have defined it as a spasmodic, unorganized, limited resistance to military authority on the part of small groups of soldiers. The 'Delhi' series also anticipates later claims that the insurgency was not only widespread but highly organized, pointing out that soldiers acted in 'perfect concert and cohesion'.[31]

In addition, this narrative locates the origin of the revolution not in the army but in 'the people'. This claim, again rejecting a fundamental feature of contemporaneous accounts of 'the Mutiny', when integrated into a synoptic theoretical account of imperialism, anticipates a basic and contested component of the critiques of imperialist and elitist historiography by the Subaltern Studies collective. The project of decolonizing Indian history for them begins in the very process of its writing.[32] Unlike the work of scholars in the tradition of Subaltern Studies, 'Delhi' and other articles like it do not critique the nation form but rather invest in it, seeking at times to read the 1857 insurgency as a form of nationalism or the emergence of 'Indian nationality'.[33] In fact, by 3 October, in an article titled 'The British Liar', the *Nation* condemned the *Times* for its 'fraudulent congratulation, that the Indian catastrophe is a military mutiny, not a *national revolt*'.[34] In the quoted passage, the emphasis on 'the people' as the source of resistance and insurgency and as the agents of history, and the soldiers as no more than the expression of the popular will, exposes the key transition in the nationalist, anti-Mutiny accounts. The repeated slippage between 'the people' and 'the nation' (and notably 'the people' are invoked far more frequently than 'the nation'), confirms David Lloyd's insight that 'it is a paradox of nationalism that though it may often summon into being a "people" which is to form and subtend the nation-state, it is always confronted with that people as a potentially disruptive *excess* over the nation and its state.'[35] As we will see, the invocation of a national subject is not sustained and comes into conflict with other categories such as 'peasant'. This vision of 'the people' as the subject of history, suggests a politics that may disrupt, challenge, exceed, or exist in a productive tension with the very nationalism of which it is a part.

Early articles during the summer of 1857 surmise that, even if the initial revolt took place among soldiers, it would 'quickly spread to the people; and should this occur England may bid a lasting farewell to India'.[36] However, this understanding of the path the 'revolution' took is quickly reversed. By 4 July, insurgency is declared to have had its origins not just in the people but specifically in the peasantry:

Indeed it is very evident that disaffection is not confined to the Sepoy—that he

30 The *Nation*, 8 August 1857, 792.
31 The *Nation*, 18 July 1857, 744.
32 For a useful account of the project of Subaltern Studies from a central member of the group, see Dipesh Chakrabarty, 'A Small History of Subaltern Studies.' in *Habitations of Modernity: Essays in the Wake of Subaltern Studies* (Chicago, 2002), 3–19.
33 The *Nation*, 12 September 1857, 25.
34 The *Nation*, 3 October 1857, 73 (*my emphasis*).
35 *Ireland After History* (Notre Dame, 1999), 33.
36 The *Nation*, 13 June 1857, 664. Although there was no way for the writers of the *Nation* to be sure of this, their account of the spread of revolt is very much in keeping with the account provided by, for example, Rudrangshu Mukherjee. See his introduction to the second edition of *Awadh in Revolt*, Chapters 3 and 4.

REPRESENTING THE 'INDIAN REVOLUTION' OF 1857:

Eastward Ho! (1859), by Henry Nelson O'Neil, depicts British soldiers boarding a ship at Tilbury, England to fight against the Indian Mutiny of 1857. Located in: Museum of London. © The Gallery Collection/Corbis

would never, possibly have renounced his allegiance to his officers without the assurance of having the sympathy and support of the general population; nay, long and deep as has been the course of outrage and indignity to which the Indian soldier has submitted, the sufferings of the people under English rule have been far greater. ... the disaffection of a century, *spreading from the peasant to the soldier*, has culminated in the terrible events which have taken place at Meerut and Delhi.[37]

The invocation of the peasant here is quite striking. It foresees important shifts

37 The *Nation*, 4 July 1857, 713 (my emphasis).

English Residents Being Slaughtered by Sepoys, Asssembly Room, Cawnpore.
© CORBIS

ENGLISH RESIDENTS BEING SLAUGHTERED BY SEPOYS, ASSEMBLY ROOM, CAWNPORE.

in the Indian historiography of the 1857 rebellion which sought to identify peasants as the agents of insurgency and of their own history.[38] Historian Rudrangshu Mukherjee reminds us that most of the sepoys who participated in the rebellion were from peasant families,[39] and so the distinction made in the passage both does and does not hold. For historians such as Mukherjee and Ranajit Guha, it is indeed difficult to make the distinction between soldier and peasant, but at the same time, perhaps the relationship of kinship, class, and culture allowed those peasants who had become soldiers to absorb the disaffection of those who had not. The accuracy of the passage is of little concern, for the writer himself acknowledges that there is no sure basis to his truth-claim. More interesting is that, while the writer's claim subverts the vision of insurgency as 'mere mutiny', it also identifies the peasantry, the group to which the majority of Irish people belonged at this time, as a potentially revolutionary class. For Irish nationalists who struggled to mobilize the peasantry throughout the nineteenth century and who lived in a nation that retained many of the economic structures of feudalism,[40] this vision of peasants as

38 For a useful account of this turn to the peasantry in Indian historiography, particularly through the work of Guha, see Mukherjee, vii–xvii. On Guha's primary argument, he writes: 'He saw them [peasants] as conscious agents working to overturn a power structure that they considered alien, exploitative and oppressive.' (xiv)
39 Mukherjee, xiv

the origin of anticolonial revolutionary struggle would have been attractive, and in fact the *Nation* articles that campaign vigorously against Irishmen enlisting in the British army draw comparisons and encourage identification between the Irish peasant boy and the sepoy. This recentering of history on the peasant also challenges the then prevailing views, in political economy and other discourses, of the Irish peasantry as idle, unproductive, atavistic, and the antithesis of modernity.[41]

Yet it is clear that the *Nation* writers ignore or are unaware of some salient features of the 1857 outbreak. Most important among these, is the fact that the sepoys were Muslims and that British policy thereafter was to reduce the number and the ratio of Muslims to other groups in the Indian army. This in itself indicates that the whole idea of a unified India eventually became a Hindu possession, although arguably it had in fact been created by the British. And the caste system that led to so many severe exclusions of the 'people' from the ruling Congress Party is in itself one of the reasons that Subaltern Studies had their startling influence in India. For there the distinction between the 'nation' (largely Hindu), and the 'people' was more durable than any comparable one in Ireland—although it certainly existed there also. Thus, while the ethical dimension of postcolonialism remains powerful, it has a very different historical inflection in India and in Ireland. Little of this was visible in the mid nineteenth century to the nationalist analysts of 1857.

As should be obvious, the alternative account of the sepoy revolution that emerges in the pages of the *Nation* is grounded first and foremost in a sustained critique of the colonialist representations and narratives against which it is written. Throughout summer and autumn, the writers of the *Nation* lament the absence of Indian narratives about the event: 'could we receive the Indians' narratives of those transactions they might perhaps appear in another light.'[42] Describing articles in the *Times* as 'falsehood', 'delusion',[43] and even 'monstrous exaggeration',[44] nationalists thus continually challenged the truth claim of the Victorian media's representations. By October, when word of the capture of Delhi by the British reached Ireland, they make the case that the British press is in fact 'a gagged press' or 'the Atrocity press'.[45] The *Nation* writers state that the press has been censored and constrained from providing any account of the revolution that is not imperialist and sensationalist. Calling attention to the history of the suspension of basic rights such as trial by jury and habeas corpus in Ireland, and following the contention of a fellow writer that there is 'one law for the oppressor, and another for the oppressed', a columnist writes in 'Gagging the Press' that

> we in Ireland know what "Freedom of the Press", in this country, means: it means freedom as long as the Government Press is able to poison and corrupt the public mind, and prevent or overpower the expression of honest opinion ... should the Government for a moment fear for its grasp upon the country—*then* we know what becomes of the vaunted Freedom of the Press.[46]

He then goes on to assert that

> the first act of the government [upon the commencement of the insurgency] was to silence the Press in India; to silence *not alone the native press but that of even the Europeans themselves [...]*! We in Ireland also know what Trial by Jury means: it means the most atrocious juggle, the most deadly weapon by which a tyrannical Government ever struck down its foes.[47]

In Althusserian terms, the mainstream British press is an ideological state apparatus which seeks to rationalize empire through the interpellation of British readers as colonialist subjects. As the call for the most extreme counter-

---

40 Terrence McDonough, 'Bulwark of Landlordism and Capitalism: The Dynamics of Feudalism in Nineteenth Century Ireland', *Research in Political Economy*, 14 (1994), 63–118.

41 See David Lloyd, 'Nomadic Figures: The "Rhetorical Excess" of Irishness in Political Economy' in Maureen O'Connor, ed., *Back to the Future of Irish Studies* (Oxford, 2010), 44–45.

42 The *Nation*, 3 October 1857, 72.

43 The *Nation*, 29 August 1857, 340

44 The *Nation*, 3 October 1857, 72.

45 The *Nation*, 24 October and 3 October 1857.

46 The *Nation*, 5 September 1857, 8

47 The *Nation*, 5 September 1857, 9 (original emphasis)

insurgent measures intensified in Britain, the writers of the *Nation* describe in detail the psychic and affective manipulation that drives this process: 'Since the days when the revolutionary sceptre of the Great Napoleon struck a terror through the British oligarchy, and it was found necessary to lash the people into fury, and influence them with hatred of the French race and name, we have had nothing to equal the inhuman animus which pervades the journals …'.[48] They read accounts of the cruelty of and murder by insurgents not so much as untrue but as deployed in very precise ways to create hatred, reinforce racism, and provoke panic in the British public.

In an article published late in 1857, 'India and the British Press', the author clarifies the exact interests served by producing this 'animus' that he and other writers for the *Nation* had condemned over several months. He contends that 'the people of England have derived but little advantage from India', which serves only the economic gain of two allied and 'closely related' oligarchies of the 'privileged classes'—a merchant 'clique, into whose pockets for a long time the wealth of the country was absorbed', and the aristocracy whose younger sons can make their fortune in India.[49] Thus the ruling classes' investment in empire explains the role of the press in representing the rebellion in ways that seek to secure the support and public opinion of the masses who otherwise have no real stake in empire.

> Hence the powerful motives which actuate the aristocracy to preserve India; hence the furious efforts made by their special press, to stimulate public feeling in England to support their interests. In short, India, in her relation to Great Britain, is, in many respects, like Ireland—a province conquered and consolidated for the especial benefit of the governing class, who fill all the public offices, command in the army, occupy fat church benefices, and reap all of the profits of conquest and annexation.[50]

This account is echoed in Marx's assertion in 1870 that Ireland is 'the bulwark of the English landed aristocracy' in that it provided them not only material wealth but also '*moral* strength'. Indeed, he argued, 'Ireland is therefore the grand moyen by which the English aristocracy maintains *its rule over England* itself.'[51] As Marx's subsequent writings on Ireland make clear,[52] not only does the sensationalist 'prose of counter-insurgency' work to secure British rule in India in the interests of a small ruling class, but it works to bind British subjects together through that counter-insurgency and through the production of panic and terror in ways that served to dissolve class consciousness and class conflict.

The writer of 'Gagging the Press' also identifies the routine suspension of rights by the state as a persistent strategy of power, even an explicit policy, of the colonial state, and he argues that this legal tactic—including the declaration of martial law—is rationalized and legitimized for the British public through newspaper writings on the rebellion. By citing examples from Irish history, for example the corruption of the process of trial by jury, the suspension of habeas corpus, and the suppression of the press, he provides an implicit theorization of the ways in which the declaration of a 'state of emergency' is crucial to the operations of British power throughout the empire; this article thus intimates a larger critique of the state form in Britain as fundamentally counter-insurgent. Eventually as reports of the torture, execution, and canon-binding of Indian rebels trickled into Ireland, the analysis that we see in 'Gagging the Press' is yoked to a recognition that British representations of sepoy revolution and of violence against British civilians operate as 'shrieks for blood'[53] and serve to condone counter-insurgent violence in its most extreme forms.[54] Another article describes the

48 The *Nation*, 5 December 1857, 217.
49 The *Nation*, 5 December 1857, 217.
50 The *Nation*, 5 December 1857, 217.
51 Letter to Sigfried Meyer and August Vogt in D. Fernbach ed., *The First International and After, Political Writings: Volume 3* (New York, 1974), 168 (original emphasis).
52 Marx was writing about the Indian rebellion and about Ireland during the same period as the *Nation* articles were published. As Joe Cleary observes, 'Ireland and India would become the two key sites for Marx's speculations on the nature of colonial capitalist development, and it was his conception of conditions in Ireland that prompted Marx's strongest comments about the regressive (rather than progressive) consequences of colonial rule', *Outrageous Fortune: Capital and Culture in Modern Ireland* (Dublin, 2007), 43. For an excellent analysis of Marx's writings on India and Ireland, see Kevin M. Anderson. *Marx at the Margins: On Nationalism, Ethnicity, and Non-Western Societies* (Chicago, 2010), 37–41 and 115–53.
53 The title of an article published on 12 September.
54 In 'The Prose of Counter-Insurgency', 64, Guha describes the official discourse as a form of colonialist knowledge which reproduces colonial relations of power in that '[t]he historian's attitude to rebels is in this instance indistinguishable from that of the State—the attitude of the hunter to his quarry. Regarded thus, an insurgent is not a subject of understanding or interpretation but of extermination, and the discourse of history, far from being neutral, serves directly to instigate official violence'.
55 The *Nation*, 12 September 1857, 25.

A political cartoon portraying the Governor General of India, Earl Charles Canning patronizing a small Sepoy soldier at the time of the 1857 uprising.
© Hulton-Deutsch Collection/CORBIS

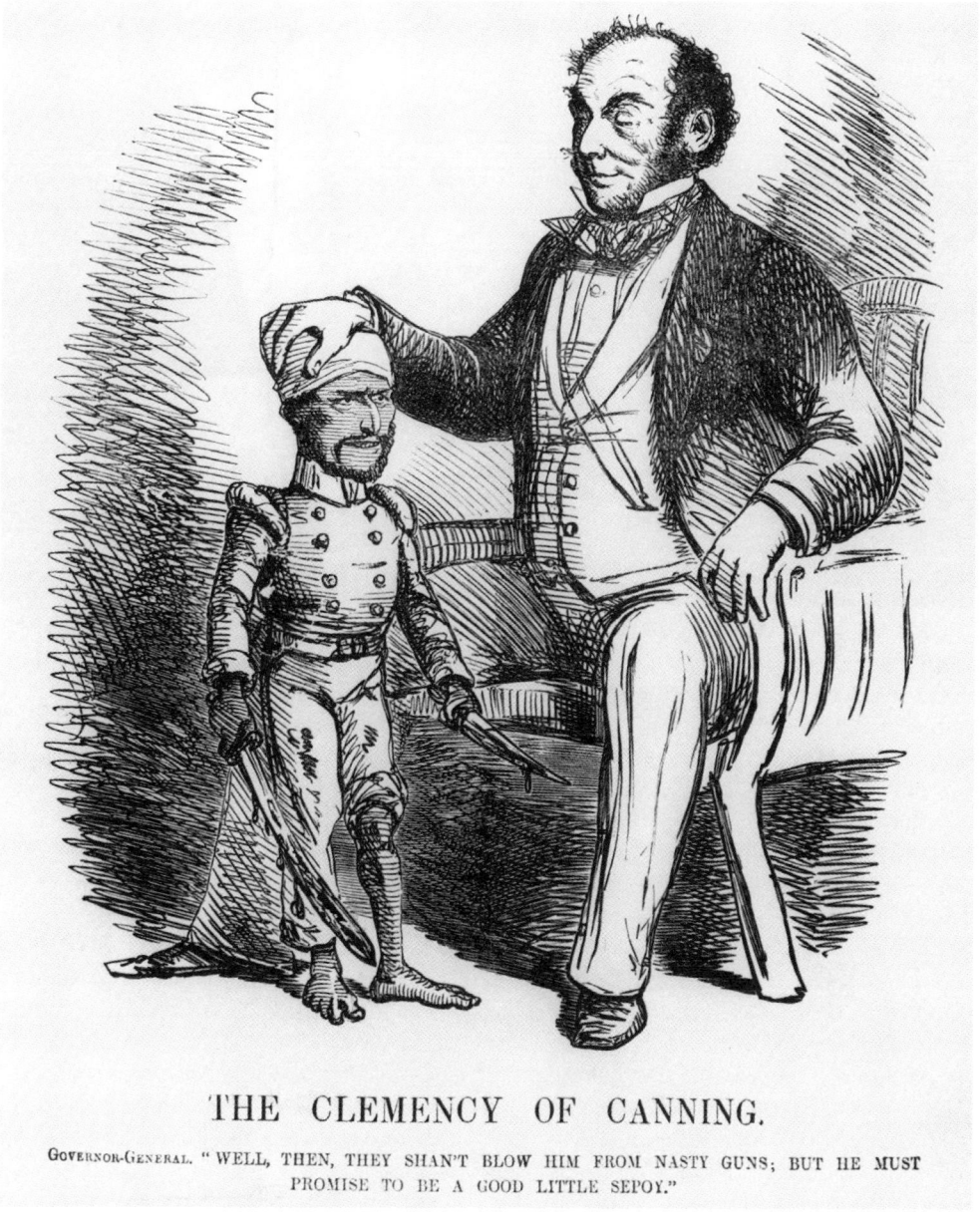

THE CLEMENCY OF CANNING.

GOVERNOR-GENERAL. "WELL, THEN, THEY SHAN'T BLOW HIM FROM NASTY GUNS; BUT HE MUST PROMISE TO BE A GOOD LITTLE SEPOY."

56 The *Nation*, 24 October 1857.

response of the *Times* to the rebellion thus: 'It is slay, slay, slay'.[55]

Nationalists insist, however, that while the violence of Indian insurgents is reported frequently and sensationalized, there is absolute silence about the repressive actions of British authorities. This observation flowers into a theorization of the writing of violence in imperialist representation and history—the violence of those colonial subjects who resist or revolt is represented hyperbolically, yet these representations call for a counter-insurgent violence about which there is then silence, which it is impossible to represent in the narrative forms of British imperialism. As one Irish writer asserts, '… a gagged press tells no tales; Sepoy atrocities may be told—or invented—but those of the British must not see the light'.[56] Writing of 'The Massacre at Delhi' on 26 November 1857, the problem of silence, amnesia, and repression in

Sepoy Rebellion (1857–58): Execution of rebellious Sepoys by British troops.
© Bettmann/CORBIS

the production of imperialist knowledge comes to the fore: 'Very possibly mankind will never be made cognizant of the entire enormity of the crime. Like the history of British rule in India, it will, for the most part, be hidden in darkness, with little other record than that of Hell itself.'[57] This chimes with the observation of Mahmood Farooqui that '[the] massacres committed by the British leave no written traces, their memory is ground to a certain amnesia, buttressed by the colonial censor on sedition and on invoking 1857'.[58] He then suggests that this amnesia posed a particular problem concerning the 'sack of Delhi'. Facing the 'darkness' of British accounts on the subject of colonial violence and the massacre of civilians in particular, the *Nation* writers identify a problematic concerning memories and histories of the rebellion for India and for historians of 1857 in general.

Indeed, the relationship between contemporaneous accounts of the rebellion and what will be the subsequent project of history-writing (nationalist or otherwise) is made explicit in these *Nation* writings. Beyond a frequent lament over the absence of Indian accounts of events, only one column attempts to provide a brief alternative history of British colonialism in India. This is framed by the following attempt to read the history of the conqueror against the grain:

> Unhappily we have only the History of the British Conquest of Hindostan by English writers. If we had also that of the Indian annalists we could come nearer the truth. At least between the narratives of the Conqueror and the Conquered it would be possible to form a fairer estimate of the transaction than with our present means we can possibly do. But even from the undeniable leading facts detailed by the former, and with all careful suppression of the numerous accessories connected with the event, we have a picture of bloodshed, perfidy, and rapine, which it would be hard to parallel in the history of this world.[59]

Nationalists seek to recover a history of colonialism that locates the origins of violence not in the race, culture and barbarism of the insurgent, but in the originary violence of colonial power. Documenting this brutality and violence

57 The *Nation*, 26 November 1857.
58 Farooqui, 4

59 The *Nation*, 11 July 1857.
60 Guha, 45–46.
61 The *Nation*, 5 December 1857, 217.
62 Guha, 46.
63 For a succinct and most useful account of how Subaltern Studies historians challenged the designation of 'prepolitical' to describe peasant insurgency, see Chakrabarty, 8–10.

is both an ethical and a political project. Empire is revealed as a global project founded in and through violence of every kind—bodily, cultural, religious, and psychic. These early attempts to write the history of 'the Conquered' through the lens of 1857, however tenuous and fragmentary, allow for a rich exploration of colonial violence in all its forms and open up possibilities for modes of representing the experiences of and writing the history of those subject to this violence.

Colonial and Anticolonial Violence

The Irish nationalist representations of colonial violence in India and the attempts to write its history as a counter-narrative to British accounts of the atrocities of 'the Mutiny' serve a double agenda. Colonialism and empire are revealed as fundamentally violent enterprises driven by and resulting in human destruction. At the same time, repeated accusations of colonial violence attempt to mount a challenge to the causes of insurgency identified by the British press. These writers seem to recognize exactly what is at stake in claims about causality in the imperialist narratives of counter-insurgency, and thus over and over they dispute the commonly accepted causes of the rebellion.

Again, the work of Ranajit Guha is instructive. 'The prose of counter-insurgency' found in imperialist, elitist, and even Marxist historiography, he has argued, represents peasant revolts, including the rebellion of 1857, as 'purely spontaneous and unpremeditated affairs'; this is often indicated by the use of metaphors drawn from nature to represent suddenness, unpredictability, and inexplicability—such as, for example, a thunderstorm.[60] In an article published on 5 December 1857, one Irish journalist works explicitly to subvert the use of such metaphors and their implications: 'If the tidings of the Indian excesses were received with a feeling of horror wherever the human heart beat, the impression, if not obliterated, was at least quickly tempered, whenever the human intellect reflected on the causes of that volcanic outburst of a trampled people'.[61] While most natural images used to describe revolt imply that it is a phenomenon not associated with 'will or reason',[62] here the 'volcanic' is understood not as natural but as political history, not as mutiny or excess or an occasion for horror but as revolutionary praxis. This attempt to claim a political rationality for the rebellion runs throughout this series of articles; the revolution, as they call it, is political rather the pre-political or apolitical. The *Nation* articles redefine the category of the political itself as it is defined in imperialist discourse.[63] The eruption of resistance is not a mark of racial savagery or irrationality, but is an accumulated response to the systemic demoralization produced by the violence, plunder, and cultural assimilation of colonialism. Empire itself is a form of barbarism rather than a manifestation of progress. Insurgency is a *necessarily* violent response to decades of psychic, cultural, and bodily violence and exploitation, a system which some writers call 'terrorism'.[64]

During 1857, journalists writing in the *Nation* tried to produce what is a fragmentary history of British violence in India, all the while acknowledging the problems inherent in challenging a field of knowledge produced almost entirely by British annalists and historians and disseminated selectively by the British press. They use two primary strategies in writing alternative history. First, in what becomes an aborted attempt at counter-history, a series of articles retell the hegemonic narrative of 'the Conquest of India', in particular the role of Clive, 'the founder of the British Empire in India'.[65] Second, the writers of the *Nation* argue that the 'excesses' of the Indian insurgents are a reaction to and reflection of British colonial violence. To this end, they use examples of colonial violence from both Indian and Irish history, engaging in a comparative, cross-cultural analysis of the experiences of colonialism in each to establish the foundational violence of empire. They dispute the causes of the rebellion as identified in the British press, seeming to recognize what many later historians of 1857 do—that the accounts of causality are political manoeuvres, central to how the events of 1857 are read and evaluated politically. As Guha reminds us, '[t]o know the cause of a phenomenon is already a step taken in the direction of controlling it. To *investigate* and thereby *understand* the cause of rural disturbances is an aid to measures 'deemed expedient to *prevent a recurrence of similar disorders*'.66 To suggest alternative causes is to challenge not only the assumptions of colonialist knowledge but also the institutional practices and forms of repression, discipline, and biopower that emerge from that knowledge.

There are many examples of impassioned arguments about the causes of the Sepoy Rebellion during 1857 in the pages of the *Nation*. The earliest article in the series, 'Military Revolution in India', begins by reminding the reader of the conditions from which the revolt emerged—that '[a]fter generations of Englishmen had become rich from rapine in the devoted peninsula, it was found necessary to organise an army from the very people they had impoverished'.67 This leads to an extraordinary passage which rejects any understanding of the soldiers' actions as purely religious:

> Nothing can be more unsatisfactory than the causes assigned by the British press for this alarming change in the Indian army. That Hindoo soldiers should entertain a prejudice against the lard and tallow with which their cartridges are greased, may be possible; but they have been brought into contact with this unholy material so long that it is rather absurd to trace their revolutionary feelings to such an origin. The causes lie altogether deeper; and it is much more rational to conclude—as, indeed, from all the late accounts from India we are justified in doing—that those men, having become conscious of their power, and seeing the country to which they are bound by the natural association of birth and religion held in a state of slavery through their means, should at length, throw aside their allegiance to those hard taskmasters from whom they have received nothing but bread and blows, and make a stand for the people from whom they are sprung.68

The writer reads the rebellion as a kind of politics of the people, a bid for justice, and a natural consequence of the injustices of British rule. He describes the condition of Indians in 1857 as one of enslavement, conjuring the moral outrage of the abolitionist as well as of the republican traditions. This also suggests that the actual causes of the Indian revolution lie in a wider, English system of imperial violence; 'England sowed cruelty and she now reaps vengeance'.69 Another declares, '[a]s the East has been the principle region in which the great national crimes of England have been committed, so it seems but just that retribution should strike her from that quarter.'70

For colonial subjects, the world is structured by and saturated with violence in every imaginable form:

> The pent up wrath of centuries; the treasured wrongs of generations; each brutal insult; each keen humiliation; each work or look of scorn that passed unresented at the moment, yet eat its way into the conquered Indian's heart, now maddens—fires—the brains; blood—rivers of Ferenghi blood—alone can wipe out the dread account. . ... It is at least one hour of supremacy for them out of years of galling subjection; at least one hour of ignominous humiliation out of a century of British conquest and aggression.71

64 For example, The *Nation*, 13 June 1857, 665.
65 See The *Nation*, 11 July 1857, 728–29.
66 Guha, 74. (my emphasis).
67 The *Nation*, 13 June 1857, 665
68 The *Nation*, 13 June 1857, 665
69 The *Nation*, 14 September 1857, 42
70 The *Nation*, 4 July 1857, 713
71 The *Nation*, 29 August 1857, 340.
72 See for example, Gibbons, *Edmund Burke and Ireland* and *Gaelic Gothic: Race, Colonization, and Irish Culture* (Galway, 2004).
73 See Frantz Fanon. 'The Lived Experience of the Black Man' in *Black Skin, White Masks*, Richard Philcox, trans. (New York, 2008), 89–119; and 'On Violence' in *The Wretched of the Earth*, Richard Philcox, trans. (New York, 2004), 1–62.
74 *Postcolonialism*, 302. Notably, Young summarizes Fanon's theory of violence in his chapter on Algeria and Ireland in *Postcolonialism*, drawing his own connections between the FLN's struggle for Algerian liberation and the politics of the Easter Rebellion of 1916 in Ireland.
75 The *Nation*, 13 June 1857, 665

REPRESENTING THE 'INDIAN REVOLUTION' OF 1857:

After their capture of Delhi the Indian mutineers lost the city to British forces who extracted swift reprisals by hanging the leaders. Two of them are hanging from a gallows. (Photo by Felice Beato/Getty Images)

76 The *Nation*, 4 July 1857, 713
77 The *Nation*, 19 September 1857, 42

This is a rewriting of the usual charges of mob madness and racial insanity so familiar in Ireland.[72] If this is madness, it is legitimate and its causes are apparent to the maddened.

It resonates with Fanon's phenomenology of racism and his subsequent argument that violence is enabling, the only means of claiming agency for the racialized colonial subject.[73] As Robert Young writes, 'Fanon transforms the historical fact that violence was the only political option in Algeria almost into a general philosophy of anti-colonialism, an existential form of colonial experience, and the means through which the colonized transcends the humiliation of his or her colonial condition…'[74] In 1857, we see a strikingly similar understanding of violence as the inevitable form that anti-colonialism will take, even if only for 'one hour' compared to the 'years or 'century' of the Empire's institutionalized system. Some articles emphasize that the system of humiliation is accomplished not only by physical violence but also by 'the Anglicising system'[75] that has 'the great object of Anglicising India' by Christianization and relentless economic exploitation.[76] Others suggest that in their violence, sepoy soldiers are simply following the example of and training provided by the British army officers who have led them—'the deadliest blow is struck at the British power by those who have been fed and trained in the English school of treachery'.[77]

In September of 1857, the by now established theory of violence and anticolonialism allowed nationalists to counter the numerous reports of the murder and torture of English civilians that filled the British press. In response, one columnist writes:

143

In India, doubtless, a number of innocent [English] persons have perished; but they are as much the victims of the English government system that created the condition which generated the impulse to those atrocious deeds as of the wretched men who committed them. The instigator to murder is as guilty in the eyes of God as he that strikes the blow, and the Government which massacres, robs, and oppresses a people until that inevitable limit is reached, when they rise and trample their tyrants in the dust, is a participator in every criminality they may under such enactions commit. The crime of the tyrant finds its exact measure in the revenge of the slave, when the period of endurance is past. and we may estimate the character of British rule in India by its present consequence. Every heart shudders over the narrative of women and children, sacrificed as they have been to the insane fury of this emancipated soldiery. The atrocities of the Sepoy are presented to us in a heap; as we number up the victims we are appalled and pained as by a blow, and tremble at the accounts of horrors … But we forget the misery to which this race have been subjected for a hundred years; nor can we realise at a glance the sufferings of a hundred millions of people for that period, or the crimes of generations of Englishmen, who have so long violated, tortured, plundered, and remorselessly tyranised [sic] over them. [78]

The argument here is typical of many articles in the *Nation* which seek to reinterpret the reports of massacre at Cawnpore and elsewhere. If the origins of violent conflict can be found in the brutality of conquest and rule, the writer argues, then responsibility for all ensuing murder is shared by 'the instigator'. In distinctly republican and revolutionary logic, the 'crime of the tyrant finds its exact measure in the revenge of the slave'.

At the same time, the counter-narrative works to extend the pathos afforded the British victims of insurgency to those who have 'been subjected for a hundred years' during which insurgents were tortured and executed for acts of insurgency deemed criminal. The writers of the *Nation* go to great pains never to suggest that the civilian victims of insurgent violence are appropriate targets and even write of their horror at some of the reports. They seek instead to place these acts in a wider context of the complex, relentless forms of violence and counter-violence that are foundational to colonial rule.

Such counter-narratives are often bolstered by references to Irish history.[79] In a remarkable series of historical associations, an article on Cawnpore claims: '[f]or the massacre at Cawnpore, we can find an exact example in CROMWELL's conduct at Wexford—and the revolting outrages of British soldiers at Kertch and Bushire, are of late memory'.[80] These comparisons serve multiple political purposes. They mobilize sympathy for colonized subjects or other victims of British violence in Ireland, Iran, Crimea, and India as a kind of counterbalance to sympathy for those killed at the hands of Indian insurgents. This network of atrocities is eventually described as a 'system':

> They [sepoy atrocities] *are* a system, and this it is which invests them with so horrible a singularity; but, horrible as they are, there is no use in concealing the fact that they are the retaliation of a system equally diabolical. If the Sepoys have trampled upon every law, human and divine, they have only followed the example continually set them by the English for the last century.[81]

78 The *Nation*, 12 September 1857, 25
79 For another example, see 'Atrocities of the British—Slaughter of Women and Children', which sets contemporary accounts of the murder of women and children by rebels against accounts of the murder and torture of men, women, children, and priests during the suppression of the rebellion of 1798. The *Nation*, 5 September 1857, 11.
80 The *Nation*, 22 August 1857, 324.
81 The *Nation*, 17 October 1857, 104.
82 Dugger, Julie M., 'Black Ireland's Race: Thomas Carlyle and the Young Ireland Movement', *Victorian Studies* 48 (3) (Spring 2006), 461–85. See also, Richard Davis, *The Young Ireland Movement* (Dublin, 1987).

'Tragical Adventure in the Subseemundee—sketched by Captain G. F. Atkinson', *Illustrated London News*, October 10, 1857

83   See *Chartism* in *The Works of Thomas Carlyle*, Centenary ed. (London, 1899), 29. Both Engels and Marx drew on Carlyle's critique of capitalism in their own work.

84   *The Nation*, 19 September 1857, 43 and 46.

Empire as Global Economic System and A Vision of Internationalist Resistance: Towards A Conclusion

The writers of the *Nation* are clear throughout the pages of writings on the rebellion that the British Empire is a global system that is fundamentally economic and exploitative. This is not to suggest that they were proto-Marxists or socialists. On the contrary, the Sullivans and most of the nationalists who wrote for them were rather conservative concerning economics and class politics, and some hoped to transfer power in Ireland, once wrested from the British, to an Irish Catholic elite. However, most still understood the tenant-landlord system in Ireland as a corrupt economic system of accumulation. In addition, as we know from the example of Thomas Carlyle, whose influence on Irish nationalists is well-documented,[82] profoundly conservative thinkers could recognize the excesses and exploitation inherent in the capitalist mode of production.[83] Therefore, the newspaper's repeated recognition of the Empire as a manifestation of the pure greed of British capitalism and its ruling classes seems significant when one considers the radicalism and anti-capitalism that ran through various incarnations of Fenianism, the IRB, and offshoots of the IRB in the ensuing decades.

The *Nation* reports on the various mechanisms for economic exploitation of the Indian peasantry, in particular tax-gathering[84] and the deliberate propagation of famine as a means of coercing peasants to pay taxes. This attention is not surprising given the system of landlordism and the extraction of rent from the Irish peasantry through methods of coercion. Such specific articles exist against the backdrop of more general accounts of the plunder of wealth involved in colonial rule and the system of confiscation and 'piracy' established by Clive in India.[85] A column providing news of events in India for the week of 5 September 1857 explains: 'For more than a hundred years have the British been pursuing a course of robbery and spoilation, duplicity, injustice, and cruelty in India …' This very real economic gain for Britain continues into the contemporary moment of writing: 'We can understand how it may suit the convenience of England to hold possession of Indian, and squeeze revenue out of the poor Ryots—we can perceive the advantage of having an Indian market for Manchester cotton … the Sepoys are winning back possession of their native land'.[86] The ryotwari zone, in which taxes were paid directly to the State, and the zamindari sector, where they were collected in the form of rent by landlords, were not distinguished in these articles, although by the crucial year, 1922, when Gandhi called off a tax strike that threatened the collapse of the British Raj, the Irish had followed the logic of their own position on violence and got rid of the British in two-thirds of the country. The Nation's diagnosis of the 'Mutiny' was much more effective in its application to Ireland than to India. After all, initially the Raj was felled, not by Indian revolutionary violence, but by the Japanese attacks in South East Asia in 1942.

After months of siege in Delhi, the Nation published in September 'How England Rules and Triumphs'. In this essay, the writer identifies economic exploitation and expropriation as the true motives of colonialism, rejecting its claims to the civilizing mission.[87] Only such economic objectives could explain the desperation of England to hold onto India. In an earlier critique of British imperialist discourse, one column quotes at length from the Times on the planning of a statue in the memory of Clive on the 100th anniversary of the battle of Plassey: 'And what is it that he had founded? Not only a dominion from which we may import at our pleasure almost all the precious commodities of the world, but an empire in which thousands of Englishmen of every generation can find scope for their enterprise and recompense for their toil. Ship, colonies, and commerce have not been of more service to us than this famous land …'. The writer dismantles this mythos of empire in which the Times claims that India accomplishes 'the progress of the nation and the happiness of the country' and declares, to the contrary, that the monument memorializes 'crime, fraud, perjury, robbery, oppression, and cruelty'.[88] Against this narrative of capitalist exploitation, another columnist identifies the possibility introduced by the insurgents of 'a government which would develop her resources instead of exhausting them'.[89]

This vision of an expansive, still expanding system of capitalist exploitation and the violence by which this was maintained may be embryonic and underdeveloped, but it signals the possibility of an anticolonialism that is internationalist, one in which Irish nationalists looked to non-white colonized subjects as models and as potential allies and one in which the international socialism emerging in this period might someday play a role. All of these writings on the Sepoy Rebellion have a common goal—the overthrow of the Empire. The critique of the monument to Clive ends by asserting: '"This dazzling structure of power", as the British organ has called the empire so foully acquired, may, after the present disruption be patched together for a little time again, but it will not hold; the rottenness spreading from its core has reached the surface, new breaches will open from day to day, till at last the whole sinks into irreparable ruin.'[90] This stands as just one instance of the many times that the collapse of empire is not only wished but foretold: 'The dissolution of the accursed Empire of Great Britain is inevitable, and after these transactions it is near at hand.'[91] Some writers claim this as the collective desire of the Irish people: 'The Irish millions wish to see England subdued; her insolence chastised; her barbarous

85 The *Nation*, 11 July 1857, 729.
86 The *Nation*, 5 September 1857, 8
87 The *Nation*, 25 September 1857, 62. Although well beyond the scope of this essay, it is worth noting that just two weeks before the first articles of the Sepoy Rebellion appear in the *Nation*, there is a lengthy analysis of the hypocrisy of Britain's abolitionism, which contains a quite thorough, detailed analysis of how Britain continued to benefit economically from the American slavery trade despite its protestations against it. This is meant to explain Britain's policy of non-interference with ships carrying slaves.

and tyrannical power broken to pieces ... They look upon English aggression there as similar to the onslaught made centuries ago upon their own forefathers ...'.[92] However, Indian insurgency, while securing the collapse of British rule in India itself, is an insufficient source of the destruction of the Empire itself. For that, a broader coalition of anti-colonial struggle must begin to be imagined. Invoking the revolutionary discontent of people in Persia, Russia, Iran, China, Africa, and Ireland as well as those of Muslim scholars and clerics and suggesting that the news of India might serve as a spark around the world, one column describes a bold political possibility: 'Meantime, there appears to be some likelihood that nations and peoples in various parts of the world who feel the scourge of British tyranny will learn the value of a pull together. Such a pull for one week would dismember the British Empire, and render England powerless for mischief ever more.'[93]

History tells us that such a 'pull together' was not to be in 1857, although after World War II, a variety of such internationalist projects of anti-imperial unification, focused primarily on the Third World, did emerge.[94] But such internationalist anti-colonial politics, their formulations, and their practice became more explicit in Ireland after 1857. While such internationalism certainly did not dominate Irish nationalism, it is a significant part of its history in the second half of the nineteenth century. Looking back at these Irish writings about the 'Indian revolution' provide another link in the genealogy of such a politics, which has much to teach us about the potentialities of nationalisms which exceed themselves[95] and of solidarities that sought to challenge a global system of colonial capitalism that, while transformed in many ways, persists today.

---

88 The *Nation*, 4 July 1857, 712
89 The *Nation*, 12 September 1857, 25.
90 The *Nation*, 4 July 1857, 712
91 The *Nation*, 18 July 1857, 744.
92 The *Nation*, 5 September 1857, 14.
93 The *Nation*, 29 August 1857, 340.
94 See Vijay Prashad, *The Darker Nations: A People's History of the Third World* (New York, 2008).
95 See David Lloyd. 'Nationalisms Against the State.' in *Ireland After History*, 19–36.

Aerial view over Inishmaan in the Aran Islands
© Ocean/Corbis

Review

Atlas of the Irish Rural Landscape (2nd Ed) and Historical Geography

Willie Smyth

The first edition of *Atlas of the Irish Rural Landscape* (1997) was an award-winning bestseller that was reprinted six times. This second edition is not simply a reissue. At least one-third of the content is entirely new, quite a number of first edition maps are redrawn and/or enhanced and there are many new maps, photographs and landscape paintings included. The new edition also provides a listing of the top fifty books on the Irish landscape and provides a guide to the best websites addressing all the major themes of the *Atlas*. Beautifully designed with cutting-edge cartography by Matthew Stout and simply superb illustrations, this edition is characterized by written contributions that are up-to-date, incisive, often witty and mostly critical.

The first edition of the *Atlas of the Irish Rural Landscape* has been a model and an inspiration for two further atlases —those of Cork City[1] and the Iveragh Peninsula[2] —also published by Cork University Press in 2005 and 2009, respectively. And this second edition has been followed this summer by the publication of the *Atlas of the Great Irish Famine*.[3] What these four atlases share is not only the same innovative and supportive publisher in Cork University Press and a flair for highly original and brilliantly produced maps and landscape images but also a succession of editors trained in the discipline of human geography and, most particularly, historical geography. As noted above, one interesting addition to the second edition—arrived at after a wide consultation—is a list of the top fifty books on the Irish rural landscape (414). Excluding a somewhat eclectic collection of works by pre–twentieth-century observers and topographers (going back to Giraldus Cambrensis), it is noticeable that at least half of this list of works by research scholars is by geographers; archaeologists, architects, ecologists, folklorists, historians, Irish and English language specialists, natural scientists and writers of literature comprise the other half—an interdisciplinary range well represented by the contributors to this *Atlas*. Obviously, the editors faced different choices in making this selection of the top fifty. I note that T. W. Freeman's outstanding *Pre-Famine Ireland* is included but his path-breaking and internationally recognized *Ireland: A Social and Regional Geography*,[4] which now represents a unique and comprehensive view of Ireland's landscapes and societies in the middle of the last century, is not included. While recognizing that Estyn Evans's *Irish Folkways* (it could equally have been his *Irish Heritage*) and *Mourne Country* are judged worthy of inclusion, it is very surprising that his final magisterial synthesis of habitat, heritage and history, *The Personality of Ireland*,[5] did not receive precedence. (More of this anon!). The omission of Tony Orme's *Ireland*[6] from the World Landscapes Series also seems puzzling as indeed is that of the *Atlas of the Iveragh Peninsula*. I make these remarks as a prelude to the review and exploration of the intellectual roots of this Atlas and the place of such syntheses in the understanding and nurturing of Ireland's rich and diverse landscape heritage.

Readers may be anxious to know the level of continuities and the nature of the changes from the first edition. Sections that have remained substantially the same are Aalen's 'The Irish landscape: synthesis of habitat and history', the Stouts's 'Early landscapes: from prehistory to plantation' and Whelan's 'The modern landscape: from plantation to present'. Likewise, the sections on the 'Components of the Irish landscape'—bogs, forests and woodlands, houses and buildings, towns and villages, communications and mining, power and water are largely replicated. But these sections are now greatly enhanced by new images and photos and excellent caption summaries for each map and photo. In addition, there are a number of new vignettes on aerial perspectives on removing antiquities, on Ardee bog in County Louth, on handball alleys, on Slane village, on road art and on millstone quarries on the Hook peninsula. There are two really major transformations to the first edition. Firstly, 'The Challenge of Change' section (now by Kevin Whelan and not Fred Aalen) has been completely rewritten and is now the pivot of the *Atlas*. A new subset to this section has been written on Celtic Tiger housing by Ruth McManus. Secondly, five new, highly original regional case studies of the Wicklow uplands, Tory Island (Donegal), Aughris headland (Sligo), Inistioge (Kilkenny) and Point Lance (Newfoundland) have replaced these on the Hook (Wexford), Lecale (Co. Down), The Burren (Clare), The Bend of the Boyne (Meath), The Ring of Gullion (Armagh)

1 John Crowley, Robert Devoy, Denis Linehan and Patrick O'Flanagan (eds.) with Michael Murphy as cartographic editor, *Atlas of Cork City* (Cork, 2005).
2 John Crowley and John Sheehan (eds.); Michael Murphy (cartographic editor), *The Iveragh Peninsula: A Cultural Atlas of the Ring of Kerry* (Cork, 2009).
3 John Crowley, William J. Smyth and Michael Murphy (eds.), *Atlas of the Great Irish Famine* (Cork, 2012).
4 T. W. Freeman, *Ireland: Its Physical, Historical, Social and Economic Geography* (London, 1950). This book brought Ireland's geography to the attention of the international geographical community for the first time.
5 E. Estyn Evans, *The Personality of Ireland: Habitat, Heritage and History* (Cambridge, 1973). In assessing Evans's overall achievement see also John Campbell, *Geography at Queens: An historical survey* (Belfast, 1978). At least three *Festschriften* were written in tribute to him and his work.
6 A. R. Orme, *Ireland* (Chicago and London, 1970).

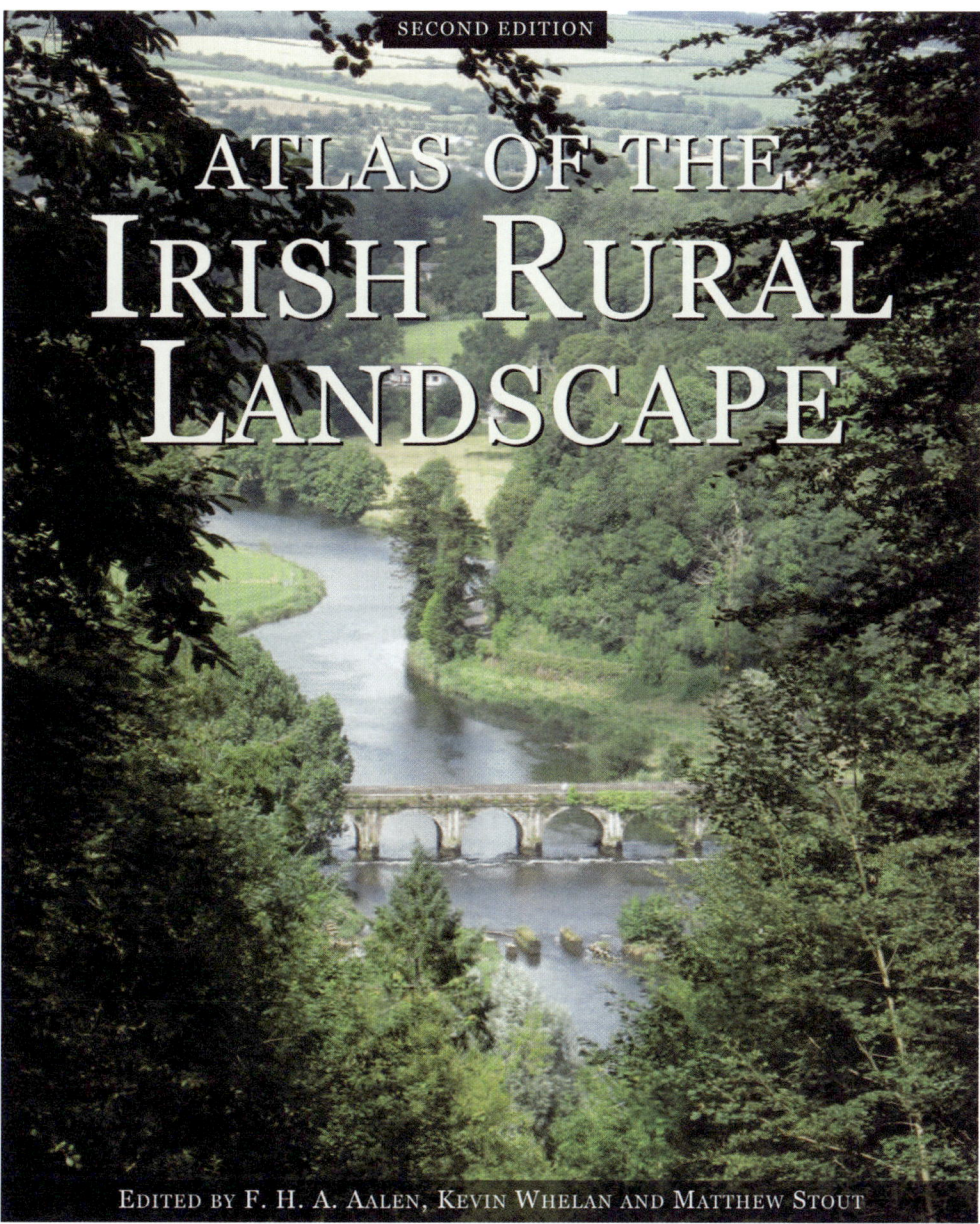

Atlas of the Irish Rural Landscape, 2nd ed. (Cork, 2011), Cover image

and Connemara (Galway). Some of the latter have subsequently been published as monographs but it is a pity that none of the new regional case studies are located in Northern Ireland.

Fred Aalen was central in providing the motivation and stimulus for the making of the original *Atlas* and his philosophical, caring attitude towards every aspect of the Irish landscape carries through to this second volume. Leading off the first section, 'The Making of the Irish Landscape', he sets the scene carefully, assisted by superb aerial photography by Daphne Pochin Mould, amongst others. He is well aware that both new technology and a global economic system 'have an invasive capacity of unprecedented power, far beyond anything previously imagined' (7). Consequently, fragile landscape quality can only be maintained by conscious design and comprehensive and sustained action.

Aalen recognizes that the protection of the Irish landscape has remained a low priority with 'still widespread insensitivity to deterioration and spineless acquiescence in brutal acts of spoliation' (29). Recognizing Ireland's profound European heritage, Aalen sees the island's culture as very much part of the Atlantic world, emphasizing that the creation of its landscapes involved a dialogue between insular and continental, as well as indigenous vis-à-vis exogenous forces. The resultant Irish landscape, therefore, reveals subtle gradations in, and hybrid forms of, settlement, agrarian systems and societies. In short, the Irish cultural landscape is plural.

This section is full of good insights and sound generalizations. 'Everywhere in Ireland', Aalen notes, 'the dominant farm economy is livestock based on permanent grassland.' The cultural and social implications of this seemingly innocent statement are immense. He confirms that 'the early medieval period (AD 400–1000) witnessed profound transformations in Ireland associated with a new religious culture and technological innovation. Ireland evolved a close-knit but decentralized society in which cultural unity coexisted with political fragmentation' (21). Like Estyn Evans, Aalen thus emphasizes the formidable complex of material cultural changes that came with the Early Iron Age and 'Celtic Christianity'. These developments saw the establishment of a highly sedentary elite all over the island as evidenced by settlement items like raths and monasteries and by the ubiquity of placenames steeped in familism. There is an excellent map (17) of the significant placename 'cloon', Irish *cluain*—dry meadow land in boggy or wooded land) and on pages 55 and 57, respectively, of placenames ending in 'grange' and 'ton/town'. But one of the weaknesses of this second edition is the lack of attention to placenames and family names. The phenomenon of Irish people enshrining their images and world views in the landscape, investing most Irish places with the symbols of their own identity, crystallized in the early medieval period and reached a climax in the high Middle Ages. Placenames and family names are integral, if not central, elements in the Irish landscape. Their distributions and meanings await exploration and clarification.

Long before it became fashionable, Estyn Evans—and Kevin Danaher in the Irish Folklore Commission—were exploring the vernacular building traditions of the island.[7] In both *Irish Heritage* (1943) and *Irish Folkways* (1957), Evans explores the nature and meaning of the old-style vernacular houses 'as a shelter for man and beast and as a vehicle for family lore and regional tradition'.[8] Separate chapters in these books deal with 'the thatched house', 'hearth and home', 'furniture fittings' and 'farmyards, buildings and fences'.[9] In Northern Ireland, students of Evans like Alan Gailey and Des McCourt expanded on this scholarly tradition.[10] In the Republic, Fred Aalen made the study of vernacular buildings his life-work.[11] The *Atlas* section on dwelling houses and buildings reflect both his extensive and superb fieldwork and his careful photography. As Aalen notes, 'Irish vernacular buildings utilised plain proportions with an almost classical restraint. They were also carefully integrated into their environment. Good proportions and environmental balance in combination conferred a notable aesthetic appeal' (214). Weaving text and image together in a very attractive way and always locating his materials within a North Atlantic and British/Irish framework, Aalen explores regional styles in vernacular dwellings, the emergence of developed substantial two-storey houses as well as later public housing and the new standardizing vernacular house—the bungalow. Basic farmyard types as well as public buildings such as churches, schools and halls all receive their share of attention. In relation to churches, Aalen notes that 'the strong sense of continuity given to many English and continental villages by an

7   See, for example, E. Estyn Evans *Irish Heritage* (Dundalk, 1943); Kevin Danaher, *Ireland's Vernacular Architecture* (Cork, 1975) and his 'Farmyard forms and their distribution in Ireland', *Ulster Folklife* (1981), vol. 27, 63–75.
8   E. Estyn Evans, *Irish Folkways* (London, 1957), 66–67
9   Evans, *Irish Folkways*
10 Alan Gailey, *Rural Houses in the North of Ireland* (Edinburgh, 1984); Desmond McCourt, 'Innovation diffusion in Ireland: an historical case-study' in *Proceedings of the Royal Irish Academy*, lxxii (1973), 1–19.
11 F. H. A. Aalen, *Man and the landscape in Ireland* (London, 1978) and, in particular, see his 'The Evolution of the Traditional House in Western Ireland' in *Journal of the Royal Society of Antiquaries in Ireland* (1966), 47–58.

Atlas of the Irish Rural Landscape, 2nd ed. (Cork, 2011), map page 46

12 See, for example, William J. Smyth, *Map-making, Landscapes and Memory: A Geography of Colonial and Early Modern Ireland c. 1530–1750* (Cork, 2006), chapters 4 and 10; T. Jones Hughes, *Landholding, Society and Settlement in Nineteenth-Century Ireland: A historical geographical perspective* (Dublin, 1910), 170–227 and 291–99.

enduring place of worship encapsulating the total history of the community' is missing in Ireland. 'The Irish countryside is studded with ecclesiastical ruins from many periods which poignantly reflect a troubled past' (239). The Irish landscape is thus littered with lost or ghost villages that died and disappeared consequent on the sixteenth- and seventeenth-century upheavals.[12]

In the preface of this second edition, the editors acknowledge that intellectually they 'belong to, and the thrust of this atlas comes from, a generation of historical geographers led by Tom Jones Hughes [UCD] and John Andrews [TCD]'. They also acknowledge that they are heirs to a venerable tradition of writing about the landscape ranging from the *dindshenchas* (lore of places) to twentieth-century scholars like Robert Lloyd Praeger, Estyn Evans and Kevin Danaher, and inspiring contemporaries like Tim Robinson,

Michael Viney and John Feehan. Behind the *Atlas* lies another powerful influence: the French geographic tradition. It is noteworthy that Fred Aalen twice (30, 40) invokes the ideas and influence of the great French human geographer, Paul Vidal de la Blache, who once stated that cultural landscapes are like medals struck in the image of the people. (In Ireland's case, a number of 'medals' or 'cultural codes' made for a highly contested domain and a fragmented and complex landscape mosaic). It is important to understand how widely influential French human geography was over the first half of the twentieth century and indeed long after. Based at the Sorbonne, Vidal de la Blache was the founder of *la géographie humaine*, author of a number of wonderful books on France, including the posthumously published and highly influential *Principes de géographie humaine*.[13] He fostered the concept of different peoples' *genres de vie,* or ways of living, and the notion of the *pays*—of distinctive local and regional ensembles and identities. The founders of geography departments in 19 of 20 French universities were graduates of the Vidalian School of Geography at the Sorbonne. The Vidalian approach was also hugely influential in the development of the very distinctive *Annales* approach to history.[14] In this long tradition of a philosophical-humanistic approach to geography in France, many kinds of social structures—whether of family, tribe, nation, state, language or religious group—are seen to have their own geographies. The established objective scientific approach is seen as only presenting a partial view of reality; to understand the nature of specific landscapes, one must seek to understand the social organization of those who inherit and inhabit these places, their beliefs and images of the world they live in.[15]

Breton-French geographer, Pierre Flatrès, was to bring this distinctive geographic tradition directly to bear on Ireland with his publication in 1957 of *Géographie Rurale de Quatre Contrées: Irlande, Galles, Cornwall et Man,*[16] an astounding achievement by a single researcher, comparing as it does the peoples, landscapes and settlements of what were defined as four Celtic countries (Scotland was not included). He is remembered as a truly superb fieldworker who taught a number of Irish geographers many a lesson on the significance of things in the field—and the way to identify and interpret these features. For example, Flatrès was to emphasize the nature of the occupation and ownership of the land—demonstrating that the impact of the landlord was far greater in Ireland than in any other West European country. English geographers emphasized land use *only*. Likewise, the German *landschaft* tradition was brought to bear on Irish studies by, amongst others, Ingeborg Leister. This Marburg-based scholar was the first geographer to work intensively on the rich documentation arising from the medieval Anglo-Norman settlement, the seventeenth-century ledger books and later landlord estate records and maps—medieval and early modern documentation written by outsiders for their own particular aggrandizing purposes. Her great work on Ireland published in Marburg in 1963, *Das Werden der Agrarlandschaft in der Grafschaft Tipperary (Irland)*[17] and her later 1976 monograph on peasant open-field farming in Ireland marked important advances in Irish historical geography. German-born UCD geographer Anngret Simms, who trained under Harald Uhlig at Giessen, has nobly sustained this kind of historical geography in Ireland. She has been an inspiration to a whole generation of young scholars and again an outstanding field worker and landscape analyst.[18] She has been the central innovator, mobilizer and editor to the very distinguished *Irish Historic Towns Atlas* series[19] and has for long represented Ireland at European-wide forums on urban-historical geography. Ireland's human geographers, therefore, have been directly and profoundly influenced by continental European traditions in the discipline, traditions which in turn have modified and mediated the

13 P. Vidal de la Blache, *Tableau de la géographie de la France* (Paris, 1911); *La France de l'Est* (Paris, 1917) and *Principes de géographie humaine* (Paris, 1921), the latter published in English as *Principles of Human Geography* (New York, 1926).

14 See, for example, Lucien Febvre, *A Geographical Introduction to History*, translated by E. G. Mountford and J. H. Paxton (London, 1932), which documents and celebrates the Vidalian impulses within the *Annales* school of history.

15 Anne Buttimer, *Society and Milieu in the French Geographic Tradition* (Chicago, 1971).

16 Published at Rennes by the University.

17 Published by the University of Marburg; see also I. Leister's *Peasant open-field farming and territorial organisation in County Tipperary* (Marburg, 1976).

18 Kevin Whelan, interviewed by Tommy Graham, acknowledges the influence of Anngret Simms in 'Interview: The colossus of Clonegal' in *History Ireland*, 9, No.4 (Winter, 2001), 42–45. He also refers in this interview to the relevance of the *Annales* school of history to his work.

19 Anngret Simms, H. B. Clarke and Raymond Gillespie (eds.) *Irish Historic Towns Atlas* series (Dublin, ongoing since 1986). See also Howard B. Clarke, Jacinta Prunty and Mark Hennessy, *Surveying Ireland's Past: Multidisciplinary Essays in Honour of Anngret Simms* (Dublin, 2004).

generous contributions of British trained geographers working in and on Ireland.

Two of Ireland's foremost human-cum-cultural geographers, E. Estyn Evans and Tom Jones Hughes, were trained in the Department of Geography and Anthropology at the University of Wales in Aberystwyth. The bringer of French ideas to Aberystwyth was the French-speaking Channel Islander, the great humanist and pacifist, Herbert J. Fleure.[20] It was Fleure who inspired the Evans style of anthropogeography with its intensive concerns with the long-term interrelationships between environment, landscapes and cultural life, with the idea of 'regional personality' and the importance of 'unwritten history' and 'the little tradition' in understanding Ireland. As acknowledged above, the work of Estyn Evans, founder of a distinctive School of Geography at Queens University Belfast, underpins part of the spirit and landscape content of the *Atlas*. Scholars have justifiably queried the northern and north-western bias in much of Evans's work, his over-reliance on material landscape as opposed to other forms of evidence and his ahistorical framework which emphasizes ethnicity as opposed to class and other factors in explaining patterns of landscape and cultural transformation in Ireland. Like the great American cultural geographer, Carl Sauer,[21] Evans always adopted broad Darwinian time-scales and explanatory frameworks in seeking to more fully understand the origins and evolution of Irish society's interaction with its distinctive island habitat. Such an approach placed much more reliance on the oral and material culture of the country people, or sources such as travellers' descriptions, rather than on official and dated documentation. Evans was, therefore, very sensitive to the pervasive 'underground' traditions which had remained invisible to the eye and pen of English officialdom. While sharply critical of a narrow nationalist definition of Irish culture, Evans still recognized the origins of part of this ideology in the efflorescence of both European folklore and romantic movements, two intellectual impulses that appear to have left their mark on the geographer himself.

Both Evans's *Irish Heritage* and his final lengthy essay, *The Personality of Ireland*,[22] remain essential reading to any person seeking to understand the foundations and subtleties of Ireland's cultures and landscapes. Such work, like Aalen's own work in the *Atlas*, make us explore the cultural consequences arising from Ireland's insular position on the edge of the wet Atlantic world, eternally engaged in some form of dialogue with the large island of Britain. Evans also reminded us how oscillations in Ireland's relative openness to external exchanges would appear to have released or depressed energies and renewed or inhibited a whole host of regional linkages from the time of the megalith builders to the island's current attempts to negotiate a viable space between America and mainland Europe. Evans also stressed the critical importance of the bogs (and the drumlins) in defining both parochial and broader regional entities such as the provinces. The *Atlas* also does this, and it focuses on the central significance of the great midland region as both a buffer and a culturally strategic zone.

The writing of the next section, 'From prehistory to plantation', belongs to a different intellectual tradition—that of archaeology (a disciplinary tradition which Estyn Evans also enhanced). Synthesizing the work of a large number of archaeologists from Anthony Lucas's painstaking work *Cattle in Ancient Ireland* (1989)[23] and Seán P. Ó Riordáin's enduring *Antiquities of the Irish Countryside* (1979)[24] through to Chris Lynn and J. McDowell's work on ring forts (2011)[25] and Tomás Ó Carragáin's on early medieval churches,[26] the Stouts—Geraldine and Matthew—bring the reader on a thrilling journey through Ireland's early landscapes from Mesolithic sites, Neolithic forts,

20 G. Bowen, H. Carter and J. A. Taylor (eds.), *Geography at Aberystwyth* (Cardiff, 1968), xii–xxiii; David Livingstone, *The Geographical Tradition* (Oxford, 1992), 282–89. See also, Anne Buttimer, *Geography and the Human Spirit* (Baltimore and London, 1993), 175–77.

21 See, for example, Carl O. Sauer, 'Foreword to historical geography', *Annals of the Association of American Geographers*, 31 (1941), 11–14 and his *Sixteenth Century North America: The Land and the People as seen by the Europeans* (Berkeley, 1971); David Livingstone, *The Geographic Tradition*, 294–310.

22 E. Estyn Evans, *The Personality of Ireland*; see also Brian Graham and L. J. Proudfoot (eds.), *An Historical Geography of Ireland* (London and Toronto, 1993).

23 A. Lucas, *Cattle in Ancient Ireland* (Kilkenny, 1989).

24 S. P. Ó Riordáin, *Antiquities of the Irish Countryside*, revised by R. de Valera (London, 1979).

25 Chris Lynn and J. McDowell, *Deer Park Farms: The Excavation of a Raised Rath in the Glenarm Valley, County Antrim* (Belfast, 2011).

26 Tomás Ó Carragáin, *Churches in Early Medieval Ireland: Architecture, Ritual and Memory* (New Haven, 2010).

Bronze Age settlement expansion and early cultural-cum-political nuclei such as the great hillforts onto the mysterious 'Celts' and the less mysterious Anglo-Normans. Much more dependent than the historical geographer on the analysis of site-specific artifacts found in the field or discovered in all kinds of excavations (including the many rescue excavations so characteristic of the road construction and building boom in the last few decades), the great majority of maps for this section are of the distribution of *individual* sites, monuments or items. Given the nature of this evidence, choropleth maps involving comprehensive data-sources covering this whole island are therefore rare in the kind of scholarly exploration. One of the exceptions to this constraint is the mapping comparison made of ecclesiastical sites per km^2 and ringforts per km^2, which throws up intriguing contrasts between a ringfort distribution concentrated in the western half of the island (plus the drumlin belt) vis-à-vis a church distribution that is more solidly anchored in the eastern and southern half of the island (50). Mysteries abound. Why are ringfort numbers so low in Leinster, while a large number of churches occupy the better lands of the province? Like all good maps, these patterns raise more questions than answers.

Overall, this section contains some of the most outstanding and beautiful maps in a book distinguished by so many of the same. The map of the 47,000 ring forts (46) is one such map and the deft, if faint, inclusion of modern county boundaries allows the reader to evaluate localized densities and variations. Likewise, the map of early medieval churches (5,534 pre-Norman examples) is stunning in both its range of sites—from the lowliest ecclesiastical settings to the great monastic centres often with high cross(es) and round tower—and in its intriguing variations in density patterns. Strangely enough, I still prefer the wonderful first edition map of the tower houses; in the second edition, the tower house distribution has to compete with the newly inserted, intricate web of small and large late medieval lordships, and this map, in consequence, seems more than a little congested.

This is also a section full of both intriguing insights and questions as one might expect from an essay covering over eight-and-a-half thousand years and dealing with *c.* 160,000 sites identified as belonging to before AD 1700. The Mesolithic colonization looks likely to have begun in the north-east of the island—yet why do the myths and stories of a lost culture off the peninsulas and rias of south-west Munster still echo in my mind? Did the scale of sea-level rise in the post-glacial period simply destroy any evidence of such early occupation in much of the south-west? Apart from the late wedge-tombs, why does Munster stand apart in all the maps of Neolithic tombs? Insightful analysis points up the significance of settlement expansion into lowland areas during the Bronze Age and the emergence of critical cultural-cum-political cores by the late Bronze Age. For example, the distribution of barrows from the Bronze and Iron Ages but with Neolithic roots (40), seems to point up what were later to become both the Eoganacht heartland in East Limerick and Connacht's royal focus on the plains of north Roscommon. The 'Celts' present problems for the Stouts, as they do for all other scholars. [Incidentally it is rather strange that neither 'Celts' nor 'Celtic' turn up in the index whereas the term 'Celtic Tiger' rears its bloated head at least 15 times]. The authors note that some scholars have denied a Celtic invasion due to negative results from DNA analyses and argue that the modern Irish population is 'genetically not distinctive "Celtic" but the dilution could be expected after 2,500 years' (41–42). There seems to be some misconceptions here about the DNA evidence. The dominant Y-chromosome pattern for the great majority of the Irish population is one of the oldest in Europe and has persisted for many thousands of years emphasizing how deep and

27 See Brian McEvoy, Martin Richards, Peter Forster and Daniel G. Bradley, 'The *Longue Durée* of Genetic Ancestry: Multiple Genetic Marker Systems and Celtic Origins in the Atlantic Façade of Europe', *American Journal of Human Genetics*, 75 (2004), 693–702, which concludes that these marker systems indicate a shared ancestry throughout the Atlantic zone that dates back to the end of the last Ice Age.

Atlas of the Irish Rural Landscape, 2nd ed. (Cork, 2011), map page 51

28 E. Estyn Evans, 'Some Survivals of the Irish Openfield system', *Geography*, xxiv (1939), 24–36; see also, Desmond McCourt, 'The Dynamic Quality of Irish Rural Settlement' in R. Buchanan, E. Jones and D. McCourt (eds.), *Man and His Habitat: Essays Presented to Emyr Estyn Evans* (London, 1971).

continuous is this early prehistoric genetic heritage.[27] We need to distinguish between genetic and cultural heritage—the latter is much more subject to a whole series of mutations and transformations through the ages, the former only weakly so. Geraldine and Matthew Stout invariably and helpfully locate Ireland's cultural patterns within a wider European framework, as for example, in the marvellous map (44) showing promontory forts extending from the Shetlands to Brittany and curving around to include much of Ireland's southern and western coasts. They are equally insightful about the radicalizing impact of Christianity on Ireland's belief systems, economy and settlement structure. Overall, this section greatly enlarges our vision of millennium old settlement patterns and rich landscape layers that have survived intact into the twenty-first century—a state of completeness unique in Western Europe. The challenge for the Irish people is how to sustain such a rich landscape heritage in the face of immense global and technological forces.

In the analysis of the modern landscape, we encounter the crisp, eloquent writing of Kevin Whelan. His command of the cultural and historical geography of this colonial era is immense; he has a very sure understanding of the ecology of Irish settlement and farming practices and his use of the Irish language is always effective. One could give numerous examples of the aptness of his writing: 'the notoriously impoverished housing' of cottiers 'was located in straggles of roadside cabins, in dishevelled cross-road clusters, in shanties on the edge of towns, piled up in dilapidated back lanes and disreputable alleyways or squeezed into commonages' (82). And on the same page, the big farm/small farm divide in Co. Cork 'also demonstrates the hurling/football divide. Christy Ring's succinct advice as to how to best promote hurling in Cork was to stick a knife in every football found east of this line'. Key insights are provided with flair and panache: 'Together, the potato (tolerant, prolific, nutritious) and the lazy-bed (adaptable, effective, productive) maximised the resource potential of marginal land' (91); 'Heavy potato consumption among the impoverished Irish labourers fattened the British urban consumer, recipient of the island's cereal and bacon exports' (93). A brilliant, and often succinct, writer, Kevin likes dramatic statements: 'the potato, not Cromwell, peopled the west of Ireland' (89). The continuing survival of Irish landlords there, the Gaelic partible inheritance system, proto-industrialization and smallpox innoculations may also have helped. His too brief analysis of the revolutionary nature of the catastrophic Great Famine is still excellent but he rather overemphasizes the correlation between clustered settlement and Famine deaths. Likewise, holdings valued at under £4 were not just the most westerly small holdings—east Ulster, Leinster and mid Munster also had their share of such lowly valued holdings 'now legally rendered a parasitic encumbrance on landlord property' (97).

Perhaps Kevin Whelan overemphasizes the novelty of some key elements and groups in the Irish landscape. It is doubtful whether farm labourers were 'a new social class' in tillage areas (83); rather, the late eighteenth and early nineteenth centuries saw a rapid increase in a long-established labouring class in these regions. The argument that the west of Ireland 'was generally an area of new rather than ancient settlement' (89) also seems a little wide of the mark. Even a cursory examination of the history and mapping of settlement in the west as outlined by the Stouts in the previous section highlights the depth and range of both settlement and society in this region. What is true is that the western half of Ireland witnessed a demographic revolution from the mid-eighteenth century onwards, which saw a dramatic expansion of settlement and colonisation out of the long-settled townlands into the more marginal areas previously used for extensive grazing and other purposes—processes well documented in this section. Whelan has perhaps given too much weight to the importance of rundale systems of farming and their associated clustered settlements. Landlord leases, allowing partnership farming amongst kin and/or neighbourhood groups within townlands, and *without* all the trappings of rundale and clustered settlement arrangements, may well have been equally important. He is correct to argue 'that rundale systems were not the degraded relics of an archaic settlement form, practicing primitive agriculture in refuge areas' (89), i.e. the distribution of clustered settlement in mid nineteenth-century Ireland was *not* a residual one as argued by the Evans

29 William J. Smyth, 'The dynamic quality of Irish "village" life—a reassessment' in *Hommes et terres du nord* (Lille, 1988); William Nolan, 'Patterns of Living in Tipperary 1750–1850' in William Nolan (ed.), *Tipperary: Historic Society* (Dublin, 1988).

30 Kevin Whelan, 'Beyond a Paper Landscape: John Andrews and Irish Historical Geography' in F. H. A. Aalen and Kevin Whelan (eds.), *Dublin City and County: From Prehistory to Present* (Dublin, 1992), 415.

31 See, for example, J. H. Andrews, 'The use of half-inch Ordnance Survey maps in Irish historical geography, with special reference to road patterns', *Geographical Viewpoint* (1976), V, 20–29 and 'Maps and the Irish local historian', *Bulletin of the Group for the Study of Irish Historic Settlement* (1983), No. 6, 22–31.

32 Whelan, 'John Andrews', 398–415.
33 Whelan, 'John Andrews', 418
34 These points are further elaborated upon in William J. Smyth's 'Tom Jones Hughes and historical geography: an introduction' in T. J. Hughes, *Landholding, Society and Settlement in Nineteenth-Century Ireland*, x–xxvi.
35 Smyth in T. J. Hughes, *Landholding, settlement and society,* xvi–xxii.
36 Hugh F. Kearney, *Ireland: Contested Ideas of Nationalism and History* (Cork, 2007), 13–18.
37 William J. Smyth and Kevin Whelan (eds.), *Common Ground: Essays on the Historical Geography of Ireland* (Cork, 1988), xv.
38 Kevin Whelan interviewed by Tommy Graham, 'The Colossos of Clonegal', *History Ireland* 9, 4 (Winter 2001), 43
39 J. H. Andrews, 'Jones Hughes's Ireland: A Literary Quest' in Whelan and Smyth (eds.), *Common Ground*, 6.

school.[28] Rather the rundale system and associated clustered settlement could be seen as 'a sophisticated response to specific ecological conditions' which maximised 'the carrying capacity of a fragile environment in an expanding demographic regime' (89). But this is not to argue that clustered settlement and associated field systems were novel features in the Irish landscape—the tradition of such a settlement and field system may be very old in Irish culture. Likewise, an overemphasis on such small farming systems may obscure the greater social and geographical significance of families resident on medium-sized and big farms, the historic sustainers of a whole series of key institutions in the culture—schools, churches, agrarian and political organizations, scribal traditions, and sporting and leisure pursuits. The diverse origins, economic functions, social structures and morphologies of clustered or nucleated farm settlements could be more fully explored and recognized.[29]

But all of the above, are, for the most part, minor quibbles, given the force and originality of Kevin Whelan's writing. And in his writing, one also encounters his clearly acknowledged debt to two of the masters of Irish historical geography—John Andrews and Tom Jones Hughes. London-born, Cambridge and University of London trained, John Andrews, who was appointed to TCD's Geography Department in 1954—has been Ireland's outstanding cartographic historian and a major contributor to Irish historical geography. Always original, lucid and immensely prolific in his writings, Andrews has been a generous facilitator to many colleagues and graduate students, piloting, in Whelan's words, 'generations of Irish historical geographers across cartographic waters'[30] and helping many of us to navigate many other terrains, both geographical and intellectual. Maps are central to this atlas and have always been central to John Andrews's scholarship. Andrews would argue that maps represent space very directly and so they should be at the heart of historical geography.

Equally important, such historical maps—especially a sequence of such maps for the same locality, region or island—need to be contextualized if they are to be properly understood. Hence the need for Andrews's astonishing command of both diverse and relevant archival sources. In historical geography, both Andrews and Whelan see maps as performing three key functions: they provide a picture of the landscape itself, they provide clues to the processes of transformation in landscape and society, and they raise questions about the history of ideas about landscape and geographical planning.[31] In short, maps address the material, social and ideological components and forces shaping landscape and society. Elsewhere, Whelan identifies five major themes in Andrews's contributions to Irish historical geography. Firstly, plantation geographies have been explored by Andrews, revealing a concern with spatial planning and its limitations, especially in the Elizabethan era. Secondly, Andrews has demonstrated how the townland framework was moved towards standardization under the impetus of cartographic and related plantation/appropriation processes while also recognising that the townland system displayed astonishing resilience in spite of ever-changing circumstances. Thirdly, the only coherent historical framework for a discussion of the Irish road system has been provided by Andrews—distinguishing between old, evolved roads and a series of planned roads from the seventeenth century onwards. Fourthly, Andrews has made a significant contribution to our understanding and appreciation of the growth and complex geographies of his adopted city, Dublin, including unravelling the intricacies of John Rocque's brilliant and elaborate mid eighteenth-century rendering of the city. Finally, Andrews challenged the Evans model and its emphasis on age-old continuities in the nature of Irish settlement and field systems, especially in relation to the claim that the clachans or clustered settlements were residual features by the mid nineteenth century.³² Andrews is a stern critic of the lazy generalisation, a stickler for precise details, for particularisation in time and space; the landscape remains a central focus of his work—'a distinctively geographical theme whose elucidation in all its variegated totality is the central issue'.³³ The editors of this book would concur.

Tom Jones Hughes belongs to an earlier and even more formative phase in the shaping of Kevin Whelan's perspectives and methods of examining and interpreting Irish worlds. Welsh-born and originally only Welsh-speaking, Tom Jones Hughes—like Evans, a graduate of the Department of Geography and Anthropology at Aberystwyth—was appointed in 1950 to establish the Department of Geography at UCD. Jones Hughes shared Evans's attention to what anthropologists have called 'the little tradition'. Unlike Evans, however, Jones Hughes did not take the same Darwinian/evolutionary, sweeping view of human history and did not make the material landscape evidence so central to his interpretations of Irish life.³⁴ Making pioneering use of the Griffith Valuation, which identifies the exact location, size, valuation, name of each tenant and landowner of every Irish property in the mid-nineteenth century, engaging in detailed fieldwork across every part of the island (for Jones Hughes, fieldwork in historical geography was seen as essential), and learning to penetrate deep into Irish society and culture (which at first baffled and challenged him) through his intimate interaction with and encouragement of his postgraduate students, he was to achieve a mastery of Ireland's historical and social geography unmatched by any of his contemporaries.³⁵ As historian Hugh Kearney noted to his colleagues in History at UCD, Jones Hughes remained an outsider, his value unappreciated and his future importance unforeseen. In truth, as Kearney further noted, he was to become 'the founder of the most influential school of historical geography'³⁶ in the Republic, if not in the whole island, mentoring at least two generations of scholars in this tradition and whose work and mapping has been frequently assimilated into this volume.

Kevin Whelan has written of his memories of Jones Hughes as a postgraduate supervisor:

> ... Supervision was done obliquely—his insatiable curiosity led to a barrage of questions and clarifications which in turn engendered increasingly deeper understandings by the student ... his finest gifts were those of encouragement and stimulation, the product of a generous, caring personality. His was a gentle dominion, the more effective for being so understated. Not surprisingly, Jones Hughes's influence permeates his students' work.³⁷

Elsewhere, Kevin notes that Jones Hughes, alert to the world of social geography, moved away from the cold facts of land and landscape 'bringing class, religion and language onto the Irish historical geography agenda'.³⁸ John Andrews has likewise commented on the difference of Jones Hughes's approach to that of T. W. Freeman whose fine book *Pre-Famine Ireland* sought to explain the complex equations between population densities, farm size and land quality, in mid nineteenth-century Ireland. Andrews states: 'Freeman's writing remained fundamentally English and conservative. Jones Hughes's mission was to socialise and thereby revolutionise the Irish past.'³⁹ And one of Jones Hughes's most telling interventions was to note the long-term impact of the colonial estate system as an early and persistent motif in his work. Other scholars, particularly many historians, have been reluctant to accept the colonial model as relevant to an understanding of Ireland. But Jones Hughes was not burdened by Irish historiography or its assumptions; he brought a radical insider/outsider view to the Irish scene. He deserves much credit for bravely putting such contested ideas at the

40 Kevin Whelan's other works includes *Wexford: History and Society* (1987); *Tree of Liberty* (Cork, 1996) and *Fellowship of Freedom* (Dublin, 1998) as well as numerous essays in a wide range of international journals.

41 See review by Paul Krugman and Robin Wells of Jeff Madrick, *Age of Greed: The Triumph of Finance and the Decline of America* (New York, 2010) in *The New York Review of Books*, vol. lviii, No. 12, 2011, 28–29, and review by Jeff Madrick and Frank Partroy of US Senate Report, *Wall Street and the Financial Crisis: Anatomy of a Financial Collapse* (Washington, 2011) in *The New York Review of Books*, vol. lviii, No. 17, 2011, 23–26; see also, Paul A. Volker, 'Financial Reform: Unfinished Business', *The New York Review of Books*, vol. lviii, No. 18, 2011.

42 See, for example, Richard A. Posner, *A Failure of Capitalism: The crisis of '08 and the Descent Into Depression* (Cambridge, Mass., 2009); Miroslav Beblavý, David Cobham and Ludovit Ódor, *The Euro and the Financial Crisis* (Cambridge and New York, 2011).

heart of Irish historical and cultural studies and for helping to stimulate a raft of new studies and interpretations. Kevin Whelan has not shied away from these challenges and concepts but has further probed, enlarged and enhanced our understanding of these and related issues both in this atlas and elsewhere. To his training as a historical geographer, he has added an arsenal of skills including an even deeper historical awareness, a powerful command of manuscript sources and literature and a theoretical finesse that is rather structuralist in its sympathies.[40]

It is in the newly written section, 'The Challenge of Change', that one encounters the full force of both Kevin Whelan's writing and his passion for the Irish landscape. He begins by noting that consequent on 'the flood of cheap money … between 1995 and 2005 over half-a-million (584,073) new houses were built and in this decade the average price of new houses tripled, the most rapid rise anywhere in the world' (115). His view that the 'economy was bingeing on property, force-fed by easy money, tax breaks, a promiscuous planning regime, profligate lending standards and reckless government' (115) seems entirely valid. Yet this provides, for the most part, a local and partial description. Kevin Whelan's writings, in this atlas and elsewhere on the eighteenth- and nineteenth-century Atlantic and European worlds—which profoundly influenced Ireland's economic and social structures—are both nuanced and contextualized. Such a contextualization seems weaker for the recent 'Celtic Tiger' era. Both Ireland's economic boom and collapse were also consequent on a new international economic ideology, American-led, which placed an 'unjustified faith in rational expectations, market efficiencies and the techniques of modern finance'.[41] This ideology helped to justify an explosion of weak credit, sponsored failures in national economic policies in many countries and reflected the absence of a disciplined international monetary system—including that of the European Central Bank for the eurozone. The so-called peripheral and weaker economies of the European Union—Greece, Italy, Ireland, Portugal and Spain—were facilitated in borrowing at very low rates to spend and import beyond their means while core European countries like France and Germany (as Kevin Whelan notes) saved at home and invested in the peripheries, so reinforcing a gap in productivity between national economies.[42] The interweaving, therefore, of unregulated banking systems and public policy failures at global, European and national levels led to a major financial crisis that severely wounded the real world economy. Ireland, a young and clearly still immature state, behaved like a child whose Christmases come every day. The disastrous aftermath of all this is now well known.

But the chapter on 'The Challenge of Change' is not just a critique of the failures of this period; it also puts forward a whole series of sensible policy initiatives so as to ensure that viable landscape and housing policies are pursued throughout the island. For example, the promotion of a dynamic vernacular architectural tradition and the conservation of a rapidly depleting stock of surviving vernacular buildings are recommended, and the development of Ireland's international reputation as a 'green' country is encouraged to boost both food production and tourism activities. Impressive features of this section are its comparative and very up-to-date European and global perspectives, its emphasis on local and regional responsibilities in caring for landscapes, and its absolutely essential emphasis on nurturing *cultural landscapes as a whole*, as opposed to an overly site-specific focus—planners and Heritage Council please note. One has sympathy with his view that the (Catholic?) parish—like the French commune—is an apposite scale for the study and planning of interactions between people and their habitat, particularly in predominantly 'rural' regions. But in commuter zones and metropolitan regions, it is unlikely that planning at this scale is feasible. Perhaps the reintroduction of the Rural District (abolished in the 1920s) as the most sustainable administrative planning level might help. Geographer Paddy Duffy here contributes a characteristic archetypal case-study of Kilclone in Co. Meath, where the countryside and the commuter zone collide and where bungalows abound on former Land Commission holdings while the big farmers resist such intrusions.[43]

Ruth McManus's subsection on Celtic Tiger housing details both the context and impact of the property boom as 'new housing estates, fuelled by a land rezoning frenzy, formed accretions on the edges of rural towns and villages' (156). She provides very useful insights into the social and psychological reasons and the consequences for young suburban couples of finding affordable homes in Dublin's distant commuter zone. McManus correctly stresses that government tax incentives and capital allowances encouraged both 'ridiculous expansion under the Seaside Resort scheme' (158) and a massive splurge of hotel building, often in the wrong locations. However, the use of terms like 'muck-mansions' may reveal a lack of sympathy for and understanding of the motivations of people seeking better homes. Perhaps the excesses of the Celtic Tiger era are now being matched by excessive reactions. Much was achieved during this expansive era. Poor housing stock was refurbished and people live in more comfortable dwellings, historic buildings, infrastructure and institutional facilities were improved or restored, and a significant growth in population was sustained. Think of the cooperation between local authorities and the Arts Council in bringing arts centres—striking in both their architecture and functions—to many county towns, most notably in the Midlands. And should we not celebrate the maturation of a more diverse, dynamic, open, multi-ethnic, better educated and skilled society which has shaken off the limitations and repressions of a post-Famine derived world? Curiously, this section does not address the saddest feature of the post–Celtic Tiger era—that many of our young people, those who are most central to both the vitality and the shaping and caring for our culture and cultural landscapes, are emigrating once again.

However, the reconstruction and interpretation of past and present-day landscapes is not only the preserve of historical and human geography. Physical geographers, as well as colleagues in a number of cognate disciplines are also involved in helping us understand the origins and evolution of natural landscapes and their continual modification by human activities. The *Atlas* has wonderful sections on Irish boglands and woodlands. Agriculturalist and landscape historian John Feehan, provides an illuminating survey, noting that one-sixth of Ireland's land area is bogland, the highest proportion of any country in Europe except Finland. The cutting away of the large raised bogs is seeing the creation of a most extensive new cultural landscape across the midlands. But the biggest challenge relates to European regulations, since 21 of the 31 bogs designated as Special Areas of Conservation have suffered damage because of human interventions and there are 3,000 people who still cut turf across the country. As Feehan notes: 'Bogs are among the most iconic element in the Irish countryside'. Their preservation presents many challenges to both policy-makers and users. Queen's geographer Roy Tomlinson reminds us that the ancient Irish landscape was not continuous woodland because raised bogs had formed over basins left after the ice-sheets retreated. Yet, by the Bronze Age, the poorly wooded character of Ireland had already been established. Clearances accelerated in the early medieval period and reached a climax in the sixteenth and seventeenth centuries. Some recovery took place in the eighteenth century when 50,000 hectares were planted in private woodlands and by 1841 there

43 See also Patrick J. Duffy, *Exploring the History and Heritage of Irish Landscapes* (Dublin, 2006).

Atlas of the Irish Rural Landscape, 2nd ed. (Cork, 2011), map page 188

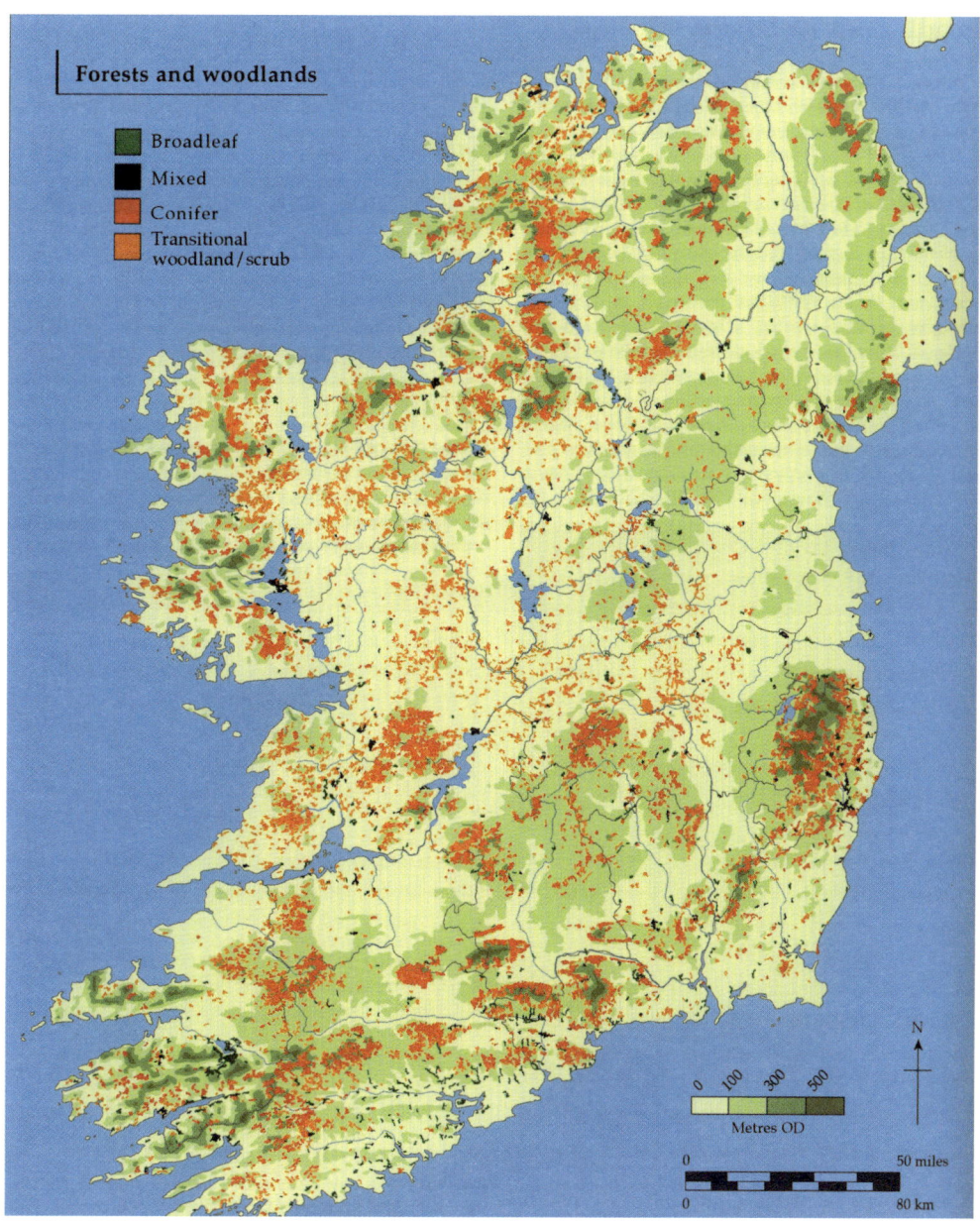

were 140,000 hectares of plantations. Of these four-fifths were mixed plantations, oak constituted only 9% and conifers even less at 7%. Today public policy in both the Republic and Northern Ireland emphasizes the need to expand the forested area by public and, especially, private forest initiatives. As Tomlinson argues, meeting these complex and conflicting demands while satisfying 'environmental, visual and social needs, offers a daunting challenge for sustainable landscape planning' (186).

The planning of communication networks—of canals, railways and particularly of roads—receives detailed attention by geographers James Killen and Enda Murphy. Road planning in the eighteenth- and early nineteenth century involved the Grand Jury and turnpike roads as well as government investment in 'regional and road planning' for the remote western and south-western counties after 1822. More recently, the Celtic Tiger boom has seen a major investment in sometimes controversially routed motorways. And, as such road building continues, 'the rural road network will continue to moulder, as the rural population relocates to sites adjoining the main roads and the urban centres' (299). Archaeologists Fred Hamond and Colin Rynne, in turn, remind us that mining, quarrying and modes of generating energy have been and continue to be significant in the transformation of particular rural landscapes. Wind farms are more recent dramatic features of these landscapes—and they now look likely to reverse the long-established dominance of water in supplying the country's energy needs. Both these authors provide well-illustrated insights into extraction and energy–generating activities, but perhaps the recent very significant industrialization of rural landscapes deserves more of their attention. All these sections demonstrate a central philosophy of the *Atlas*: that the landscape is the finest and most democratic record of human endeavours. The landscape is seen as 'history in slow motion'—and the *Atlas* reflects this by celebrating the ordinary and the usual which we often take for granted in our everyday worlds.

The concluding section of regional case studies is superb, involving a range of disciplinary perspectives. Geographer Arnold Horner, born in the foothills of the Dublin mountains, turns his attention southwards to explore the Wicklow uplands, its geology, its historical geography, including that of the pilgrims who converged 'on the famous annual pattern of the Seven Churches (Glendalough), the type of large but transient gathering that were highly significant in the Gaelic world but had no census measures' (327). Administrator Jim Hunter skilfully reconstructs the historical and social geography of Tory Island, with its two 'villages' of West Town and East Town acting as the foci of ancient field systems and long-standing kin-groups. However, his view of the island today may be just a little romanticized. This once authentic and resilient farming and fishing community is now almost totally dependent on state support and summer tourism. Its fields seem to house more abandoned cars than cattle and its excellent artistic heritage, fostered by Derek Hill and led by James Dixon, no longer appears so vibrant.[44] Archaeologist Elizabeth Fitzpatrick's recreation of the extraordinary rich heritage of the small Aughris headland in Co. Sligo is a loving and superb portrait. Her knowledge of every square inch and every monument in this once pivotal assembly place—complete with horse-racing at the Óenach of the Uí Dhubhda, Kings of Ui Fhiachrach Muaidhe—shines through as text and images are skilfully interwoven to form a wonderful vista. Equally, ethnographer Fidelma and historian Edward McCarron's recreation of the ethnography and historical geography of that beautiful and strategic village of Inistioge—located at the head of the tide on the River Nore—makes for pleasurable reading. The river forms a central thread as they weave the stories of this ever so well-documented region, of its rich medieval heritage, the later estate village and its landscapes of emigration as the families of Inistioge's townlands wend their way all over the English-speaking world, beginning with Newfoundland. And Newfoundland provides the final case study. Here, geographer John Mannion brings a lifetime's harvest of research on Irish settlement in Newfoundland (and other parts of Canada) to bear on the farmer-fishing settlement of Point Lance at the top of the Avalon peninsula. This settlement was begun by Phil Careen and his brother (probably hailing from west Waterford) after the Napoleonic wars. Mannion highlights that the apparent loose and haphazard arrangement of the Point Lance farm settlement is very deceptive—underpinned in this instance by a strictly organized kinship and social network, which the author documents in great detail

44 Bruce Arnold, *Derek Hill* (London, 2010); see also IMMA Catalogue, *Two Painters: Works of Alfred Wallis and James Dixon* (Dublin, 2006).

while skilfully locating this settlement in the wider context of Irish migration and cultural transfers to the New World.

There are many other gems in this second edition of the *Atlas*. The now newly integrated subsection called 'The Joy of Small Things' is a poetic cum-photographic celebration of a host of neglected landscape features. Architect Anne Ryan's piece on handball alleys is particularly outstanding. It reminds us all—including Departments of the Environment and Heritage Councils—that vernacular features such as the handball alley, farm villages in South Kilkenny and elsewhere, and composite if fragile cultural landscapes like the Burren in Clare, the Glens of Antrim and that of the Dingle peninsula all require careful nurturing. It is lovely to read and peruse the text and images of the vernacular buildings and houses so faithfully researched by Fred Aalen; the sections on the bogs, woodlands, demesnes, towns and villages are equally attractive. Quibbles and curiosities that might raise an eyebrow: references to the literature are very up-to-date, but the *Atlas* does not always reflect absorption of the most relevant maps and images; now and again a few maps appear rather garish and/or crowded (97, 120, 149, 292); and 'failed' appears in brackets after the names of two Irish politicians in the index, whereas all other named personages escape unscathed! Overall, this book is a treasure trove of images, insights and critical interpretations of the diverse and rich cultural and natural landscapes of Ireland. It is a big, gorgeous, accessible and very learned book—a most interesting and brilliant combination.

William J. Smyth

Woman reading *Il Manifesto*, 2006 (Photo by Eric VANDEVILLE/Gamma-Rapho via Getty Images)

The Alternative Communism of Lucio Magri

Joseph A. Buttigieg

More than two decades ago, in the immediate aftermath of the momentous events that transformed Eastern Europe in 1989, an intense debate erupted in Italy over the future of the Communist Party (PCI). Within a couple of years, the PCI ceased to exist: in February 1991 it formally dissolved itself, having already changed its name a few months earlier to Democratic Party of the Left. Nobody opposed the PCI's suicide more vigorously and eloquently than Lucio Magri; nor did anyone have stronger credentials to refute the leadership's claim that it represented a new departure rather than a capitulation to its historical adversaries. Magri could hardly be accused of nostalgia, much less orthodoxy. His long and turbulent relationship with the

Lucio Magri (Photo: oggi.it)

PCI had been marked, precisely, by his trenchant critique of its reluctance or inability to renew itself in tandem with the increasingly complex processes of modernization, the evolution of capitalism, and the emergence of new oppositional formations.

Best known, perhaps, for his prominent role in the *Manifesto* group that was expelled from the PCI in 1969 for openly challenging the party's ossified hierarchical structures and narrow-minded strategies, Magri had long been recognized as one of the boldest innovative thinkers and political activists of the Italian left. Far from expressing a desire to cling to the past, his ultimately unsuccessful struggle against the PCI's self-destruction stemmed from a conviction that the leadership's quest for 'newness' was nothing more than a poorly disguised abandonment of the notion that the left could or should strive to offer a democratic alternative to capitalism. In other words, Magri would not concede that capitalism is a *sine qua non* of democracy or vice versa, and he adamantly refused to embrace the thesis that 1989 signaled the end of history—i.e., in the words of Francis Fukuyama, 'the end point of mankind's ideological evolution and the universalization of Western liberal democracy as the final form of human government.'[1] In a last ditch effort to at least slow down the headlong rush by the party's general secretary, Achille Occhetto, and his supporters to abolish the PCI, Lucio Magri helped organize a gathering of some three hundred political leaders,

1 'The End of History?', *The National Interest*, Vol. 16, Summer 1989, 4.

intellectuals, and activists representing divergent views from a broad spectrum of the Italian left to discuss how best to confront the crisis. In his opening speech to the group assembled in a small town near Lake Garda in late September 1990, Magri went straight to the heart of the matter: had communism become obsolete and untenable? Communism, Magri argued, had long been indefensible insofar as it signified violent revolution, dictatorship of the proletariat, wholesale nationalization of the means of production, central planning, repression of individual rights, and suppression of democratic practices. Hence, there should be no hesitation in repudiating communism as it had been installed within the recently defunct Soviet Bloc. For all but a handful of diehard traditionalists this had long been all too obvious and, undoubtedly, many of them recalled Magri's ferocious indictment of the USSR, its allies and sympathizers in his article 'Praga è sola' (Prague is alone) in the *Manifesto* of September 1969. Despite its many flaws, historical missteps, and blind spots, however, the communist movement in Italy could not be legitimately conflated with its counterparts in the Soviet Union and elsewhere. To be sure, Magri argued, the Italian communist movement needed to undertake a radical self-critique and even reformulate or rearticulate its basic tenets in order to 're-found' itself. This difficult process had to take for its starting point the specificity of the PCI's history, its distinctive character, the indispensable role it had played in creating the post-Fascist Italian Republic and in formulating its democratic Constitution. To do otherwise would lead one into the false dilemma posed by Occhetto of choosing between the preservation of a vetero-communist party and its abolition in favor of a social democratic entity. For Magri and many others of like mind, what the situation called for was a revitalized party capable of bringing together multiple oppositional currents and movements to participate in a long-term project of radical political and social transformation.[2]

The Italian Communist Party that Antonio Gramsci had co-founded in January 1921, played the leading role in combating Fascism and the German occupation, grew into the second largest political party in Italy (despite the near certainty that it would never be allowed to govern as long as Italy remained a NATO member), and dissolved itself almost exactly on its seventieth birthday, when it still boasted over 1.4 million members. In the general election of 1987, its performance had fallen below expectations but it still won over 10 million votes (26 per cent of the total compared to 34 per cent for the Christian Democrats and 14 per cent for the Socialist Party). The party's total break with its communist genealogy, spurred by Occhetto, who had assumed the party's leadership a year later, was supposed to broaden its appeal among the electorate, or at least reassure voters that it was on the side of democracy against totalitarian communism. At the same time, though, Occhetto's manoeuvre implied that there was reason to doubt the PCI's principled commitment to democracy when, in fact, illustrations of the deficits of democracy in post-war Italy could most readily be found in the actions and practices of parties that had governed it. In any case, 'the turn', as it was called, yielded very poor results: hundreds of thousands of former dues-paying PCI members refrained from joining the Democratic Party of the Left, and in the April 1992 elections it barely mustered 16 per cent of the popular vote. Lucio Magri won re-election but immediately switched to Rifondazione Comunista, as did many others who had once adhered to the Partito di Unità Proletaria per il Comunismo (PdUP) that he had led for a decade before rejoining the PCI in 1984. For a while, other prominent opponents of the turn soldiered on within the Democratic Party of the Left but were unable to prevent it from drifting ever closer to the political center.

[2] The text of Magri's speech at the September 1990 gathering is reproduced in *In nome delle cose. Materiali di dibattito per la rifondazione communista* (Rome, no publisher and no date, but 1990).

The political earthquake caused by the Tangentopoli corruption scandal in the early 1990s wiped out the two parties—the Christian Democrats and the Socialists—that were primarily responsible for preventing the PCI from ever participating in the national government. Yet, it was Silvio Berlusconi's right-wing alliance that emerged victorious in the 1994 elections. Since then, the Democratic Party of the Left (which now constitutes the core of a cluster of centrist and progressive groups called the Democratic Party) has participated in a few short-lived governing coalitions. Most notably, Massimo D'Alema, who campaigned vigorously for the dissolution of the PCI, served as prime minister for eighteen months; they were hardly memorable. When it came to defending basic democratic principles and practices against the onslaught of Silvio Berlusconi's administration, however, the Democrats failed miserably. As the media mogul used the parliamentary majority of his coalition to protect his effective monopoly of television and to shield him from the criminal justice system, the impotence of the Democrats became increasingly obvious. The Berlusconi years impoverished Italy politically, morally, and culturally, as well as economically, while the left fell into total disarray. In the 2008 elections, not a single deputy from a leftist party was elected to parliament. After that, the most troublesome opponents that Berlusconi had to contend with, other than the judiciary, were street demonstrators from an array of progressive groups, and the relentlessly antagonistic daily, *La Repubblica*.

The fortunes of the Italian left had not quite yet reached rock bottom in 1999 when Lucio Magri embarked on what turned out to be his last significant political project. With the support of a distinguished group of veteran leaders representing various strands of the political left, he drew up a plan for a monthly review devoted to the exploration and elaboration of theoretical and strategic convergences that could constitute the beginning of a long process aimed at producing an oppositional force simultaneously unified and respectful of differences. The monthly was called *La Rivista del Manifesto* and its steering committee included, among others, Rossana Rossanda, Luigi Pintor, Luciana Castellina, and Valentino Parlato, who thirty years earlier, together with Magri, had launched *Il Manifesto*, also as a monthly. (It became a daily, as it remains to this day, in April 1971). Other veterans of the political left, such as Pietro Ingrao, Aldo Tortorella, and Fausto Bertinotti, joined the new venture.

The circumstances surrounding the launching of the two *Manifesto* monthlies could hardly have been more different. The original *Manifesto* group had incurred the ire of the PCI hierarchy because it demanded space for dissent, criticized the party's unwillingness to become engaged in the social and political oppositional movements that had emerged independently of it, and lambasted its exceedingly cautious expression of displeasure with the Soviet invasion of Czechoslovakia. At the time, though, the PCI was still a formidable mass party—it obtained around 27 per cent of the popular vote in both the 1968 and 1972 general elections—that the *Manifesto* group hoped to invigorate by promoting debate and thereby reversing the smug, self-debilitating notion that there could be no viable leftist formation outside it. The *Manifesto* group, Rossanda explained in the concluding sentences of her fascinating memoir, 'hoped to serve as a bridge between the youthful ideas that were emerging and the wisdom of the old left, which had had its hours of glory. It didn't work out that way. But that's another story.'[3]

The catastrophic ending of the story that Rossanda does not recount motivated the project of *La Rivista del Manifesto*: with the organized left marginalized and in fragments, the urgent task was to figure out how to construct a political force capable of offering a viable alternative to the retrograde populism of Berlusconi

3 Rossana Rossanda, *The Comrade from Milan* (London, 2010), 333.

Seated R–L: Rossana Rossanda, Fausto Bertinotti, Pietro Ingrao
Standing R–L: Aldo Tortorella, Valentino Parlato, Lucio Magri
(Photo: 'Addio a Lucio Magri', la Repubblica.it)

4   'La sinistra, rivista,' *La Rivista del Manifesto*, no. 0 (November 1999), 7.

and to the anodyne centrism of the Blair-Schroeder-Clinton 'third way' that had the Democratic Party of the Left in its thrall. It was a long-term objective that required a gradual and thoughtful approach. The first step, Magri wrote in his editorial for the inaugural issue, 'cannot take the form of organizational shortcuts; it requires a shared labor of reflection, research, and open debate that is as unconstrained as possible, by the immediate goals and self-interest of any group.' He then went on to outline the three major topics to which the review would devote special attention, of which the first is particularly revealing insofar as it brings into relief Magri's discerning relationship with communism:

> A historical and theoretical reflection on the history of the labor movement and, especially, its communist element in the twentieth century. [...] Nor should one shun an unsparing reflection on political choices taken long ago, as well as more recent ones in which each of us was a participant and, in some cases, the protagonist. In the present situation self-criticism is necessary to avoid renunciation and make critique effective.[4]

The other two areas of special interest he highlighted in the first editorial were: (a) the analysis of the salient characteristics of the current situation and identification of long term trends; (b) a discussion that would sketch some basic features of the kind of society one should aspire to in the more distant future, that is, an effort to articulate the values that animate the left and give it an identity.

The emphasis on rigorous critique; the demand for thorough analyses and deeper awareness of the profound political, economic and social transformations underway on a global scale; and the impulse to sketch the basic lineaments of an alternative social order—they are all reminiscent of the Magri of the late 1960s. In those politically exhilarating days he was participating in an effort to energize the PCI so that it would be adequate to the task of functioning as the propulsive force in the pursuit of a distinctive form of socialism in Italy. His efforts at the turn of the millennium, by contrast, were motivated by

L–R: Rossana Rosanda, Luigi Pintor, Lucio Magri (Photo: dagospia.com)

the forlorn hope of transforming defeat into an occasion to start constructiung a new foundation for an alternative communism and a springboard for relaunching leftist politics more generally.

In many respects, *La Rivista del Manifesto* was a success. Its average circulation of about 8,000 far exceeded expectations and it was able to generate widespread interest by consistently publishing lively and accessible articles on major issues of concern to progressives of different stripes. Its contributors included many prominent leftist or oppositional figures from the political arena as well as academia in Italy and elsewhere. Etienne Balibar, Perry Anderson, Arundhati Roy, Tariq Ali, Judith Butler, and Samir Amin were among its better known international contributors. The pages of the review reflected Magri's openness to diverse and contrasting ideas, and they amply illustrated his conviction that no single left formation on its own could adequately address the enormity of the injustices perpetuated and exacerbated by the complex operations and structures of global capital. As for the specific situation in Italy, the discussions hosted by the review served to heighten the sense of urgency with which the archipelago of leftist formations needed to coordinate efforts and formulate a coherent strategy for there to be any possibility of slowing down, let alone preventing, the utter moral and political degradation of the nation.

The endeavor lasted a little over five years. When *La Rivista* was shut down in December 2004, it was not because of a significant decline in circulation but because the fragmentation of the left proved insurmountable. On one level, some progress was achieved as various groups, including the Democrats, agreed to join forces in an effort to defeat Berlusconi. Magri acknowledged this in his final editorial with an optimistic observation: 'it is not unreasonable to believe that we can in the end free ourselves from him.'[5] The electoral coalition, called The Union, under the leadership of Romano Prodi, succeeded in returning Berlusconi's minions to the opposition benches in 2004. Yet, Magri also detected what would turn out to be a debilitating flaw: 'The coalition lacks [...] either the ideas or the will to design the compromises needed to square the totality of positions at stake, and circumscribe

5 'Parting Words,' *New Left Review*, 31 (January–February 2005), 99. The original version of Magri's editorial, 'Le ragioni di un comiato' appeared in the final issue of *La Rivista del Manifesto*, 56 (December, 2004), 3–7.

L–R: Paolo Bufalini, Lucio Magri, Enrico Berlinguer (Photo: 'Addio a Lucio Magri', la Repubblica.it)

6   *New Left Review*, 31 (January–February 2005), 99
7   *New Left Review*, 31, 102

the irreducible tenets by which each of its constituents could feel represented' [6]. Within a couple of years, the radical left failed to gain a single seat in parliament and Berlusconi was back with a solid majority that, despite a string of major scandals, enabled him to stay in power until the profound economic crisis forced him to make way for Mario Monti's technocratic government in November 2011.

Especially disappointing for Magri were the tactics employed by the largest organized political force of the radical left, Rifondazione Comunista, led by Fausto Bertinotti. Instead of engaging with other movements and formations in the complex and arduous task of reconstructing a political left on new foundations, Rifondazione sought to position itself as the radical left tout court. Magri could not support it unless 'its shifts of political line be made less suddenly and after more discussion, and the leadership of the party be less concentrated in its General Secretary' [7]. Essentially these were the same expectations Magri had of the PCI many decades earlier when he was rebuffed but persisted in the struggle through the *Manifesto* and the PdUP. This time, however, he decided to withdraw from the political struggle, his disenchantment exacerbated by the deep inroads that historical and ideological revisionism had made into the left as a whole.

In the concluding paragraphs of his final editorial Magri explained why his alternative communism was incompatible with a sweeping repudiation of the communist legacy. After insisting on the 'value those teachings which the political history and theoretical traditions—Gramsci and a too often mutilated Marx—of Italian communism can offer, in method and in merit, for analysis of the present and projection of the future', Magri elaborates on the irreconcilable differences that spelled the end of the project that initially animated *La Rivista del Manifesto*:

More recently [...]—perhaps prey to the force of a wind blowing hard enough to inhibit even those who would resist it—fatal differences have emerged between us. Legitimately, there are those who feel—as a kind of debt of loyalty—the need for a more explicit and radical self-criticism, a break with a past in which we were compromised and which we were too slow and cautious

Lucio Magri (Photo: 'Addio a Lucio Magri', la Repubblica.it)

The Italian Communist Party General Secretary Enrico Berlinguer during the Festa dell'Unita. Venice, 19 July 1981 (Photo by Mondadori Portfolio via Getty Images).

8   *New Left Review*, 31, 105
9   Lucio Magri, *The Tailor of Ulm: A History of Communism*, trans. Patrick Camiller (London, 2011), 4.

to oppose. I will mention only the name of Pietro Ingrao […].

Others—including, ironically, an often apostate communist like myself—feel, conversely, the need and the duty to go against the grain, and not to cross that line which divides even the harshest criticism from a blanket dismissal and wholesale rejection of the communist heritage. Not only because of the importance of roots, even when the terrain changes and one wants to graft a new shoot onto the stem of the plant; and not only because of the absurdity that, in an Italy where so many outmoded and discredited traditions have been revived with a little sprucing up, the only tradition to be avoided and exorcised should be its communism. But because I believe that a differentiated analysis, a counter-factual history of the communist tradition and its overcoming, is the most difficult and truly innovative task for a new left in a new world.[8]

Upon withdrawing from the political arena, Magri devoted his energies to detailed research and unsparing critical reflection on the post–WWII history of the PCI. As a believer in the communist project he considered it his 'duty to draw up a balance sheet, if only a personal one, and to ask whether the burial has not been a little too hasty, and whether a different way of ascertaining *rigor mortis* might be required.'[9] Notwithstanding many painful setbacks, in particular the long incurable illness and loss of his wife, he persevered and produced *The Tailor of Ulm*. As the subtitle—'a possible history of the PCI'—of the original Italian edition suggests, the work examines the road taken and the roads not taken by what was once the most influential communist party in Western Europe and, for four decades, the second most powerful political force in Italy. Despite his underlying melancholy, Magri refrains from speculative flights of fantasy into the realm of the 'what if'? His extensive analyses and critiques, however, provide ample support for making the case that the PCI's self-dissolution was not the inevitable outcome of the march of history. For the English version, the subtitle was changed to 'communism in

Lucio Magri (Photo: Ansa)

the twentieth century' which is indicative of the numerous pages the author devotes to the vicissitudes of communism in the rest of the world, and especially in Eastern Europe and China. While those pages help contextualize the history of the PCI and bring into relief the degree to which the Italian party's strategies and tactics were influenced and, in some very important instances, determined by events and situations of an international dimension (e.g., the Cold War), they are not always convincing and tend to distract the reader from the main focus on the distinctive democratic character of the Italian communist movement.

The distinctiveness of the PCI resided in what Magri calls 'the Gramsci genome.' A great admirer of Lenin, Gramsci nonetheless believed that the Bolshevik strategy of direct assault on the seat of state power, though successful in tsarist Russia, was not a useful model for a revolutionary struggle in a liberal democracy. In a note on 'War of position and war of maneuver, or frontal war,' Gramsci observed:

10 Antonio Gramsci, *Prison Notebooks*, Vol. 3 (New York, 2007), 169.
11 Antonio Gramsci, *Lettere dal carcere*, ed. A. Santucci (Palermo 1996), 458–59.
12 Magri, *the Tailor of Ulm* 42
13 Magri, *the Tailor of Ulm*, 41

> In the East, the state was everything, civil society was primordial and gelatinous; in the West, there was a proper relation between state and civil society, and when the state tottered, a sturdy structure of civil society was immediately revealed. The state was just the forward trench; behind it stood a succession of sturdy fortresses and emplacements—needless to say, the configuration varied from state to state, which is precisely why an accurate reconnaissance on a national scale was needed.[10]

In a liberal democracy, the state does not need to exercize its coercive power overtly, as long as it derives its legitimacy from the consent of the governed. Its resilience comes from 'an equilibrium between political society and civil society' that sustains 'the hegemony of a social group over the entire national society, exercised through so-called private organizations, such as the church, the trade unions, the schools, etc.'[11] The struggle to displace the prevailing hegemony, then, must take place on the terrain of civil society; it will have to be a war of position that, in Magri's words, 'requires a protracted labour of capturing fortresses and earthworks and constructing a historic bloc of various classes, each with distinctive interests and cultural and political roots'.[12]

Gramsci's theoretical and strategic insights provided the PCI with what Magri describes as 'the basis for a middle way between Leninist orthodoxy and classical Social Democracy'.[13] 'Middle way' is too bland a phrase to convey the enormity of an endeavor that had no precedent: building a new kind of communist party with a mass base strong enough to vie for power democratically in a strategically vital member of the NATO alliance that is also the epicenter of Catholicism. Nor were the hurdles only external. Charting a middle course also meant negotiating the internal tensions produced within the party by strong currents that tended in different directions. Distancing the party from Moscow risked alienating, even antagonizing, the many stalwarts who bravely fought Fascism under the banner of the international communist movement under the aegis of the Soviet Union. At the same time, relenting to the pressures exerted by those who envisioned a reunification of the PCI and the Socialist Party would have meant sliding down the slippery path of democratic socialism and abandoning the project of an alternative communism. As the party grew and the social, political, and economic landscape changed, other pressures and tensions arose. What new openings and alliances were needed and what form should they take? The proven electoral strength of the party also gave rise to questions that had a direct bearing on the importance or desirability of protecting its distinctive character. Did it have to be forever consigned to an oppositional role, or should it make compromises to be included in governing coalitions? These are the intertwined issues that Magri treats with the thoroughness of a historian rather than the subjective hindsight of a memorialist.

Of the many shifts and turns of the PCI that Magri examines, one of the most fascinating occurred in the 1970s and early 1980s. Under the leadership of Enrico Berlinguer, the party attempted a bold experiment: a historic compromise with the Christian Democratic Party (DC) aimed at forging the grand coalition that was deemed necessary to successfully address the nation's profound social and economic crisis, and to implement the fundamental reforms that would rescue Italy from becoming ungovernable. The move entailed a complex strategy with many intricate manoeuvers and it generated passionate and divisive reactions. It ended in failure not, as is commonly believed, because of Aldo Moro's kidnapping and murder but, as Magri shows in his thorough and lucid exposition, because the DC was never really willing to share power with its historical rival and used every available political tactic to keep the PCI in a subordinate role. In the wake of the debacle, Berlinguer changed course. The 'second Berlinguer,' as Magri describes him,

> 'attempted to make a turn that was not only tactical but strategic, not only political but cultural. The idea [...] was not only, or not mainly, to recover a past identity, but also to renew that identity in a profound way that took account of a rapidly (and dangerously) changing reality'[14].

The initiative undertaken by the second Berlinguer had three major components: strengthening the party's ties with the working classes through active participation in their battle against redundancies and the abolition of wage-indexation; treating the abuse of power, clientelism, and corruption of the political parties as a moral question (echoing Gramsci's call for moral reform in the 1920s); breaking unequivocally with the Soviet Union, with Berlinguer declaring that: 'The impetus [of] the October Revolution is now exhausted. We have reached the point at which that phase is ending.'[15] Not everyone within the party was enthused by Berlinguer's new course, but the effort to revitalize the PCI by reasserting its distinctive identity provided it with new momentum. Berlinguer died unexpectedly and prematurely in June 1984 before he could tackle the much needed and delicate task of restructuring the party and rejuvenating its upper echelons. Still, in Magri's estimation, Berlinguer left the PCI well-positioned to weather the collapse of real existing socialism in Eastern Europe and even to 're-found a Communist-inspired Left that was vibrant and meaningful'.[16] It was no coincidence that Magri rejoined the PCI in 1984.

The dilution of Berlinguer's vision of a party with a distinct identity that occupied the moral high ground in the political arena started not long after his untimely death. The recurring urge to forge an alliance that would permit the PCI to participate in a government majority surfaced yet again. It would have meant reaching some accommodation with the Socialists led by Bettino Craxi who had moved his party rightwards to form a government coalition with the Christian Democrats and whose tenure as prime minister was characterized by battles against workers' movements, massive deficit spending, and rampant clientelism. Such a move would have been a complete betrayal of Berlinguer's campaign for a morally principled reform of Italian politics; it would have also signaled the abandonment of the PCI's claim that it offered a democratic alternative to the ruling coalitions that had governed Italy since 1948. It proved to be a vain aspiration anyway since neither the Socialists nor the Christian Democrats had anything to gain from sharing power with the Communists. Nevertheless, the emergence of an impulse to reverse the course charted by the second Berlinguer marked the beginning of the end of the PCI.

The Tiananmen massacre and the collapse of the Berlin wall did not cause Achille Occhetto's headlong rush first to change the PCI's name and then to dissolve it; rather, they provided him with the opportunity to renounce the party's communist identity in order to make it an acceptable partner in a governing coalition. In crude terms, Occhetto's logic amounted to this: If you can't beat them, join them. As Magri points out, Occhetto's project constituted first and foremost an ideological revision that necessitated a revision of 'how the Party saw its own past'.[17] By way of illustration, he quotes a snippet from an interview in which Occhetto stated: 'The PCI feels itself to be the child of the French Revolution (the revolution of 1789, that is, but without the unfortunate Jacobins) and not, as is always said, the heir of the October Revolution'.[18] On other occasions, Occhetto characterized Togliatti as Stalin's innocent dupe and Berlinguer as a fantast of an alternative society. Iconoclasm and historical revisionism became the order of the day. The political philosopher,

14 Magri, *The Tailor of Ulm*, 338
15 Quoted by Magri, *The Tailor of Ulm*, 336.
16 *The Tailor of Ulm*, 347
17 *The Tailor of Ulm*, 169
18 *The Tailor of Ulm*, 169–70

19 Quoted by Magri, *The Tailor of Ulm*, 370.
20 Gramsci, *Prison Notebooks*, Vol. 2 (New York 1996), 40–41.
21 The historical tailor of Ulm, Albrecht Berblinger, plunged into the Danube in his failed attempt to fly; but he never tried again.
22 *The Tailor of Ulm*, 2.
23 *The Tailor of Ulm*, 368

Norberto Bobbio, observed at the time: 'I ask myself whether what is happening in the PCI is not a real about-turn. One has a sense that there is a lot of confusion there. The haste with which they have been throwing their old cargo overboard seems suspect to me.'[19] The confusion stemmed from the conflicting impulses to erase the party's distinctive identity while simultaneously converting the remaining husk into a political formation capable of contesting elections and vying for a place in a governing majority.

If Magri were inclined towards bitterness and recrimination he would have invoked a note by Gramsci on the failure of the Italian left to mount an effective resistance to the rise of fascism:

> The fable of the beaver (the beaver pursued by hunters who want his testicles for the extraction of medicinal substances, tears off his own testicles to save his life). Why was there no defense? The parties lacked a sense of human and political dignity: but these factors are not facts of nature, they are not deficiencies inherent in a people as permanent characteristics. They are 'historical facts' that have their explanation in past history and in current social conditions.[20]

Instead, Magri alludes to a more ambiguous tale of failure or defeat. The tailor of Ulm, in Brecht's eponymous short poem, crashes to his death when attempting to disprove his bishop's assertion that humans cannot fly and never will. Yet humans did learn to fly, Pietro Ingrao reminded Occhetto during the debate on whether to call the party something other than 'communist'. Magri was not so sure that the story of the tailor of Ulm[21] was a source of consolation, and he asked: 'Can we be sure that, if the fall had only crippled the tailor instead of killing him, he would have immediately picked himself up and tried again, or that his friends would not have tried to restrain him?'.[22]

Following the dissolution of the PCI, Magri did pick himself up and try again by launching *La Rivista del Manifesto*. That effort too ended in failure. By the time he finished writing the *Tailor of Ulm*, the PCI had become a distant memory and the remnants of the left had become almost invisible. He remained convinced that 'the Left [is] more necessary than ever' but he was no longer able to participate in relaunching it: 'the reconstruction of a genuine Left will be a problem for future generations'.[23] He had done his part. In November 2011, he ended his life by assisted suicide in Switzerland.

Old Library at Trinity College, Dublin.
© Dave Bartruff/CORBIS

'Sub Nomine Columbae / In the Name of Columba'

Ronan Sheehan

[This essay is based on the paper 'Downloading The Book of Kells', which was delivered to the Irish Jurisprudence Society at Trinity College Dublin, 15 December 2011; it, in turn, was based on the essay 'Colmcille and the Irish Copyright Tradition', which appeared in the *The Bar Review* (January 2009). The essay takes its title from the conference *Colmcille and the Irish Copyright Tradition*, hosted by the John Philpot Curran Foundation at the National Museum of Ireland in October 2006. It overlaps with an essay in *European Intellectual Property Review* (July 2012) and with talks given on this subject at various venues, including Milan 2009, Edinburgh 2011, Bantry 2011, Dublin 2011, Kells 2012, London 2012.]

If you think you know a little law and find yourself in debate with citizens of Dublin upon matters of politics, economics, the courts, literature, sport or whatever, there is a temptation to quote *Bunreacht na hEireann*, the constitution of the Irish Republic. In my experience, the response is invariably blunt. You will be told to get lost. If you try a favourite piece of legislation, say *The Offences Against The Person Act* (1867), the response is in kind. 'Did you not hear me the first time? I told you what to do with the constitution. You can do the same with what comes out of Dáil Éireann. You can stuff it'. Decisions of the European Court Of Justice, the Supreme Court, hallowed judicial precepts, honoured legal text-books, meet the same fate. But if you say 'this is what my father used to say', or, 'this is what my mother told me', the response may be different. Quiet, curious, respectful even, at least by Dublin standards.

****

My mother put the portrait of her great-grandfather John Adye-Curran BL (1802–67), Alderman of Dublin Corporation, upon the wall of a room at the back of our house in Rathmines where her children's coats, footballs, medals, photographs and various items of sporting equipment were kept. Beside it was a portrait of his wife Frances, of the ancient Yorkshire Catholic family of Dolman.[1] And there was a random collection of sporting photographs including a Gonzaga College under-13 rugby side *c*. 1960 with the long-since-demolished stand of Shamrock Rovers at Milltown in the background. My eldest brother Garrett crouches in the middle of the front row, holding the ball, the captain. In the row behind him, turning away from the camera somewhat shyly, stands his friend and classmate, Peter Sutherland.

Peter's father Billy was a partner in the insurance firm Mathews, Mulcahy and Sutherland of South Leinster Street, just across the road from Guinan and Sheehan, Solicitors, 1 Clare Street, which I entered as an apprentice in 1975. Billy (who always had a word of encouragement for a young person) and my father might be found in consultation in his office on the first floor, which offered a superb view of Nassau Street. Not necessarily, I imagine, upon matters of great moment.

My father's partner Dermot Guinan had inherited a love of theatre from his father John who had written popular plays for The Abbey, including the much-loved *Black Oliver* (1927). A collection of books, including account books relating to royalties, were gathered on a little wooden bookshelf in a room on the top floor at the back of the house where I was stationed. These were the business of the then virtually defunct Irish Playwrights' Association. Occasional queries relating to the authors and the plays were referred to me. I would draft a letter in reply, for the approval or disapproval of a partner.

'To every cow its calf', my father would say, in a grave tone.

As the years progressed, I succumbed to the temptation to quote law cases to him. This usually enraged him.

'Did you read the whole case? Not just the judgement. The whole case!'

One day, Niall Montgomery telephoned to make an appointment to consult me upon a question of copyright law. I was in awe of Niall. Architect, artist, poet, among the first Dublin Joyceans, begetter of the famous Rosc exhibition of 1967 with Michael Scott and others, possessor of a superb prose style in his essays upon, inter alia, Georgian Dublin, friend and correspondent of Samuel Beckett, friend of Brian O'Nolan for whom he had occasionally written his multilingual 'Cruiskeen Lawn' column. I had heard Niall deliver a brilliant lecture on poetry to the English Literary Society in University College Dublin (UCD) a

1 Among notable members of the Dolman family were John (1556–?), a barrister who witnessed the execution of the Jesuit Saint, Edmund Campion, at Tyburn, 1 December 1581, then became a Jesuit himself; Robert (1659–1730), who was charged and acquitted in the 'Popish Plot'; Charles (1807–63), a publisher of Roman Catholic periodicals, including the well-known *The Dublin Review*, a quarterly founded by Nicolas Wiseman, M. J. Quinn and Daniel O'Connell.

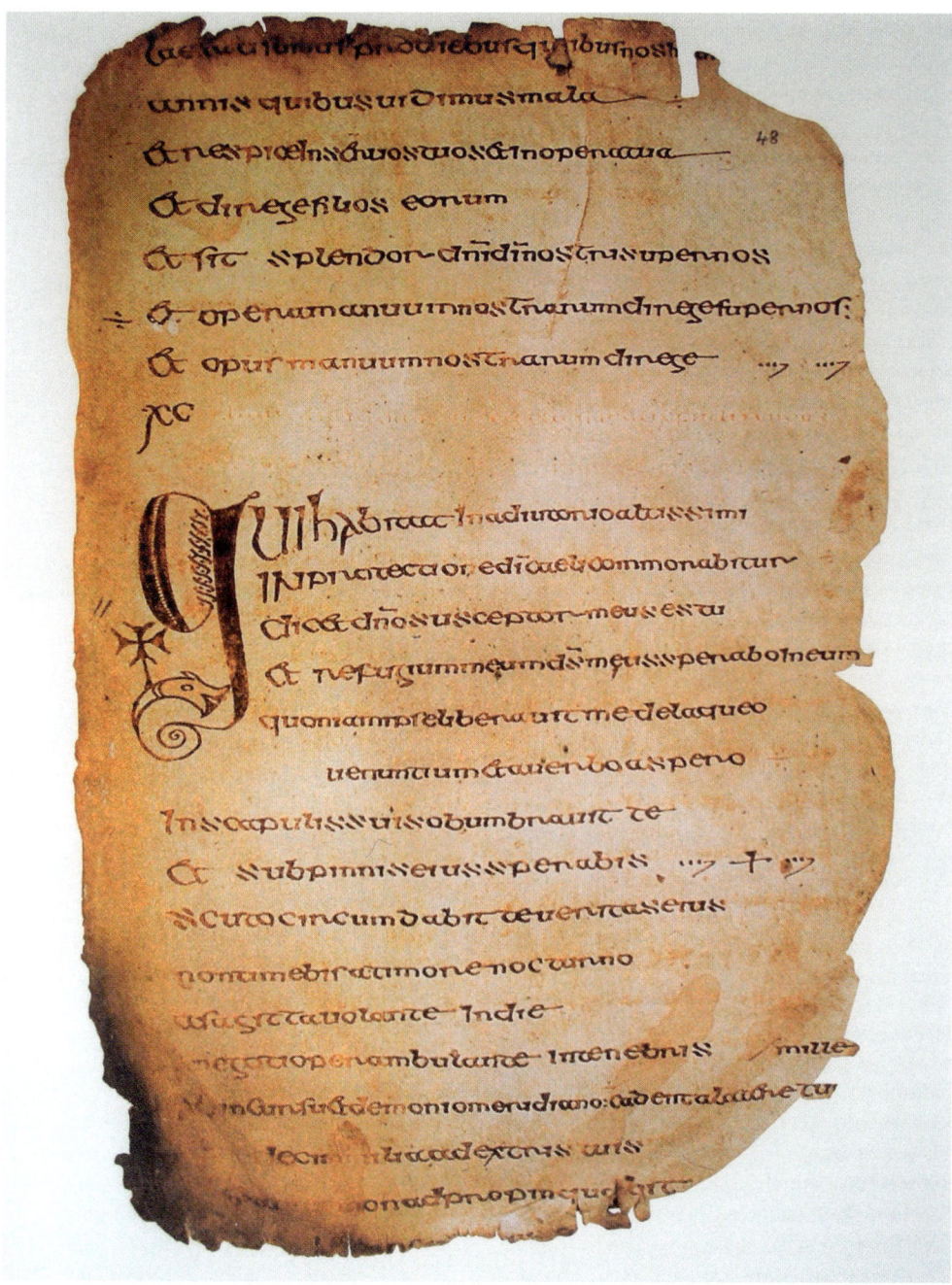

A sample of text from the *Cathach* of St. Columba

few years previously: *Bird Lives/To Hell with D'Alembert*. My father and Niall had been friends at UCD in the thirties, with the radical journalist and activist, Charlie Donnelly, who had been in the same class as my father at the O'Connell school. Years later, a question concerning Charlie's literary estate was brought to us for advice. Donnelly was killed at the battle of Jarama in the Spanish Civil War in 1937. He had begun working on a biography of James Connolly and fought in Spain as a member of the James Connolly Column. His reported last words were 'Even the olives are bleeding'. Joe O'Connor, now a well-known novelist, made these words the title of his fine biography, *Even The Olives Are Bleeding: the Life and Times of Charles Donnelly*, in 1992.

In the late seventies or early eighties my father was instructed in the purchase of a Wilde family home. Not the one down the street from us on the corner of Merrion Square, but Moytura Lodge in County Galway, once the scene of a fire in which two natural daughters of Sir William Wilde had perished. I suspect it was out of curiosity rather than any conveyancing obligation that my father decided to investigate the pre-Land Act title of the property which was to be found in the archives of the Land Commission in Merrion Street. The place had received few enquiries since the Second World War, yet its attendants sitting around the turf fire in the foyer were legendary among Dublin's law clerks and apprentices. Among the deeds, affidavits, certificates and miscellaneous correspondence pertaining to Moytura Lodge, he found the original summons which had been served upon Oscar Wilde in Reading Jail to commence bankruptcy proceedings against him on behalf of The Marquess of Queensberry. Oscar's signature — his endorsement of the service of the summons — was on the back of the document. Someone else might have put the summons in their pocket and walked off with it. My father replaced it. It belonged to the people of Ireland.

Oscar Wilde's litigation with the Marquess of Queensberry is well-known. Lesser-known is the case of *Burrow-Giles Lithographic Company v Sarony*, heard in New York in 1884, an action which claimed damages for the infringement of copyright in a photograph of Oscar Wilde. This was the first case to decide that the American constitutional provision affirming copyright was broad enough to cover an act authorizing copyright of photographs, so far as they are representative of original conceptions of the author.[2]

Looking to the right from my window on the north side of Clare Street lies South Leinster Street and the hotel where Nora Barnacle worked, its name, Finn's Hotel, still faintly but legibly displayed on the brickwork over Nassau Street. As Joyceans know, the day Joyce collected her there is the day of *Ulysses*. I advised Pat Murphy, film director, to whom Stephen Joyce refused permission to quote from the writings of either of his grandparents in her excellent film *Nora*, which explores and celebrates their life together — an heroic quest for freedom.

Stephen Joyce tried to prevent the National Library placing upon exhibition (an act expressing copyright) the *Ulysses* manuscripts it purchased for a fabulous sum over ten years ago from a friend of Joyce or the child of a friend to whom he had entrusted the manuscript. Possession of a manuscript and copyright in it are often different things. In response to Stephen Joyce, the National Library orchestrated a piece of writing which authorized it to do just that: an act of Dáil Éireann, specially drafted to enable the library to exhibit the manuscript without the permission of the copyright owner.

As Pádraig Pearse was at pains to show, we are a sovereign people.

Number 6 Clare Street once housed the offices of Beckett and Metcalf, Quantity Surveyors. The Beckett concerned was William, the father of the playwright; he died very suddenly in 1933. Sam had lived on the top floor of the building for a period during the 1930s and wrote *Murphy* (1938) there.

He also wrote an affidavit on behalf of the plaintiff in the libel action, *Sinclair versus Gogarty*. Sam swore that he had left his apartment at 6 Clare Street and crossed the street to Greene's bookshop where he purchased a book named *As I Was Going Down Sackville Street: A Phantasy in Fact* (1937), by Oliver Saint John Gogarty, the Buck Mulligan figure in *Ulysses*. He saw that Arthur Sinclair was the intended target of a passage in which Gogarty referred to an antiques dealer in Nassau

2 Alan Latman, Robert A. Gorman, Jane C. Ginsburg, *Copyright For The Eighties* (Charlottesville, 1985), 19–23.

Street who was fonder of young mistresses than of old masters. The case was brought by Henry Sinclair, on behalf of his brother Arthur, who died in May 1937. Beckett was treated with such ferocity and contempt by both prosecuting counsel and judge that he decided he could no longer live in Ireland. He 'belonged', Gogarty's counsel said, to 'a coterie of bawds and blasphemers'. Gogarty lost the case and Ireland lost Beckett.

Beckett had loved his cousin, Arthur's daughter, Peggy, who had died of tuberculosis in Germany in 1933.

My great-aunt Agnes Russell (née Becker) had subsidized publication of Gogarty's book. Gogarty liked flying. He had become friends with Charlie Russell, Agnes's deceased husband, one of the first officers of the Irish Air Corps. Charlie and his plane had been on standby in 1921 during the Ango-Irish Treaty negotiations in London, ready to fly Michael Collins back to Ireland in case of an emergency.

'Never volunteer information', was one of my father's precepts.

Once or twice I heard him describe himself as a 'Michael Collins man', without being quite sure what he meant. Was it information or disinformation?

Clare Street runs into Merrion Square, past Oscar Wilde's house, past Niall Montgomery's office, into Lower Mount Street and beyond. It was chiefly in this area that Collins's squad — aka the Apostles — wiped out a division of British intelligence in a series of adroitly co-ordinated operations on Bloody Sunday November 1921. On that day, IRA volunteers Seán MacBride and Ernie O'Malley found a safehouse in the apartment of Lennox Robinson, playwright and manager of The Abbey Theatre, who lived on the top floor of 1 Clare Street.

Seventy-five years, later my friend Neil Jordan made his film *Michael Colli*ns, which recreated the events of that day. A copyright challenge was offered to the script in the course of pre-production. Neil kindly referred the matter to me — he might have sought the advice of a more senior lawyer. I am pleased to say my reading and analysis of the script and various biographies of Collins produced a common source defence to the claim which was persuasive. The law only acknowledges copyright in an original work. There are several biographies of Michael Collins. None could claim copyright in the details of his life. All recounted the salient details, which featured in Neil's script.

A Michael Collins man was my father's first cousin on his mother's side, Luke Foley of the South Dublin battalion of the IRA, who led his men and women in the Battle of Pigeon House Road. My father's sister Rose told me about it and I called my first child after him. So too was my wife Imelda's maternal side grandfather, James Cahill. An Apostle, he had despatched two 'G men' before his seventeenth birthday. The first man to wear the uniform of the Irish army. I remember my father approaching him, with great courtesy and respect, at our wedding. Did Colonel Cahill remember Luke Foley?

I was sitting with Neil Jordan in a bar near the Project Arts Centre in East Essex Street, Dublin, one afternoon in the mid 1980s. Katherine Kavanagh, née Katherine Barry Moloney, a niece of Kevin Barry, was there. She and her companion the writer Leland Bardwell were getting grief from the barman for some reason and we intervened on their behalf. There followed a delightful couple of hours with Katherine in the course of which she asked me to represent her in her efforts to recover copyright in Patrick Kavanagh's work from his brother Peter. I said I would do it.

It was a complicated business which dragged on for almost fifteen years. Ultimately, an order was made in favour of the Trustees of the Kavanagh Estate by Mr. Justice Declan Costello, then President of the High Court of Ireland, who had famously drafted the Copyright Act of 1963. He was the son of Taoiseach John Costello, who had declared the Irish Republic in 1948. Most lawyers, young or

Senior professors of the Dublin Institute for Advanced Studies, 30 March 1981. L–R: John T. Lewis, James R. McConnell, Lochlainn S. O'Raifeartaigh.

old, were at least slightly in awe of Declan Costello. When he gave his judgement upon those issues, which had puzzled and sometimes baffled two teams of lawyers (with the exception of the outstanding Fidelma Macken BL, acting for Peter Kavanagh, and Frank Callanan SC, with me) for so many years, in a lucid exposition lasting ten minutes, I wondered why they were only *slightly* in awe of him.

James McConnell was in the same class in the O'Connell School, North Richmond Street in the 1920s, as my father. His father, from Ballymena, had died when James was four. My paternal grandfather had died in 1918, when my father was four. I imagine this helped to forge the lifelong bond between them. One day in 1921, James McConnell was in Talbot Street with his mother when Sean Treacy and his comrades were attacked by British troops. Treacy was killed. The trauma appears to have caused the child to take a kind of mental photograph of the entire street, because for the rest of his life, at a moment's notice, he could, as it were, take you on a walk down Talbot Street on that day, shop by shop. First one side of the street, then the other.

James studied mathematics and became a priest. He worked with Erwin Schrödinger in the Dublin Institute of Advanced Studies where in due course he became a professor; he also worked in Maynooth where he became professor of mathematical physics in 1945, then dean of the faculty of Science and Registrar of the college. He acted as Director of the Institute from 1969 to 1972. He was meticulous in his priestly duties, except for one — he refused to hear confessions. He signed a copy of his book *Quantum Particle Dynamics*[3] for my parents, which I now hold in trust.

Its object was to enable those who had no previous acquaintance with relativity or quantum theory to acquire sufficient knowledge of quantum mechanics, quantum electrodynamics and meson theory to understand the main features of the theory of elementary particles. After an introductory chapter on the special theory of relativity, the subjects treated include Schrödinger and Werner Heisenberg's quantum mechanics, Paul Dirac's theory of the electron, properties of spinors which are used in radiation theory, the quantization of the electromagnetic field, perturbation theory, photoelectric effect, Compton scattering, bremsstrahlung, production and annihilation of positrons, Yukawa's meson theory, production and scattering of pions, and the theory of anti-nucleons and of strange particles. My father told me that one of his friend's equations had been used in the production of the hydrogen bomb.

Fr. McConnell married my parents one day in September 1945 in the Church of the Three Patrons, Rathgar, beneath the statues of Patrick, Brigid and Columba (the Latin name for Colmcille). In September 1992, my father died. A couple of days later, I walked down the aisle of the same church to where Fr. McConnell was standing at the altar-rail. He wasn't looking very well himself.

'We are pleased you could come to say the Mass, father', I said in greeting.
'Hello, Ronan', he replied. He pointed to a side altar. 'Didn't I baptize you over there just a few minutes ago?'
'You did, father. Indeed you did.'

I had taken instructions from him some time before to draft his will. And I had presented it to him for execution at the Institute for Advanced Studies on Burlington Road. He bequeathed his intellectual property to *Propaganda Fidei*.

Shortly after my father's death, Fr. McConnell's descent into dementia commenced. Unhappy was the day I made an application to the High Court to make this mathematical genius a ward of court and myself guardian of his person and property, including intellectual property. I knew his book had been taught in Princeton, in Beijing, in Cracow. Where else? What had become of the H-bomb equation? What precisely were my duties in the matter? My responsibility did not last long enough to make answers to these questions an obligation. He died soon after. Responsibility for the management of his property passed to his executor.

His book does not bear the usual copyright formula: ©James McConnell 1958. Three lines on a page inside the jacket say that no part of it may be reproduced without permission of the publisher, but no legal authority is cited for the warning.

*****

The second of our two sons was named James, after my father — 'JJ' for short. The year after his grandfather's death, he won a prize in the Texaco Children's Art Competition for a figure painting titled *Batty Bat*. I arrived home one evening to find an invitation from US ambassador Jean Kennedy Smith to see the prize-winning Texaco paintings on exhibition in the American Embassy in Ballsbridge, Dublin

On June 27, 1993, Laila Al'Attar, a leading painter of Iraq and of the Middle East, was killed with her husband and their housekeeper, and her daughter blinded, when President Clinton ordered that a Tomahawk missile be fired at the Mukhabarat, the headquarters of the Iraqi Intelligence Service in Baghdad, held to be

[3] James McConnell, *Quantum Particle Dynamics* (Amsterdam 1958). Chapter 3 is titled 'Schrödinger's Wave Mechanics', 33–51.

responsible for planning an assassination attempt (itself fictional anyway) on George Bush, Clinton's predecessor. Her house was next door to the Mukhabarat. Michael McDowell and Proinsias de Rossa both denounced the action in Dáil Éireann. The only possible justification for such an action in international law was that it was done in self-defence. Neither Laila Al'Attar nor Iraq had offered a threat to the United States.[4]

To place a work on exhibition is, as we have seen, an expression of copyright. So here was a situation where the ambassador of a country guilty of the unlawful killing of Laila Al'Attar and her husband was commandeering, without permission, the artwork of Irish children and placing it on exhibition in their embassy.

I wrote the ambassador a 'cease and desist' letter. Having identified myself as the father of the child artist, I demanded that the Ambassador take JJ's painting off exhibition forthwith. She had not got my permission. I refused permission — as a protest at the unlawful killing of Laila Al'Attar and her husband. There followed a brief, intense correspondence between myself, Texaco and the embassy. *Batty Bat* came off exhibition and was delivered to 1 Clare Street.

The victory was real — the ambassador's removal of the painting from exhibition was an admission of error. But I could only persuade two people to support the idea of an Irish protest for Laila — the painter Robert Ballagh and John Gormley of the Green Party, who had met her in Baghdad. Other artists, male and female, were not interested. So I dropped the idea. Although the removal of the painting was a fact and although the art columns of the papers were often short on news and long on trivia, I could not persuade one newspaper to publish the fact of our protest. So it might as well never have happened.

I waited.

Twelve years later I interviewed my namesake Cindy Sheehan (whose son Casey had passed through Shannon en route to Iraq and death) for the American magazine/website *Counterpunch*, edited by Alexander Cockburn, brother of Patrick, son of Claude, of the radical Church of Ireland tradition.[5] With Cindy's permission, I told the story of the copyright protest. In due course the editor reported that the interview had received one million hits on their website. It also appeared on a Baghdad website uruknet.info/information from occupied Iraq. Hopefully some surviving members of Laila's family, friends and supporters learned that in Dublin too there was a protest over her killing. In our case, a copyright protest.

2

After completing a term directing competition policy in the European Commission, Peter Sutherland was appointed Director General of the General Agreement on Tariffs and Trade (GATT) in 1993. His task was to conduct the Uruguay Round of negotiations with the object of producing a global trade agreement. Intellectual property issues played an important part in this business. It led Sutherland to the headquarters in Geneva of the World Intellectual Property Organization (WIPO), a specialized agency (one of 16) of the United Nations that administers 23 international treaties dealing with different aspects of intellectual property protection and which embraces 183 nations as member states.[6] Here he discovered, among the agency's disparate iconography and exhibitions, an image of Colmcille, which included the words 'To every cow its calf, to every book its copy'.[7]

That pithy, poetic expression is forever associated with Colmcille, although no-one claims that he said it. And, while the date upon which it was said, or whether it was even said at all, may be a matter of conjecture and dispute, Europe has no copyright expression of older vintage. In S. M. Stewart's *International Copyright and Neighbouring Rights* (1989), it is the single legal decision cited from antiquity

4   See *Irish Times*, 28 and 29 June 1993.
5   Alexander Cockburn died 20 July 2012.
6   WIPO website: www.wipo.int (accessed September 28, 2012)
7   Peter Sutherland, conversation with Ronan Sheehan.

World Intellectual Property Organisation, Geneva, Switzerland, where copyright problems are settled (Photo by Francois Lochon/Time & Life Pictures/Getty Images).

8   S. M. Stewart, *International Copyright and Neighbouring Rights* (1989), 14

and the Middle Ages, that is of the era before the printing press. It articulates the fundamental concern of copyright law: Who is entitled to make a copy? It offers the answer to that question which western traditions of copyright law generally give: the person who is entitled to the original work is entitled to the copy of that work.[8] It is ironic that the principle, which, according to the record, he disputed, should be associated with his name. But that is why Colmcille features in WIPO headquarters in the role of father-figure to the legal tradition which the organization espouses.

A standard American textbook, *Copyright for the Eighties*, notes the significance of Colmcille's case in its historical perspective upon copyright:

> Our whole law relating to literary and artistic property is essentially an inheritance from England. It seems that from the time 'whereof the memory of man runneth not to the contrary' the author's right to his or her manuscript was recognized on principles of natural justice, being the product of intellectual labour and as much the author's own property as the substance on which it was written. Blackstone's

Book of Kells, Folio 32v, Christ Enthroned.

Commentaries associates it with the Law Of Occupancy, which involves personal labor and results in 'property', something peculiarly one's own (as implied by the Latin root 'proprius').[9]

But ages before Blackstone, an Irish king had enunciated the same principle in settling the question of property rights to a manuscript: 'To every cow its calf, to every book its copy'.

Patrick, Brigid and Colmcille are the three patron saints of Ireland. Colmcille was born in or about the year 521 in Gartan, Donegal. His father Fedelmith was a grandson of Conall who gave his name to the Cenel Conaill dynasty. Conall and his brothers were sons of Niall of the Nine Hostages whose descendants became the Uí Néill dynasty which dominated most of the northern half of Ireland from the sixth

9 *Copyright for The Eighties* (Charlottesville, Virginia, 1985), 1

10 Brian Lacey, *Columcille and The Columban Tradition* (Dublin, 1997). See Joseph Szövérffy, 'Some stages of the Saint Columba tradition in the Middle Ages', paper presented at the VIIIth Celtic Symposium at Harvard University, in J. Szövérffy and U. Kindermann, eds., *Sequenzen in Osterreich* (Brookline, Leyden, 1988), 49–78; Ian Finlay, *Columba* (London, 1979).

century onwards. Colmcille was therefore an aristocrat.[10]

By tradition, he was fostered according to the Gaelic custom at Kilmacrennan and studied at Saint Mobhi's in Glasnevin to the north of Dublin. By tradition, he founded a monastery at Derry, which in the Irish language is called Doire Cholmcille. In 563, he left Ireland for Britain. He founded a monastery upon the island of Iona. From there, Christianity reached Scotland and the North of England, specifically Northumbria. In Ireland, Scotland and England, a confederation of Columban monasteries developed, famously at Kells in County Meath.

Literature about Colmcille includes a life, *Vita Columbae*, by Adamnán (628–704) his successor as abbot on Iona. The Venerable Bede records the achievement of Colmcille in his *Historia Ecclesiastica Anglorum* (c. 731AD). An anonymous Derry scribe wrote a life in the 12th century. Manus O'Donnell's classic Irish language work *Beatha Colaim Cille* (*The Life Of Colmcille*) appeared in 1532. Geoffrey Keating's *Foras Feasa Ar Eirinn, History Of Ireland* (c.1634) offers an account of the saint and the copyright dispute, which in some respects confirms O'Donnell's, although it draws on different sources. Here is a summary of the event, from Brian Lacey's translation of O'Donnell's *Life of Colmcille*:

Colmcille visited the monastery at Dromyn, near Ardee, County Louth, where Finnian was abbot. He asked to borrow a book and it was given to him. He would stay behind to copy the book after Mass, without Finnian's knowledge. When Finnian heard about this, he protested to Colmcille. This should not have happened without his agreement.

'I will need the King Of Ireland's ruling about this', said Colmcille. 'That is the judgement of Diarmaid MacCerbaill.'

'I'll accept that', said Finnian.

After that they both went to Tara of the Kings, to Diarmad. Finnian told his version of the events to the king first.

'Colmcille copied my book unknown to me and I say that the "son" (copy) of my book is mine.'

Colmcille replied:

'I say that Finnian's book that I copied is none the worse for it. And it is not right that the divine words in that book should perish. Or that I, or anyone else, should be hindered from copying or reading them or spreading them among the people. Moreover, I claim that I was entitled to copy it. Because if I gained any benefit through the copying I would give that to the people. There would be no loss to Finnian, or damage to his book.'

Then Diarmad gave his famous judgement:

'To every cow its little cow, that is its calf, and to every book its little book (copy). Because of that Colmcille, the book you copied is Finnian's.'

'That is a bad judgement', said Colmcille. 'And you will be punished for it.'

For this judgement, and for the reason that the king executed a hostage who was under Colmcille's protection, Colmcille called his kinsmen, the Cenél Conaill and Cenél nEógain, to arms. The Battle of Cúl Dreimne (in Sligo) ensued.

These were the three kings of the Cenél Conaill and Cenél nEógain at that time: Ainmire son of Sedna, king of the Cenél Conaill. And Fergus and Domnall, the two kings of Cenél nEógain: that is two sons of Muircertach son of Muiredach, son of Eógain, son of Niall of the Nine Hostages. Moreover, Eochaid Tirmcharna, king of Connacht and the Uí Maine of Connacht came there in support of Colm Cille. On the night before the battle Colm Cille fasted for God to give him victory over the king of Ireland so that no harm would come to his kinsmen or their followers.'

O'Donnell emphasizes the importance of the *Cathach*:

'The Cathach (the battler, the Battle Book) is the name of that book over which the battle was fought. It is the greatest treasure of Colmcille in the territory of

the Cenél Conaill. It is covered with silver and gold. It is not lawful to open it and if it is taken three times right-handwise around the host of the Cenél Conaill when they are going into battle, they will come back safe and triumphant. And it is on the chest of the abbot or cleric who is, so far as possible, without mortal sin, that the Cathach should be carried around the host.'

****

Robert Clark and Shane Smyth's *Intellectual Property Law in Ireland* is the standard legal textbook upon Irish copyright law.[11] It devotes half of one of its 837 pages to the question of copyright in Early Irish Law:

The creation of any tangible object can be seen as an expression of skill, effort or individuality which raises in turn issues about ownership of that work, the freedom of others to imitate or utilize the work, or the right of the original creators of the work to control such imitations or uses. While these matters are now regulated by statute, early Irish manuscripts provide a well-known illustration of this conflict. Saint Colmcille is recorded as having illicitly copied a gospel manuscript which belonged to Saint Finnian. When Saint Finnian discovered this unauthorised act of reproduction he claimed, before Diarmad, arguing by analogy, that he held 'for every cow its calf': thus 'to every book its copy'. Scholars dispute the true outcome of the litigation. Under some traditions it is said to have led to the battle of Cúil Dreimne. One scholar at least is of the view that the entire 'decision' is probably fictitious and Phillips is unable to identify any convincing proof that the trial of Columcille was actually about unauthorised copying.

Clark and Smyth thus dismiss the dispute between Colmcille and Finnian, suggesting that at best the matter may be regarded as a story, 'a tale which resonates down the ages'. But it is not law. As a consequence, the authors provide no enquiry into the legal basis for the production of manuscripts in medieval Ireland, or in the monasteries founded by Irish missionaries on the continent, at Saint Gall and Bobbio; no enquiry into the legal basis for the production of manuscripts in the North of England and Scotland. And, on foot of all that, there is no need to consider the intellectual property status of the Book of Kells.

It was, not surprisingly, in the new 'medium' of the Internet that major intellectual property issues contested before the High Court in Dublin two years ago were produced. Mr Justice Peter Charleton's decision in the so-called downloading case entitled *EMI Records (Ireland) Ltd v UPC Communications Ireland Ltd*[12] was made on 11 October 2010. On foot of the judgement, the Minister for Enterprise, Trade and Innovation began a consultation process towards an amendment he contemplated to the *Copyright and Related Rights Act* of 2000. The Internet enables the copying of different kinds of material, including music. In the jargon of the internet, an uploader makes a piece of music available on the Internet and a downloader brings it to his computer. According to the record companies, the first action infringes the intellectual property right to make the music available and the second action infringes the right to reproduce it.

The record companies sought an injunction whereby an Internet service provider would be obliged to monitor users, whom they claimed were infringing their copyright in this way, with a view to withdrawing the service from them. The idea, expressed in the jargon of American baseball, is that an Internet user should lose the service if shown to have infringed three times — 'three strikes and

11 Robert Clarke, Shane Smyth, *Intellectual Property Law in Ireland* (London, 1997)
12 *EMI Records (Ireland) Ltd. v UPC Communications Ireland Ltd.* (2010) IEHC 108 HC (Irl)

you're out'.[13] Two EC directives, in the plaintiff's view, provided for the sanction. Mr. Justice Charleton declined to make the order sought. He ruled that there was no provision in the act of 2000 which empowered him to do so.

A remarkable passage in Mr. Justice Charleton's judgement in the related case *EMI Records (Ireland) Ltd et al v Eircom Limited* (16/4/2010) (3) attracted no media comment:

> There is a fundamental right to copyright in Irish law. This has existed in Irish legal tradition since the time of Saint Colmcille. He is often quoted in connection with the aphorism: le gach bó a buinín agus le gach leabhar a chóip (to each cow its calf and to every book its copy). I regard the right to be identified with and to reasonably exploit one's own original creative endeavour as a human right.

This was the first time that an Irish court had formally adopted the Colmcille tradition as law.

What is the law of Colmcille?

In 2006, Liam Breathnach of the Dublin Institute of Advanced Studies, author of *A Companion to Corpus Iuris Hibernici* (2005), a commentary on Daniel Binchy's 6 volume *Corpus Iuris Hibernici* (1978), explored the Colmcille tradition at a seminar organized by the John Philpot Curran Foundation[14] at the National Museum of Ireland, Collins Barracks. What follows derives from that.

What, he asks, is the expression of a legal principle doing in the life of a saint? The question must be considered in the context of Irish law as a whole. A large body of legal writing reveals a tradition which extends from the seventh to the seventeenth century. The jurisdiction of the brehons encompassed the whole island from earliest times until the Norman invasion of the twelfth century. From then until the seventeenth century it was used in a significant portion of the country.

Many of the legal texts we have comprise compilations specially put together for lawyers. Law and literature were not exclusive categories. No lawyer's book consists solely of law texts. They include sagas and lives of saints. The professions of law and poetry were affiliated. Some legal texts were in verse; one example is a thirteenth-century work on distraint. A sixteenth-century compilation from County Clare contains the texts of several sagas. Some stories are set in a legal context. The story of the ill-fated king Fergus Mac Leti, for example, occurs in both legal and literary contexts.[15] The enunciation of legal principles by the illustrious dead is one notable feature of the texts, while a common theme is the false judgement. Here is one typical story:

> One day Cormac Mac Art set out for Tara. He met a woman who was weeping. The reason was that her sheep had broken into the queen's woad garden and eaten the leaves off the plants. The king MacCon had ordered that the sheep be forfeit for their offence. Cormac immediately pointed out that the judgement should have been 'one shearing for another'. In other words, the woman should only have been obliged to hand over one shearing of her sheep in recompense for the shearing of the woad plants. When MacCon was informed of Cormac's judgement, he realized he was guilty of an injustice and that Cormac was the rightful king.

The famous story about how Cú Chulainn got his name is also structured to make a legal point — about compensation. On a journey north, Setanta encounters a guard dog. It belongs to Culainn. He kills the dog. Now he is obliged to provide a substitute dog. Until the appropriate mastiff

---

13 Gerard Kelly, 'Three Strikes is Ruled: the Decision in *EMI Records (Ireland) Ltd. and Others v UPC Communications Ireland Ltd.*', *Irish Intellectual Property Law Quarterly* (March 2011), 63.

14 John Philpot Curran (1750–1817), orator, lawyer, poet, founder member of the Monks of the Order of St. Patrick (popularly known as 'The Monks of the Screw') and of the Irish Whig Party. He was a lifelong opponent of John Fitzgibbon, and defended several members of the United Irishmen. His daughter Sarah Curran was the beloved of Robert Emmet; Curran disowned her and gave up the defence of Emmet. He was friend of the English radical anarchist and novelist, William Godwin, Shelley's father-in-law. Curran was described by Karl Marx as 'the greatest lawyer of the eighteenth century' and by Byron as a 'machine of the imagination'. He was member of the Irish Parliament for Rathcormack and forebear, by tradition, of John Adye-Curran. The Irish Parliament refused to recognize English publishers' copyright claims; this gave birth to a flourishing reprint industry in Dublin.

15 See Katherine Simms, 'The Poetic Brehon Lawyers of Early Sixteenth-Century Ireland', *Ériu* 57 (2007), 12–32.

is found, that substitute must be Setanta himself who accordingly changes his name. Thus cú (dog) Chulainn (of Culainn).

Works such as Muirghius O'Davoren's (Dubdaboiren) *Eeincland na trí seacht n grad* served various purposes. The title translates as 'Safeguard of the Twenty One Orders' and the manuscript lists the several taxes to be paid to the various orders (bishops, priests, etc.) that would sustain and protect them. But it is one of many texts that operate as a mnemonic that would help fix in the law student's mind the varying amount of taxes for different orders, the honour prices, or the procedures to be followed when distraining the property of an accused person. In their intricacy, works such as this were an exercise in literary rhetoric that advertised the skill and status of the person who wrote them. Status was a central and complex concept. For someone who was both judge and poet, the honour price of both professions was combined to indicate his worth in a dispute. Thus lawyers had to be learned in the literary, historical and mythological traditions of their country, because these were sources of law. *Uraicecht Becc* (*Little Primer c.* AD 900), a primer for law students, begins in a manner similar to the *Institutes* of Gaius, or Justinian, by defining the bases of law as 'roscadaib & fasagaib & teistemnaib fraib' which means 'upon maxims and precedents and true scriptural testimonies'.

Old Irish law texts cite the opinion of ancient judges in past disputes generally drawn from mythology. Doubtful cases and contentions are drawn from literary myths and sagas, a practice not unlike that employed in the ancient Roman schools of rhetoric. The relationship between law and poetry had its roots in pre-Christian Irish culture. Poets were seers who performed public rites—like the *sacra vates* of Virgil, whose inspired words represented a moment of intersection between the divine and the human. The judge's verdict was also such a moment. The pagan belief that the moment a judge uttered his verdict was an encounter between the human and the divine and that the will of God was outraged by an unjust judgement, while just judgements, on the other hand, drew down divine blessings, is already testified among the Celts of Gaul in the first century BC, where Strabo remarks that the druids were chiefly trusted to try cases of homicide. And that 'when there is an abundance of these, they consider that there is also an abundance of the land', presumably because their many just judgements draw down God's blessing on the crops. In medieval Ireland the judge who gave false judgements also brought a curse on the surrounding population: 'seol n-eta blechta & mesa [...] gallra & ancesa' ('a failure of grain and of milk and of mast [...] diseases and difficulties').

The age of the copyright dispute is a material point. Manus O'Donnell's is the oldest version we have. The ancient 'Lives' do not mention it. But that factor is not decisive. It may be that it is a survival. O'Donnell states that his book is based on a comprehensive review of older books. Geoffrey Keating as we saw, records the dispute between Colmcille and Finnian in *Foras Feasa Ar Éirinn*. His version is based on the lost Book Of Malacca and has the gospel, not the psalms, as the subject matter of the dispute. It may therefore be assumed to derive from a different tradition from O'Donnell, his predecessor. Both, however, focus upon the unjust judgement — that 'there is no harm in copying'.

Colmcille, not Manus O'Donnell, says this. In the lives of the saints, when a saint makes such a statement, it is conclusive. That is taken to be the truth of the matter. Both the O'Donnell and the Keating versions concur in rejecting the claim to copyright. On this basis, Liam Breathnach affirmed that the right we call copyright did not exist in the law of Ireland under the system of jurisprudence known to the Irish people as the Brehon Laws.

The word copyright is ambivalent. It can mean the right to restrict copying, which Finnian claims, and it can mean the right to copy, which Colmcille claims.

Photograph engraving of Queen Alexandra wearing the Koh-i-noor diamond in her coronation crown, 9 August 1902. (Photo: W. and D. Downey)

Points of Contact

(a) *The Statute of Anne*

A detailed account of the *Cathach* was recently commissioned by the Royal Irish Academy. This shows that the right to keepership of the relic has been a crucial issue since earliest times.

The O'Donnells claimed Colmcille as their ancestor. Deriving from the ninth century Domhnall, they were a branch of the Uí Néill. Tír Chonail, their territory, takes its name from Conall, son of Niall Noigiallach, 'Niall of The Nine Hostages'. Manus O'Donnell, the historian, was grandfather of Aodh Rua O'Donnell, the 'dauntless red Hugh' of Elizabethan times. After the fall of Limerick (1691) the Catholic Jacobite army retreated to France. Colonel Daniel O'Donnell of Ramelton (1666–1735), like Aeneas leaving the ruins of Troy with his household gods, brought the *Cathach* to the continent.

He fought in the Irish Brigade in the service of France. He campaigned in France, Germany, Italy and the Low Countries. He fought Marlborough, Churchill's ancestor, at Oudenarde in 1708. He commanded the regiment of O'Donnell in the Irish Brigade in the campaigns of 1709–12. These actions included the battle of Malplaquet and the defence of the lines of Atleux, Denain, Douai, Bouchain and Quesney. He served under Marshal Louis Hector de Villars in Germany at the sieges of Loudun and Freiburg and at the forcing of General Vaubonnes entrenchment. This led, in March, 1714, to the peace of Rasstat between Germany and France.

So, at the time when the English parliament was enacting the first copyright statute, the *Statute of Anne* 1709, which afforded the owner of a book the right to copy it, Daniel O'Donnell was sustaining upon the battlefield his allegiance to a far older law. He was made a Brigadier-General on 1 February 1719. He died in his bed at St. Germain-en-Laye, where the exiled Stuarts and their supporters, many of them Irish, lived for many years at the invitation (originally) of Louis XIV, who was born there. O'Donnell had deposited the *Cathach* with a convent of Irish Benedictine nuns at Ypres in Flanders with the stipulation that it should be given to the chief of the clan when applied for.

Conal O'Donnell brought it back to Ireland in 1813. It was found to contain the pages of a psalter written in Irish majuscule script. It may date from the sixth century, and it appears to have been written by one hand. The number of errors and corrections in the text suggest that it may have been written in some haste. It may indeed have been written by Colmcille.

The manuscript may be seen in the Royal Irish Academy. The casket in which it was contained is in the National Museum of Ireland. The *Cathach* may be cited in support of the view that that the legal tradition is based on actual historical events. It is worth noting that, after the siege of Limerick, the *Cathach* was not given for safekeeping to Trinity College Dublin, to keep company with the other great relic of Colmcille, the Book of Kells.

(b) *Irish Folklore*

The archives of the Department of Irish Folklore in UCD reveal a long tradition concerning the copyright dispute. Bairbre Ní Fhloinn of that department gave an account of this tradition to the seminar cited above:

> Six years ago an old man living at Altagowlan, Arigna, County Roscommon was asked what he knew of Colmcille, to which he replied 'Every cow is calved. And every book is copied'.[16] Of all the various stories and legends about St. Columba that have survived, that of the copyright dispute is the most widely dispersed. It is, very appropriately, a part of written as well as oral tradition.

In 1867, Michael Harkin, a teacher and journalist from Donegal published a

[16] John James Mulhern in conversation with Wendy Elliott (UCD) (August, 2006). See Joseph Szövérffy, 'Manus O'Donnell and Irish Folk Tradition', *Éigse*, 8 (1956/57), 108–32; 'The Well of the Holy Women: Some St. Columba Traditions in the West of Ireland', *Journal of American Folklore*, 68 (1955), 111–22.

volume on the history and antiquities of the peninsula of Inishowen, particularly associated with Colmcille (or Columbkille, as Harkin refers to him). St. Finnian, Colmcille's opponent in the dispute, was founder of the abbey of Moville during the reign of Dermot of the Owen family, monarchs of the kingdom. Harkin's version of the famous aphorism is 'Le gach bóin a bóinín, agus le gach leabhar a leabhrán'. He too, as is perhaps more the case in Donegal tradition, emphasizes Colmcille's punishment — the canonical penance for being accessory to the battle of Cúl Dreimhne by which the saint was forced into exile, away from his beloved Derry and Donegal, to Iona—where the Book of Kells was probably begun. That too, we must remember, was an act of copying, as well as an act or project of communal genius.[17]

(c) The Public Interest Defence
In an article entitled 'The Public Interest Defence in Contemporary Copyright law', Alexandra Sims cites an observation of Lord Jauncey in *Attorney General v Guardian Newspapers Ltd* (no. 2):

> The courts of the United Kingdom will not enforce copyright claims in relation to every literary work. Therefore courts do play an active role in copyright's operation and will intervene to deny protection when the public interest would be harmed. The public interest defence differs from the public interest in the broad sense. The public interest defence does not deny copyright protection in a work; it merely prevents the claimant from enforcing copyright against the defendant.'[18]

What Colmcille copied was a psalter, the *Cathach*. Martin MacNamara argues that the psalter was:

> '... at the very centre of monastic life, indeed of the life of the literate community. The earliest specimens of writing in Ireland were the so-called Springmount Bog tablets (Co. Antrim, early seventh century). They are wax tablets bearing psalms 30–32, used it would appear, to initiate pupils as was customary through the psalms into the arts of writing and reading. [...] The psalter as a book in Ireland was loved and venerated. It was at the centre of monastic literature and learning.'[19]

This observation suggests that Colmcille's case was concerned with, inter alia, a matter of public interest.

It is appropriate to note at this point the great excitement over the chance discovery in Tipperary in 2006 of the Faddan Mór psalter, said to be the first discovery of a medieval manuscript in Ireland in over 200 years. Its survival is something of a miracle, and the skills and care devoted to its (partial) restoration are only one indicator of the book's treasured status.

The psalter in Ireland was also known as *na trí cóicat*, 'the three Fifties', the traditional division in Ireland for the 150 psalms. Then, the chanting of 150 Paters as a devotional ritual was modified, after the thirteenth century, to include fifty Aves as well; this seems to have happened in France, Germany and Ireland, perhaps in that sequence. The singing or chanting of fifty psalms for the dead became an intercessionary ritual, like the saying of Mass for the dead. This chant itself developed, probably through the influence of St. Dominic, into the devotion of the rosary.

Thus, the traditional division of the rosary (ten Aves followed by a Pater followed by a Gloria) derives from the original division of the Psalms; the prayers ('bedes', beads) took the place of the words of the psalms themselves, more specifically in Catholic countries, while the singing of the psalms became a characteristic of the territories of the Reformation. The rosary of prayers was often developed in the image of the garland or necklace, the beads often made of precious woods, metals, even

---

17 Harkin used the pen-name 'Maghtochair'. The chapters of the book had appeared initially in the *Derry Journal*. See *Inishowen: Its History, Traditions, and Antiquities* (Dublin, 1985), 28–30.
18 Alexandra Sims, 'The Public Interest Defence in Contemporary Copyright Law', *European Intellectual Property Review*, 28.6 (2006), 335; *Attorney General v Guardian Newspapers Ltd.* (no. 2) (1990) 1 AC 109 HL.
19 Martin McNamara, *The Psalms in the Early Irish Church* (Sheffield, 2000).

pearls; in some instances it was a garland of verses in which the element of devotion or adoration was prominent. Colmcille's last act was the copying of a psalter; his most contentious act the copying of the *Cathach*.

(d) Muslim Law

'It is not right that the divine words in that book should perish.'
(*Beatha Cholmcille*)

Intellectual property law did not play an important role in the Indonesian economy until the 1980s.[20] The Live Aid Concert organized in 1985 by the Irish rock singer, Bob Geldof, became the starting point for discussion about intellectual property law in that country. Soon after the release of the Live Aid record, 1.5 million tapes with a market value of US$3 million were produced in Indonesia. Owing to poor copyright protection, the Live Aid organization did not get a single cent of this money and Geldof called for a boycott of Indonesia as a holiday destination.

In a newspaper article of 2008, the Indonesian lawyer Mohamed Mova Al'Afghani criticized *fatwas* issued by the Indonesian Ulemas Council because they contained the judgement that intellectual property violations are *haram* (forbidden), in effect that the unlawful use of intellectual property violates the law of God and is therefore sinful.[21] The Council had argued that intellectual property is one of the types of property protected under Islamic law. Al'Afghani argued that the council should have investigated whether this was a *sui generis* Islamic concept rooted in the primary sources of Islamic law, the Koran and *hadith* (oral tradition). They would have found that few verses supported their tradition. On the contrary, there is abundant authority for the proposition that all knowledge belongs to God and that seeking and sharing knowledge is an obligation for all Muslims. There had been a system of 'knowledge acknowledgement' known as *yaza*, from the author. This system of a chain of authority was designed to ensure authenticity in the passing of knowledge from one person to another and also as a form of respect for authors. It was not created for financial benefit, but rather for the sanctity of science. It only protects the moral right of the author to a certain degree. The knowledge itself belongs to God, not to any individual. The *yaza* system certainly is not a form of copyright.

In Mohamed Al'Afghan's view, copyright is a response to the Gutenberg printing revolution of the European Middle Ages. The concept of the patent — an intellectual product — stemmed from that. Intellectual property is a concept developed in the West. It is not a *sui generis* Islamic legal concept. Does intellectual property protection serve Indonesian society's best interests? On the contrary, it has been the cause of much abuse. It would serve Islamic society to limit the concept of intellectual property, if not completely to abolish it in the future. Extensive intellectual property protection is only in the interests of big corporations and advanced nations.

Islamic values favour the promotion, transfer and dissemination of knowledge rather than treating it as property. Islamic legal scholars should enlighten and liberate Muslim society by limiting and reducing the protection granted under the concept of intellectual property. Imparting a capitalistic legal concept and stamping God's word on it will not bring any benefits to society.

(e) Chinese law

'*It is not right that I, or any other, should be hindered from copying them or reading them or spreading them among the people. I claim that I am entitled to copy it for if there was any profit for me in copying it, I would want to give that profit to the people.*'
(Beatha Cholmcille)

In Colmcille's view, the people are entitled to the value of the book. The copy grants them their entitlement. The

20 Christopher Antons, *Traditional Knowledge, Traditional Cultural Expressions and Intellectual Property Rights In the Asia-Pacific Region* (Leyden, 2009).
21 *The Jakarta Post*, 17 November 2008.

22 Li Xiang Cheng, (lawyer of the China Legal Affairs Centre, Beijing; Associated with Simmons and Simmons, London), 'Waiting for Supplements: Comments on China's Copyright Law', *European Intellectual Property Review*, 5 (1991), 171.
23 Li Xiang Cheng, 'Waiting For Supplements', 171–77.
24 Cheng, 'Waiting for Supplements', 173.
25 Cheng, 'Waiting for Supplements', 175.
26 Cheng, 'Waiting for Supplements', 171.

defence expresses a cultural, moral and philosophical attitude to knowledge, one we may assume was widely held in his society. The book, the Psalms, should be freely available to everyone.

China once had a similar view. This is recorded by Li Xiang Cheng of the China Legal Affairs centre, Beijing, in an article which assesses the enactment of the New Copyright Law by China's Congress in that year (1991). The Bill was designed to bring China into line with the West. It might be one thing, Li Xiang Cheng suggests, to change the law, and quite another thing to change the long-established cultural attitudes of an ancient civilization:

> Before discussing the legal issues arising from the Copyright Law, it is of interest to consider the historical and political circumstances leading up to its introduction. Historically, the development of copyright law is recognized as a consequence of the invention of printing techniques and the development of book-publishing. However, although printing was first invented in China and publishing traditions date back further in China than in Europe, a comprehensive copyright system was never established in China.[22]

Among the various reasons for this, Chinese cultural attitudes constitute one that cannot be overemphasized. Morality concerning intellectual property differed from that concerning other types of property. It is a tradition in China that 'in matters of calligraphy and printing, one is not to discuss a price'.[23] Chinese intellectuals, the authors of many copyright works, were not interested in the economic value of their works. By the same token, it is also necessary to highlight that the potential value of original works might not have been understood by the user of copyright works. Therefore, it remains to be seen whether traditional Chinese attitudes towards copyright works may now affect the operation of the new Western-style copyright law. If the shades of Finnian and Colmcille are reflected here, that of Cúil Dreimne may be discerned in the course of China's engagement with the concept of intellectual property. The British Navy was involved at the start.

In fact the copyright law was not the first copyright law of China. The first such law can be traced back to 1910, one year before the last emperor was overthrown. The reason for its introduction was probably not changing Chinese attitudes towards the protection of original works, but more likely can be attributed to foreign influences, including the presence of the British Fleet.[24]

Since there had been no copyright law in China for 40 years prior to 1990, its introduction involved a new concept for most Chinese. Li Xiang Cheng warns that this fact should be borne in mind by those who contemplate the exploitation and protection of their copyright in China.[25]

Foreign influences played a role in the discussions which preceded the Copyright Law. An important role was played by the US government armed with GATT, section 301, and Super 301 of the US Trade Act 1974. Zeng Chenghsi, the distinguished jurist, noted that there was a strong call for change by domestic intellectuals. The situation reflected not only changing attitudes but also the serious extent of the infringements.[26]

(f) Copyright and Related Rights Act (Ireland) 2000

'Then Diarmad gave the famous judgement: "To every cow its little cow, that is its calf, and to every book its little book (copy) and because of that, Colmcille, the book you copied is Finnian's."' (Beatha Cholmcille)

Diarmad's judgement and order prefigure our contemporary legislation. Section 102 enacts that the author of a work shall be identified as the author and that the right shall also apply in relation to an adaptation of the work. The right conferred by this section shall be known as the paternity right.

Section 126 enacts that when a person has in his possession an infringing copy of a work or an article designed for making copies of a work, the owner of the copyright in the work may apply to the appropriate court for an order that the infringing copy or article may be delivered up to him or such other person as the court may direct.

(g) The Book Of Kells

> '*Why should the Irish people pay to see pictures they already own?*' [27]
> '*It is not right that the divine words in that book should perish or that I, or any other, should be hindered from copying or recording them or spreading them among the people.*' (Beatha Cholmcille)

Either Iona (I Cholmcille) or the monastery at Kells, County Meath, produced the Book of Kells in the 8th or 9th century. Some believe the work started on Iona and transferred to Kells to escape the Viking marauders. An illuminated manuscript of the four gospels, it is on display in the library of Trinity College Dublin. While the book's awe-inspiring visual dimensions have made it a wonder of the world for a thousand years and more, it is essentially a Latin gospel and may be regarded as the cornerstone of Ireland's Latin heritage. In the Irish language it is Leabhar Cholmcille, the Book of Colmcille. Upon postcards, facsimiles, calendars and various other places, the trustees of the library of Trinity College assert a copyright interest in the book, an interest which is more emphatically exercized through the entrance fee charged to visitors to the library, which earns the college a substantial income every year.

Whose book is it? Whose copyright, if there is copyright in it at all?

The first reference to it we have is in the *Annals of Ulster* (Year 1007), when the theft of the most precious object in the world is described. In the following century, Giraldus Cambrensis thought the great 'Gospel Of Colmcille' the work, not of man, but of angels.

Michael Slavin outlines the book's history.[28] A land grant at the back of the book places it in Kells *c*. 1140. In about 1260, the monastery was transferred from Columban to Augustinian hands. At the suppression of the monasteries in 1539, its fate becomes unclear. The best guess is that the book passed into the hands of the family of the last abbot, Richard Plunkett. From 1558 to 1604, someone who has not been identified used the book to record annals. In 1621, James Ussher, Church of Ireland Bishop of Meath, made an entry in the book. Ussher's successor in the see, Henry Jones, gave the book to Trinity College, along with the Book of Durrow.

According to Michael Slavin, this might have been done for the protection of the book:

> It is quite possible that both volumes were in any case housed at Trinity for safe-keeping. Kells is known to have been a hotbed of Puritan extremism — these individuals, who had an abhorrence of graven images, would surely have loved to get their hands on either book with a view to destroying them.[29]

Trinity College officially concurs with this account, which puts the college in possession of the book legitimately. It has retained the book and the benefits of that possession for 300 years. The people of Kells wish to bring home the book which had been there for 800 years.

Henry Jones (1605–82) seems an unlikely saviour from Puritan or indeed

27 Charles Haughey, Taoiseach, declining a proposal that the National Gallery charge an entrance fee.
28 Michael Slavin, *The Ancient Books Of Ireland* (Dublin, 2005), 30–31
29 Slavin, *Ancient Books of Ireland*, 132

Dr Herbert Parke, chief librarian of Trinity College Dublin, holds the 8th-century illuminated manuscript the Book of Kells at the Trinity College exhibition at Burlington House, London, 11 January 1961. (Photo by Keystone/Getty Images)

30 Aidan Clarke, entry for Henry Jones (1605–82), *Oxford Dictionary Of National Biography* (2004).

any brand of extremism. Scoutmaster General in Cromwell's army, he attended meetings of the army council, an institution responsible for ordering the massacre of Irish Catholics at Drogheda and elsewhere, and for rounding up and transporting tens of thousands of people as slaves to the Barbados. He established and served upon a special court which tried people for their alleged involvement in atrocities. He administered the transplantation of Catholics to Connacht. According to Aidan Clarke:

> He was rewarded by elevation to the bishopric of Clogher in 1645 and appointment as vice-chancellor of Dublin University in 1646 in place of his uncle, Archbishop Ussher, a position which he held until 1660 and the tacit obligations of which he more than fulfilled by the presentation to the college library of the books of Kells and Durrow.[30]

Under Cromwell, he acquired forfeited estates in Summerhill, County Meath, together with the wardship of the heir of a wealthy landowner within the Pale and grants of tithes of nine abbeys rectories (these last directly ordered by Cromwell). He was complicit in the persecution of Archbishop Saint Oliver Plunkett.

What valid title, in real property, in personal property, in intellectual property, could pass through the hands of Henry Jones? His business was the plunder of a devastated country.

****

In 1848, after a protracted struggle, the British Army defeated the Sikhs in northern India. General Hardinge seized their fabulous diamond, the Koh-I-Noor, a symbol of Sikh sovereignty. It was duly presented to Victoria and set in her crown. The Book of Kells was and is a symbol of Irish sovereignty. It was and remains the quintessential expression of the Gaelic Catholic civilization, which Trinity College was by its constitution mandated to destroy. The seizure of the Book of Kells in the seventeenth century and its transfer to Trinity College was the equivalent of the transfer of the Koh-I-Noor diamond in the nineteenth century. When Victoria and Albert visited Dublin in 1900, they were invited to sign the Book of Kells. Any vestige of Irish sovereignty had to be appropriated.

(h) Downloading The Book of Kells
The tradition of Kells holds that there was a time when the book was on the altar of the church, available for all to see. On certain feast days it was carried around the town to the various high crosses, whose colours would have corresponded with those of the book. Once in Trinity, the book effectively disappeared from public view for centuries. The ordinary pejorative meaning of the term 'downloading' is to make something privately owned publicly available, without compensation. The Trinity College download of the Book of Kells is a reverse procedure. It is to make something that was publicly owned or quasi-publicly owned, in that it was held absolutely for the benefit of the people and was publicly available for nothing, into something privately owned and available at a charge.

Should this copyright question regarding the Book of Kells, by far the most valuable piece of intellectual property in Ireland, be a matter of concern to those whose business is the defence of the national intellectual property interest? Two years ago, Lady Pearson of Addison Publications Ltd. (London) wrote to me noting my interest in the book and offering to sell me a facsimile copy of it (produced in association with TCD) for £10,500. She did not say that, like Colmcille, she was passing any profit she made in selling a copy of his book to the people. Perhaps, unlike me, she does not feel that Colmcille's law should go with Colmcille's book. And neither, it seems, does INFACT, which, so far as I am aware, has yet to issue injunction proceedings against Lady Pearson.

(i) Video Recordings Act 1989 (Ireland)

'I say that Finnian's book that I copied is none the worse for it.'
(Beatha Cholmcille)

The passage of this Act had perhaps as much to do with foreign influence, specifically that exercised by the Motion Picture Association of America, which represents giant corporations like Disney, Warner Brothers, Dreamworks, Columbia Pictures — which in turn feature such luminaries as Michael Eisner, Jeffrey Katzenberg, Rupert Murdoch, Harvey Weinstein — as it had to do with a change of cultural attitudes on the part of the Irish people. The act purported to criminalize matters of copyright infringement in the context of the cinema. In imitation of the British organization FACT (Fight Against Copyright Theft (established 1983)), INFACT, the Irish National Fight Against Copyright Theft, was established at the time of the Act.

It has been objected that FACT's name is a misnomer since there is no such offence within the United Kingdom as 'copyright theft' under the Theft Act 1968. When copyrighted material is copied, this act is not permanently removing the material from its owner. Copyright infringement is not theft, stealing or taking without consent. It is possession of a copy, or copies, of copyrighted material without a suitable licence from the owner.

In 2005, Denise Fitzpatrick (with Terry Prone) published *Cease and Desist*, an account of her struggle to assert her intellectual property rights against the Disney Corporation. A native of Skryne, County Meath, she conceived of a character called Piggley Pooh and tried to transform it into a TV series. She claimed that the idea was born of the rural Irish culture of her childhood. The Disney Corporation saw the matter in a different light. *Winnie the Pooh,* a children's story by A. A. Milne, was published in 1926 and was followed two years later by *The House at Pooh Corner.* Milne gave the name of his son, Christopher Robin, to the child who plays with the animal characters in the books: Winnie the Pooh (a toy bear), Rabbit, Piglet, Eeyore, etc. Disney acquired intellectual property rights to the Milne characters.

Disney's claim was that Denise's pig represented an infringement of the company's rights in A. A. Milne's bear. It issued a 'cease and desist' letter, a threat to sue her unless she stopped trying to turn her pig into a television series. *Cease and Desist* records the sheer misery and virtual ruin to which Denise and her family were subjected by the Disney Corporation, whose vast resources were deployed against her for many years in myriad legal procedures

Denise never relinquished her right to her intellectual property — her characters. After more than a decade of soul-destroying struggle, the European Court at Alicante upheld that right. The victory was soured by an unforeseen aspect of the children's entertainment business, its realpolitik. Were Denise to use the word 'Pooh' in her title, Disney might boycott — and ruin — everyone who dealt with her. From the jaws of victory a character named 'Piggley Winks' was born.

In this contest, which concerned the intellectual property rights of an Irish citizen, the Irish citizen was not assisted by the organization styling itself the protector of Irish intellectual property interests, which had usurped that name and that role before the contest began. To this legislatively assisted act, our representatives should return, perhaps by the Sligo road.

Appendix 1

Legal opinion of Paul McNally BL upon the title of Trinity College Dublin to the Book of Kells, Michaelmas 2012.

THE REMOVAL OF *THE BOOK OF KELLS* TO TRINITY COLLEGE

Following the sacking of the island of Iona by the Vikings in 806, Kells became the principal house of the Columban order. It is not clear whether the Book of Kells was commenced and finished in Iona, whether it was started in Iona and finished in Kells, or whether it was commenced and completed in Kells. Whatever the case, the book was located in the monastery in Kells throughout the Middle Ages where it was venerated as a relic of St Columcille.[31] However, according to Aubrey Gwynn, by the mid sixteenth century the it had ceased to be venerated as a relic and was examined as a venerable and beautiful manuscript.[32] By that time the Abbey had been suppressed. However according to Aubrey Gwynn this 'had no immediate effect on the fate of the Book which continued to be the chief treasure of the Church of St. Columba'.[33] From the date of the suppression, the Protestant Bishops and archdeacons became the legal custodians of the Book.[34]

The Diocese of Kells and the town of Kells were badly disrupted by the seventeenth-century conflicts. The town was taken over by the Irish on a number of occasions following the 1641 rising. Anthony Martin, Bishop of Meath, left his diocese for Dublin in 1641. He was an anti-parliamentarian and when the Cromwellians came to power in Dublin he was imprisoned. He died in the plague of 1650. In 1660 Henry Leslie, Bishop of Down and Connor was transferred to the Bishopric of Meath and, following his death, Henry Jones, scoutmaster general to Cromwell's army and bishop of Clogher, was transferred to the Bishopric of Meath after the restoration of the monarchy in

---

31 Bernard Meehan, 'The history of the manuscript' in *The Book of Kells: An Illustrated Introduction to the Manuscript in Trinity College Dublin* (London, 1995), 14.
32 Aubrey Gwynn, 'Some notes on the history of the Book of Kells' *Irish Historical Studies* 9.34 (September 1954), 131–61
33 'Some notes', 152
34 'Some notes', 153.

1661. During the period 1650 to 1660, there was no Bishop of Meath and during the period 1641 to 1650, Bishop Anthony Martin was non-resident.

Aubrey Gwynn believes that the Book of Kells found its way into the possession of Trinity College, Dublin by way of being sent to Dublin in 1653 by an act of the Cromwellian Government in Ireland during a time when there was neither a Bishop nor Archdeacon of Meath in place.[35] His belief in this respect, which was contrary to the prevailing view of the time he wrote his article — that the Book came to Dublin and Trinity College in 1860 as part of Bishop James Ussher's library — is based on a report of Samuel O'Neale who was one of the surveyors for the Parish and Barony of Kells carrying out preliminary work on the survey who stated as follows:

> The inhabitants of this town [Kells] have for many hundred years past had the keeping of a large parchment manuscript in Irish written as they say by Columbkill's own hand, but of such character that none of this age can read it. The said writing was about a year and a half ago sent to the late commissioners of the commonwealth by the Governor of Kells …

In a footnote, Aubrey Gwynn says that 'The confusion of O'Neale between Latin and Irish is not surprising in an account written by a man who admits that he is unable to read the script'.[36] While Aubrey Gwynn's belief about how the Book came to Dublin appears to be generally accepted, his belief about how the book came into the possession of Trinity College in 1660 is contested. Gwynn believed that it was Henry Cromwell, who had been made Chancellor of the University of Dublin (Trinity College) in 1653/4, who gave the book to Trinity College although he had no substantive evidence that this is what happened. He believed it occurred in 1654 or later, and that when Bishop Ussher's library came to Trinity College in 1861, the book was easily absorbed into that collection.[37] In an article published a few years after Fr. Gwynn's essay, William O'Sullivan contradicts Gwynn, stating that the book was given to Trinity College by Bishop Henry Jones after he had become Bishop of Meath in 1661. Henry Jones had been appointed Vice-Chancellor of the University in 1646 and had been a benefactor of the college. William O'Sullivan supports his contention by quoting a letter of William Pallister, a Fellow of the College, to Henry Dodwell, another Fellow, as follows:

> I had not the opportunity since the receipt of your letter of speaking to the Bishop of Meath […]. I was with him not long ago and he assured me that S. Columkills and the Cupboard M.S. were those mentioned by the primate (James Ussher) in his de Primord p. 691, there judged of equal antiquity, and that himself was assistant to the primate in collating them, and bestowed both upon our library.[38]

Bernard Meehan states that the Governor of Kells referred to in Samuel O'Neale's report, as quoted by Aubrey Gwynn, was Charles Lambert, First Earl of Cavan. He then states that the Book was moved to Dublin from Kells in the 'interests of the safety of the manuscript'. He does not substantiate his grounds for this belief other than by stating that 'the town of Kells suffered badly in the political upheavals of the seventeenth century. The 'great stone church' appears to have been damaged in the rebellion of 1641 and not immediately repaired'.[39] Kells was on the border of the Pale and must have suffered the ongoing conflict between the English colonists and the native Irish through the centuries without the Book of Kells suffering any harm. We can assume that both cultures had similar regard and reverence for the book. According to Aubrey Gwynn, 'Fleetwood and his fellow commissioners were not the kind of men who would take

35 'Some notes', 159.
36 'Some notes', 158.
37 'Some notes', 160.
38 William O'Sullivan, 'The Donor of the Book of Kells', *Irish Historical Studies*, 11.41 (March, 1958), 5–7 (6).
39 Bernard Meehan, '*The history of the manuscript in The Book of Kells*': MS58 Trinity College Library (Dublin, 1995).

40 'Some notes', 159.
41 Thomas Mac Nevin, *The Confiscation of Ulster* (Dublin, 1846), 129.

an interest in the fate of a large parchment manuscript in Irish written as they say by Columbkill's own hand'.[40] On that basis the Book was no safer in their hands than in its ancient resting place in Kells and perhaps less so. Gwynn clearly believes that the book was taken from Kells by the Cromwellian civil authority without the consent of the custodians of the Book, the Protestant Bishop and Archdeacons when, during the 1650s, there was neither a Bishop nor Archdeacon of Meath. The only factor which gives possible legitimacy to the transfer of the Book of Kells to Trinity College is the role played by Henry Jones, the Bishop of Meath, as established by William O'Sullivan and confirmed by Bernard Meehan. However, it could be argued that Henry Jones's role in legitimizing the transfer as Bishop of Meath was compromised by his involvement with the Cromwellian campaign.

In law somebody who has possession of a moveable item has a relative interest in that item if the absolute ownership of the item rests in somebody else. The person in possession will have a better title in the item against everybody else other than the person who holds the absolute ownership. In the case of the Book of Kells, on the basis that the absolute ownership of the book was never transferred to Trinity College because at the time in the mid seventeenth century, according to Gwynn, the people who had the best title to the book, the custodians of the book in the persons of the Protestant Archbishop of Meath and also his Archdeacon, never consented to the it being transferred to Dublin and ultimately to Trinity College as there was neither an appointed Bishop nor Archdeacon at the time and if, according to Gwynn, the book was taken by the Cromwellian government without authority, then it can be argued that the possessory title of Trinity College in the book is secondary to the absolute ownership of the Church in the book. However the length of time that Trinity College has held the book strengthens its rights in the book and dissipates the rights of other parties. Also, 400 years later, it is not clear which Church or which part of the Church could claim ownership. In addition, the role of Henry Jones who was appointed Bishop of Meath in 1661, in giving the Book to Trinity College also strengthens Trinity's rights in respect of the Book.

Thomas Mc Nevin in his book *The Confiscation of Ulster* (1846) about the plantation of Ulster under James I in the early part of the seventeenth century, states as follows:

> It has been a matter of dispute as to the extent to which the Dublin University can be considered a purely Protestant institution [...] but it must be admitted that she derived much of her great and, in many senses, untold wealth, from the plundered estates of the Catholic Chieftains and people of Ulster. In Tyrowen, the University was by this Project to have 813 acres; in Coleraine it was to have 1,125 acres out of the Monastery lands; in Armagh it was to have 1,200 acres; in all over 3,000 acres. In addition, it was to have six advowsons in every county, three of the best and three of second value. Thus the spoils of the ancient Church and the pillage of the Monasteries, went to enrich what is called a purely Protestant foundation, and whose enormous wealth is supposed to have sprung from the beneficent gifts of Protestant sovereigns.[41]

The comparison between the benefits Trinity College obtained from the confiscated lands of Ulster to the detriment of the native Irish and the removal of the Book of Kells — the most historic, sacred and beautiful manuscript — from its native Irish resting place to Trinity College is clear.

A German submarine rises to the surface in rough seas. c. 1914–18. |Photographer: F. Schensky © CORBIS

The End of the World

SEAMUS DEANE

HELGA

The steamship *Helga* took part in the first Clare Island Survey of 1909–11; then, refitted as a gunboat, she shelled the centre of Dublin during the 1916 Rising. She later became a troopship and transported some of the notorious Black and Tans to different ports in Ireland when the roads were blocked. Eventually, the new Free State bought the ship while the Black and Tans and RIC men, hardened by their Irish experience, left to continue their rampages among the unfortunate villagers of Iraq in 1922. The *Helga* thus passed out of the history of world domination and into the quiet desuetude of the Irish Free State naval service.

The SS *LUSITANIA* homeward bound on her last voyage, April 1915
Art Archive / Imperial War Museum

LUSITANIA

The son of Lady Gregory's sister Adelaide, Sir Hugh Lane, the art dealer, once Director of the Irish National Gallery, Gregory's favourite nephew and a friend of Yeats, left for the United States on 12 February 1915 from Liverpool on board the *Lusitania*. It was then, just before the journey out, that he decided to change his will for a second time and to bequeath his important collection of Impressionist paintings to the Dublin Municipal Gallery, as he had initially done. But the codicil he added was never witnessed. The collection was claimed by the National Gallery in London, to whom Lane, in disgust at the failure of the Dublin municipal authorities to build a gallery for the paintings had, in his second will, assigned the collection. Lane took the *Lusitania* on its return journey to Liverpool and perished, with 1,201 others, off the coast of County Cork on the afternoon of 7 May 1915, when the liner was struck by a torpedo fired from a German U-boat. A long dispute over the will, in which Lady Gregory was prominent, followed; but her persuasive *Case for the Return of Sir Hugh Lane's Pictures to Dublin* of 1926, although it did contribute to the eventual settlement of the dispute, was not successful at the time.

The Lane pictures controversy was no more than a sideshow to the controversy which followed the sinking. It was a powerful exercise in propaganda, carefully aimed at an American audience. The strike was presented as a uniquely barbaric act; a ship with no military purpose or capacity attacked without warning in an extension of war to innocent civilians, a fearful harbinger of what was to come. Centrally, since 128 of the dead were Americans, it was taken by many as an act of war by Germany on the USA. The initial statement by President Woodrow Wilson in 1914 of the American position on the war, 'to be neutral in fact as well as in name', allowed him to be re-elected in November 1916 as the man who 'kept us out of the war'. But Wilson's increasingly aggressive diplomatic notes to Germany about the *Lusitania* attack made war inevitable. His Secretary of State William Jennings Bryan resigned over the issue, claiming that it was British policy to use US passengers on civilian liners to disguise the shipment of military contraband. By 1917, Wilson abandoned his earlier position, declared the era and time of neutrality had passed, that the causes of world peace and the freedom of peoples made America's intervention in the war necessary.

The impetus for this turn also came from internal American politics. In Wilson's bitter struggle against the Unions, especially against the International Workers of the World, the famous IWW, he had made the legal justification of 'Emergency Powers' for either the President or Congress a strategic goal. Joe Hill, the IWW leader, was 'the author of a cartoon in *Class War News* figuring an IWW submarine firing on the ship of "Capitalism"'.[1] (The first animated cartoon made for propaganda purposes was on the sinking of the *Lusitania*.)

Certainly, the distinction between making 'the world safe for democracy' and making it safe for Americans became so slight that, as one of its almost immediate effects, it quickly became a widespread belief that most or all of those who perished on the *Lusitania* were American. Meyers points up the similarities between this event and September 11, and how emergency powers for internal purposes and for war abroad were fused in both cases in the atmosphere of 'civic war'[2] that obtained, in this instance, between the sinking of the *Lusitania* and the American declaration of war on 6 April 1917. The fact that the German embassy in the USA had warned on 1 May 1915, when the *Lusitania* was leaving New York, that civilian ships were being used by the Allies to transport munitions and that they would be on that account regarded as legitimate targets was dismissed as in any way excusing the sinking.

Even at the time, there were suspicions. The liner exploded with a force that seemed remarkable for one torpedo hit. It sank just eighteen minutes after being struck. It also seemed suspicious that it had sailed so close to the Irish coast, against specific instructions for liners in that stretch of dangerous water, that it had no armed escort, that it pursued a straight rather than the usual zigzag course advised for large ships, that the regular armed escort for that area had been ordered away some hours before by Churchill. Was the ship deliberately sacrificed to bring America into the war? Seven hundred and sixty one passengers were saved, but the newspapers concentrated on those who died, particularly on Alfred of the famous Vanderbilt family, much more than on Hugh Lane and the collection of famous paintings in lead-lined tubes that he reputedly had on board — Impressionist paintings, maybe even a Rembrandt, a Rubens, a Titian? One wealthy passenger, Welsh mining magnate, D. A. Thomas, survived; a newspaper printed the headline: 'Terrible Disaster: D. A. Thomas Saved'.[3] One who did not survive, Thomas Atkinson, from London, was not wealthy. With three sixpences in his jacket pocket, he was brought ashore behind a small currach, his body attached to a buoy, floating vertically in the water, at the Blasket Islands off the coast of Kerry to where he and sections of the ship's structure and cargo were swept by the tides over the next few days. The bodies of two passengers were swept up on the beach of Aran Island and buried in the corner of the communal graveyard. And there was another echoic return to this area of the sea off Kerry. The torpedo officer who pressed the button that sank the *Lusitania* was Raimund Weisbach who, 6 months later, was the captain of the U-19 that brought Roger Casement to Banna Strand on Good Friday 1916. U-20 was in fact the submarine on which Casement set out; but it developed engine trouble, so the Irish party was transferred to U-19.[4]

****

---

1 Peter Alexander Meyers, *Civic War and the Corruption of the Citizen* (Chicago and London, 2008), 105
2 *Civic War*, 107
3 For a review of books on the *Lusitania*, see David Reynolds, 'Too Proud to Fight', *London Review of Books*, 24.23 (November, 2002), 29–31; Philippe Masson, *Les Naufrageurs du Lusitanie et la Guerre de l'Ombre* (Paris, 1987); Raymond Hitchcock, *Attack the Lusitania* (London, 1980) — a novel in which Churchill and naval intelligence decide to sink the ship and say the Germans did it.
4 I am grateful to Dr. Tim Hogan who gave me this information on Weisbach and U-19 and U-20 at a Conference in the Royal Irish Academy in September 2012.

Roger Casement on board a German Submarine, 1916. Private Collection / The Bridgeman Art Library

The Irish novelist Violet Martin (of Somerville and Ross fame) while out for a walk had seen the *Lusitania* pass half an hour before its sinking. In the sixth volume *Le Temps Retrouvé*, of *A la Recherche du Temps Perdu*, published in 1927, the ghastly Mme Verdurin is presented as reading of the sinking the day after in the newspaper. In this passage, Proust is — among other things — satirizing and relishing the sumptuous selfishness of those who live comfortably and ignorantly in the midst of disaster; the barbarians are at the gates, and yet they pursue nothing but their own private satisfactions. Charlus, the novel's chief grotesque, pursues his sexual pleasures 'never dreaming that the Germans — albeit immobilized by a bloody yet constantly replenished barrier — were an hour by car from Paris'. The Verdurins have a political salon every week, so they

5 *In Search of Lost Time*, vol. 6, *Finding Time Again*, trans. Ian Patterson, Gen. Ed. Christopher Patterson (London, 2002), 80–81

6 Elias Canetti, *The Conscience of Words* (New York, 1979), 32

must have thought about it [...] And they did, it is true, think about the hecatombs of regiments annihilated and passengers swallowed by the sea [...} but a reciprocal process so far multiplies whatever concerns our own well-being, and divides by such a formidable number whatever does not concern us, that the death of millions of unknown people hardly troubles us, and we find it scarcely as disagreeable as a cold draught. Mme Verdurin, suffering from migraines again now that there were no croissants to dip in her coffee, had finally obtained an order...allowing her to have them made for her [...] She received the first of these croissants on the morning when the newspapers reported the wreck of the *Lusitania*. As she dipped it in her coffee, and flicked her newspaper with one hand so that it would stay open without her having to remove her other hand from the croissant she was soaking, she said, 'How awful! It's worse than the most horrific tragedy'. But [...] even while she uttered, through a mouthful of croissant, these distressing thoughts, the look which lingered on her face, probably induced by the taste of the croissant, so valuable in preventing migraine, was more like one of quiet satisfaction.⁵

The croissant had been created in Vienna after the defeat of the Muslim armies at the great siege of 1683 as a mock version of the Islamic crescent; the Viennese ate the crescent bread for breakfast the day after the siege was lifted. It became for a time an emblem of the successful expulsion of the barbarian from the gates of Christian Europe. The echo of that rumour lingers in Proust's final volume and in a Europe deafened by the British propaganda about the German barbarities in gallant little Belgium. Medically speaking, Mme Verdurin's cure for migraine should have stimulated the condition, but the consumption of that particular croissant and the news of the *Lusitania* together seem to have created a perfect cure. She consumes the news that the newspaper provides. The Viennese journalist Karl Kraus, always alert to the mass media's inexhaustible capacity to turn 'the most horrific tragedy' into cliché, to reduce disaster into the sheer materiality of printer's ink, the 'covering' of the page becoming the 'covering' of the event, believed that the miracles of technological advance catastrophically reduced the ethical capacity of the audiences they created. This is the abiding preoccupation of his epic collage-play of 1918, *The Last Days of Mankind* in which the voices of the drowned children of the *Lusitania* are heard singing in the general uproar. Elias Canetti wrote that Kraus had a capacity for 'acoustic quotation' which allowed him to read the 'newspapers as though he were *hearing* them. The black, printed dead words were audible to him. When he quoted them, he seemed to be letting voices speak acoustic quotations.'⁶ In Kraus's view, anyone who speaks a language of congealed cliché and stock phrases, whose consciousness is dominated by the newspaper, advertising and bureaucratic officialese, is equipped to accept massacre in a placid, robotic spirit. It's on the surface of society, where the media dominate, that the roots of society's problems lie — specifically the capacity to endorse, even enjoy, the mass killing of others, preferably with a croissant in hand.

Kraus was speaking of Europe in general but of Austria, and especially Vienna, in particular. In Germany and in Austria the news of the *Lusitania* was received with delight as a proof that submarine warfare was working against the British attempt to impose mass starvation by naval blockade. (Thomas Mann rejoiced at the news in his *Reflections of an Unpolitical Man*). Still, the image of the doomed *Lusitania* was a gift for British recruiting posters; since they controlled the transatlantic cable, British newspaper owners influenced American news. This was a propaganda feast. There were riots in Liverpool, Manchester and

London after news of the sinking was broadcast. Most of the coal trimmers and stokers on the liner were Liverpool Irish from the north end of the city; the first riots began there with attacks on shops (particularly pork butchers) owned by long-settled German families. Crowds in other English cities followed suit as the wave of outrage rose. The Government finally intervened by introducing internment for 'enemy aliens' and repatriating large numbers of ethnic Germans.[7] The Hun, the barbarian, in France the Boche — this was the common enemy of humankind. In the final volume of his great novel, Proust predicted that the name,'Boche', like that of Dreyfusard, would become almost meaningless within a few years — hard as that was to believe for those who had lived through the storms of the Dreyfus affair.[8] He overstated the case. The 'sale Boche' survived intact for some decades.[9] Still, having barbarians as enemies had its advantages. Cavafy's famous poem of 1904, 'Waiting for the Barbarians', concludes, 'In a way, those people were a solution.'

* * * * * *

Some years later, one of Freud's patients, an American, who claimed he loved his wife very much, invited her to take the *Lusitania* and join him in Europe. He had meant to say the name of the sister-ship, the *Mauretania,* on which he himself had come over. But, Freud told him, this showed that he really wanted to kill his wife. Such a diagnosis, based on this example of what Freud called 'parapraxis', really irritated the Italian Marxist Sebastiano Timpanaro whose book *The Freudian Slip: Psychoanalysis and Textual Criticism* (1974; trans. 1976) attacked Freud's

> mania for psychologising, a conviction that the most trivial error always answers to some 'intention', leads to the invention of a non-existent [...] essence at a level of reality which cannot be investigated.

Timpanaro went on to cite this particular case:

> The transatlantic steamer, *Lusitania*, which was sunk in the war by a German submarine and thus became the subject of much emotion and hostility, was much better known than her sister-ship the *Mauretania* — all the more so in the case of the 'slip' cited by Freud, whose author was an American, since it was for the most part Americans who had perished in the disaster of the *Lusitania*.[10]

Just over ten per cent of the dead were Americans. Timpanaro here makes the political slip, a mark of the incident's reputation for having directly brought the USA into the War. Freud's 'slip', as Timpanaro called it, provoked Timpanaro's.

Writing in the 1970s, Timpanaro felt it important to affirm materialism in the face of so many sophistries that claimed to be in alliance with Marxism. 'Psychoanalysis', he wrote, 'is neither a natural nor a human science, but a self-confession by the bourgeoisie of its own misery and perfidy, which blends the bitter insight and ideological blindness of a class in decline'.[11] Moreover, Timpanaro accuses Freud of relying on intuition, or at least of not revealing the code of his system.[12] Perhaps now, in retrospect, Timpanaro's objection to this kind of detective work on Freud's part seems justified, although his general description of psychoanalysis is more troubling. Certainly, when we re-read Freud and Proust together, the death of the European bourgeoisie is more evidently than ever a shared theme. In the nuanced gap between the physical taste of Mme Verdurin's croissant and her sense of gratification at having it, we can smell the sharp odour of decay. It surrounds the story of the ascent of the Verdurins and the disintegration of the world that once despised them. This is the story of a class, like the middle classes of Freud's Vienna.

7   6 Nicolette Gullace, 'Friendly Aliens and Enemies: Fictive Communities and the *Lusitania* Riots of 1915', *Journal of Social History*, 39.2 (Winter, 2005), 345–67
8   Proust, *Finding Time Again*, 35
9   Unsurprisingly, it was much used by Charles Maurras; see, for instance, his newspaper article of 1946, 'Enseignon M. Teitgen sur la Résistance', where he speaks of French revulsion 'a [à] l'odeur du sale Boche, "foetor Germanicus"'; at http://maurras.net/texts/209.html 12 September, 2012
10 Sebastiano Timpanaro, *The Freudian Slip*: *Psychoanalysis and Textual Criticism* (London, 1976), 144, 146
11 *The Freudian Slip*, 224
12 *The Freudian Slip*, 222

13 *Finding Time Again*, 16
14 Theodor Adorno, *Philosophy of Modern Music* (1948), trans. Anne G. Mitchell and Wesley V. Blomster (London, 1973, repr. 1987), 133.

But in both instances, with the analysis of a particular class, we also have the analysis of a more wide-ranging crisis that affects all civilization.)

So Timpanaro's charge survives his own slip. It has been often said that psychoanalysis (or psychology, with which it is frequently conflated) is an ideal pseudo-science for and of the bourgeoisie in the last phase of its historical domination of Europe —and, by extension, of much of the world. But it is indeed a world, not just a class, that is falling and our fascination is with the close-up that shows the moment of eclipse as well as the long shot that opens the wider horizon. With that bite of the croissant, as Mme Verdurin reads the newspaper account of the sinking and exclaims how dreadful it all is, and as a European public reads this in 1927 twelve years after the event (and in English in 1931), the *Lusitania* sinks definitively, emblem and image of an earlier, lost world, into the density of literature. It was watched for those last eighteen minutes from the Old Head of Kinsale by a picnic party and from underwater through a periscope glass, as it reared up in shock at the fatal blow and then toppled into the waves, reappearing the next day in photographs, and then again and again, in poster images, paintings, sculpted memorials, year on year. Whatever the sinking was — a diabolic act, engineered by the British to bring in the Americans, a barbarous act by the U-boat commander in a scenario that we now read as thoroughly vulgar Freudians — the disaster sliding under the surface of civilized life — its 'meaning' was quickly captured by the media and deeply imprinted in public opinion thereafter. A great divide had opened into which the old world suddenly vanished, as the passengers and the lifeboats, miniaturized in the general consciousness by all those representations of the giant liner, were tilted into the now-distant sea. In Paris, wrote Proust, 'one of the most fashionable ideas was the claim that the pre-war period was separated from the war by something as deep, something seemingly as long-lasting, as a geological period'.13 This 'fashionable idea' became almost proverbial in modernism. Adorno ended his essay of 1941 'Schoenberg and Progress' on the fate of modern music which

> has taken upon itself all the darkness and guilt of the world [...] music which has not been heard falls into empty time like an impotent bullet [...] Modern music sees absolute oblivion as its goal. It is the surviving message of despair from the shipwrecked.14

The Irish-American Fenian Brotherhood financed the first submarine, 'Holland Boat Number 1', launched on the Passaic River, New Jersey on 22 May 1878. The vessel was named after John Holland from Liscannor in Co. Clare, the inventor and designer of the new submersible. The Fenians hoped that the new invention would be a threat to British naval supremacy; once their financing of the project became known, the New York newspapers named the underwater craft the *Fenian Ram*. But it was the US Navy, not the Fenians, who eventually bought USS-*Holland VI*, its first submarine, from Holland's firm, by then owned by a German-born businessman. The successful trial runs Holland conducted off Staten Island on St. Patrick's Day 1898, convinced the American authorities, including Theodore Roosevelt, of its potential usefulness against the Spanish fleet in Cuba in the Spanish-American war of that year. The *Holland* was never used against the Spanish but its successors were used against Germany in the First World War, which broke out two weeks before Holland's death on 12 August 1914. Submarine Day in the US Fleet, 11 April 1900, is the day of the submarine's (USS-1) purchase.

Could the submarine be anything but a machine of war? It was a vexed question. Were the *Bremen* or the *Deutschland* merchant vessels, 'commercial submarines' when they travelled unarmed with cargo to

John P. Holland standing in the conning tower of his submarine, *Holland VI*, later known as the USS *Holland*, April 1898, Perth Amboy, New Jersey, 1 April 1898.
© Bettmann/CORBIS

New York?[15] So too with a ship that was torpedoed, especially during a blockade. If it was named as a legitimate target, did that make it so? If it was, like the *Lusitania*, both a civilian liner and a warship, what was its status in international law? The character of the war at sea was drastically altered by the submarine, not only in its legal aspects but also in popular perception. The menace from below, the silent intent shadow pursuing a prey that seemed by contrast to be unsuspectingly

15 14 See Carl Schmitt, *The Nomos of the Earth in the International Law of the Jus publicum Europaeum* (1950) trans. G. L. Ulmen (New York, 2005), 314.

The body of an American citizen is carried through the streets of Queenstown (modern Cobh) in Ireland, one of the victims of the sinking of the RMS *Lusitania* by a German U-Boat, May 1915. Original Publication: *The Illustrated War News*, 12 May 1915 (Photo by Hulton Archive/Getty Images)

16 *Nomos of the Earth*, 315, 307

vulnerable on the surface, intensified the nightmare of war more than the tank did on land, only exceeded in menace later by the scream of the dive bomber and the continuous thunder of approaching mass attacks from the air. In the case of the *Lusitania*, it was the nomination rather than the identification of the victims that became crucial in the propaganda war. Most of the dead were Europeans but were 'remembered' as Americans. Dead Americans were the political point; the 'ethical' issue was subordinate. The survival of the dead in popular memory as Americans indicated an abrupt shift in world power to the USA.

Moreover, with the arrival of the submarine, the sea had become a theatre of war in a new sense. Submarines did not, could not take ships or crews prisoner as 'prize'. The emergence of a new international legal order at the expense of the European Public Law (*Jus Publicum Europaeum*) was almost as sudden as the American reversal of foreign policy. 'The purely maritime character of an important component of the conduct of sea war

[...] had been changed fundamentally and conclusively by the introduction of submarines.' So wrote Carl Schmitt, caustic, envious and clear-sighted, the fascist jurist who recognized that the US had gained the power, by its dexterity in the quarrel over the use of the submarine, that Germany had believed was necessary for its own survival — to rewrite the law of the sea. The Great War had been a European affair; it became a World War with the American intervention. In 1928, the Kellogg Pact in effect made the US the arbiter of the international system. The old balance of powers had given way to a new hegemony. Universality, Globalization and the World became the key terms of the vocabulary that began to rival, then replace, the legal idioms of the nation-state and the European balance of power. 'The praxis of the *Jus Publicum Europaeum* had sought to encompass conflicts within the framework of a system of equilibrium. Now they were universalized in the name of world unity'.[16]

The USA, in justifying its intervention in the First World War on the basis of

German Cruiser *Bluecher* sinks during the naval engagement between German and British dreadnoughts in the North Sea, 24 January 1915. This photo was taken from the deck of the British Cruiser *Arethusia*.
© CORBIS

what it claimed were international human rights — a repeated 'justification' for many future wars and, according to Hedley Bull and others, 'a direct offshoot of the missionary and colonizing tradition of the West, with its roots in the early nineteenth century, the period of US intervention in Cuba and the European intervention in the Ottoman Empire',[17] criminalized war. Was Walther Schweiger, the U-boat commander, a war criminal? Was the declaration of unrestricted submarine warfare by Germany in 1917 outside the law? And what of all those submarine commanders, German, British and American, who sank ships without warning in the Atlantic, North Sea and the Baltic in both World Wars and in the Pacific in the Second? Not to mention Captain Alexander Marinesko, of the Soviet S-13, whose three torpedoes brought down the German ship *Wilhelm Gustloff* in the Baltic off Danzig in 1945; it was crammed with refugees; 9,500 died, 4,000 of them children. Günter Grass's novel *Im Krebsgang* (*Crabwalk*) of 2002 not only commemorated that event but tried (by his own account) to deny the opportunistic charge by right wing parties in Germany that this was a war crime. Grass's view was that this was 'war', and *therefore* not a crime. Did this reasoning also apply in the case of the Argentine destroyer *Belgrano* which, as the US *Phoenix*, had survived Pearl Harbour, only to be sunk, without warning but after consultation with Prime Minister Thatcher, by the British nuclear submarine *Conqueror*, outside a declared war zone, with the loss of 323 lives, in May 1982? The *Lusitania* had a desolate and bloody heritage.

* * * * * *

17 Quoted in Danilo Zolo, *Invoking Humanity: War, Law and Global Order* (London, 2002), 87.

18 Muiris Ó Súilleabháin, *Twenty Years A-Growing* (Dublin, 1933), 140
19 Ó Súilleabháin, *Twenty Years*, 142
20 *Twenty Years*, 143

THE BLASKETS

Ourselves, oursouls alone. At the site of salvocean [...] Based on traumscrapt from Maston, Boss.

Finnegans Wake, 623

[*An Blascaod Mór, the Great Blasket, is the largest of an archipelago of seven islands, just less than 2 kilometres off the coast of Kerry in south west Ireland. It is one kilometre wide, 5 kilometres long. Its profile is perhaps 300 metres high, stretching south westerly between the Blasket Sound and the Great Sound that separates it from the mainland at Dunquin and one of its smaller companion islands, Inis na Bró. The population never exceeded 200; in the early twentieth century this seems to have fallen to just over 100, but since 1953 the island has been uninhabited. In 1933,* Fiche Bliain ag Fás *(Twenty Years A-Growing), by Muiris Ó Súilleabháin, (Maurice O'Sullivan, 1904–50), was published in Irish in Dublin and in English translation (with a couple of passages omitted) in London. E. M. Forster contributed an Introductory Note to the English translation and the translators themselves, Moya Llewelyn Davies and George Thomson, added a Preface. Pádraig O Fiannachta and George Thomson co-edited the second edition of* Fiche Bliain *in 1976; Oxford University Press published a revised translation in 1953, with reissues in paperback in 1983 and in 2000. The book is a memoir in which the author gives an account of his first twenty years on the Great Blasket. Dylan Thomas wrote a filmscript, published in 1964, but no movie of the book was ever made.*]

We read in the memoir that shortly after the news reached the island that England and Germany were 'hurled against each other'[18] in war, came the harvest of the marine battle. German submarines (two of which were sunk near the Blaskets by Q Boats between 1915 and 1917) took a heavy toll of shipping off the Irish coast. Cargoes were often completely lost — coal, munitions, chemicals — but others regularly washed up on the beaches. The first great haul was timber. Almost the entire population of the island, over a hundred people, came down to the shore one day to collect a great forest of wooden planking that had filled the bay quite suddenly and that a storm tide then heaped upon the sand, some of the beams sixty feet long. This was wealth untold for the islanders. It was a day later that they learned it was fragments of the *Lusitania* that were dangerously overloading their currachs in their repeated plunges to the shore.

'By God', one man would say, 'war is good.'
'Arra, man', said another, 'if it continues, this island will be the Land of The Young.'[19]

That evening the 'King' of the Island announced that 'the end of the world is coming [...] and England is going to send out conscription through the whole of Ireland'. But such news was beside the point for those listening. Impatiently a listener asked, 'did you hear of any ship being sunk in any place since?' It is then the 'King' tells them of the

'*Lusitania*, the finest ship the Americans ever had. They say there were millionaires in plenty on board and isn't it a terrible thing that not a sinner of them came ashore alive. If this breeze lasts from, the south tonight, the coast of the island will be full of drowned men tomorrow.' And everyone that night and next morning was out 'in search of the millionaires.'[20]

But only one body came in after the wreckage of the liner. O'Sullivan's father pulled the corpse of Henry Atkinson of London, identified by his pocket book as 'First-class Officer, S.S. *Lusitania*' from the sea, 'the eyes plucked out by the gulls, the face swollen, and the clothes ready to burst with the swelling of the body'; he had three sixpences in his pocket, which the islander who had drawn the pocket book from the foul-smelling corpse was allowed to keep by the police who came to collect the body. Thereafter, on at least two occasions, shipwrecked sailors made it to shore on lifeboats. Their survival perhaps indicated that the Germans were now giving warning before firing on merchant ships, as they had agreed to do in response to President Woodrow Wilson's protest over the sinking of the *Lusitania*. After that, for several weeks, the cargoes washed ashore — boxed chocolates, barrels of apples, flour, wine, bacon, castor oil, pocket watches, clothes, leather strips and cowhides, cotton bales, wooden planks; 'there was plenty and abundance in the Island — food of all sorts, clothes from head to heel [...] not a penny leaving home; everything a mouth could ask for coming in with the tide from day to day — all except the sugar, which melted as soon as it touched water.' One rescued sailor, telling how he had jumped from his doomed ship and gained land, says

> We thought then that it was some backward country with no one alive in it. But, 'upon my word', said he, glancing around, 'you are here — fine, well-favoured people, mannerly, intelligent, generous, and hospitable'.[21]

The search of the islanders for millionaires was unsuccessful, but it was an American millionaire who eventually gained possession of the sunken liner and carried out a thorough and expensive investigation of the wreck. Gregg Bemis, a Texan millionare, was granted a five-year license by a Heritage Order of 2007, issued under the National Monuments Act of 1995, which had declared the site and the wreck of the liner a national monument, to undertake this task. The long search culminated in a two-hour television programme, 'Dark Secrets of the Lusitania', first aired on 14 July 2012 by National Geographic Broadcasters. (The Discovery Channel had aired an American-German production, 'The Sinking of the Lusitania: Terror at Sea' in 2007.) The 'secrets' had long been available. The *Lusitania* was both a civilian liner and a warship. In this dual role she was used to sustain the supply of war material and goods to Britain, which itself was blockading all supplies to Germany, particularly in the North Sea and the Baltic Sea. Some artefacts from the ship's bridge were recovered and donated to the Irish State and were accepted as memorials of 'a key moment' in that series of 'historic events that shaped the course of Irish history between 1912 and 1922',[22] which have now entered upon their centenary commemorations. The difficulties of underwater survey and retrieval had been enormously increased by the bombing of the site with depth charges by the British Navy in the 1950s; some of these hedgehog mines have been clearly seen on the monitor screens of the diving operation. Yet, with all the evidence that has piled up against the accusation that the torpedoing was an unprecedented act of barbarism, outside the limits of international law, the *Lusitania* has remained an emblem of the pitiful consequences of war for humankind. (The evidence of a conspiracy or of opportunism of course makes it an even darker portent.) The names and numbers of the dead and of the survivors are known, but the numbers of those seduced by the unceasing propaganda about it into armed service are unknowable — one key constituency targeted in the recruitment drive that followed, especially given the Irish resistance to conscription, were Irishmen who were exhorted to AVENGE THE LUSITANIA / JOIN AN IRISH REGIMENT.

******

21 *Twenty Years*, 146, 145, 161, 160
22 Jimmy Deenihan, Minister for Arts, Heritage and the Gaeltacht, on 26 April 2012, welcoming the gift to the State by Mr. Greg Bemis, owner of the wreck of the *Lusitania*, of a number of important artefacts recovered from the ship.

'Irishmen, Avenge the Lusitania, Join an Irish Regiment Today', poster issued by the Central Organization of Recruiting in Ireland (colour litho), Irish School (20th-century). Private Collection / Ken Welsh / The Bridgeman Art Library

'Mar ná beidh ár leithéidí arís ann ...'

The literature of the Blasket Islands and indeed of all the western islands of Ireland (from Gola in Donegal to Aran in Galway) in the twentieth century is woven, sometimes exquisitely, around a belief by and about the islanders themselves;

> I have written minutely of much that we did, for it was my wish that somewhere there should be a memorial of it all, and I have done my best to set down the character of the people around me so that some record of us might live after us, for the like of us will never be again.[23]

Tomás Ó Criomhthain's *An t-Oileánach* (1929), translated by Robin Flower as *The Islandman* (1937), is the abiding classic of this elusive genre which is a memorial to the island people, to the Irish language, and to the European idea of an 'organic' community. The moment of extinction, when the elements of wind and sea will prevail over an abandoned island, is mobilized from the beginning of the narrative to render the sense of the personal life or of the habitual life of the community more precious. Against the natural, the human is as helpless as a body in a vast, running sea. Only these final images, we are told, will be left to us of a heroic, eloquent and lovable people; we gaze at them now and they gaze at us like Easter Island statues across the ocean that walled them in throughout history. The communal time stretches from beyond the Christian era to the earliest stages of human existence. The lure of these writings is increased, not only by their extraordinary idiomatic eloquence but also by the implication of a natural equality, that this gift is a 'natural' acquisition, perhaps even an instinct (not that the word 'instinct' explains anything, but has the merit of claiming there is no longer any need for explanation). Here we have a living language in the most enhanced sense of the term, especially as it is Irish, a language that had been almost exterminated and was still in the 1930s trying to sustain, as a political as well as a cultural project, the revival that had begun in the 1890s. Some of the islanders could remember how they had once been despised by the people of Dunquin on the mainland because they had Irish only and no English. But since the first language revival and especially since the publication and warm reception of *The Islandman*, the islanders had become respected and celebrated, not least because of the increased tourist trade they had begun to attract. In February 2009, the Irish Government purchased the Great Blasket from a private company (Blascaod Mór Teoranta) for €2 million and it became a National Historic Park under the aegis of the Office of Public Works, which has now completed the restoration of the deserted village. Dunquin opened a Heritage Centre devoted to the abandoned island facing it.

The life realized in these writings is the more enchanting because it has been 'discovered', has always been there and yet has only now arrived in the modern consciousness. This is as unexpected and more troubling than a geographic/anthropological discovery. 'Only in the middle of the twentieth century CE did two Australian prospectors stumble, to mutual astonishment, on the hitherto unknown societies of the New Guinea Highlands.'[24] Synge had of course 'discovered' the Aran islands in the last years of the nineteenth century; *The Aran Islands*, *The Playboy of the Western World* and *North Kerry* all belong to 1907, and all enact that thrill of discovery that was supposed to belong only to the anthropologist and was equally supposed, in the highly globalized late nineteenth or early twentieth century, not to be any longer possible, since the world was so comprehensively known, mapped, invaded, dominated and recognizable. And yet in Europe, in the first quarter of the twentieth century, two such 'places' had been discovered, both of them part of the

23   22 Tomás Ó Crohan, *The Islandman* (1929), translated by Robin Flower (1937; Oxford, rev. transl. 1951, 1953, reissued 2000), 244. A new translation appeared too late for inclusion here: Tomás O Crohan, *The Islander*, A Translation of *An tOileánach*, by Garry Bannister and David Sowby (Dublin, 2012).

24   W. G. Runciman, *The Theory of Cultural and Social Selection* (Cambridge, 2009), 191

Irish Postal Stamp depicting Tomás Ó Criomhtháin

geography, history and ideology of the old and the new Ireland.

It could be argued that for painters, writers and patriots — especially of the counter-revolutionary family — Brittany, as a 'Romantic' territory, had anticipated these discovered Irish islands. Yet because it was part of a or of *the* continent (or Continent, *le Vieux Continent*), because it had figured prominently in French history since the Revolutionary era, it was 'known' and so lacked the surprise element of the Blaskets. It was indeed as 'Celtic' as anyone in search for an enchantment to counter-modernity could wish for. But it had been too long embroiled in the crises of modernity, however faithful it was to its ancient religious and pagan traditions. It was in thrall to the sea, but not surrounded by it; it had had, since the middle of the nineteenth century, the staged symbolism of Chateaubriand's grave alternately appearing above and disappearing under the waves. And Frédéric Mistral's campaign for the recovery of Occitan in Provence and the idea of that language and territory as the enchanted realm of the ancient and Graeco-Roman-French spirit of the pre-modern world had ensnared many in 'the false brilliance of a bogus history'[25] peddled by the French Right of Barrès and Maurras.[26] And another image of perfection, as in Alain Fournier's *Le Grand Meaulnes* (1913), appearing just before the war in which its creator died, was heartbreakingly unreachable, a realm not a place, a flash photograph of what had never existed until it was, in that moment of capture, as war began, revealed as lost.

The Blaskets were different. They were a place that became an image, an actuality that became an ideal type. This micro archipelago looked to its largest island, the Great Blasket; in turn it looked to a yet larger island, Ireland; and Ireland to a continent that it could belong to or that could belong to it. As this serial synecdoche was pursued, Ireland once more in the twentieth century offered to modernity an opportunity for re-enchantment. Yeats and Synge in their generation had already seized it in the image of the Aran islands and the Irish West. That was before political independence; now here it was to be seized again, after political independence. Although both seizures belong in a continuum, they are nevertheless distinct phases. They have the same structure. A part (an island) that stands in for the whole (Ireland); that is then repeated, as Ireland (an island) stands in for the whole (Europe); and within this structure of replication and enlargement in geography, there is the accompanying transition in historical time, from the present moment to the most distant past (ancient or medieval Ireland or ancient Greece); then the dimension of the historical itself dissolves into the pre-historical or eternal (where the human and the natural become fused in an originary human nature). In this latter case, whereby the Blaskets become the site of a national project, closely allied to that of the Revival, the process of memorializing — dependent throughout on the *acknowledgement* of extinction that is itself a creative act, a cultural stimulant to which the Irish had developed a necessary addiction — is intricate, hidden within the fiction of its spontaneity.

Ireland had two revivals in the first fifty years of the twentieth century. They are structurally so similar that in them the same thing appears to happen twice; or, as has been said of the two acts in *Waiting for Godot*, 'nothing happens — twice'. But this 'nothing' is the feeble word we use for the pressure that builds within to disintegrate the meaning of 'happens'. The key Blasket island memoirs conflate the period they recall with the process of remembering it. That period is historical, in that it has datable moments and even more in the sense that for the narrators everything swings on the pivot of time, 'that time when', (*fadó* in Irish, *olim* in Latin) and yet it is the dimension of time that melts, like a frozen sea in a climbing temperature, into a sempiternity that, only when it has successfully replaced historical time, reveals and performs its historical function. That, in short, is the function of legitimizing the newly formed Irish State (which of course only reaches its specific gravity in 1932 with the accession of De Valera to power) as the domain of the ancient European civilization, which had elsewhere collapsed — and had Europe but known it was, in 1929–33, finally to fall away, as in a geological disaster, from the continent that it had created and that had created it.

Twice, versions of the West and of the immemorial, had become in Ireland new sites for the creative act by which 'a people is a people'.[27] In each case, the immemorial was a code for the utopian. But in the second case, the 1930s, the centrality of the memoir secured the notion of the generic individual as the inhabitant of this condition and had, as its stated aim, the commemoration of a community that was about to disappear and the (unstated) aim of thereby creating in it a heightened consciousness of itself. It produces a utopian political community by lamenting the disappearance of an historic

25 Marc Bloch, *Métier d'historien* (1949), *The Historian's Craft*, trans. Peter Putnam (Manchester, 2012), 72

26 'See for example, Charles Maurras, 'Vingt-Cinq Ans de Monarchisme' (1924) in *Oeuvres Capitales, Essais Politiques* (Paris, 1954) 456, 506.

27 J.-J. Rousseau, *Du Contrat Social*, Book I (1762), Chapter V, par.2, 'Of The Social Contract' in *Rousseau: The Political Writings*, ed. C. E. Vaughan, 2 vols. (Oxford, 1962), II.31; '... l'acte par lequel un peuple est un peuple; car cet acte [...] est le vrai fondement de société.'

28 Gilles Deleuze, 'Literature and Life' trans. Daniel W. Smith and Michael A. Greco, *Critical Inquiry*, 23.2 (Winter, 1997), 225–30 (229). For the present purpose, I am taking this essay rather than the book he co-authored with Félix Guattari, *Kafka: Towards a Minor Literature* (1975; trans. 1986) as the best account of his thinking on these matters.

29 Deleuze, 'Literature and Life', 228, 229. See also, Ronald Bogue, 'Minor Writing and Minor Literature', *symploké* 5.1/2 (1997), 99–118.

one. Its goal was the collective, not any version of the realization of the 'self'. In a sense, the genre of the 'memoir', which is highly problematic (ethnographic, auto-ethnographic?) reveals the function of the form more readily than any specifiable protocols. The generic mode, although it certainly allows for and even promotes the idea of the heroic, also promotes the concept of equality. This is not heroic individuality, not Christy Mahon becoming a playboy as the community reverts to nullity. This is an heroic community that is being created, an island people becoming, for Ireland, *le peuple*; what is set down here is not an 'I' but 'the character of the people around me', in Ó Criomthain's phrase.

* * * * *

A MINOR LITERATURE, A MAJOR LANGUAGE

Ever since 'general theory' gave way to cultural studies, there has been by the latter an occasional attempt to smuggle in by the back door what had been expelled by the front. This has been peculiarly the case in relation to the Deleuze/Guattari idea of a 'minor' literature, which has had an irresistible appeal for postcolonial studies, since it seems to reformulate the relationship between a dominant major literature and the literature of an oppressed group. This misreading would be particularly unfortunate in the present case, although Irish or Irish-English seems ready-made for the occasion, because the central issues are so easily coarsened into banality by dividing them into a set of binary oppositions. For the idea of a minor literature, when more amply understood, has a bearing on the phenomenon of the Blaskets literature. Deleuze turns to Proust for support.

> We can see more clearly the effect of literature on language: as Proust says, it opens a kind of foreign language within language, which is neither another language nor a rediscovered patois, but a becoming-other of language, a 'minorization' of this major language, a delirium that carries it off, a witch's line that escapes the dominant system.[28]

Two of Deleuze's examples are from American literature — Thomas Wolfe and Herman Melville — since they demonstrate 'health as literature', which 'consists in inventing a people that is missing. It is the task of the fabulating function to invent a people.' Another example is T. E. Lawrence in *The Seven Pillars of Wisdom*. Drawing on E. M. Forster's distinction between 'granular' and 'fluid' writing, Deleuze shows how, out of the blazing light and emptiness of the desert, Lawrence invents a revolutionary people — in this case, the Arabs. Kafka is of course his central example. He and Melville, for Central Europe and America, respectively, 'present literature as the collective enunciation of a minor people, or of all minor people, who find their expression only in and through the writer'. It's a struggle for Deleuze to sustain the notion that a people so enunciated is always 'minor'. Writing at high intensity ('delirium') loses its force and becomes 'the disease par excellence, whenever it erects a race it claims is pure and dominant'. This is domination, racism. But the measure of writing's 'health' is taken when 'this oppressed bastard race that ceaselessly stirs beneath dominations' appears instead. This is 'a race that is outlined in relief in literature as process'. It is often the case that one kind of delirium, of domination, 'will be mixed with a bastard delirium', and in that mix, the racial can become racism, literature is pushed 'towards a larval fascism'.[29] (This is perhaps the outcome of reflection on Rousseau's *Du Contrat Social* (1762)). Deleuze certainly makes the association of a 'major' literature with domination seem inescapable at times; and a 'minor' literature aspires to subversion, to refusal or at least sporadically realizes its ambition not to be canonized or even canonizable.

The pertinence of this to Irish writing is that translation, mostly between Irish and English but also, in Beckett's case, between French and English, is such a central activity, that it regularly raises questions of major and minor writings, of colonial and native, of original and copy, themselves regular victims of ambush in the guerilla wars between the folkloric and the historical over the legitimacy of the the oral or the written. Do all of these form a set, a series, a hierarchy, an echelon or a double helix? Moreover, it provides a theoretical basis for Pascale Casanova's work on the *Republic of Letters* in which the distinction between minor and major has to be worked hard and Ireland's prestigious place in that Republic illuminated.[30] Deleuze's work also leaves its mark in his student Anne Querrien's 'The Metropolis and the Capital' (1986) in which the metropolis is receptive to migration and multiversity while the capital dominates in the name of a single or consolidated set of interests. Inevitably, an island literature like that of the Blaskets will be claimed both by capital and by metropole, national and global readings. It will be weighed in relation to the 'minor' Irish language and 'major' English language traditions, although the demonstration that there is a major tradition of writing in the Irish language, preceding any such in English, or that there are more than enough Oedipal figures in Irish writing in English, makes everything more fissile and can lead readers to cry halt and settle for a plain and gross binary division that keeps life simple and literature simpler.

By the thirties, the Revival's claims for a natural (primitive, originary) eloquence had lost some of the power they had won in the early century. At least, the claims had changed and once more the emphasis moved from the achievement of an individuality through eloquence to the realization of a community's self-consciousness in language. The latent political function of the claim to eloquence was realized by a system of mediated writing, by which the question of individual authorship is raised not to weaken but rather to extend the text's communal authority. Language is a cultural wealth that is in inverse proportion to economic prosperity, the riches-in-rags story that had so many nuanced versions in the tramps of Synge, Yeats and (again in the thirties, Beckett) that had for over a century been an embedded feature of commentators on Irish-language speakers — 'natives', 'peasants'. Even in the late eighteenth and early nineteenth century, the impoverished Irish peasant had had a reputation for eloquence — in Latin — usually the only other language he/she shared with an English-speaking observer. This eloquence and learning were explained by the enormous impact of the ruined and learned Gaelic poets on the populace into whose weak and welcoming arms they fell after the final destruction of their courtly civilization in the seventeenth century. By keeping Ireland economically poor, the Union could advance the claim to be keeping it culturally rich — at least until the deadly and classic colonial use of famine as a weapon against a threateningly disobedient population, much used by the British in India also. That finally destroyed any notion that there was a near-mystical correlation between eloquence and poverty. The consequences for the Irish people and their language were almost fatal. Whatever was to be salvaged of the old civilization had to be 'collected' as quickly as possible — folklore, stories, curious turns of speech (*cora cainte*), customs, rituals. These memoirs stand within that tradition of collection which, as far as folkstories are concerned, goes back to the 1820s, again in the shadow of famine (and of Malthus), although its first impulse, belonging to the Enlightenment and not to romanticism, comes from the Royal Irish Academy (1786). Eventually, the catastrophic economic relationship segued, attended by an anxious scholarship, from an imperial into a national stride in the Revival and then again, into its second wind, in the thirties.

30 See Christopher Prendergast, 'Negotiating World Literature', *New Left Review*, 8 (March/April 2001), 100–21; Stanley Corngold, ' Kafka and the Dialect of Minor Literatures', *College Literature*, 21.10. (Feb., 1994), 89–101.

31 Robin Flower, 'Foreword', *The Islandman*, x

****

Eloquence in Irish in the colonial mode had unexpected consequences. Since the language Revival, most notably in and since An t-athair Peadar Ó Laoghaire's *Mo Sgéal Féin* (*My Story*, 1915), much admired for its idiomatic richness, the quality of writing in Irish has been judged by its closeness to the spoken word. Writing here is secondary to speaking, in part because the speaking of the language had been since the Famine such a contested issue and because the superiority of the native as opposed to the school speaker was plainly audible in its ease, richness and power, unmediated by enforced compromises with English or by any of the painful social embarrassments or self-consciousness that attended the choice of speaking a minority language that was supposedly outmoded. Therefore, the more isolated the area the more likely was the Irish spoken there to be the real thing. And, since the Celtic languages had become of such strategic importance in the great Indo-European language tree largely created by German scholarship in the nineteenth century, a 'pure' example of this Celtic language, a surviving remnant, was a philological treasure. In the case of the Blaskets, the philological 'find' also became a civilizational find, a lost world discovered — with its enormous inner richness audible in its speech rather than in written texts. So even when the written texts appear, as with these memoirs of Peig Sayers, Ó Súilleabháin or Ó Criomthain, they enact for the reader a contest for priority between the spoken and written. Some adaptation of Karl Kraus's acoustic gift would help, so that we could read them as though we were hearing them. But the usual difficulties of translation are, in such instances, so magnified that the act seems pointless. How can we 'hear' in English a language which has been compelled, for its survival, to proclaim a kind of acoustic autarky? All the translators of these texts are acutely aware of the near-impossibility of their position. Robin Flower, who translated *An t-Oileánach* claims in his Foreword that 'Irish and English are so widely separated in their mode of expression that nothing like a literal rendering from the one language to the other is possible'. Although translation had of course been central to the Revival, Flower — important and emphatic in the making of this distinction — rejects the 'literary dialect', 'the mixture of Irish and English idioms' that had formerly been used 'for translation from the Irish or for the purpose of giving the effect of Irish speech'. No Synge song for this work. 'This literary dialect could not be used to render the forthright, colloquial simplicity of the original of this book.'[31] In fact, all the most obvious features of the earlier Irish English, its rich, slow obesity above all, needed to be replaced by an idiom that was sharp and fit, moulded by the harsh necessities of its social world.

Thus in these works, Irish has a mythical presence — something between a god of language and the language of God. Like any such presence it is knowable to the subordinate world through privileged or chosen speakers only. The language can be learned by members of a caste or élite, but it can only be mediated to the world at large in another language and another medium (print). The act of mediation or translation carries with it the inescapable whiff of betrayal; an oral culture is no longer so when recorded in writing — or later, on tape recorder or radio. Or at least what we have in these media is either the trace of the oral culture or another kind of culture that is born out of the contest between mediacy and immediacy. The choice is to lose it or record it but, in recording it, to change it. The contest between the oral culture and a recorded or collected version of it is thereby claimed to be fought on the demarcation line between nature and culture, with twentieth-century Irish uniquely bearing in itself the sound of that battle. Thus the scholars and antiquarians who have learned Irish and have come to recognize it as having a special place and role in the history, not just of linguistics but of civilization itself, are witnesses to and participants in a moment of birth. They are coaxing Ó Criomhthain and Ó Súilleabháin to bear witness indeed but in doing so to re-enact the process by which culture ratifies itself — by revealing its source and spirit in nature.

The Blasket writings are not autobiographies or ethnographies, neither folklore nor legends. (*The Islandman* was originally a series of letters.) They are, so to speak, before genre, before the kinds of writing that can be distinguished by their several sets of laws and requirements. But they have something else — their freshness, newness, miraculous present-ness which is also something ancient, already-known. This language, like its speakers, is about to go into exile; for its recorders the emigration, which they cannot prevent, is to the world of culture. Irish is the world of nature and the Blaskets are the place in which the passage from one to the other is, incredibly but actually, happening — and they are watching and encouraging it. So the mediation of such writing by people drawn to the islands from beyond magnifies the strong maieutic effect of the works. The spark of cognition is attended by the light of re-cognition. In this dappled linguistic weather, Irish and English lights are interwoven, often beautifully. But the overall action is one of modulation from one system to another, analogue to digital. Irish turns into English, a community becomes a set of emigrants, Dunquin becomes Springfield, Massachusetts. The rate of emigration quickened in the thirties; by 1942, what mackerel remained were being vacuumed up by Spanish fishing trawlers and the destitution of the islanders was radical. The young aged quickly, the death rate was as alarming as the emigration rate. One woman, Eibhlís Ní Súilleabháin, whose English was rudimentary, described their condition on 5 February, 1942: basic cataloguing is now effective eloquence. There was

No sugar [...] no soap, no tea, no tobacco and the worst of all no flour nor bread nor biscuits nor paraffin oil for light nor a candle. [32]

'Here', wrote Seán Ó Coileáin in 1978, 'the struggle is not for the luxury of meaning in existence, but for existence itself...'[33] Instead of visitors, from Synge in 1905 to Carl Marstrander in 1907 to Flower (1910) and Thomson (1923), whose love for the place had transformed it, the islands now have tourists, what Ní Súilleabháin calls the 'Lá bréaghs'—that is those who had learned to say 'Fine day' in Irish and no more. The brutal hardship and poverty which was for a time one of the conditions for the exaltation of the island's 'spiritual' staus, lost that function in the late thirties and brought what earlier had been the dramatic prospect of extinction to the numb reality of it.

PEIG

In all the writing about the Blaskets, this contrast between actual conditions and some 'idealized' version of them drones on, as is also the case for 'De Valera's Ireland', an inexhaustible cliché of the commentariat. The linkage between the two is common knowledge. Certainly, De Valera, his colleagues and many of his notable contemporaries, made it clear that there was a traditional Ireland, of which only traces remained, but which it was the (noble) ideology of the state to incarnate and preserve as far as possible. Thus the Irish Folklore Commission was founded in 1935 with Dev's approval. Under its chairman James Delargy (Séamus Ó Duilearga), it embarked on the task of recovering as much as possible of the old rural culture of the country; Delargy was also the editor of the important folklore journal *Béaloideas*, founded in 1927, for its first forty-six years. Its motto, from John 6.12., could have been that of the Irish Free State, 'Colligite quae superaverunt fragmenta ne pereant' ('Gather up what

32 Eibhlís Ní Shuilleabháin, *Letters from the Great Blasket* (Dublin and Cork, 1978), 83

33 Introduction, *Letters from the Great Blasket*, 12

34 *Peig: The Autobiography of Peig Sayers of the Great Blasket Island*, trans. Bryan MacMahon (Dublin, 1974, repr. 1983); John Eastlake, 'The (Original) Islandman? Examining the Origin in Blasket Autobiography' in *Anáil an Bhéil Beo: Orality and Modern Irish Culture*, eds. Nessa Cronin, Seán Crosson and John Eastlake (Newcastle, 2009), 241–49; Angela Bourke et al., eds, *The Field Day Anthology of Irish Writing* IV, *Irish Women's Writing and Traditions* (Cork, 2002), Angela Bourke, 'Oral Traditions', 1191–98; 'Life Stories', 1198; Éilís Ní Dhuibhne, 'International Folktales', 1214–18; W. R. Rodgers, ed., 'An Old Woman's Reflections' (London, 1962); Patricia Lysaght, 'Tá an seana-shaol imithe go maith: the changing folk narrative environment in Ireland', *Proceedings of the International Society for Folk Narrative Research* (Mysore, India, 1999), 19–37; Patricia Coughlan, 'Rereading Peig Sayers: Women's Autobiography, Social History and Narrative Art' in *Opening the Field: Irish Women, Texts and Contexts*, eds. Patricia Boyle Haberstroh, Christine St. Peter Christine (Cork, 2007), 58–73; 'An Léiriú ar Shaol na mBan i dTéacsanna Dírbheathaisnéise Peig Sayers' (The Representation of Women's Lives in the Autobiographical Texts of Peig Sayers) in Máire Ní Chéileachair, ed., *Peig Sayers: Scéalaí 1873–1958* (Dublin, 1999), 20–57; Lillis Ó Laoire, 'Augmenting Memory, Dispelling Amnesia', *Dublin Review of Books*, 17 (Spring 2011).

fragments remain that none may be lost'). Douglas Hyde, who had relinquished his leadership of the Gaelic League in 1915 after it decided to support military measures to achieve national independence, returned to the political arena at Dev's instigation to become President in 1938, a dexterous manoeuver on Dev's part. But his most ingenious recruit was folklore, or the memoir as the innovative form of folklore. It was accompanied by a hesitant, half-fearful recognition of film which was, anyway, too expensive and for which there was not, to say the least, any comparable body of expertise. The most famous of all storytellers chosen by the State as part of its ideological appeal, was Peig Sayers.

Sayers (1873–1958) was encouraged by Flower and another linguist and folklorist, Kenneth Jackson, to dictate her three autobiographical narratives, two to her son Mícheál Ó Gaoithín — *Peig* (1936) and *Beatha Pheig Sayers* (*The Life of Peig Sayers*, 1970), and the third, *Machtnamh Seana-mhná* (*Reflections of an Old Woman*, 1939), to Máire Ní Chinnéide. The first, *Peig*, was chosen as a text for the Leaving Certificate State examination and remained on the syllabus for almost sixty years. As a consequence, almost all the disputes about the language, its compulsory status in schools and for entrance to university, polarized around this book. In addition, the implicit endorsement by the State of the form of patriarchal society the memoir revealed aroused increasing protest, so much so that the Irish language became for many an emblem of coercion and regression. No book in Irish ever damaged the cause of the language revival so effectively as this one. Yet Peig was one of the finest of all storytellers, blessed with a greater repertoire of stories than any other individual, a signal contributor to the wealth of the National Folklore Archives. Her book had been under the spell of the State for so long that only when it was lifted in 1995, when she was taken off the syllabus, did the impact of her (written) work as a whole begin to

be felt. Yet since she dictated and did not write her account of her own life, she is not in an important sense its author. Nor are those who recorded it. As a work on the national syllabus, we may say that its silent author was the State, its influence pervasive and deadly.[34]

As a consequence, the stoicism of the narrators of these memoirs, for which the State acted as the currency converter, did not translate effectively in the case of Peig. Yet it did, with some qualification, for Ó Criomthain and Ó Súilleabháin. The stoic resignation to God's will, in the Christian idiom, or national endurance in the political, or even — in George Thomson's case — as its historical version in Ancient Greece, had the appeal of a noble confrontation with a universal fate. That dimension, salient in *Peig*, is what in her case became most derided. It was 'translated' by her captive student audience into a purblind peasant ignorance. Thus, annexed by the State as exemplary, *Peig* was polemically read for decades as an instance of the regression and boredom the State had unwittingly exposed as its presiding ethos. Flann O'Brien's *An Béal Bocht* (1941)/*The Poor Mouth* (1964) is a savage satire of the whole genre and of the mode of relentless lamentation indicated in its title. Its immediate target is *An t-Oileánach*; its recurrent theme of 'we'll never see the like again' became a deadly and scornful refrain. It made fun of the state policy of reviving Irish and suffocating almost every thing else, including the language's real capacities. O'Brien's humour and satire cast a long shadow over the whole genre of the memoir and the mannerisms of proverbial wisdom that are common in oral traditions. Thus a telling source of amusement to him and his audience was the love affair between public discourse and the cliché, the decanted wisdom of the intellectually impoverished — and the drunk. Precisely because much of his work was journalism, the cliché's residence of choice, the medium was the message for O'Brien as for Karl Kraus. The usual antidote to the cliché is the aphorism, but in O'Brien's case it was another cliché — and then another, nested within the first. The vulnerability of these memoirs to parody of this sort indicates how risky the whole venture was; getting to print from an oral tradition and becoming an ideal to counter modernity was a hazardous process of which *Peig* was a prominent victim. For all that, the ethical dimension, taken to include the courage and the dignity of a stoical outlook, was worth reaching for. The capture of the idea of universality is a key moment in any ideological formation, especially when it can be presented, simultaneously, as a fresh discovery and an ancient lore, the composite which the new State, as the embodiment of an ancient nation, wanted to claim as the blend of the historical and the timeless which was specific to it.

* * * * * *

THERAPEUTIC REALISM

It would have been impossible for most people outside his own Parisian cénacle, in the period between the publication of *Ulysses* and Joyce's death, to believe that he, of all people, would ever become a singular example of literary and ethical heroism. Dispute and disrepute dominated the reception of his work; it now seems odd that *Ulysses* appeared in the same decade as *An t-Oileánach* and that both these Irish works have been taken to be — amidst much else — 'classic' instances of realism. For the outraged, it was not only the appalling sexual candour of Joyce that shocked but also his multiple violations of literary and social propriety, ominously related in their jolting way to the alluring arts that the technologies of photography and cinema had helped create. (Fritz Lang's *Metropolis* appeared in 1927, the same year as the final volume of Proust.) This sort of realism, whose formidable precursor was Flaubert, was seen as a relentless inventory, an encyclopedic debauch, inevitably a slander on the providentially ordained structure of the world. Early cinema was not criticized on similar grounds. It was a different matter when a more traditional art adapted new techniques, especially when they emphasized the crass or inhuman aspects of urban life. The animus against literary realism was (is?) not confined to the popular newspapers. It retained political and cultural prestige within modernist and anti-modernist circles, the latter including a great many authors who would not be pleased to see themselves regarded now as modernists. So, the modernist epic *Ulysses* was taken to be a scandalous perversion of what epic had been and a demonstration of what modernism had become — bereft of serenity or wisdom, stricken by incontinence in language and form. It did not help that the array of the typical features of realism in Joyce is so rich and the range of the term thereby so extended by him that the notion of typicality itself begins to wobble. In such circumstances, one predictable refuge is to find a secure definition of what a novel, an epic or 'a classic' is. In Ireland, the modernist epic met its antithesis, the folk memoir. The dissonances of modernity were confronted with a formidable opponent, ' the concept of true or original or uncorrupted absolute human nature as opposed to history'.[35] Human nature had blossomed in some earlier historical periods — Ancient Greece, Medieval Europe — although these were really more like existential states, paradisal in their stability, from which we had been expelled. In such periods/states the epic (Homer, Dante) flourished. Mikhail Bakhtin declares '[t]he world of the epic is the national heroic past, it is a world of "beginnings" and "peak times" in the national history, a world of fathers and founders of families, a world of "firsts" and "bests".'[36]

In 1934, Dev and his cabinet attended the premiere of Robert Flaherty's *Man of Aran* in which the new medium of modernity commemorated the immemorial world of Ireland in the brilliant genre

35 Erich Auerbach, 'Vico and Aesthetic Historism' in *Scenes from the Drama of European Literature* (1959) (Minneapolis, 1984), 184.

36 Mikhail Bakhtin, 'Epic and Novel', in *The Dialogic Imagination: Four Essays*, ed. Michael Holquist, trans. Caryl Emerson and Michael Holquist (Austin, 1981), 13

christened 'fictional documentary', a title which could plausibly include the Blasket memoirs as well. Flaherty was quite candid about the effects he wished to produce, whether these involved him in anachronisms or not. Therefore, it is not entirely to the point to say that shark hunting had long died out as a practice in the Aran islands.[37] That only tells us that the film, like all of Flaherty's 'documentaries', is very carefully staged to embody a struggle between the human person, or the generic human family, and the elemental, indifferent forces of nature. The immense seas that pound the cliffs and shores from the opening shot and the tiny currach with its human figures lifted by this moving wall of noise and energy need only the most basic story line to imprint their 'meaning'. However, Flaherty's film performs an additional function. It is about a heroic dying community indeed; but the world of Tiger King and his family is not entering upon a meaningless dissolution. Their world has an end (telos), not just an ending. The harpooning of the basking shark, the endless collection of seaweed to create a bed for a crop of potatoes, the sheer effort of daily existence all enhance that element of documentary realism, which is actually intensified because it so readily translates or converts into an epic register. Oddly, the realism is the more realism when, by the sheer repetitiveness of daily routines, it gets closer to abstraction, This is the source of the therapeutic element in such works. It is when the quotidian is convertible into the immemorial that its curative, religious element is mobilised. All action, especially repeated action, is meaningful; the art of both this film and the Blasket memoirs is to slow down the regular pace of the day-to-day to the point where it becomes a ritual. The ritual, never to be altered because its repetitive sameness has now become sacred, is an appeasement of the Gods. Monotonous labour provides the gestural basis for a sacred rite — the monotony remains but for the listener or reader especially the ritual element begins to predominate. This cinematic feature, especially its ritual-dramatic-mythic element, the musical signature that regularly identifies it, had already been noticed by George Thomson and became central to his 'Hellenization' of the Blaskets.

✶✶✶✶✶✶

A THERAPEUTIC LANGUAGE

What might be the capacity of either English or Irish, or of a middle, interstitial language which is neither and both at the same time to register the specific historical experience of the Irish people is a question almost as difficult to formulate as to answer. The critical works that addressed it most memorably are Thomas MacDonagh's *Literature in Ireland: Studies Irish and Anglo-Irish* (1916), Robin Flower's *The Irish Tradition* (1947) and Daniel Corkery's *Synge and Anglo-Irish Literature* (1931). The publication date of *The Irish Tradition* is a little misleading. Flower's work was in fact, as the Preface tells us, 'a selection he had put together of what he had already said or written on the subject on various occasions over a long period of years'. The central essay, chapter V of the book, 'Ireland and Medieval Europe', had been given in 1927 as the John Rhys Memorial Lecture at the British Academy and published the following year. Ill health dogged Flower from 1930, delayed his translation of *An t-Oileánach* until 1937, and made him despair of ever writing a long-planned history of Irish literature. Much of the remaining chapters of the book were given as the Donnellan Lectures, delivered at Trinity College in 1938. So this book properly belongs to the period 1927–38.

---

37 Among the first to say this was R. Lloyd Praeger, *The Way That I Went* (1937) (Dublin, 1997), 153: 'Before the days of petroleum, the islanders of the west coast hunted them [basking sharks] for the sake of the oil contained in the liver, which furnished many a house with its only source of light — a practice resurrected by Robert Flaherty to add picturesqueness to his film *Man of Aran* a few years ago, but belonging in fact to a bygone time.' For commentary on the film, see Luke Gibbons, 'Romanticism, Realism and Irish Cinema' in *Cinema and Ireland*, eds. Kevin Rockett, Luke Gibbons and John Hill (London, 1987), 200–03.

Thomas MacDonagh
From 'Last Address of Thomas McDonagh', ILB 300 P6 (Item 17). Reproduced courtesy of the National Library of Ireland.

THOMAS MACDONAGH

MacDonagh was dead within four months of his book's publication, shot by the British as a rebel leader. His political status has almost entirely obliterated the memory of his academic careeer as a teacher of English at University College Dublin and his pursuit of what he called 'The Irish Mode' — a literature in two languages, Gaelic and Anglo-Irish. He wrote these studies before the summer of 1914.

38 Thomas MacDonagh, *Literature in Ireland: Studies Irish and Anglo-Irish* (Dublin, 1916), ix
39 MacDonagh, *Literature in Ireland*, 169
40 *Literature in Ireland*, 55
41 *Literature in Ireland*, 169

The present European wars have altered our outlook on many things, but as they have not altered the truth or the probability of what I have written here, I have not altered my words. As will be seen, I anticipated turbulence and change in the arts. These wars and their sequel may turn literature definitely into ways towards which I looked, confirming the promise of our high destiny here.[38]

MacDonagh regards the Irish language as having suffered a 'temporary abandonment' after the Famine. Although the Gaelic League had now brought the people back to it, he clearly regarded this revived Irish as somewhat artificial or mechanical. It was not from its committees and organization that he expected the new creative work in Irish to come. Here, as is inevitably the case with any discussion about revival, the condition to be revived is always beyond the reach of the revivers. They can only achieve an approximation. In the modern history of the Irish language this creates that characteristic structure of dissatisfaction with the present and more than usually intense apotheosis of the original, of the past, of the authentic which has an ultimately disheartening effect on all the serial efforts to sustain the process of revival or even the hope of survival. But MacDonagh's view in 1914–16 is sanguine.

> But above all we are fresh in language, which the most city-hating English lover of nature cannot be. We are the children of a race that, through need or choice, turned from Irish or English. We have now so well mastered this language of our adoption that we use it with a freshness and power that the English of these days rarely have. But now also we have begun to turn back to the old language, not old to us. The future poets of the country will probably be the sons and daughters of a generation that learned Irish as a strange tongue; the words and phrases of Irish will have a new wonder for them; the figures of speech will have all their first poetry.[39]

MacDonagh sees as a preliminary the need to distinguish the Irish Mode in both languages, especially in Anglo-Irish, which has a different acoustic from English and requires in its poetry a different metrical system, perhaps with the line rather than the foot as the basic unit. He explored the possibility of defining the metrical effect of a number of chosen poems to give substance to his notion of an Irish Mode (a composite inheritance of the intricate sound patterns of Gaelic metres, Anglo-Irish speech patterns and folk songs) and thereby to replace the notorious vagueness of the 'Celtic Note', introduced by Matthew Arnold in his essay 'On the Study of Celtic Literature' (1867), which MacDonagh describes as 'largely a work of fiction'.[40] Flower makes a much more emphatic and sustained repudiation of the Arnoldian 'Celtic' and he, unlike MacDonagh, lived long enough to see in the Blaskets memoirs, as he believed, the modern incarnation of the genuine tradition of Irish letters in which 'the figures of speech will have all their first poetry'.[41] Flower's own position is as ambiguous as it is important. He is remembered best as a scholar, translator, collector, of refined judgement and of an indisputably English tradition which was itself undergoing a contemporary Christian (and anti-modernist) revival. The Blaskets writings initially (that is in the period *c.* 1930–50) belong to that as much as to any Irish tradition.

DANIEL CORKERY

Corkery is the ideal ideologue; his search is for the essential and, for all that he owes to MacDonagh, his stance is that of the pioneer who, because he is the first, is ready to say that therefore he is a traveller in the realms of gold where no individual has gone before but where the community of race awaits him. The question is — even though he is writing in English — can any other Irish writer in English be admitted to that territory and be greeted as a native? The answer, tortuous in its reasoning, but blunt in its finality, is no. The ideology is in his style and syntax in which a laborious archaism passes itself off as profundity. For all the similarity of theme between him, MacDonagh and Flower, he is far from them because of the ultimate dishonesty of the reasoning by which he justifies exclusion.

Corkery's book on Synge has one anxious question to ask. Why is Synge, for all his virtues, not a 'classic' writer? The answer is wrapped in a vocabulary and syntax that Dev might have envied but never emulated. Synge's defect, we learn, is that he was not fully a member of the community of the Aran islands because he, like his class, 'have always been reared on an alien porridge'.[42] Yet his allegiance to Aran has made his work much more enduring than the rootless achievements of 'the Internationalists'. It is indeed 'almost as old-fashioned as that of Periclean Greece'. Synge is compared favourably with Shaw who is the quintessence of the shallow cosmopolite (for Yeats too). Terence McSwiney, the Lord Mayor of Cork, who died on hunger strike, an exemplary nationalist, although 'not enamoured of certain of Synge's plays [...] saw that his work was rich in those qualities that literature cannot do without'. Once we wriggle free of Corkery's syntax, we find that these qualities 'give us respite from the vexing criss-cross of daily life'[43] — they offer therapy. Synge may not have the full serenity of the ancient Greeks, but he does provide a version of it. Moreover, through him, Corkery is enabled to distinguish weak from strong books. In 'weak books' the common idiom is replaced by bookish words. The more bookish writing is, the more easily is it translated, 'the more easily will it make its way from tongue to tongue, from land to land; and the more easily also will it shame-facedly slip away after a short time into the eternal silence'. Therefore, the fake ideal of a universal language that would do away with all the thorny problems of translation, is the very antithesis of the universal appeal of the 'common idiom' which is rooted in the local and stubbornly remains there.

> To have nationalism ruling the world is to have the natural pieties — of which Greek literature is full to overflowing — organised to stand in the way of International literature, just as languages do, languages themselves also being natural pieties.

As for Synge's work, 'wrought out in the ancient and natural way', it 'may be destined', he says with much rhetorical pursing of the lips, 'to exert on the world's literature such influence as a work of a classical nature cannot help doing'. But no further than that. Corkery's phrasing and syntax become more and more contorted, affecting to bear the weight of an argument while averring banalities and producing grand abstractions such as 'natural pieties' like rabbits out of a hat. A negative is being insinuated into the body of the prose but, to be effective, it has to have the same generic valency as all the positives about language, Greeks, 'classical nature' and the like. 'If universality be felt as wanting to his creations, therein is the cause.' For Synge's

> people, except those in *Riders to the Sea*, are inclined to be naturalistic rather than human, for it is human to practice inhibitions for the sake of ideas, to curb appetite by traditions, dreams, faiths well or ill-founded (if so we may put the matter under its most general aspect).[44]

Such sentences should be extracted and kept as specimens in a jar, 'if so we may put the matter'. What Corkery is saying, but trying not to appear to be saying, is that Synge does not quite make it into the classical pantheon because he does not recognize the need for censorship. Thus

42 Daniel Corkery, *Synge and Anglo-Irish Literature* (1931) (Cork, 5th Impression, 1966), 240
43 Corkery, *Synge*, 235
44 Corkery, *Synge*, 237–39

the censorship of the Free State finds its justification in classical Greece, human nature, etc. The abrupt appearance of 'naturalistic' as the antonym of 'human' is a reminder of earlier debates about the immorality of 'naturalism' (documentary realism) as a genre, when the names of Zola and George Moore, his scandalous Irish disciple, dominated the tirades of the 1890s on 'the modern novel'.

ROBIN FLOWER

In *The Irish Tradition* Robin Flower tells the legend of Cenn Faelad son of Ailill and Betan, who suffered a head wound in battle and had the organ of forgetting struck out of him. He was carried to an abbot's house and compulsively began to write everything he knew down on slates. The legend is taken to be an account of how the recording of vernacular knowledge began — a heroic warrior in effect becoming a cleric, pagan becoming Christian.[45]

Flower was intrigued by the passage from oral to written culture, especially as the first was pagan and the latter Christian. Not everything historical is Christian but everything Christian is historical.

> The 7th century monks had oral pagan traditions, and Church material from Israel, Greeece and Rome; they sought to blend both in the new writing, since it was imperative to give a validity to the oral tradition upon which they depended for the Irish events of their chronicle. How was this to be done? It has often been imagined since the advent of wireless telegraphy that those vibrations which are our voices, once surrendered to the air, never come to rest but wander about for ever in the ether, as potentialities of sound. Thus, it is argued, if only an appropriate machinery could be devised and the wave-lengths of the innumerable periods of the past be established, we might listen in to history and eavesdrop upon all that part of action which is committed to the living voice. Even if this fond dream were realized, it would be a one-sided communication, for we could not catechize the voices of the past. Our Irish historians improved upon this idea: they brought the saints who were their warrants for history into a personal relation with those who had figured in past events, and fabled that their accounts were authenticated by the actual testimony and eye-witnesses and participants of the great deeds of the past [...] Either the informant might be recalled from the dead, or by God's grace his life might be miraculously prolonged until the time of the saints and the coming of the written record.

Flower gives as one example of the recall from the dead the story of how Pope Gregory, Gregory Goldenmouth, brought the Emperor Trajan out of hell and baptized and blessed him. This is one variant of the story of the skull with a tongue (adapted by Yeats and in the talking head motif in Beckett); it is found in the Glossary of Cormac of the 9th century, in early commentary on Dante;[46] at either end of Aran island Gríor Béal an Óir (Gregory Goldenmouth) is commemorated (his supposed tomb overlooking Gregory's Sound at one end, and at the other, a valley, hillock and a terrace sloping into the sea called An Gríor, the Gregory). This hermit saint was said in the chronicles to have 'gnawed off his lower lip in a spasm of anguish over the sins of his early life [...] or simply because he was hungry [...] and a golden lip grew in its place'.[47] The conceit of the golden mouth or lip is a perfect image too, like the speaking skull, of the oral tradition being preserved in or replaced by the written. The shape-changers that engage in the heroic battles are also images of the person of knowledge in all its changeable forms; the dead are called in various shapes to bear witness to the truth of the heroic past and of its congruence with the Christian present. This is the full and copious world of

---

45 Robin Flower, *The Irish Tradition* (Oxford, 1947), 10–11
46 *The Irish Tradition*, 6–7
47 Tim Robinson, *Stones of Aran: Pilgrimage* (London, 1980), 22

epic deed and record. The secular and the religious dimensions are interfused, making the chronicles resonate with the sound of past and present, the goal of the 'principle of divarication, typical of medieval art between classical themes reproduced anachronistically and ancient images Christianized'.[48] Dialogues with the Dead was renewed as a literary genre with Fontenelle (*Nouveaus dialogues des morts*, 1683, dedicated to his Roman predecessor Lucian); Flower's image of the labyrinth of radio voices typically emphasizes the range of oral history — obviously by far the greater part of the past — 'that part of action which is committed to the living voice'. The act of listening to the storyteller is in part always an eavesdropping. So, on the Great Blasket, when an old man digging potatoes calls him over for conversation and then flawlessly recites to him Ossianic lays, Flower both hears and overhears the dead speak again in the voice of the living at this world's end which is also the end of a world:

> I listened spellbound and, as I listened, it came to me suddenly that there on the last inhabited piece of European land, looking out to the Atlantic horizon, I was hearing the oldest living tradition in the British Isles. So far as the record goes this matter in one form or another is older than the Anglo-Saxon Beowulf, and yet it lives still upon the lips of the peasantry, a real and vivid experience, while, except to a few painful scholars, Beowulf has long passed out of memory. Tomorrow this too will be dead, and the world will be the poorer when this last shade of that which once was great has passed away. The voice ceased, and I awoke out of reverie as the old man said: 'I have kept you from your dinner with my tales of the *fianna*.' 'You have done well,' I said. 'for a tale is better than food', and thanked him before we went our several ways.[49]

Flower, more than MacDonagh or Corkery, is at pains to distinguish his idea of the Irish Tradition from everything that 'Celtic' has meant in literary criticism since the days of Macpherson's Ossian and the later solecisms of Renan and Arnold 'neither of whom, I believe, knew any Celtic language'.

> The concrete cast of language, the epigrammatic concision of speech, the pleasure in sharp, bright colour which we find everywhere in the best of the literature, is confused in the worst periods and examples by strange pedantries of rhetorical expansion, which appear to derive from a native tendency to display, fostered by the influence of the more degenerate kinds of late Latin rhetoric. But these characters, never far away and emerging everywhere whenever nature can get the better of the conventions of the schools, are inherent in the very being of the language as a spoken tongue and cannot be carried over into translation. They are the extreme antithesis of the twilight vagueness which in popular criticism is often associated with the word 'Celtic' ... [50]

Again, this is the product of Flower's fascination with the transition from oral to written. No matter how it is done, poorly or well, the most basic characteristics, 'inherent in the very being of the language as a spoken tongue [...] cannot be carried over into translation'. That loyalty to the spoken, as I have indicated, remains alive in Irish writing today, really a potent and paradoxical disclaimer of any kind of translation at all, not into any specific foreign language but into any *written* language at all. For there is no written language that does not have a spoken predecessor, even if the predecessor is 'created' by the act of writing. Flower, conscious of the contradictions in his own roles as translator and recorder, nevertheless presents these as inescapable features of, perhaps even constitutive

48 Carlo Ginzburg, *Threads and Traces; True False Fictive*, trans. Anne C. Tedeschi and John Tedeschi (Berkeley, Los Angeles, London, 2012), 186, 152–53.
49 *The Irish Tradition*, 105–06
50 *The Irish Tradition*, 110–11

of the acts of memory which have created European culture in the ongoing exchanges between speaking, listening, recording. In Ireland's case the noise of the vulgarizing 'Celtic note', itself an example of the modern world's arrival, blurred the reception of Irish and, globally, all kinds of static polluted the atmosphere as the dread dawn of modernism broke. In his book of 1944, *The Western Island, or, The Great Blasket* given initially by Flower in 1935 as the Lowell lectures in Boston, in a typical moment, a storyteller, filled with the ancient lore, complains that the traditional stories are being driven out of his head because his son is forever reading to him out of the newspaper; this jabbering of the ephemeral news drives tradition into forgetfulness. In Ireland, there is the double threat of the newspapers on one hand and on the other, the 'Celtic'-influenced ignoramuses who regard themselves as guardians of the language.

These are the ultimate target of Flann O'Brien's wrath in *The Poor Mouth*. To reduce the freshness of the original to the stale cliché of the contemporary is the standard and unavoidable sin in the Irish language world. Patrick Power, who translated *An Béal Bocht* into English catches in his 'Translator's Preface' some of the impossible ironies that bedevil the translator: 'It is time that this book, which should have acted as a cauterisation of the wounds inflicted on Gaelic Ireland by its official friends, might do its work in the second official language of Ireland. That it may do so is the translator's wish and hope.' O'Brien, in the guise of the 'Editor', closes the foreword to the 1964 edition, dated like the Foreword of the 1941 original, 'The Day of Doom', with these words: 'I recommend that this book be in every habitation and mansion where love for our country's traditions lives at this hour when, as Standish Hayes O'Grady says, 'the day is drawing to a close and the sweet wee maternal tongue has almost ebbed'.[51]

Flower, as keeeper of manuscripts in the British Museum, had continued Standish Hayes O'Grady's work on the catalogue of Irish Manuscripts there. As product of his life's work, the vision of the monastic Ireland of the seventh to ninth centuries as the prelude to the European middle ages was created as a key element of the ancient nation's heritage and its rediscovery one of the cultural achievements of the new State, further enriched by the poetry of Austin Clarke in which that Ireland became the dynamic of his poetry, including the fierce reaction to the sexual oppressions of the time which Clarke contrasted with the candour of the early Irish sources. Flann O'Brien shared this view of the emancipated values implict in the old language. Flower's scholarship, and his translations of Irish poems, *Love's Bitter-Sweet*, are of a piece with this; more, he is the source of this vision of Ireland. In scholarship, it culminates in Ludwig Bieler's *Ireland: Harbinger of the Middle Ages* of 1961. Yet, at the heart of his scholarly and imaginative venture, lay the Blaskets, already doomed by the time he died in 1946; as he had asked, his ashes were scattered on the Great Blasket.

Still, the 'medievalism' of the twenties and thirties was an English as well as an Irish phenomenon and Flower contributed to both. The rechristianizing of the genre of epic, the inclusion within it of myth and allegory as types of a 'human' and 'Christian' thinking, had as its base a belief in language as in itself a mode of creation, radical to any religious sense of the world, now under threat from the diabolic agencies of a culture that had, as a deliberate aim or policy, the impoverishment of language. 'All language proceeds from mythology and an "ancient unity" of meanings', declared Owen Barfield in *Poetic Diction*, his influential book of 1927. In the preface to the second edition of the following year, he wrote:

> Of all the devices for dragooning the human spirit, the least clumsy is to

---

51 Flann O'Brien, *An Béal Bocht* (1941), *The Poor Mouth* ([1973] London, 1988), 6, 9.

procure its abortion in the womb of language; and we should recognise [...] that those [...] who are driven by an impulse to reduce the specifically human to a mechanical or animal regularity, will continue to be increasingly irritated by the nature of the mother tongue and make it their point of attack.

The paranoid tone and front-loaded vocabulary (spirit, abortion, womb, animal, nature, mother) remain features of the English 'medievalism'. Flower's rhetoric never aspires to such aggression. Barfield's friendship with C. S. Lewis and J. R. R. Tolkien is well-known; he was a member of the Inklings, the Oxford group that successfully, in literary criticism and in children's books, popularized the relationship between the 'modern world' and the past as a clash between the forces of Evil and the Good, an epic re-enactment of the ancient story. Flower's work belongs in this context; so too does the 'Blasket moment' in Irish writing.

GEORGE THOMSON

Two kinds of extinction throw their shadows across the Blaskets as a human habitation. One is the Great Famine (not to mention the periodic famines which were a feature of British rule in Ireland). The Blaskets re-enact the story of the nation's extinction, in hunger, emigration and gradual abandonment of the language for the language of England and America. The other is the World Wars and the growing consciousness, to be confirmed in the Cold War, that the extinction of civilization itself had become a real possibility — not only in the cultural sense (for many that had already happened), but in the sheerly physical sense. Thus as an individual death is absorbed into the death of a small community, that of the community itself seems to merge with the imminent death of the 'Big World' beyond. From there had come a brief flare of prosperity to the island, with the rich debris of the *Lusitania* catastrophe and others. The re-enactment of the experiences of the Famine in the Blaskets, the loss of people and of language, actually operates as part of a vivifying ideology for the new State, the synecdoche of what it must overcome, the replacement of a policy of immiseration by one of preservation, the stoic endurance in the face of adversity, the teleological confidence of national and Christian convictions. It is a demonstration of the State's failure that the policy of preservation with respect to people and language was eventually replaced — as a substitute — by one of pious (if sporadic) conservation of parts of the built environment and of the natural habitat. It is also evident that, at least since the late sixties, the idea of preservation as a political policy has passed from right wing to left wing parties, emerging more and more from the latter as ecological warnings and demands, softened usually for easy mass consumption into the pulp of 'heritage'.

When George Thomson, a classicist from the University of Birmingham, came to the Blaskets in 1923 he turned the idea of an imminent extinction inside out and claimed to have found there, not the Free State, but a pre-State civilization of the kind Homer had known. His translation of *Fiche Bliain ag Fás* carried an Introductory Note by E. M. Forster (who must have known of this kind of 'discovery' before in India in Sir Henry Maine's apotheosis of the Indian village as the cradle of all civilization) in which Forster warns the reader of

> what a very odd document he [sic] has got hold of. He is about to read an account of neolithic civilisation from the inside. Synge and others have described it from the outside, and very sympathetically, but I know of no other instance where it has itself become vocal, and addressed modernity.' [52]

Maine's thesis about the 'immemorial' Indian village community, introduced in 1871, wilted somewhat under a

52 *Twenty Years*, 5

combined Indian and Irish readiness to attack imperial versions of property law precisely in the name of an immemorial communal ownership.[53]

Immemoriality could be taken too far. But not in Thomson's case. He was a classicist *and* a Marxist. He saw the poverty of the Blaskets (and Ireland) as an example of capitalist underdevelopment. The Blaskets had remained so wholly an archaic community that the typically capitalist-liberal notion of self-autonomy had never been known there. This lost communal world, he claimed in *An Blascaod a bhí* (1977; expanded version *The Blasket that Was* (1982)), immured in poverty by industrial capitalism, was in some respects 'medieval' and yet, because of its history, was even more like the 'pre-capitalist' world of Homer's ancient Greece than any other. In the Preface to the first edition of *Aeschylus and Athens*, Thomson acknowledges his debt

> to my friends the peasant-fishermen of the Blasket Island in West Kerry, who taught me [...] what it is like to live in a pre-capitalist society. It is true that nominally they fall within the orbit of the capitalist system, because they are liable for rent, but most of them refuse to pay it; and in general their traditions, especially their poetry, date from a time when social relations were profoundly different from those in which I have been brought up.[54]

Marx's sixth thesis on Feuerbach, a utopian vision when written in 1845, (and unknown to Thomson, since it was not published until 1924), expressed Marxism's rejection of liberal individualism: 'The human essence is no abstraction inherent in each individual. It is the *ensemble* of human relations.' The Blaskets were, at one and the same time, an image for the future as well as an image from the past. The cherishing of the communal life and the repudiation of individuality was both a conservative and nationalist, as well as a radical and collectivist political position. (The 'Conclusion' to Corkery's *The Hidden Ireland* (1924) opens with an account of the absence of 'individuality' in ancient Greek sculpture).[55] Thomson thought the 'idea' of the Blaskets could survive, but that the immiseration of the people should be ended. In the dialectic between 'the growing individuation of society' and the division of labour, 'the emotional and intellectual life of the people' in a modern society has been so deepened and enriched that, faced with the theatrical spectacle of a tragedy, for instance, the 'higher level of sublimation' they can achieve secures the endorsement of the established order. 'The emotional stresses set up by the class struggle are relieved by a spectacle in which they are sublimated as a conflict between man and God, or Fate, or Necessity.' When the behaviour of an Athenian audience is compared to that of a London theatre, the atmosphere of the latter is greatly subdued; 'but in the cinemas of the west of Ireland, where the spectator are peasants, the atmosphere is far more intense. At the critical moments of the plot, almost every face wears a terrified look and continuous sobbing may be heard. In this respect, an Athenian would undoubtedly have felt more at home in the west of Ireland than in the West End of London'.[56] Thomson's analysis of tragedy in Greece and of storytelling in Ireland is in each case an account of the social function of catharsis or purging by which the performance of the actor or storyteller revealed a patterned variation between solo virtuosity and communal, choric consensus that produced a therapeutic sense of relief in the audience.

He, like all visitors to the island in those decades, was fascinated by the speech, or perhaps more exactly, the conversational protocols of the islanders. He did not regard their flourishes, invocations of the deity, appeals to human experience, as routine additions that had become traditional and could even be regarded as immemorial in the sense of being proverbial or simply well-worn. Instead he heard these

---

53 See Henry Maine, *Village Communities in East and West* (London, 1871); *The Effects of Observation on India in Modern European Thought* (London, 1875); Thomas R. Metcalf, *Ideologies of the Raj* (Cambridge, 1995), 66–159; Mahmood Mamdani, 'What is a Tribe?' *London Review of Books*, 34.17 (September, 2012), 20–22.

54 George Thomson, *Aeschylus and Athens: A Study in the Social Origins of Drama* (London, 1941), vii. The Preface is dated 'September, 1940'.

55 Corkery, *The Hidden Ireland* (Dublin, 1924), 302–04.

56 Thomson, *Aeschylus and Athens*, 380–83

flourishes and the conduct of conversation in general as a participation in a ritual. The storyteller, a key figure in the shared life, is not the holder of a hidden, inscrutable essence; she is not conjugating as story a paraphrasable 'world view'; the role of memorization and of dramatic adaptation does not have the function of conveying this or any other comparable type of information. Pascal Boyer pointed out that 'if traditions were about world views, the study of traditional discourse should have no difficulty in uncovering them. It turns out that [...] traditions [...] cannot be linked to underlying conceptions without systematically distorting the data.'[57] Thus, formal and ritual features are primary, not secondary. Rites are repeated exactly so that their specific meaning is both expressed and preserved in the repetition. There is no target language into which to translate them. It is difficult to say how much of this Thomson drew from the researches and writings of the 'Cambridge school' of anthropology, founded by Jane Harrison. Richard Seaford regards his work as its 'culmination'.[58] Certainly, Harrison's *Ancient Art and Ritual* (1913) helped create the ethnographic modernism that began seriously to undermine the accepted romantic conception of popular or epic poetry as a product of folk genius.[59] Thomson's disavowal of that distinguishes his notion of 'community' from most writings on the Blaskets. But the notion that myth is founded on ritual — Harrison's central point — enabled Thomson's concentration on the poetry and speech and, of course, on the Irish language of the Blaskets people. The purity of the genre of storytelling (in particular that of Peig Sayers) depended on the enforced backwardness of the conditions of the islanders; but it was also for him a revelation of the origins of European civilization here being re-enacted at its ending. He was consistent in urging that this form of 'backwardness' be preserved while a form of economic development compatible with it be discovered or achieved by the new Irish state. And it became part of his life's work to canvass for the economic help that they needed (and didn't get) and the cultural help the language needed to survive.

Yet there is inevitably a sense in which he reified this community as an object to be understood; this outsider gained through it what he considered to be an insider's view of the ancient Greek community and this in part enabled his powerful study of ancient Greece in which he reproduces the idea of an enormous rift between a 'medieval' and a 'renaissance' Greece. Perhaps more to the point, the vision of the tragedies of Aeschylus as marking the point of final transition in the evolutionary process from a tribal to a state culture is clearly indebted to Thomson's understanding of the Blaskets. They are integrated into Thomson's own philosophy of history which pivots (as do many modernist accounts of the emergence of modernism itself), on the notion of a break, usually catastrophic, in which one ancient civilization ends and another, barbaric in its energy, appears. That 'break' or moment of transition for him began with his first visit to the islands. But the ethnographic riddle, insider or outsider, was not solved by his becoming more of an insider than almost any outsider could be. It seems proper that E. M. Forster wrote the Introductory note to his translation of *Twenty Years A-Growing*. His *Passage to India* was as problematical as Thomson's passage to the Blaskets. The telling sense of slight anomaly, Ireland as Greece, touchingly appears in Thomson's act of dedicating his great edition of the *Oresteia* (1938) of Aeschylus to his friend Maurice O'Sullivan. He learned modern Greek as he learned modern Irish so that he could know the continuities of both cultures; it was 'in the cultural unconscious of peasants and fishermen that he discovered the survival of ancient cults and practices'.[60] In both cases, however, and more particularly in the Irish case, his belief in continuity was provoked by the simultaneous and unavoidable

57 Pascal Boyer, *Tradition, Truth and Communication* (Cambridge, 1992), 107. Boyer's title is Henry Luce Professor of Individual and Collective Memory.

58 Richard Seaford, 'George Thomson and Ancient Greece', *Classics Ireland*, 4 (1997), 121–33 (131); on Thomson, Greece and Ireland see also J. V. Luce, 'Homeric Qualities in the Life and Literature of the Great Blasket Island', *Greece and Rome*, Second Series, 16. 2 (1969), 151–68; Seán Ó Lúing, 'George Thomson', *Classics Ireland*, 3 (1996), 141–62.

59 See Cary J. Snyder, *British Fiction and Cross-Cultural Encounters: Ethnographic Modernism from Wells to Woolf* (New York, 2008). See also Diarmuid Ó Giolláin, *Locating Irish Folklore: Tradition, Modernity, Identity* (Cork, 2000).

60 Dimitris Tziovas, 'George Thomson and the Dialectics of Hellenism', *Byzantine and Modern Greek Studies*, 13 (1989), 296–305 (303).

THE END OF THE WORLD

61 Thomas Campbell, *Strictures on the Ecclesiastical and Literary History of Ireland from the most ancient times till the introduction of the Roman Ritual, and the establishment of Papal Supremacy, by Henry II King of England* (Dublin, 1789), 6–8.

62 I am indebted for this paragraph to a lecture by Tim Robinson, given at Terre Haute, Indiana in 1995.

sense of an ending. He could hardly have imagined the disappearance of that community into Springfield, Massachusetts, the world, not of the Greek Homer, but of Homer Simpson.

HELGA: SEAS OF GLASS AND SHIPS OF AMBER

The antiquarian Thomas Campbell's work of satiric antiquarianism, *Strictures on the Ecclesiastical and Literary History of Ireland* (1789), derided claims for the island's ancient civilization, saying that 'the glory of an illustrious origin' is neither of much use nor provable and, moreover, that the search for it invariably ends in 'downright ignorance of the matter, or in a nest of pirates, or a band of freebooters, or the hut of the barbarian, or the forest of the savage'. The date of his dedication of the work to Edmund Burke, 'March 17, 1789', was then a nod to the national saint and to arguments about early Christian civilization. Now it reminds us how suddenly the impact of the French Revolution, then only four months away, transmitted to such internal disputes a rhetorical and political ferocity, forever after associated with Burke's defence of traditional, ancient civilizations, including the Irish. Campbell, a Church of Ireland clergyman, anxious to promote a union with Great Britain and a relaxation of the Penal Laws, wanted Irish policy to be based on a claim to an 'intrinsic glory' which would be 'more firmly established, by considering it [Ireland] as a *new*, than as an *old*, nation ... . If antiquity means anything honourable to any nation, it must mean that, that nation has been for a long time removed from the infantine state of society ... '. So antiquarianism should confine itself to those eras in which there is indisputable evidence of 'higher efforts of art, and less equivocal symptoms of nascent civilisation' — like those 'symptoms' claimed for ancient Ireland. 'All beyond are seas of glass, and ships of amber.'[61]

The Aran islands have been more frequently used than anywhere else as offering an idea of a possible alternative history of Ireland. Just to list a selection of the names of the best-known visitors who sought a version or vision of Aran, shows the importance of these islands: from John O'Donovan's visit in 1835, as a researcher for the Topographical Department of the Ordnance Survey, to the extraordinary meeting of the British Association in 1857, at the invitation of Sir William Wilde (father of Oscar), then secretary of Foreign Correspondence at the Royal Irish Academy, which included a dinner (hampers were brought with them) at the ancient fort of Dún Aonghasa. O'Donovan again was there, along with Eugene O'Curry, George Petrie, Samuel Ferguson and many others. Padraig Pearse first visited in 1898, when he founded the local branch of the Gaelic League, and other leaders of the League came, among them Eoin MacNeill, Thomas MacDonagh, Una Ní Fhaircheallaigh; then the well-known visits of Synge and Lady Gregory between 1899 and 1907; of Heinrich Zimmer in 1880, the great Celticist, there to research his thesis on St. Enda; of Kuno Meyer of Leipzig, founder of the School of Irish Studies in Dublin, in 1889; of Jeremiah Curtin the Irish-American, who collected materials there for his *Myths and Folklore of Ireland* (1899); and of the Danish linguists Holger Pedersen and Franz Nikolaus Finck in the late 1890s, authors of, respectively, the *Comparative Grammar of the Celtic Language*s and *Die araner mundart* (1899), the latter the first study of an Irish dialect. The most casual reading of that list immediately shows links between language revival, revolutionary aspirations, philological research, antiquarianism and the fascination these islands had for naturalists.[62] To bring the islands right back to Woodrow Wilson's great domestic enemy, we might remember that the Aran novelist Liam O'Flaherty had been involved with the International Workers of the World, during his sojourn in America in 1918.

The Clare Island Survey of 1910–11, followed by a centenary survey of 2010–11, have made the biota of Clare Island, off the coast of Mayo, one of the most thoroughly studied in the world. It would have been interesting if we had a comparable study of the Great Blasket to accompany the various studies of the island's people and culture we have had now for more than 80 years. It almost happened. According to R. Lloyd Praeger, the leader of the first survey:

> Clare Island was selected, as board and lodging for working parties were possible there, and transport not too difficult — qualifications which scarcely held for the Great Blasket, a close runner-up.[63]

The *Helga* was the ship chosen for the expedition.

> Also, by the co-operation of the Fisheries department, their steamer *Helga*, specially fitted for biological research, joined in the work, and greatly enhanced the results obtained fron dredging and trawling round the island.[64]

Five years later, as we have seen, refitted again as a gunboat, she would be shelling central Dublin.

Lloyd Praeger did visit the Great Blasket in the first year of the Clare Island expedition. He remembered when he 'botanized' there in 1910 that his usual dinner was 'one herring and potatoes'. It had in fact become just possible to stay there 'if fish and potatoes are deemed a sufficient diet'. Manstrander and von Sydow and others had settled for that a few years earlier, since the Great Blasket already was 'to philologists [...] a prized sanctuary of the Irish language, a place of pilgrimage for students of the ancient tongue'. Of course, Praeger reminds us, the Blaskets and the western coastal areas of mountain and sea are not really the characteristic Ireland which 'is to be found in the wide bogs and pastures of the Central Plain'. But it is 'the Atlantic fringe [...] which remains a lodestar to people of many lands — a magic region which, once viewed by the stranger, rests for ever in his memory'.[65] This enchantment cast on the visitor is always being counterposed against the conditions of the native. Even in the early twentieth century, during a childhood spent entirely on the Great Blasket, a girl or boy would never have seen a tree, a motorized vehicle or electric light. No sound would have competed with the endless wind and the folding sea. Books and money were just about unknown. When the Blaskets were abandoned in 1953, soon after an incident in which a young man had died because a storm had cut the island off at a crucial moment from medical help, the main complaint was isolation, not poverty.

It was in the Blaskets memoirs that the question of outsider and insider, already an issue that had been debated by novelists and critics of literature (and that Corkery, for example, had transposed to the Irish versus Anglo-Irish register, much more irenically treated by MacDonagh, Flower and Thomson), is opened to ethnography and to the role of language in the formation of cultures. They also gave to the new state one of its most intensely imagined versions of an identity, locked securely in those 'seas of glass' on which the ships of amber floated. Ireland's achievement of cultural independence from Britain, which began about 1890, with the Literary Revival and the Gaelic League, ended about 1970, with the Northern Troubles and the first Oil Crisis. It was itself part of the transition between two empires, the falling British Empire to which it had given a telling blow in 1916, as the *Helga* fired her shells, and the rising American Empire which began to dawn over Europe the day the *Lusitania* sank.

Had we a composite study of the type of the Clare Island Survey and of the life and literature of the Blaskets, we might be better able to see the force of Eric

63 R. Lloyd Prager, *The Way That I Went*, 185
64 *The Way That I Went*, 186
65 *The Way That I Went*, 380–83

Hobsbawm's remark that history is 'the continuance of the biological evolution of *homo sapiens*, but by other means'.[66] Praeger's *The Way That I Went* is resolutely apolitical until its last pages, where he wishes the people of Ireland could learn to live at peace with one another. Also, in a manner that becomes familiar in writing of this kind, he disavows the contemporary world and modern art, accepting happily the charge of being an old fogey.

> The present time is one of rush and clatter, of fuss and noise and glare; and I fancy I see repercussions of this or of the mentality which has produced it, and which it has produced, in the strange literature and art and music and music of the day. My medieval mind will not rise to modern heights. I frankly confess to preferring Mozart to Ravel, Constable to the cubists, Browning to James Joyce ... [67]

This is endearing in its way, but disingenuous. The material and botanical life of a place is not more fully understood or appreciated by being separated from the cultural and political. But what does show here is the unavoidable unease created by different dimensions of time. In the light of the history of rocks or plants, human affairs are always going to seem dismissable as no more than momentary flickerings. Yet it is from that perspective that the 'botanizing' is carried on. The Blaskets writing that we have looked at bears that burden too. Its appeal is centred precisely on that discrepancy between the hurry and change of the here-and-now and the sempiternity of the surrounding land and seascapes. That balancing of times demands a form of awareness and a genre of writing rarely found, except in the novel — Hardy, Woolf, Proust, Joyce, Sebald.

But there is at least one example in the last forty years of a work that captures that awareness, not for the Great Blasket, but for the other storied western island, Aran. Tim Robinson's *Stones of Aran: Pilgrimage* (1980) is still a pioneering work and yet also a culmination of much of what has gone before. This is not the island of saints and scholars, although it includes that concept; this is 'Aran of the Saints and Stones' and in the final step of the walk around the island, reviewing the 'cast' he has gathered — 'myself the walker, you the reader, they the farmers and fishermen, landlords and bailiffs, rabbits and stoats, gulls, cormorants, dolphins, plants, fossils; the gamut from saint to stone' — this is what he is left with, 'the ordinary stone of Aran'. Yet, catching sight of the tower that marks the grave of St. Gregory of the Golden Mouth, he thinks of beginning again, a second circuit. This last step is the end of that book and of that transfigured world which he has created out of human imaginings and evolutionary processes.[68] There has been a remarkable advance in the understanding of the evolutionary and human history of these western islands in the last 115 years and in their relationship to Ireland. Famine, war and cultural revival have all contributed. Yet, '[in] a post-Darwinian world', wrote W. G. Runciman, 'understanding of the underlying processes which has made species, cultures, and societies into what they are comes at the price of surrendering any vestigial hope of predicting what they are going to become.'[69]

---

[66] Quoted in W. G. Runciman, *The Theory of Cultural and Social Selection* (Cambridge, 2009), 220.
[67] *The Way That I Went*, 384–85
[68] Robinson, *Stones of Aran*, 280–82
[69] Runciman, *Theory of Cultural and Social Selection*, 216

Notes on Contributors

Angus Mitchell
Angus Mitchell's biography of Roger Casement will be published in the 16 Lives series in 2013.

Willie Smyth
Author of the prize-winning *Map-making, Landscapes and Memory: A Geography of Colonial and Early Modern Ireland* c. *1530–1750* (Cork University Press, 2006) and joint-editor (with John Crowley and Mike Murphy) of the *Atlas of the Great Irish Famine* (Cork University Press, 2012).

Amy E. Martin
Amy E. Martin is Associate Professor of English at Mount Holyoke College. Her book, *Alter-Nations: Nationalisms, Terror, and the State in Nineteenth Century Britain and Ireland*, is forthcoming early 2013 from Ohio State University Press. Her work has appeared in *Field Day Review*, *Victorian Literature and Culture*, and several collections of essays on nineteenth-century Ireland.

Ronan Sheehan is a novelist, short story writer and essayist. A recipient of the Rooney Prize for Irish Literature (1984), he was a practising lawyer until 2005.

Joseph A. Buttigieg is William R. Kenan Jr. Professor of English, Director, PhD in Literature Program Director, The Hesburgh-Yusko Scholars Program and Co-Director, Italian Studies at the University of Notre Dame. His main interests are modern literature, critical theory, and the relationship between culture and politics. His books on James Joyce's aesthetics, *A Portrait of the Artist in Different Perspective* and *Criticism Without Boundaries: Directions and Crosscurrents in Postmodern Critical Theory* were published in 1987. He is also the editor and translator of the multi-volume complete critical edition of *Antonio Gramsci's Prison Notebooks*, Vols. 1 – 3 (New York: 1992–2007); see also Borg, Carmel, Joseph A. Buttigieg, and Peter Mayo, eds., *Gramsci and Education* (2002). He was a founding member of the International Gramsci Society, of which he is president, and is a member of the editorial collective of *boundary 2*.

Seamus Deane is Keough Emeritus Chair of Irish Studies at the University of Notre Dame.

MURLOUGH BAY AND FAIR HEAD, CO. ANTRIM.